SILENT FIELDS

SILENT FIELDS

The Long Decline of a Nation's Wildlife

ROGER LOVEGROVE

Line illustrations by Ross Lovegrove

OXFORD

UNIVERSITY PRESS

OXFORD
UNIVERSITY PRESS

Great Clarendon Street, Oxford OX2 6DP

Oxford University Press is a department of the University of Oxford.
It furthers the University's objective of excellence in research, scholarship,
and education by publishing worldwide in

Oxford New York

Auckland Cape Town Dar es Salaam Hong Kong Karachi
Kuala Lumpur Madrid Melbourne Mexico City Nairobi
New Delhi Shanghai Taipei Toronto

With offices in

Argentina Austria Brazil Chile Czech Republic France Greece
Guatemala Hungary Italy Japan Poland Portugal Singapore
South Korea Switzerland Thailand Turkey Ukraine Vietnam

Oxford is a registered trade mark of Oxford University Press
in the UK and in certain other countries

Published in the United States
by Oxford University Press Inc., New York

The moral rights of the author have been asserted
Database right Oxford University Press (maker)

First published 2007

British Library Cataloguing in Publication Data

Data available

Library of Congress Cataloging in Publication Data

Data available

Typeset by RefineCatch Limited, Bungay, Suffolk
Printed in Great Britain
on acid-free paper by
Clays Ltd., St Ives plc

ISBN 978-0-19-852071-9

2

To my friend Fred Farrell,
with whom I spent the joyous years of youth
roaming the hills, marshes, fields, and woods
of Cumberland

Acknowledgements

It was many years ago that I was first intrigued by the references in the late Colin Tubbs' fine monograph on the Buzzard, to the existence of countless historical vermin records in churchwardens' accounts throughout the parishes of England and Wales. Colin had dipped into these in researching his book and it was a tantalizing peep into what he clearly regarded as an untapped treasure-trove of past records of wildlife that were to be found as victims of parish bounty payments. I often meditated about this and discussed it with others. It retained a restless allure for me. As I later slid quietly into retirement, several people urged me to take on the task of combing through such records and publishing the findings. For several years I resisted, exciting though the prospect was, simply because the scale of the work would be so daunting. In the end I succumbed, and so my first thanks are due posthumously to Colin Tubbs for having unwittingly sown the seeds of this book, and to those others who have steered me in this direction.

Once I had decided to embark on the project two people in particular were instrumental in their support and encouragement. Professor Chris Smout initially assured me that the project was a valuable one and had the potential for filling an important gap in our knowledge of British wildlife. Subsequently, he has been a wise counsel and kindly agreed to read a full draft of the text on which he has made numerous invaluable comments; he has subsequently dealt patiently with a flow of other queries. Derek Barber (Lord Barber of Tewkesbury) has also been a tower of strength over the years with clear views as to the directions in which I should be heading. On top of this, he has not only loaned me half his library of books from time to time but has also plied me ceaselessly with invaluable clippings, articles, thoughts, and suggestions. To both I owe enormous debts of gratitude and only hope that where I have dissented from their advice or frustrated their expectations they will not be too disappointed with the final result.

An enormous number of other people have contributed in a multitude of ways. In particular I am greatly indebted to those who have had input to individual species accounts and have read and commented on drafts of those, correcting my errors and in many cases, ensuring cogent additions: Libby Andrews, Johnny Birks, Ian Bullock, Paul Chanin, Mark Cocker, Roy Dennis, Robert Dodgshon, David Drummond, Stephen Harris, Don Jefferies, Andrew Kitchener, Nigel Matthews, Pat Morris, Mike Shrubb, Stephen Tapper, Derek Yalden. Rosemary Mason took on the laborious job of proofreading the drafts and making innumerable suggestions. My sincere thanks are due to them all.

Ann Egan, the chief librarian at Powys County Council, has been an ever-present support over six years or so: patient, friendly, unassuming, and with an apparent genius for persuasion in obtaining the most obscure references, often in next to no time. Without her help the book would have taken a year longer. Similarly Ian Dawson and Lynne Giddins, librarians at RSPB headquarters, have dealt with a steady stream of enquiries with their invariable patience and kindness. There are far too many archivists in the record offices and national libraries throughout the country to mention them all by name but they have all been extremely helpful, many of them putting themselves to undue trouble on my behalf, none more so than Anne Rowe at Kendal and Richard Smout on the Isle of Wight. Similarly many estate owners and their staff in England and Scotland have answered endless enquiries and have trawled their records to try to locate vermin records. Tony Pearson has marvellously countered my computing deficiencies, recovering vanished texts and rescuing me in a host of other ways. My friend Geoff Morgan gave up many days in extracting records from the Exeter and Truro archives offices and another friend, Jim Flint, toured Oxfordshire parishes searching for woodpecker holes in church steeples.

The following have all given me crucial help in a variety of fields by making their particular expertises available to me and answering questions. Without their help the project could not have been completed. John Armitage, the late Colin Bibby, Roger Broad, Linda Brooks, Andy Bunten, Louise Cavender, Dave Dick, Graham Elliott, Richard Farmer, Julian Hughes, Duncan MacNiven, Tony Prater, Ken Smith—all former colleagues at RSPB. Also, Malcolm Bangor-Jones, Mike Blunt, Lord Burton, Ian Carter, Sgt Pete Charleston, Prof. Sandy Crosbie, Tony Cross, Prof. Chris Dyer, Graham Ekins, Gwen Evans (SNH), Gillian Falla, Chris Feare, Andrew Fisher, Mark Fletcher, Richard Grogan, Jim Flegg, Rob Fuller, Sgt Ian Guildford, Martin Hancox, Bill Hale, Derek Hughes, Hugh Insley, Frances Kerner, Elaine King, Richard Kuhta, Gwyn Lloyd, Murdo MacDonald, Alan Macnicoll, Adrian Meyer, Ian Morgan, Linda Peabody, Steve Petty, John Phillips, Robin Prytherch, Roger Quy, the late Derek Ratcliffe, Geoff Relph, Nick Rossiter, Tony Rouse, Graham Scholey, Graham Smith, Anthony Squires, Paul Stamper, Margaret Storrie, Richard Strand, Denis Summers-Smith, Prof. Joan Thirsk, Barry Todhunter, Norman Tyler, Lord Williams of Elvel, Victor Williamson, Anne Wilson.

In addition to the help I have had from archive offices throughout the country, I acknowledge the assistance I have given at the British Library and especially the National Museums of Scotland (who kindly made available all the Harvie-Brown papers), the National Archives of Scotland, and the National Library of Scotland. Other individuals and bodies have also been kind enough to allow me to reproduce items under their copyright: the Fred Archer Trust, Sue Boyes-Korkis and Malcolm Clarke, Bob Cook, county archive offices in Cheshire, Cornwall, Dorset, Shropshire, Norman Moore, the Richard Green Galleries, RSPB, A. E. Smith, Stephen Tapper, Tyne and Wear Museums, Tom Williamson,

Finally, my enduring thanks are due to my wife Mary who has not only tolerated six years or so dominated by this all-consuming project, but has travelled the country with me and has put in hundreds of hours extracting records from dusty archives. She has also constructively redirected the approaches to many of my earlier drafts. Nonetheless, I acknowledge that she regards these sacrifices as a far better alternative than the prospect of having me at home with idle hands every day.

Contents

Introduction

THIS book charts the history of Man's deliberate killing of terrestrial wildlife in Britain—specifically native birds and mammals—from about 450 years ago, up to the present. It is the story of his attempts to control, and at times to eliminate completely, species that he has deemed to be undesirable or unnecessary. The story that links past campaigns of vermin control to the modern practice of wildlife management (which is, in fact, control by any other name), is traceable from the very earliest organized records in the sixteenth century, through to present times. Thus we can follow the vicissitudes and effects of Man's relationship with some of the most familiar species of wildlife with which he has shared this island since those times. There would only ever be one winner. Wildlife has suffered to an extreme extent, never more so than since the middle of the nineteenth century, when an onslaught on predatory species began with little or no regard for long-term consequences. We have moved full-circle now, into an era when public opinion demands a very different set of priorities and principles. Since the middle of the sixteenth century, four distinct phases in our approaches to wildlife management can easily be identified. Phase one was the 250-year period which lasted from the first legislation (1532) relating to vermin control, up to around 1800, throughout which time organized vermin control was carried out in the parishes of England and Wales, based on a system of financial rewards. The second phase was an indiscriminate war of attrition against predatory species embarked on by the new sporting estates in England, Scotland, and Wales, from the late years of the eighteenth century up to the time of the Second World War. In the post-war decades, the third phase was characterized by an upsurge of public concern about wildlife. One of the results of this was a labyrinth of twentieth-century legislation that was designed to respond to this concern, and to protect many species that had previously been subject to a permanent open season. Finally, in the early years of the twenty-first century we enter a difficult period of growing controversy about what constitutes the legitimate control of wildlife species. Man has never accepted that nature can be left to look after itself without his intervention; that belief is as true today as it was in the distant past. However, nowadays wildlife management becomes an ever more sensitive topic and the longer we fail to address these difficult issues, the more difficult they will become to resolve.

Several hundred years ago, organized vermin killing gradually became big business. Under the Tudor monarchs, Henry VIII and Elizabeth I, it assumed national importance, the legacy of which has persisted through to the present day. The native fauna of our islands has been affected by Man's activities ever since he first arrived from mainland Europe. Unquestionably, the major factor impacting on our wildlife populations has been alteration of the land surface, through clearance of the original woodlands, drainage of wetlands, introduction of domestic stock, and the cultivation of crops. Many centuries later, following the dawn of the Industrial Revolution, other factors such as pollution of land and waterways, spreading urban development, and, most recently, intensive agriculture, have exacerbated the situation and made life more difficult, if not impossible, for many wildlife species. However, across all these years, super-imposed on these Man-made environmental factors, there has been an incessant campaign against a wide range of species of birds and mammals that have been considered to conflict with Man's shifting interests and perceived priorities. A series of campaigns against 'vermin', varying in intensity and with time, have been conducted over the years. Occasionally they have been broadened to include introduced species such as American Mink, Grey Squirrel, Coypu, and Ruddy Duck. However in tracing the history of vermin control in Britain over the last 450 years, it is the native species listed in the Tudor legislation (see p. 82), which initiated the sixteenth-century campaigns in England and Wales. It is those species, therefore, that form the focus of this book

It is widely recognized that the responsibility for the extermination of some of our finest species of native birds and mammals in Great Britain can be laid at the doors of Victorian and Edwardian gamekeepers and their masters. Although this is undoubtedly true, what is less widely appreciated is that serious inroads had already been made into many wildlife populations several hundred years before. Many of these losses had been caused by land use change, but much had also resulted from direct human effort in killing those species that people chose to regard as vermin. Moreover the programme of structured vermin control starting in the sixteenth century was enshrined in law, encouraged by remuneration, and pursued with intent. The clear aim of that initiative was the elimination of 'problem' species—an aim that generally fell well short, except perhaps locally, until the evolution of game estates and the arrival of gamekeepers.

The determination as to what species constitute vermin varies from person to person. Everyone has a different definition: 'vermin' implies different things to different people. Few people nowadays would disagree with the Brown Rat being regarded as a genuine pest. Rabbits and other introduced mammals such as Grey Squirrels and American Mink are also widely accepted as undesirable. However, other interests still regard some legally protected species such as Hen Harrier, Sparrowhawk, Otter, or Badger, as serious pests. The authors of the 1886 volume of *The Badminton Library of Sports and Pastimes* produced their own idiosyncratic definition:

'We would then divide it (vermin) into three classes.

First—those that do nothing but harm, *e.g.* Crow, Magpie, Sparrowhawk, Stoat, Weasel, Cat, Polecat, Rat.

Second—those that do little harm and some good and are killed only to keep numbers down, *e.g.* Jay, Jackdaw, Kestrel, Hedgehog.

Third—those that destroy a certain amount of game but afford good sport themselves— Fox, Badger, Peregrine, Buzzard, Harrier, Raven, owls.'

Nowadays, 'vermin' is all too frequently an emotive word with echoes of the Fox-hunting controversy, bats in houses, Magpies and garden birds, Hedgehog killing in the Hebrides, or Herons and garden ponds. It was not always so. Vermin issues were woven tightly into the fabric of rural life in the seventeenth and eighteenth centuries. Its necessary control was uncontroversial and unrestricted. The killing of a wide range of creatures in the name of vermin was regarded as normal, in a way that it is more difficult for us to understand today. The word itself has its roots far back in the Latin word '*vermis*' meaning worm and subsequently after the Norman Conquest, the old French word '*vermine*' came into general use as anything serpentine, slimy, or otherwise repulsive. Since then it has been used in the dictionary definition to describe 'any animal of noxious or objectionable kind'.

The present composition of the native fauna in Britain bears little resemblance to that which existed in a very different countryside, with a human population of only 2–3 million, 500 years or so ago. Many species we now recognize only as rarities were then ubiquitous and of daily familiarity; others that are still familiar to us today were even more abundant in those times. The catastrophic losses which took place in the nineteenth and early twentieth centuries, characterized by the extermination of species such as Sea Eagle and Osprey, together with the almost total elimination of Wild Cat, Pine Marten, Red Kite, and others, occurred not by accident but as the result of determined campaigns to remove them entirely from the British fauna. However, the story of the deliberate attempts to eradicate certain species reaches back several centuries earlier than that, and forms the central theme of the book. The earliest statute aimed specifically at controlling wildlife was in Scotland in the early fifteenth century. In England and Wales, the first legislation was not enacted until a hundred years or so later. Earlier than those times, of course, Man had already successfully removed the largest native predators such as Bear, Lynx, and most of the Wolves, as well as Beaver (although for its fur and the medicinal chemicals in its glands, rather than as vermin), and the original large ungulates.

After the earliest Scottish Act in 1424, James II of Scotland passed a stronger Act in 1457 (p. 62) which listed various birds that were to be targeted although, sadly, little is known of its implementation or effectiveness. In England and Wales in 1532, it was Henry VIII who introduced the first of a series of Acts which were followed by others under his daughter Elizabeth I in 1566, and subsequently renewed. These became known familiarly as the Tudor Vermin Acts. The most important of these was undoubtedly that of 1566, which listed all those species of birds and mammals that were to be considered as vermin, and for which statutory payments would be made by the churchwardens in all parishes. That list, nominally aimed at the protection of agricultural crops, went wider than that, to include a range of indigenous species which had nothing to do with agriculture (for example Wild Cat, Shag, Kingfisher), but were presumably deemed to be of nuisance in other respects. Paradoxically some of those species listed were clearly beneficial to agriculture in that they preyed regularly on genuine agricultural pests. The 1566 list (p. 82) is the definitive one on which the content of the book is based. It remained the guideline for continuing persecution through the parishes for several centuries, up to the early decades of the nineteenth century and in some cases even later than that. Thus, the focus is entirely on species which are truly native to Britain. It is interesting, but perhaps unsurprising, that almost all of the native species that are still regarded as genuine pests today, were present on the Tudor list. Others on that list are fully protected nowadays although some are still widely, but illegally, persecuted.

Sources of data—parish records

The control of vermin has been undertaken ever since Man first interacted with nature, but it is only since the sixteenth century that we have a clear written record of the extent to which various species were persecuted. The primary source of historical records is the churchwardens' annual accounts in the surviving parish records throughout England and Wales. Similar records do not exist in Scotland although the Old and New Statistical Accounts are of limited help. The second important source is the vermin records which were kept by the heavily 'keepered shooting estates after they became established from the late eighteenth century onwards. From that time those estates, which increasingly occupied the majority of open countryside in all three countries, in effect absorbed the function of the parishes in controlling unwanted species. However, any suggestion that the parishes simply stood aside and left vermin control to the gamekeepers is a little simplistic. Other considerations undoubtedly came into it too; financial costs were probably one reason. Why, for example, should land-owners and tenants pay a vermin tax if there was an alternative route, *viz* the new sporting estates, by which the same result could be achieved? The Rev Walker described how, in 1892, a portion of the money received at Dry Drayton (Cambs) for the letting of roadside grazing (it was probably 'owned' by the parish) was applied to killing sparrows. At the rate of a halfpenny for each bird, as much as £7 or £8 was spent in a year. Jefferies (pers com) suggests that this indicated a useful alternative income to the unpopular levy on landowners and that a change in the availability of this income probably contributed to the winding down of parish payments at Dry Drayton and possibly elsewhere. Certainly, at Rampton, in the same county, vermin payments were made from rental income from church lands rather than as a levy on landowners and tenants.

Churchwardens' accounts are held in the archives of county and municipal record offices throughout England and Wales. These records are generally available for public perusal and additional ones still occasionally turn up, excavated from parish offices or from the dusty recesses of rural vestries. A few are still kept in parishes in which proper conditions exist for their conservation and where they provide a modest income in permitting their use by genealogical and other researchers. My original hope in researching this book was to extract the relevant data from *all* the historical accounts that still exist in the various archive offices. However this slightly naive aim could never be achieved for several reasons. There are many more documents than I had imagined, and the sheer amount of time and volume of work that would have been involved, made it unrealistic. Also, in a considerable number of cases archive officers withhold fragile original documents from public use for valid reasons of conservation, therefore those accounts are not available unless they have been reproduced on microfiche or microfilm. Many are not yet in either form (and even where they are, they are heartbreakingly slow and difficult to use). In addition, the available lists of churchwardens' documents are themselves a moving target; some of the examples quoted by J. C. Cox in his classic 1913 book, *Churchwardens' Accounts from the Fourteenth Century to the Close of the Seventeenth Century*, cannot now be traced while at the same time, as mentioned above, additional documents are still being uncovered. I searched a significant percentage of available parish accounts up to the early decades of the nineteenth century. However, documents in urban parishes in the larger townships and cities were not usually examined, as evidence showed that they rarely contained records of vermin. Most payments, even in parishes that were assiduous in pursuing vermin, were phased out by the early decades of the nineteenth century and therefore, where parish records existed which only started in the early years of that century, I usually omitted them from my search also. A complete list of the accounts that I examined forms Appendix 1. *The full details extracted from those accounts are placed, as an archive, in the library of the Museum of English Rural Life at Reading.* I hope that one day someone may find the time to undertake the task of completing the record.

Hambleden, Buckinghamshire 1635–1808

In the eighteenth century, Hambleden parish in the Thames valley north of Henley-on-Thames, was five miles in length and four in breadth and comprised some 7,000 acres (2,833 hectares). Of these, 1,200 acres were Chiltern woodland, 5,500 acres agricultural land, and 150 acres common or 'wastes'. In 1801, the parish supported a population of 970. There were 30 farms and 154 cottages.

Between 1718 and 1831 a consistent toll was taken on various 'vermin'.

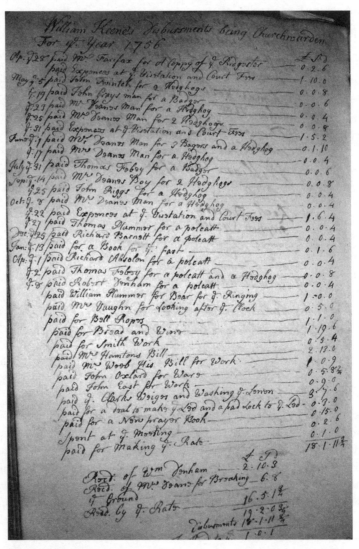

Figure 1. Sample page from Hambleden churchwardens' accounts.
Reproduced by kind permission of Hambleden churchwardens.

The vermin totals through the years running into the nineteenth century were fairly modest.

Badger: 155 in 49 years (all avg. *c*.3 per year)
Polecat: 330 in 87 years (all avg. *c*.4 per year)
Hedgehog: 1,161 in 85 years (all avg. *c*.13 per year)
House Sparrow: 23,064 in 36 years (all avg. *c*.640 per year)

Badgers and Polecats were heavily targeted from 1732 to 1785 after which Badger killing ceased. The last payment for Polecat was 1808. The peak of Hedgehog killing was in the 1780s when up to 88 per year were killed but payments ceased abruptly in 1802. House Sparrows became prime targets in 1786 and were controlled annually until 1832 with a maximum of 182 dozen in 1804.

One is often puzzled by the absence of vermin records in a parish where they might have been expected. In these instances it is sometimes confusingly the case that the payments have actually been made from the constable's account, or those of the overseer of the poor, or they may even be found, unexpectedly, 'hidden' in the vestry minutes. In terms of the sheer volume of work and time involved, it was not possible to pursue these potential sources in addition to the churchwardens' books. Although additional records would undoubtedly have been found there, the return for the time expended would have been low. The total number of parishes examined in England and Wales was 1,579.

The following is a list of those archive offices from which the data were obtained.

England	Doncaster	Matlock	Winchester
Aylesbury	Dorchester	Morpeth	Woking
Barnsley	Durham	Newport, I of W	Worcester
Barnstaple	Exeter	Northallerton	
Barrow-in-	Gloucester	Northampton	**Wales**
Furness	Halifax	Norwich	Aberystwyth
Bedford	Hereford	Nottingham	Caernarfon
Beverley	Hertford	Oxford	Cardiff
Borthwick	Huntingdon	Preston	Carmarthen
Institute, York	Ipswich	Reading	Dolgellau
Bradford	Kendal	Shrewsbury	Haverfordwest
Bury St Edmunds	Leicester	Stafford	Hawarden
Canterbury	Leigh	Taunton	Llangefni
Cathedral	Lewes	Truro	Monmouth
Carlisle	Lincoln	Trowbridge	National Library
Chelmsford	Lowestoft	Wakefield	Ruthin
Chester	Maidstone	Warwick	Swansea
Chichester	Manchester	Whitehaven	

The only county record office I did not visit was Bedford, where Steele Elliott had carried out comprehensive extraction of relevant data for seventy-two parishes in 1936, enabling me to make direct use of them.

Other more obscure sources are likely to contain further evidence of systematic killing. Manorial records are almost certainly one source, although the labour involved for the likely return was dubiously cost-effective. The Patent Rolls also shed occasional light on permissions that were granted for vermin control, but provide no evidence of results. For example in July 1552, at a time when only landowners with an income of at least £100 from land were entitled to the privilege to hunt or shoot, Edward VI made special dispensation to Sir John Cheke. Sir John was Edward's tutor and also secretary to Lady Jane Gray and thus in a privileged position. The grant stated that,

'The king hereby licences Sir John Cheke . . . to appoint one of his household servants to shote in his crossbowe, handgonne, haquebutt or dymdhake at all manner of dead marks, flowers, wedes, trees and such lyke at all kyndes of crowes, rookes, pyes, choughes, ravens, bussardes, ringtailes, henne hearnes, kytes, puttocks, jayes, cormorantes, stares, doves, pigeons, owles, bustardes, cranes, peyhennes, howse cockes, barnacles, seapyes, gulles, and all manner of sea fowles and fenne foulis, wooddoves, cowshentes, all small birds . . . and also at dogges, squyrrelles, polcattes, fulmardes, weaselles, cattes, conyes, foxes, badierdes, otters, and all fysshes. . .'

This fairly comprehensive list of British wildlife that Sir John was empowered to slay (which went on to include all deer!) is again indicative of the attitudes towards wildlife and the general hostility with which most species in the sixteenth century were regarded. Several other grants were made to landowners in the following years, during the reign of Mary I, with similarly extensive lists of named species. Such documents imply that there were other waves of persecution for which, sadly, there is no record.

So, how complete and representative is the picture that is derived from all these historical searches? Obviously it can never be complete, because for one reason, the majority of old parish records have been lost or destroyed. Furthermore, it is immediately evident from the most cursory look at the dates of those that have been examined (see Appendix 1) that none of them encompass the entire period from the enactment of the first legislation up to the early decades of the nineteenth century. Many in fact, that start and/or finish when vermin killing was clearly in full flow, cover only brief periods of the much longer time when control was evidently being undertaken. Therefore only a glimpse of a far bigger picture is available, a narrow window, curtained from a wider view by the loss of the majority of records. In these respects, when considering the numbers of creatures that were killed in the parishes, it is worth bearing in mind that very few of the records are complete and no more than c.14% of the total number of

English and Welsh parishes are represented in the analyses. The overall totals of vermin killed, revealed by my searches, are presumably little more than a tithe, which is a point that should be borne in mind.

TABLE 1. Number of churchwardens' accounts examined in each county compared with total number of parishes in that county in 1832. (Figures from *The Phillimore Atlas and Index of Parish Registers* 1995; Phillimore does not separate the Welsh parishes into counties).

Bedfordshire	71 parishes out of	137	Leicestershire	30 parishes out of	279
Berkshire	28	180	Lincolnshire	56	564
Buckinghamshire	24	224	Norfolk	50	601
Cambridgeshire	34	191	Northants/Rutland	31	371
Cheshire	24	148	Northumberland	23	110
Cornwall	45	225	Nottinghamshire	25	227
Cumberland	23	152	Oxfordshire	28	249
Derbyshire	17	295	Shropshire	36	248
Devonshire	78	413	Somerset	45	504
Dorset	37	264	Staffordshire	14	196
Durham	25	110	Suffolk	73	523
Essex	39	420	Surrey	25	170
Gloucestershire	25	375	Sussex	47	333
Hampshire	57	308	Warwickshire	23	241
Herefordshire	24	224	Westmorland	32	74
Hertfordshire	37	147	Wiltshire	40	326
Huntingdonshire	14	107	Worcestershire	31	218
Isle of Wight	17	30	Yorkshire	91	854
Kent	70	427	**Total**	1429	10819
Lancashire	33	290	Wales	146	1018

Throughout the book the pre-1974 county names are employed, as these were the counties under which the historical records were made and kept until that date.

County abbreviations used throughout the book:

England	Devon
Bedfordshire (Beds)	Dorset
Berkshire (Berks)	Essex
Buckinghamshire (Bucks)	Gloucestershire (Glos)
Cambridgeshire (Cambs)	Hampshire (Hants)
Cheshire (Ches)	Hertfordshire (Herts)
Cornwall (C'wall)	Huntingdonshire (Hunts)
County Durham (Durham)	Kent
Cumberland (Cumb)	Lancashire (Lancs)
Derbyshire (Derbys)	Leicestershire (Leics)

Lincolnshire (Lincs)
Norfolk
Northamptonshire (N'hants)
Northumberland (N'humb)
Nottinghamshire (Notts)
Oxfordshire (Oxon)
Rutland
Shropshire (Salop)
Somerset (Som)
Staffordshire (Staffs)
Suffolk
Surrey
Sussex
Warwickshire (Warks)
Westmorland (W'land)
Wiltshire (Wilts)
Worcestershire (Worcs)
Yorkshire (Yorks)

Wales (Anglicized names are used as is consistent with the period reviewed)
Anglesey (Ang)

Brecknockshire (Brec)
Caernavonshire (Caerns)
Carmarthenshire (Carms)
Cardiganshire (Cards)
Denbighshire (Denb)
Flint
Glamorgan (Glam)
Merioneth (Mer)
Monmouthshire (Mon)
Montgomeryshire (Mont)
Pembrokeshire (Pembs)
Radnorshire (Rad)

Scotland (where abbreviations are used)
Caithness (C'ness) (now part of Highland Region)
Inverness-shire (Inv'ness) (ditto)
Ross and Cromarty (Ross & C) (ditto)
Perthshire (Perth) (part of Tayside Region)
Sutherland (Suth) (part of Highland Region)

Sources of data—estate records

The Parliamentary Enclosure Acts, implemented in England and Wales between 1750 and 1870, made it possible for the owners of the newly enclosed lands to develop sporting estates. From the earliest dates, most of the larger estates—many of which still exist today—kept invaluable records of the numbers of game shot each season. Many also maintained similar records of the vermin totals killed by the 'keepers which were reported periodically to the landowners. Such records are potentially priceless sources of information about the range and extent of killing that took place on these game estates. They also help to give an insight into the wildlife populations that existed at different times and serve, to a degree, as an hourglass, measuring the demise of some species. Sadly, in England and Wales very few of these vermin records can now be traced. In Scotland, the picture is different and there is a reasonable spread, geographically and temporally, of historical vermin lists. In this respect there is a clear disjunction between our knowledge of vermin history in Scotland and that south of the border. In England and, to a lesser extent, Wales, there is an outstandingly good record of species and numbers killed, parish by parish, up to the early nineteenth century but little by way of existing estate records in the subsequent period. In Scotland the other side of the coin applies. There is scant evidence of the levels of killing before the establishment of game estates, but rather good information thereafter.

In England, the extent of slaughter of predatory birds and mammals that was perpetrated in the nineteenth century on sporting estates is legendary. This fact is echoed by almost every author of county natural histories and avifaunas around the end of the century and in the early years of the next, and is cited as evidence of, and the reason for, the loss of many species. However, with few exceptions (Chapter 8) the hard figures confirming the levels of killing on individual estates no longer exist. In searching for these records I have had help from over thirty long-established game estates in both England and Wales. However, it appears that in most cases records have been discarded in the past as being of no real interest while in other instances it is suggested that they may still exist, but are somewhere in immeasurable volumes of uncatalogued estate papers. Although the records are better in Scotland, there are still gaps, especially in the middle years of the nineteenth century. This is particularly frustrating because this was the time when the greatest impacts on the populations of species such as Pine Marten, Polecat, Osprey, and Wild Cat were being made. Examples from the oft-quoted Glengarry estate in Inverness-shire (p. 74) indicate the appalling carnage that was inflicted there, but further examples from the same period would help to give a much clearer picture. Once again many Scottish estates have been extremely co-operative, although the information yielded has been disappointingly sparse. When Harvie-Brown wrote the various regional natural histories of northern Scotland he obtained a wide range of vermin records from many different estates. Through the help of staff in the National Museums of Scotland, I have had access to his papers which produced evidence from sixty-five estates and, although these are very valuable, they refer only to the two decades of 1880 and 1890 and do not cover the key era of maximum killing in earlier decades.

The value of money

The Vermin Act of 1566 stipulated the payments that were to be made for the heads of different species of vermin presented to the churchwardens, e.g. Raven, Kite one penny; Fox or Badger twelve pence. These were considerable sums in the middle of the sixteenth century, and thereafter, and presumably reflected the seriousness with which the issue was regarded, at least by the law makers in London. Of course these amounts in England and Wales were in 'old' pre–1971 sterling currency of pounds, shillings, and pence (*£.s.d*) in which £1 = 20*s*. = 240*d*. All the sums mentioned throughout the book are necessarily in that currency. Shillings and pence are shown in the conventional form for that currency, e.g. nine shillings and five pence = 9/5.

These sums can be put in the context of average agricultural labourers' wages over the years. In 1500, the average wage in the south Midlands was *c*.4*d*. per day, while pay in the North of England was rather lower. By 1540, when the first Vermin Act was operating, the average wage for a labourer stood at much the same as in 1500. In 1593, magistrates in the East Riding of Yorkshire set weekly wages of 10*d*. for mowers, 8*d*. for reapers, and the winter wages of labourers at 4*d*., rising to 5*d*. in the summer. However, by 1640 wages had increased three-fold, to one shilling (1/-) (but the cost of living rose six-fold in the same period, in a time of severe rural privation).

In the following 100 years, wages rose by no more than one or two pence. Defoe thought a 'poor man' in Kent earned about between seven and ten shillings a week in 1704, a figure that still applied in most areas, certainly in southern England, across the remainder of that century. In the second half of the eighteenth century, a weekly wage within 20 miles of London was around 10/9, but reducing the further away, until it was no more than 6/- per week in northern counties.*

It is relevant to relate these sums to current values. One penny in the early 1500s was the equivalent of 6*d*. by the middle of the next century, when vermin payments were at their height, and would be equivalent to somewhere in excess of £1 at today's value. In a similar vein, the Economic History Services data suggest that 1*d*. in 1532, the date of the first Tudor Vermin Act, was the equivalent of *c*£1.35 today.

In Scotland by the early years of the seventeenth century there was already a clear discrepancy between 'fees' (wages) paid to workers in different parts of the country. It is important to note that between 1603 and 1707 (the date of Union) the Scottish currency was the 'lib. Scot' (now usually referred to as '£ Scots') which was valued at $\frac{1}{12}$ the English £1[†]. All the figures given below, including those for the eighteenth century are in £ Scots for consistency and therefore should be divided by twelve to make comparison with the rates in England and Wales.

In 1560, a daily wage rate for a Scottish building labourer was about 2/- Scots or less, rising to about 6/- at the start of the seventeenth century, though the value of the increase was cancelled by inflation. However, in the next half

---

* Principal source Thirsk (1967) vols IV,V,VI; subsidiary source, Rogers, *Six Centuries of Work and Wages* (1884).

† Principal source Gibson and Smout 1995.

century the increase to 8/- or more represented a real advance in the standard of living. Thereafter, for a century Scottish wages stagnated while those in England rose, accentuating the difference between the two countries. After 1760 wages rose rapidly, though unevenly, across southern Scotland. Thus, a rural labourer in Wigtownshire or Dumfriesshire earned around £24–£30 annually until 1760 after which he may have enjoyed wages rising to £80 p.a. or even higher. The rates paid in northern Scotland were consistently lower than these, infrequently reaching £20 p.a. before the 1760s, but throughout Scotland the picture is difficult to paint accurately as the 'fee' was only part of the earnings for many workers. Single men frequently received their food as part of the payment and married ones were given accommodation, possibly with cloth, shoes, or drink as well, with the result that it is very difficult to establish true figures of earnings.

Unanswered questions

Examination of the old churchwardens' accounts and shooting estate records, together with a few other sources, sheds light on the management of wildlife that has taken place in the past. At the same time, as is often the case, the findings pose almost as many questions as they answer. This is particularly so with the early parish records. One obvious question is why some parishes undertook vermin control while others evidently ignored it completely, at least so far as churchwardens' records show? There is no doubt that the influence of the squirearchy within the parishes was paramount and if they objected to the raising of yet another separate levy for vermin payments they could effectively block the scheme. This may be part of the answer but there are presumably other reasons for discontinuity across the parishes, which are lost in time. What were the philosophies or thinking that guided the decisions whether or not to undertake vermin control? The administration of the statute was on an autonomous parish basis, not county by county and yet some counties stand out as being completely out of phase with their neighbours. Why did the mere handful of parishes that controlled vermin in Essex—a county with a long-established, rich, and varied landscape, like Devon and Kent—not undertake killing of anything except a few Hedgehogs, Foxes, and occasional Badgers?

Similarly in West Sussex, four parishes killed nothing but House Sparrows while none of the other fourteen that I searched produced anything at all. This was at a time when the surrounding counties were taking a reasonable toll on a wide variety of species. The same might be said of other counties. Why, for example, when the contiguous parishes of Tarporley and Bunbury (Ches) were slaughtering Kites in unprecedented numbers, did the adjacent parishes of Whitegate and Church Minshull wholly ignore the species? Shropshire was strangely out of step with all other Marcher counties, in that Polecats were not apparently killed at all, nor were Red Kites, nor in fact many other vermin except the inevitable Hedgehogs and Foxes. It is interesting to reflect on the circumstances that led to a sudden campaign being launched against a certain mammal or bird, often intensively, and then to be terminated a year or two later just as abruptly. In pondering these issues one can only speculate as to what the effect on wildlife would have been had all parishes applied themselves with equal vigour to the statutes, in the way that some of them clearly did.

Why is there no evidence of payments for any birds of prey in the midland and eastern counties of England (save one solitary, ill-fated Buzzard in Suffolk)? It is an inexplicable puzzle. Even in Bedfordshire and Norfolk, where killing was all embracing in virtually every parish, there is not one record of a bounty for a diurnal raptor. There is, also, one critical underlying question with regard to wildlife 300 or so years ago. What were the populations of some of these species? Was the countryside the bucolic paradise we like to imagine, swarming with innumerable birds, mammals, and insects against a colourful tapestry of wild flowers? What seductive picture is painted in our flights of imagination?

We shall never really know the truth, but at least an exploration of the old parish records gives us a few pointers. To start with, the picture was clearly not a uniform one across England and Wales. The relatively intensively farmed open fields in eastern England were nothing like as rich in wildlife as the western areas and Wales. In these latter areas, and in the widely distributed heathlands and unclaimed wetlands, the wealth of wildlife must have been breathtaking compared with what existed even up to the time of the two world wars. The churchwardens' records give us glimpses of the numbers of some species that existed. Hartland parish in north Devon killed huge numbers of Polecats and Wild Cats in the seventeenth century. In Dorset 9,339 Water Voles were killed in 26 years in Puddletown while Sherborne accounted for scores of Hedgehogs for decade after decade with a maximum of 182 in 1726. Ravens suffered in many parishes, particularly in the west, but few more so than at Wirksworth in Derbyshire where parishioners were paid for 1,775 heads in a mere 18 years. Kites were extremely numerous in many areas as testified by various heavy kills: 447 at Tenterden in Kent, 523 in Eastham (Ches), 424 at St Erme (C'wall), among many others, some even more extensive than those. But these are only passing glimpses, based on our fragmentary gleaning of numbers of vermin killed in the parishes. The real picture will remain a tantalizingly clouded one.

Another key question, of course, is the extent to which the parochial campaigns actually succeeded in reducing or eliminating the target birds and mammals. This is discussed under the individual species accounts in Chapters 6 and 7, but it is clear that, overall, the campaigns actually had little effect. Some of the figures of kills recorded—such as those shown above—are fairly shocking but these are quoted for the very reason that they are extreme. Other seemingly impressive totals become less so when averaged out over the years to which they apply, and in many cases are small compared with tolls that are taken today. In the past, of course, the victims were culled from larger populations anyway. The hostility directed towards many of the vermin species was great, but the impact on populations was, fortunately, less impressive than the antipathy directed against them. This was particularly the case with most of the birds, especially the corvids and, certainly, House Sparrows. The largest birds of prey—Osprey and eagles—had mostly been removed in England and Wales before the Acts came into being. In parts of the country some of the predatory mammals may well have been reduced locally, and certainly could have been finally removed, but for the fact that many parishes did not apparently observe the statutes. Control was random and therefore recruitment from adjacent parishes was easy and regular. If all parishes in a county or other sizeable area had worked together, elimination of some species would probably have been assured. Cresswell et al. have shown that the virtual absence of Badgers in Norfolk today is the result of just such action by gamekeepers a century ago.

Bounty schemes rarely succeed in eliminating the species at which they are targeted. There is always a degree of vested interest in conserving the resource, so that future payments can be assured. The modern example of bounties of 1/- per tail (later 2/-) for Grey Squirrels illustrates the point. The scheme was terminated in 1958 because it was clear that some of those who trapped the Squirrels live, were cutting off the tails, collecting the bounty, and releasing the animal to breed more tails. Bounties also encourage people to kill when the numbers are highest, at which time it is least effective. The immense toll taken on House Sparrows in the past, without reducing their population, illustrates that point. Gamekeepers on the other hand succeeded in achieving their aim because they had a vested interest in elimination.

Thus, the answer to the key question in the era of the 'keepered game estates is much more straightforward. We know from the information in the nineteenth and early twentieth centuries that in the 130 years or so preceding the First World War, they were principally responsible for the total elimination of several species and the drastic reduction in range and numbers of many others. The groundwork may have been laid through 400 years of land use change and direct action through the parishes, but the *coup de grâce* was administered by the 'keepers.

James Knapp, writing in Gloucestershire in 1829, at a time when church payments were generally being discontinued, lamented the unnecessary amount of wanton killing that was still taking place:

'We still continue here that very ancient custom of giving parish rewards for the destruction of various creatures in the denomination of vermin. In former times it may have been found necessary to keep under or reduce the numbers of predaceous animals, which in thickly wooded country, with an inferior population might have been productive of injury: but now however our losses by such means have become a very petty grievance; our gamekeepers do their part in removing pests of this nature and the plough and the axe leave little harbour for the few that remain. An item passed in one of our late church-warden's account was "for seventeen dozen tomtit heads". In what evil hour and for what crime this poor little bird could have incurred the anathema of a parish is difficult to conjecture.'

Referencing

References for individual chapters (and the species discussed in Chapters 6 and 7) are given at the end of the book and are cited in full even when the same reference is repeated in successive chapters. In addition a further list of bibliographic references is given, indicating books and papers that have been consulted, but not necessarily used in the text. Within the text of the book, the dates of individual references are included in parentheses after an author's name only when more than one reference from that author has been quoted.

1

Lost animals:
early eliminations by Man

THIS book explores the impact of Man on some of our native fauna from the sixteenth century, in the second half of the reign of Henry VIII. This is the logical point from which to trace the history of deliberate and planned persecution of those species considered as vermin because it represents the time at which statutory legislation, backed up with financial reward, was introduced. However, in starting at this point of history, we do of course pick up the story of Man's impact on wildlife in Britain several thousand years after those interactions first began. The evolution of British wildlife in distant eras and the consequences of early human predation and conflict on it, have been thoroughly covered in other volumes (e.g. Yalden 1999, Harting 1880) and it is not the role of this book to dwell on that long period of time. Nonetheless, to put the focus of our investigation of wildlife management and vermin control into a wider context, it is pertinent to consider the chronology of Man's earlier elimination of several important species.

In the post-glacial millennia, starting some 10,000 years ago, most of the mammals which we now recognize as components of our native fauna—including those subsequently exterminated—became established as the change from sub-arctic to temperate habitats evolved. The same applied to most of our familiar bird species, the important difference being that whereas terrestrial mammals could migrate into Britain only while the land bridge to the Continent existed and therefore once established could not be added to, birds retained the ability to move in and out at will. By the time of our separation from mainland Europe the list of mammal species present thus contained all those native species with which we are now familiar. Among the animals that later appeared on the post-medieval lists of vermin (with the exception of rats, both species of which were man-assisted introductions), all the familiar mustelids were here, including Otter and Badger, together with Fox, Wild Cat, and Hedgehog. Many larger mammals roamed the land too. Red and Roe Deer were numerous and have survived in varying numbers ever since, while other larger species have subsequently disappeared at the hand of Man: Aurochs, the wild oxen, roamed the woodlands, accompanied by Elk, Wolf, Lynx, Brown Bear, and Wild Boar, while Beavers were widespread in the wetlands.

Mesolithic Man in the post-glacial millennia hunted these animals with spear and with bow and arrow, as they provided him not only with essential food but also skins for clothing, bedding, and shelter; antlers and bones for tools and other necessities. Plenty of archaeological evidence exists that testifies to the activities of these nomadic fishermen/hunter-gatherers. Like the larger mammals, they could move freely across the boggy land bridge joining us to the Continent, and evidence of their presence there is provided by relics such as harpoons, which are occasionally dredged up from the drowned peat deposits under the North Sea. Their camps were scattered around the coasts of Britain where remains of their middens have later been found. The most famous Mesolithic site, dating back to some time between 7,900 and 7,200 BC, was uncovered at Star Carr, in what is now the Vale of Pickering in East Yorkshire. It was a settlement beside an ancient post-glacial lake. Here clear evidence was found of the use of dugouts, worked bone and flint implements, harpoons, hand axes, elk-antler mattocks, etc. Furthermore, there were ample remains of mammals and birds to give us a clear picture of some of the creatures on which Man preyed in those early centuries after the withdrawal of the ice. Their principal hunted prey were evidently Red and Roe Deer but other ungulates in the midden remains were represented by Elk, Aurochs, and Wild Boar. There were also bones of Brown Bear, Pine Marten, Fox, Wolf, Badger, hare (possibly Mountain Hare), Beaver, and Hedgehog. Appropriately in such a wetland situation, the bird remains discovered at Star Carr were dominated by species such as Crane, Merganser, Red-throated Diver, Great Crested Grebe, and various ducks. Yalden has attempted to make a tentative estimate of the populations of some of the larger mammals of the Mesolithic fauna; see Table 2 below.

Although we like to think of hunter-gatherers as essentially sustainable harvesters, dependent on ensuring a continuing supply of animals, this may not necessarily have been the case. There is suspicion that during their tenure of the land several species were severely reduced and possibly brought to the brink of extinction. Elk may have been particularly affected and at one time it was thought that Lynx also disappeared then. It clearly didn't however, at least in some of the remoter areas, because Lynx was subsequently thought to have occurred in Scotland and Yorkshire as late as the time of Roman occupation. However, whatever the actual reduction of numbers that may or may not have taken place, it is evident that the first real impact on the populations of some of the larger native mammals began as long ago as the Mesolithic era.

From around 3,000 BC, the long-established Mesolithic nomads were joined by incoming Neolithic settlers. These were the first farmers and husbandmen,

TABLE 2. A tentative estimate of populations of some of the larger mammals in Britain during the Mesolithic era. Adapted from Yalden (1999) with the author's permission.

Red Deer	1,000,000+
Roe Deer	1,000,000+
Elk	67,000
Aurochs	99,000
Wild Boar	1,000,000
Wolf	20,000
Lynx	10,000
Beaver	35,000
Otter*	7,000
Weasel	423,000
Polecat	104,000
Stoat	50,000+

* excludes coastal populations

crossing over from the Continent, who brought with them their own domesticated cattle (already ancient descendants of the wild Aurochs), sheep and goats (neither of which were ever native to Britain), and domesticated pigs. Their arrival was a huge milestone in the ecological history of these islands—the arrival for the first time of domesticated herds of grazing animals that competed with native herbivores and required open areas of pastureland as well as fenced enclosures, and needed shepherding to protect them from Wolves, etc. These Neolithic settlers were the first people who had to contest Nature seriously, to challenge it, and in essence to fight against the natural processes and eliminate competing creatures. They pushed back the woodland and expanded forest clearings to provide better grazing for their stock and tillage for their crops. They also had to have a proactive approach to wildlife and combat those animals—Bear, Wolf, Fox, etc.—that posed threats to their domestic stock and thereby their livelihood. It is clear from archaeological records that domesticated animals provided the bulk of meat for the Neolithic people although wild animals still featured in their kills—Red Deer, for example, not least for the antlers to be made into tools. The necessity of hunting the predators of domestic stock certainly appears to have further reduced the numbers of Wolf and Lynx across this period. Yalden suggests that the Aurochs declined to the brink of extinction at this time, possibly because of the problem of interbreeding with domestic cattle or because they were a threat to crops.

The date of the final demise of the Aurochs in Britain is not known. The last individuals on the Continent of Europe were killed, according to Pyle, in the Jaktorowska Forest in Poland in 1627. In Britain, although there is uncertainty as to whether or not the remnants may have survived to Roman times, they had probably been exterminated in the wild a thousand years before that.

The long-term survival of large wild mammals, particularly predators, on a small island such as ours, increasingly stripped of its natural vegetation, was highly unlikely. Archaeological evidence shows that, prehistorically, the Brown Bear was widespread throughout Britain. As in the time of the Mesolithic inhabitants, Neolithic Man continued to hunt bears for meat and fur although they still roamed the forests and wildwoods through the Roman era and on into the Dark Ages. The scattered forest remnants in Scotland were one of its last strongholds, a claim that is given some credence by the claim that, during the time of the Roman occupation, Caledonian Bears were taken to Rome for fighting purposes. So, the date when the last native bear was eliminated is again unknown and the claim, quoted by Harting (1880a) and others, that they had probably gone by the tenth century, is probably optimistic. It is more likely that they disappeared before the Anglo-Saxon arrival, several hundred years earlier. Certainly it was the first of the large predators to be eliminated by Man from Britain.

Where the Bear went, the Wolf was bound to follow. If there was an inevitability about its eventual extinction, at least the Wolf lasted several centuries longer than the Bear and we therefore have a rather more accurate record of its demise. Of the various species of large mammal exterminated by Man in Britain, the Wolf was the last to survive. There is no doubt, as shown by Harting (1880b), that like the Bear, the Wolf was at one time to be found throughout the length and breadth of Britain. Since the arrival of Neolithic Man, if not earlier, it was understandably regarded as a serious nuisance, but as long as there were large tracts of impenetrable woodland and wild uncharted countryside, it was impossible to eliminate such a resourceful and elusive animal. The ancient Britons were keen Wolf hunters and it is well recorded that the Anglo Saxons too enjoyed the hunt for Wolf, Fox, and Boar as well as Deer. Wolves were at their boldest in the harsh months of winter and the Saxons referred to the month of January as the 'wolf month'. Harting in his extensive review, *Extinct British Animals*, relates the oft-quoted story of the tribute extracted by the Saxon King Edgar from the Welsh around the year 960. Following the earlier defeat of his predecessor, the Welsh King Idwal was required to furnish Edgar with the skins of 300 Wolves annually. At this time, it was reputed that the areas on either side of Offa's dyke were infested with Wolves, although the tribute was only paid for four years, after which it was claimed that there were no more Wolves to be found. This was not the end of the animal in Wales however, since it was undoubtedly still to be found in some of the wild, heavily wooded, remote valleys and mountain sides. In 1166, a rabid animal was reputed to have run amok in the Carmarthen area where it was claimed improbably to have been responsible for several human deaths.

In tenth century England, the same Edgar, still urging the control of Wolves, imposed a punishment on some criminals which required them to produce a given number of Wolves' tongues instead of more conventional penalties, although it was apparently of little effect. In the eleventh century, Canute introduced draconian forest laws, but at the same time in respect of Foxes and Wolves, decreed that 'whoever kills any of them is out of all danger of forfeiture . . .'. Subsequent monarchs through William Rufus, Henry II, King John, and Edward I all hunted the Wolf or required others to pursue its control. During the reign of Edward I, it was still regarded as common in many areas, although this probably applied mainly to peripheral and upland areas. In 1281, Edward commissioned Peter Corbet to destroy all Wolves in the counties of Gloucestershire, Worcestershire, Herefordshire, Shropshire, and Staffordshire. In the fourteenth century, Wolves were allegedly numerous in areas such as the forests of the Derbyshire Peak, although Yalden (pers com) believes that this is extremely unlikely. Harting puts the date of the last Wolf in England and Wales at around the end of the fifteenth century. However, Rackham and others believe it is more likely to have been exterminated 200 years earlier than this.

In the remote wilds of Scotland, Wolves were even more difficult to eliminate. It was long regarded as a serious and fearsome enemy, and in 1428, James I passed a law enforcing Wolf hunting although, as with a similar Act of his son James II thirty years later, it may have had some local success but relatively little effect overall. By the end of the fifteenth century wide areas of Ross, Cromarty, Inverness, Argyll, and Perth were still forested. During Mary's reign (1547–87), the queen herself was a keen huntress. One account of 1563 describes a Highland hunt in which she deployed 2,000 Highlanders to drive the woods of Athol, Mar, and Badenoch, at the climax of which they had killed some 360 deer and five Wolves. By the end of that century however, Wolves were still regarded as a major problem. The animals lingered on and by 1621 the bounty of three shillings and four pence (at least in Sutherland) was the going price for a Wolf's head. Later in the century however, it is thought that the last ones had been killed. Sibbald in his *Scotia Illustrata* published in 1684 certainly believed that they were by then extinct, a belief echoed by Thomas Pennant. However there is some evidence that a small number may have remained at least a few years beyond this, the last ones perhaps being those allegedly killed in Sutherland some twenty years later.

The two remaining large mammals that were exterminated by Man in the past were certainly not pursued as vermin. The Wild Boar was always highly esteemed as an animal of the hunt and the Beaver valued above all others for the quality of its fur. Both were widely distributed across Great Britain and were numerous, respectively, in extensive areas of deciduous woodland and the network of wetlands. Many place names, reflecting alternative names of Wild Boar—boar, swine, hog—as well as Gaelic names in Scotland, testify to its ubiquity and imply both familiarity and abundance. Before the interference of Man, the Wild Boar was probably second only to Red Deer in numerical terms.

The Wild Boar was principally seen as an animal of the chase although it was also probably killed by villagers to prevent undue damage to agricultural land and to avoid the risk of them hybridizing with domestic pigs. It was hunted in prehistoric times as archaeological evidence demonstrates and was certainly pursued by the Celtic peoples, Romans, and Normans. Reduction of woodland was doubtless one factor in the decline of an animal that is partly dependent on such habitat, but if Rackham is right, most of the deforestation had taken place before the Romans arrived. As an illustration of the importance that was attached to the Royal Prerogative for hunting favoured quarry in England, William I passed severe forest laws in 1087 which decreed that anyone killing deer or Boar should be punished by losing their eyes. Wild Boar remained a major game species in all the great forests of Britain, although Rackham asserts that by the Middle Ages it had already become very rare. He records the Christmas dinner which Henry III demanded in 1251 and which included 200 Boar from the Forest of Dean and 100 from the Forest of Pickering. After 1260, when Henry sought twelve from the Forest of Dean, records cease and Rackham believes that that date probably signalled the last of truly Wild Boar in England. Ritchie suggests that in Scotland they survived a little longer but had probably gone by the early years of the seventeenth century. The end picture, however, is confused by the repeated attempts to reintroduce Wild Boar into parklands and forest in many areas from the thirteenth century onward. There were short-term introductions in sites as diverse as Stafford, Savernake, Windsor, Alice Holt, the New Forest, and probably Forfar. In Wales as late as 1834, Baron Von Rutzens released a pair of Wild Boars in the woods at Canaston in Pembrokeshire but they were greatly resented by local landowners and soon removed. This was the fate of most of the earlier attempts of reintroduction; local resentment, usually in respect of damage on farmland, resulted in the animals being destroyed.

The downfall of the Beaver in Britain can safely be attributed to two characteristics of the animal itself. On one hand its fur has always been regarded as being superior to any other in terms of warmth and comfort, while at the same time its medicinal properties were equally valued; the original castor oil was derived from the Beaver (*Castor* is the generic name for the animal). Without doubt the Beaver was originally a widespread resident in suitable wetland habitats throughout Britain. However, it disappeared from all areas so long ago, before the written record, that we have only the most fragmentary evidence of its existence although remains from prehistory support its widespread distribution. The clearest literary account again comes from Wales where the Laws of Hywel Dda, dating from around AD 940, determined that 'the king is to have the worth of Beavers, Martens and Ermines in whatever spot they shall be killed, because from them the borders of the king's garments are made'. In view of the high value that was put on Beaver skins compared with those of other animals, we can deduce that the animal was already scarce by then. Some 250 years later than this, Giraldus Cambrensis, on his travels through Wales with the Archbishop of Canterbury in 1188, leaves a somewhat confusing account of Beavers on the Afon Teifi in West Wales, which he claimed was the only place left in England or Wales where Beavers still existed. His account seems to be based on first hand observation (or local reports) together with a mixture of fantasy. Whether the Teifi was indeed their final stronghold remains a moot point. Giraldus himself understood that there was one river in Scotland that still supported Beavers, although there is evidence of their wider existence later in medieval times, and until the early sixteenth century in the Loch Ness area. It is unclear as to when they actually became extinct in Britain.

A fashion for fur

In looking at the background of persecution of our native wildlife in the centuries leading up to the campaigns launched through the parishes, it is relevant to consider one other factor. Many of our fur-bearing animals had long been heavily exploited, not as vermin (although this clearly happened as well), but for the value of their skins. Fur trading may be the oldest trade in the world. This exploitation was at its peak in Britain for a very long period, stretching from the twelfth century to the middle of the sixteenth. By coincidence, the latter date was almost precisely that at which residual populations of fur-bearing animals were first being targeted, as vermin, for bounty payments in the parishes.

From the very earliest times, Man has hunted animals so that he could use their furs as essentials for clothing and other domestic purposes. However, by the early Middle Ages they were increasingly—and eventually outrageously—being widely incorporated in the making of sumptuous garments for the rich. By the fourteenth century, heavy fur-lined clothes were worn not only outdoors, but indoors as well, since the alternatives for keeping warm were limited and rarely efficient. As the Middle Ages progressed the great variety of colours, textures, and lustre of furs propelled European furs into the realm of essential fashion accessories and upper class status symbols. Clothes exercised a great fascination for the privileged classes, with both men and women, and were important elements in society. Some of the excesses required to satisfy the market begin to put the scale of killing into perspective. Veale, in her book *The English Fur Trade*, quotes numerous outrageous regal excesses, many of which clearly depended on imported furs as well as native ones. The royal household in the single year 1344–5 required 79,220 skins of trimmed miniver (particularly the white belly fur of squirrel) sewn into fur garments, while another 32,762 were used simply to produce the trousseau of Princess Phillipa and the liveries of her escort. When Richard II's widow withdrew to France after his death in 1399, her sombre clothes were enlivened by the incorporation of 45,722 squirrel skins and 400 white lettice skins. One of Henry IV's splendid robes-of-nine-garments was made from 12,000 squirrel and 80 ermine skins. Veale further pointed out that larger skins were similarly required in substantial numbers. Henry VI had a velvet gown lined with 250 backs of Pine Marten whilst the sleeves were made of 68 belly skins. In 1530, Henry VIII used 350 imported Sable skins to line a single satin gown and his daughter Elizabeth needed 200 ermine skins for the trimming of a single gown.

Of course, it was not only the royalty who adorned themselves in selected furs. Noblemen, bishops, and gentlemen of many ranks through the Middle Ages sought the best that they could afford, in order to maintain and advertise their status. The doctrine that the wearing of certain furs was the privilege of only the highest in the land was enshrined in a series of fourteenth century sumptuary laws that defined precisely who was entitled to wear the different furs. The first of these statutes, in 1337, was the most extreme, limiting the wearing of any furs to those of nobles of gentle birth. By 1532—the same year as he passed the first of the Vermin Acts—Henry VIII's final sumptuary Act completed moves in the opposite direction, defining far more widely who could wear what, to the extent of downgrading miniver and some of the other previously prized furs. Thereafter even humble folk could wear furs such as squirrel.

The important point is that at the same time as the eradication of Beaver and the last large predators—Lynx and Wolf—there was already a huge pressure being applied to a range of the smaller native mammals for the purpose of fuelling an almost inexhaustible medieval demand for furs—Otter, Pine Marten, Stoat, Weasel, Polecat (fitch), Fox, Squirrel, Rabbit, and Hare. As the demand increased from the fourteenth century onwards, enormous numbers of skins were imported from northern Europe where the thick and lustrous winter pelage of Beaver, Squirrel, Sable, Pine Marten, and ermine were the most valued of all. However, it is unquestionable that there was a great harvest of British skins as well. Veale stressed how villagers throughout the country produced a steady stream of furs for the domestic market in the Middle Ages—in its way an equivalent source of income to that which was yet to come from killing the same animals as vermin. She suggests that the populations of Pine Marten and Beaver were already greatly reduced by the early Middle Ages (which accords with Giraldus' belief) and quotes, in support of that claim, that in Wales by the thirteenth century there were already extremely high fixed prices for both furs— respectively set at 24 and 120 times the value of a sheep skin! As we know, Beaver was already a rare animal by this time, and it is tempting to suggest that the relatively few records of churchwarden payments for Pine Martens (p. 204) in most parts of the country may be a reflection of the heavy toll that had been taken on them too, for the fur trade in preceding years. Certainly Millais believed that the Pine Marten was indeed a rare animal by 1577. Ritchie has shown that the wearing of Marten fur in Scotland was restricted by sumptuary law as early as 1457.

Scotland was an important source of medieval furs and was famous for its exports of skins. By the seventeenth century, there was a long-established and flourishing trade in Fox, Otter, Squirrel, Marten, Wild Cat, and formerly Beaver, with Inverness having been the main centre of the trade in the north in the sixteenth century, specializing in exports of Beaver and Marten. The Mar and Kellie papers include the mention of the export of many hundreds of Scottish skins in the early seventeenth century, among which Otter and Fox alone brought an income of '£2,024 Scots' and '£88 Scots' respectively. The fur market at Dumfries, long-established, although its actual date of origin is unknown, was claimed to be the most important market in Britain for native furs up to its decline in the late nineteenth century (see Chapter 4).

Thus, even before the implementation of rewards for killing these animals as vermin, there had already been sustained killing for an entirely different purpose. There is no record of the extent of this, but it seems likely that it had already made severe inroads into the populations of several species, notably Beaver and Pine Marten and possibly Otter and Wild Cat. The smaller mustelids, with greater population densities, probably survived better.

The popularity of furs lasted for several centuries and resulted in the taking of many hundreds of thousands—possibly millions—of skins of native mammals in Britain in addition to large numbers imported from Europe. By the mid sixteenth century, the high fashion for furs had almost run its course and a new vogue for extravagant fabrics such as velvets, damasks, and brocades had taken over.

2

The social background
to persecution

THE implementation of the Tudor Acts in the mid sixteenth century not only introduced financial incentives for killing vermin, but also gave official sanction, moral emphasis, and structure to the less intensive and more haphazard war against many wild creatures that had in any case been prosecuted ad hoc over the earlier centuries since Man first settled the land. As this account will show, these Acts vastly increased the numbers of animals, birds, and even in some cases reptiles and amphibians, that were officially targeted in the name of agrarian protection. In some cases species were pursued, irrespective of the Acts, for reasons far removed from the stated agricultural considerations. Justification—should any have been needed—was readily found for example, in conflict with Man's interests (Fox, Red Kite, Rook), fear (Adder), revulsion (Toad), or even prejudice and superstition. Whatever the putative justifications, however, there are several questions that need to be addressed before examining the extent to which individual species may have been reduced, locally decimated or exterminated, or perhaps little affected. First and most importantly, what were the underlying reasons and imperatives that drove such a sustained and systematic campaign against so many wildlife species, to the extent of eventually driving several of them over the edge of either regional or national extinction? Why was such an onslaught initiated and then perpetuated for so long? What were the social issues in post-medieval centuries that drove those imperatives, and what were the human attitudes and philosophies on which the approaches to wildlife were based; how or when did they evolve with time?

Population growth and the pressure on agriculture

As a result of the ravages of the successive outbreaks of the plague in the fourteenth century, the population of England and Wales had collapsed from a previous high of 3.7 million to no more than 2.5 million or so by the last quarter of the century. The recovery of the population thereafter was remarkably slow. Indeed the population of Britain essentially stagnated for the following

150 years with the result that by 1525 there were still no more than half a million people in Scotland, 2.6 million in England, and a mere 210,000 in Wales. The demography of England and Wales showed a population that was still almost exclusively rural, the only major urban area being London (reduced to c.50,000 inhabitants around 1525). Otherwise there was only a handful of regional centres such as Norwich, York, Bristol, Edinburgh in Scotland, and a scatter of small market towns which, in England at least, had often been chartered since Saxon times. By 1550, only one provincial town had a population in excess of 10,000 and the market towns rarely had more people than a modern village. Elsewhere the daily life of the rural populations was practised in the same way that it had been by generations of their forebears. Arable crops of barley, wheat, rye, or pulses were grown on open field strips; meadow land provided hay and in many parishes cattle and sheep were brought in after the harvest from the summer grazings on the common to feed on the stubbles and aftermath. In addition to the cultivated crops, in years of harvest failure the produce of woods and fields—berries, fungi, birds' eggs, wild meat, and fruits—were crucial con-stituents of existence. The eggs of Lapwing, wild ducks, and Black-headed Gull have long been harvested traditionally in spring, but for hard-pressed rural communities opportunities went far beyond those species. Sparrows (see Chapter 6) and a wide variety of other birds and their eggs—however small—were important supplements to a frugal diet. For this rural, self-sufficient life was no bucolic idyll: far from it; harvests were never reliable, disease was an ever present and deadly cohabitant, and the poverty threshold was a daily companion for many (no systematic poor relief existed until 1601). Rural subsistence could not readily tolerate competition from a range of species preying on crops or stock. Regional differences in agricultural practice were as significant in the sixteenth and seventeenth centuries as they are today, determined by basic factors such as climate, soils, altitude, etc. These differences themselves are frequently reflected in the emphases that were soon to become apparent in the different species of vermin that were targeted, at different times, irrespective of statute, in parishes throughout England and Wales.

From about 1525, however, profound social changes were under way, stimulated by a long overdue rise in population and rural stability. The rise was steep for the first twenty years but thereafter slumped again temporarily in the 1550s principally because of a series of disastrous harvests and serious outbreaks of disease. After that, the population continued to climb steadily again to the end of the sixteenth century and into the early decades of the next.

This sudden population growth in England in particular brought with it great problems. As the price of agricultural produce rose to meet the new demand, landlords were quick to revise land rents and in many areas these spiralled upwards to put unsustainable pressure on leaseholders. This factor was further exacerbated by the landlords' opportunistic and piecemeal improvement of marginal lands to produce more and better grazings for an expanding sheep flock. More and more commons and 'wastes' were eroded, thereby inexorably reducing the land resource available for the remainder of the rural population. The price that could be gained for produce in the increasing urban market place was higher than that which had been asked previously of the local communities which therefore were frequently without many of the basic necessities of life.

Demand often outstripped supply, especially in years of poor harvests and the latter half of the sixteenth century was blighted by many such years. There was a whole succession of disastrous harvests in this period that produced serious food shortages and led to widespread malnutrition and consequent disease and death. There were poor harvests in 1544–5, and then in 1549–51 (these three years in succession were therefore particularly devastating), 1554–5, 1586–7, and then four in succession, 1594–7. Thus the most catastrophic crop failures were those in 1549–51 and later from 1594 to 1597. Population growth and the agricultural disasters of those years unquestionably stimulated the imperative for the succession of Vermin Acts across this period of the sixteenth century. One third of the population lived in poverty and another third only marginally above it; the state of the annual harvest was a constant topic across all strata of society and the spectre of famine and starvation for those at the lower end was very real. Thus one of the net results of all these social upheavals was to promulgate an aggressive war against any wildlife that was deemed to compete in any respect with agricultural, horticultural, or piscatorial production. In 1598, immediately after the latest catastrophic failures of the harvest, Elizabeth I gave final renewal (39 Eliz 18) to the 1566 legislation. She had already renewed it once in 1572 and it was firmly enshrined in public consciousness.

It is no coincidence that this period of burgeoning human demand for food in the second half of the sixteenth century, amid a series of disastrous harvests, saw the publication of a succession of books on vermin control. Many of them make fascinating and often amusing reading. The first volume was that produced by Mascall in 1590 and it was followed by a rash of others in the succeeding century and on into the next. These were books which—frequently plagiarizing each other—described elaborate trapping methods or concoctions for killing the whole range of vermin species from bedbugs and wasps to serpents, Kites, and Foxes.

So, in the late sixteenth and seventeenth centuries severe hardship was widespread. Vagrancy, driven by rural deprivation and often swollen by destitute or maimed soldiers and sailors returning from the wars, was a major problem in urban and rural communities. In these circumstances major outbreaks of disease were unsurprising. The devastating influenza epidemic of 1555–9 was so serious and extensive that it was the main cause of a significant decrease in population in England. Inflation and unemployment were major social problems throughout the latter part of the Tudor dynasty and on into the Stuart period. Two years before her death in 1601, Elizabeth had introduced the Poor Relief Act that made every parish responsible for its own poor, paid for by the raising of a special parish tax. From then on, the existing parish accounts of the churchwardens and overseers of the poor are a telling indication of the extent of poverty throughout the country.

We tend to look back on the Tudor Age as one of the golden eras of British history and indeed in many respects—military, cultural, literary, ecclesiastical— it was a momentous age. For those in the privileged classes it was, despite many examples of brutal barbarity, undoubtedly a golden period. However, for the majority of the underclasses, both rural and urban, it was unquestionably a desperate daily struggle against hunger, squalor, disease, unemployment, and death.

The major factor that affected the quality of annual harvests and the lot of the people themselves, was climate. Excessive rainfall in particular was responsible for many of the harvest failures. The weather through much of the sixteenth and seventeenth centuries was more extreme than it had been in human memory before and since. The so-called 'Little Ice Age' lasted for 500 years or more, but reached one of its worst phases in the seventeenth century, with many successive years of cold, wet weather. The severity of the weather conditions that had to be borne at times can be illustrated by the following entry abstracted from the churchwardens' accounts at Youlgreave in Derbyshire.

A memorial to the great snow 1614–15

This year January 16th 1614 began the greatyst snow which ever fell within many memo-rye. It covered the earth five quarters deep upon the plain. And for heaps and drifts of snow they were very deep: so that passengers both horse and foot, passed over the gates and hedges and walls; it fell at several tymes, and the last was the greatest. To the great admiration and feare of all the land, it came from the four parts of the world so that (it covered) all countrys from the south part as well as these mountaynes. It continued daily increasing untill the 12th day of March without the sight of any earth, either upon the hilles or valleyes upon which day (being the 'Lord's Day') it began to decrease, and so little by little consumed and wasted away till the eight and twentyeth day of May before all the heaps and drifts of snow were consumed: except one upon Kinder Scout which lay till Witsun Weeke and after.

Hynderances and losses in this peake country by the snow aforesayd

   i)   it hindered the seed time. A very cold spryng
   ii) it consumed much fodder
   iii) And many wanted fawell, otherwyse few were smothered in the fall or drowned in the passage away in regard the floode of water; (losses) were not great though many.

The name of the Lord be praysed

The Spring was so cold and so late that much cattel was in great danger and some dyed. There fell also some ten lesse Snowes in Aprill some a foot deep, some less but none continued long. Upon May Day in the morning in stead of fetching flowers the Youth brought flakes of snow which lay about a foot deep upon the moores and mountaynes. All these aforesaid snowes vanished away and thored with little or no rayne.

With or without the Vermin Acts, the rural communities throughout the times of the Tudor and Stuart dynasties had to regard virtually any competition for their food resources as unacceptable. Thus any and all of those species of bird or mammal that were known or suspected to impact on crops or stock were legitimate prey to the countryman's inventiveness to catch and destroy. Simultaneously, of course, other species could offer the opportunity for desperately needed foods in winter and at other times of need. The whole spectrum of wildlife was of infinitely greater consequence to people in those centuries, for a variety of very different purposes, than anything we can imagine today. The example of the Rabbit is a case in point.

The Normans introduced Rabbits to Britain in the early part of the twelfth century. The first warrens were established on offshore islands to combat the Rabbit's ability for rapid dispersal; island havens round the coasts solved the otherwise difficult problem of fencing them in. The earliest written record mentioned by Sheail in his history of the Rabbit concerns the establishment of a warren on the Scilly Isles in 1176. During the next century, numerous other warrens were constructed in England, Scotland, and Wales, many of the largest of them by monastic houses. Sandy soils on heathlands were particularly favoured, since they were unsuitable for the cultivation of crops, yet easy to dig. By the late nineteenth century, for example, Sheail estimates that some 11% of Breckland was occupied by warrens and extensive areas of the Hampshire Downs and Yorkshire Wolds were put to the same purpose. A successful warren was a very valuable asset for the landowner and would not only assure a healthy profit each year but would provide permanent employment for a warrener and for a person to make and maintain the nets and snares employed for trapping and ferreting. As the Rabbits spread out from the warrens to the wider country-side, they became increasingly available to the peasantry and in many areas became a vital source of supplementary food. Thirsk (1967) relates, for example, that poor people on Hatfield Chase in Yorkshire virtually lived off the abundance of Rabbits there and the same applied in many other parts of the country.

However, Rabbits have many other predators in addition to Man. They are the main prey of Buzzard, Stoat, Wild Cat, Fox, and Polecat as well as being an incidental one for a range of other predators such as Badger and Kite. Thus, with the importance that was attached to Rabbits, both commercially and as a basic food source for many rural communities, there was a further need to control predatory species beyond that which was intended by successive Acts. A good example of the extent of measures that were taken to protect warrens from natural predators is shown by the number of specially constructed traps that have been found around some of the Dartmoor warrens. Around Trowlesworthy Warren on the south bank of the upper reaches of the River Plym, thirty-one solid granite traps have been located in recent decades. Their construction must have been astonishingly laborious and they probably date from the early eighteenth century. Details of these elaborate structures are given in Chapter 3.

How the circle has turned. In modern times, the Rabbit has become regarded as a major agricultural pest and many of its predators generally better valued and protected.

Cycles of agriculture and pulses of vermin control

Thirsk (1997) has shown clearly how the cycles of British agriculture over the centuries have been driven by alternating imperatives of supply and demand. She defines four very clear periods within which supply generally outstripped demand, prices fell, and farmers were obliged to move away from the mainstream production of cereals and meat to find more profitable crops. The present phase in which British agriculture now operates (Thirsk's 'fourth era of alternative agriculture') is a perfect example, wherein during the late twentieth century we witnessed surplus 'mountains' of agricultural products, obliging legislators to use financial leverage to force cut-backs, and farmers, thereby, to seek innovative ways of using their land and diversifying into alternative crops. This phase is a mirror image of what has happened three times before.

1350 $\longrightarrow$ 1500 $\longrightarrow$ 1650 $\longrightarrow$ 1750 $\longrightarrow$ 1879 $\longrightarrow$ 1939
   alternative   mainstream   alternative   mainstream   alternative

Figure 2. Thirsk's periods of mainstream and alternative agriculture.

As can be seen in the timeline above, the three defined periods of alternative agriculture are interspersed with equally long periods wherein the mainstream production of cereals and meat predominated, with demand promoting increased supply and prices favouring the producer. The period covered by this book extends from 1532 up to the present and it can be seen that the starting point occurs within a period when the demand for increased food productivity was at a premium, as highlighted earlier in this chapter. The sixteenth century was characterized by a burgeoning population, serious human privation, and many harvest failures. Thus the introduction of Parliamentary Acts by Henry VIII and Elizabeth, designed to initiate campaigns of vermin destruction, was no coincidence, but a clear legislative measure reflecting the determination to assist production. The fact that both the 1532 Act and that of 1566 refer specifically to the protection of grain (despite the latter's wide range of offending species which have no relevance whatever to the title of the Act) reinforces this point.

Having identified a clear relationship between the timing of sixteenth century vermin legislation and the need for maximum yields from agriculture, one would expect that similar connections might be found in the next period of production pressure. Thirsk again demonstrates that the factors that stimulated a return to mainstream products of meat and cereals around 1750, after 100 years or so of depressed agriculture, were echoes of the previous phase from the 1500s up to 1650. A population of 6.2 million in England and Wales in 1751 increased by half a million ten years later and rose to 7.6 million by 1781. It then doubled to almost 18 million by the middle of the nineteenth century. The 100 years from 1750 witnessed the most widespread change to agricultural systems that could be imagined. The implementation of the parliamentary Enclosure Acts signalled the final demise of the open field system, with the simultaneous reclamation of many of the remaining 'wastes', commons, and heaths being brought into cultivation. However, despite this revolution in agriculture, there is no evidence from the parish records of a parallel increase in payments for vermin. In fact, if anything, the reverse appears to be the case as levels of persecution seem to have reduced.

I analysed the vermin payments from a sample of thirty-one parishes in sixteen English counties; counties in which relatively long runs of records of churchwardens' accounts existed, starting in the early sixteenth century (or earlier where possible) and which were notable for heavy kills of vermin. Of these only fourteen revealed sustained killing extending beyond 1750, whereas all except two were heavily focused on the period between 1650 and 1750—exactly the period of alternative, diversified agriculture. It was a long period characterized by the development of crops such as rape, woad (and other dye plants), hops, root crops, and horticulture (especially a wide variety of fruits).

E. L. Jones has shown that during this time, there was an upsurge in the killing of species such as Red Kite, Buzzard, Jay, and Bullfinch, the emphasis then being directed to those species preying on farm poultry and new-born lambs, etc. and others responsible for stripping fruit buds. This was an era in which home-grown grain was in good supply and surpluses exported to Europe with the result that prices fell, thereby encouraging diversification into a wider range of alternative crops. One reflection of this was a marked increase in the planting of orchards and a ready market for fresh fruit. The onslaught on Bullfinches in different parts of the country precisely coincides with this period from c.1650 to 1750, outside which dates very few Bullfinch records are to be found in the parish records. Jays were predominantly targeted in Devon, with lesser kills in Dorset, Kent,

Herefordshire, and Gloucestershire. Interestingly, persecution of Jays did not occur across the same period as with Bullfinches. With a few exceptions it started noticeably later, around the 1680s and 1690s and continued in some cases well into the nineteenth century and occasionally into the early years of the following one. The spread of years across which bounties for Kites were given is shown on p. 121–3.

These examples illustrate how the emphases of vermin control through the parishes reflected the shifts in agricultural demand. At the same time, it leaves the question open as to whether the squirearchy's strengthening hold on land in some parts of the country meant that they took on increasing responsibility for the removal of competing vermin through their own resources? If so it would explain the puzzling lack of bounties in many parishes in the latter half of the eighteenth century.

Enclosure: barren fields and a link to killing

One might initially question the relevance of the agricultural enclosure movement in the context of the control of vermin. In fact, it is one of the very significant factors as we shall see, in terms of its consequence both to wildlife populations and to the numbers and species that were targeted in different areas. It led directly to the impetus that resulted in the elimination of several species.

Since Saxon times, the cultivated areas over much of southern Britain were characterized, parish by parish, by the open field system of agriculture with huge areas of ploughland, meadow, and fallow, largely unseparated by hedgerows or other divisions. Each great field—usually three in each village—was farmed in long individual strips by the inhabitants of a nucleated village at their centre. Such a landscape dominated much of the countryside for a thousand years or more. The footprints of these ridge and furrow systems still exist and are most readily seen in the heavy clay lands of the Midland counties. Slowly, over time, increasing areas were enclosed by new hedgerows or stone walls into fields of different shapes and sizes, overriding the old Saxon and medieval strips, to produce the pattern of countryside with which we are now familiar. The process of change had been ongoing for many years; even areas such as the Hampshire Downs were being brought into cultivation, using new husbandries, from the late seventeenth century. However, the fulfilment of this evolutionary process was the enactment of some 2,500 Parliamentary Enclosure Acts embracing the larger, more complex villages in England, in the eighteenth and nineteenth centuries. Across this period the Acts enclosed land affecting some 3,000 English parishes alone in a great swathe of country stretching from coastal Dorset to the uplands of Yorkshire. The extent of these lands is shown on the map below.

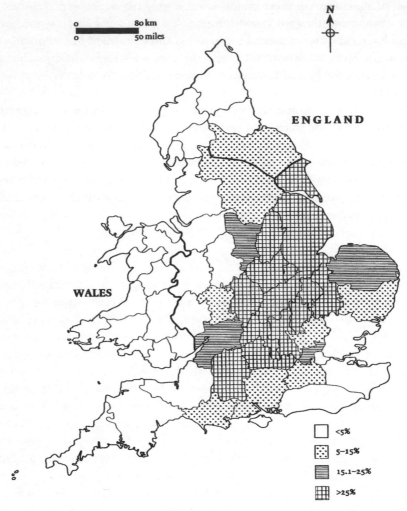

Figure 3. The percentage of open field systems enclosed by Parliamentary Act
in the eighteenth and nineteenth centuries. Reproduced from Shrubb (2003)
with the author's permission.

The changes in the nature of the countryside resulting from these enclosures had
enormous social consequences. Moreover, they also had serious implications for
the status of many of the species of our native wildlife and thereby the necessity
or otherwise for their control.

   The principal purpose of the enclosure process was to rationalize land holding
and increase agricultural productivity. This meant the breaking up and fencing
in of the great open fields and many of the commons and 'wastes', dividing the
areas into manageable hedged or fenced fields and permitting a more efficient

system of agriculture to meet the growing food needs of the nation. Stock and arable crops henceforward could be managed in separated field units. There was no longer the constant need to shepherd sheep and cattle away from arable crops in the open fields or to fold them on the commons. With the collapse of the open fields, the days of Little Bo Peep and Little Boy Blue with his horn were numbered.

The process of enclosing the open fields and rough grazings was a very protracted and complicated one. Considerable areas of southern England and the few lowland areas in Wales and the Marches had already been enclosed before the beginning of the eighteenth century and as Yelling has shown, such enclosure had been going on piecemeal since at least the fourteenth century through land exchange, purchase, and private agreement. Thus the development of what Rackham describes as the 'ancient countryside' characterized much of west and south-west England, lowland Wales, and large parts of south-east England.

In these areas, the open field systems were never fully developed and where they did occur they had slowly disappeared across time without much trace or record.

Unsurprisingly these fundamental changes to the countryside wrought by the Parliamentary Acts and the consequent lot of the rural peasantry were hardly

◼ Predominantly Ancient Countryside
▢ Predominantly Planned Countryside

Figure 4. Map of Oliver Rackham's simplified landscapes of 'ancient' and 'planned' countryside. Redrawn from Williamson (2002) with the author's permission.

welcomed by the poorer villagers. The enclosures often resulted in serious rural depopulation—including the entire disappearance of some villages—resulting in large-scale urban migration, much poverty, and misery. John Clare, himself a native of Helpston in Northamptonshire in the heartland of the Midland enclosure process, expressed his sentiments clearly and undoubtedly reflected the heart-felt view of most of the peasant class:

> Inclosure thou'rt a curse upon the land,
> And tasteless was the wretch who thy existence planned.

He lamented the loss of the countryside he knew as a boy (Helpston was finally enclosed in 1820), the disappearance of the heaths and commons, and the loss of wildlife: 'The Wild Cat (was) an animal that used to be common in our woods though rather scarce lately'. The disappearance of the Kite too he felt, with the loss of nests that he had regularly climbed to as a boy. Notwithstanding these deeply felt emotions, Clare was employed for a time in the very process of planting the enclosing hawthorn hedges in the parish. Around the same year Knapp, in Gloucestershire, lamented the continuing loss of wildlife, 'Some of our birds are annually diminishing—population, plough, enclosure, clearance, drainage'. Such sentiments and reflections would have been echoed in many parts of the country.

In the Midland areas, the conversion to enclosure was predominantly to new grasslands for sheep and cattle. Williamson gives figures which demonstrate dramatically the extent to which unrelieved grassland then dominated these counties. For example, in Warwickshire he quotes a figure of 232,000 acres (939 hectares) of new pasture by 1794 (plus another 576 acres (233 hectares) of rotational grass) with 60% of Rutland under new grasslands and only 16% of Leicestershire still under arable about the same time. The figures for Buckinghamshire north of the Chiltern scarp and other Midland counties were similar.

In association with the great open fields, there had been the extensive areas of 'wastes'—rough commons, marshes, heathlands, upland moors, etc. These wastes were crucial components of the village life and whereas their most obvious role was in providing essential grazing for the commoners' stock away from the cultivated fields, they also fulfilled other important functions. They were the source of much of the villagers' fuel, from peat and turf to wood and gorse, wild meat in the form of game and wildfowl, and bedding (bracken) and winter feed (heather) for stock. The Board of Agriculture figures for 1795 suggest that at the end of the eighteenth century there were still some 8 million acres (c.21% of the total) of these wastes in England and Wales. They were distributed widely across virtually every county; the example of Lincolnshire is shown in Figure 5.

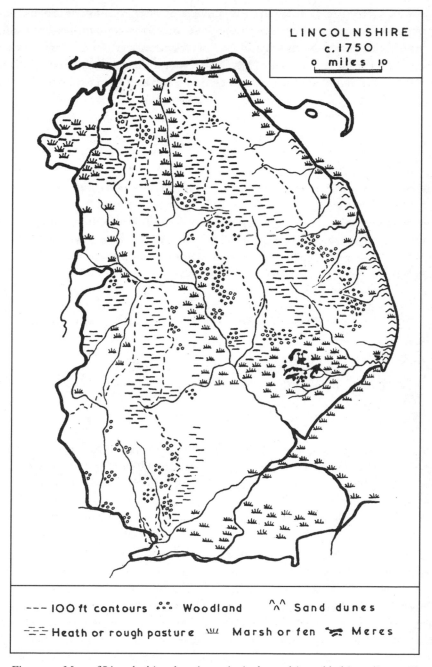

LINCOLNSHIRE
c.1750
0 miles 10

--- 100 ft contours   ⁙ Woodland   ∧∧ Sand dunes

⹀ Heath or rough pasture   ⱶⱶ Marsh or fen   ⤳ Meres

Figure 5. Map of Lincolnshire showing principal uncultivated habitats ('wastes')
c.1750. Reproduced from *The Birds of Lincolnshire* (1955) by kind
permission of Dr A. E. Smith, joint author.

However, Lincolnshire, where there was an exceptional extent of marshland and fens, was not representative of most other counties. In those counties dominated by heavy clay land—Nottinghamshire, Leicestershire, etc.—wastes were far fewer and in some areas such as south Warwickshire, virtually absent. When Daniel Defoe documented his famous *Tour of the Whole Island of Great Britain* in 1724, he was appalled at the wildness and inhospitable nature in some parts of the country. The uplands and mountains of the West Country, Wales, and the North of England were justifiably regarded as wild, dangerous, and forbidding places—certainly well beyond the pale so far as someone like Defoe was concerned. But there were vast areas of barren countryside in the lowlands of England as well; Hampshire still had some 100,000 acres (40,500 hectares) of untamed heathland (you can still sense a step back in time to this countryside as you cross the northern fringes of the New Forest) and neighbouring Berkshire had perhaps 60,000 acres (24,000 hectares). Shropshire, Dorset, and many other counties had similar expanses of rough wastes. Bagshot Heath in Surrey, a stone's throw from London, horrified Defoe:

Here is a vast tract of land some of it within seventeen or eighteen miles of the capital city; which is not only poor, but even quite steril, given up to barrenness, horrid and frightful to look on, not only good for little, but good for nothing; much of it a sandy desert . . . for in passing this heath on a windy day, I was so far in danger of smothering with the clouds of sand . . . that I could neither keep it out of my mouth, nose nor eyes . . . the product of it feeds no creatures, but some very small sheep, who feed chiefly on the said heather, and are very few of these, nor are there any villages, worth mentioning, and but a few houses or people for many miles far and wide.

The other principal component of the countryside, apart from extensive wetlands which characterized many of the lowland valleys of England, were the woodlands. These were still extensive in some areas of both uplands and lowlands but almost absent in many of the heavy clay areas and the open downlands. Rackham shows that the 15% of woodland cover at the time of the Domesday Book (1086) had shrunk to *c.*10% by 1350. However, those woodlands then remaining had a good chance of longer term survival and many were brought into stable management through coppicing. In addition there was some development of secondary woodland, such was the need for timber, in particular in the ship building industry. Woodlands, as with the other categories of 'waste', were the principal reservoirs of wildlife outside the intensively farmed land, and their removal and fragmentation therefore directly affected populations of both verminous species and those not perceived as a threat to Man. The principal period of parliamentary enclosures was to put a further strain on this resource due to the large amounts of timber that were required, not least to provide the miles of mandatory fencing that accompanied each enclosure award. These

demands necessarily encouraged the care of woodlands and stimulated replacement and regeneration in many areas.

By the early years of the eighteenth century, Williamson points out, vast areas
still remained unenclosed and that the process of enclosure accelerated, partly
by outright purchase and partly by Parliamentary Acts, from the mid 1700s
onwards. Whereas the earliest Parliamentary Acts concentrated on the open field
system, in the later ones the emphasis moved more towards the enclosure of
wastes and commons, many of them residual as they had already been subject to
encroachment for centuries.

In Wales, the historical pattern of land use and agriculture was very different
from that in the adjoining English counties. First of all Wales is a predominantly
upland country with more than 25% of its land above 300 metres. In addition,
the pattern of rural land holding was based, not on a system of nucleated villages
as in the Saxon lands of England, but (at least until the Acts of Union in 1536
and 1542) on historic systems of bond settlements (i.e. tied to a landlord)
or free holdings held on hereditary tenure. Many family groups operated
through gavelkind rather than primogeniture. Furthermore, agriculture was
predominantly pastoral, with only limited areas of arable even in the more productive lowland parts. However, some parliamentary enclosures were enacted
between 1733 and 1885 although, as may be assumed from the above, the
extent was far less significant than in England. Again the greatest effects were to
be seen in the Marcher counties (except Radnorshire and Flintshire) and mainly
occurred in the period up to the end of the Napoleonic Wars.

The ultimate social effect of enclosure in England and Wales was to concentrate the ownership of the majority of land into the hands of a smaller number
of individuals and to produce a class of prosperous capitalist tenant farmers,
thereby effectively dispossessing the small freeholders of their former living.
As a result a huge number of landless peasants either took to low-wage farm
labouring or migrated to the uncertainty of better pay prospects in the urban
areas. It was the most dramatic agricultural, landscape, and social change that
had occurred in rural Britain for a thousand years or more. It also had significant
implications for wildlife and its control.

Wildlife and the pattern of the countryside

It is axiomatic that each species of plant, bird, mammal, etc. has its own individual habitat requirement. Uniformity and monoculture support only poor
diversity. The greater the variety of habitats that the countryside supports, the
wider will be the diversity of its wildlife. The pattern of the countryside therefore—its landscape, natural habitats, different agricultural systems, settlements,
and other man-made elements—has a profound influence on the composition

of its wildlife. As a consequence of these differences across the country, the patterns, emphases, and even take-up (or not) of control of various species has been greatly influenced.

In these respects there were significant differences between the open fields and the new enclosures that succeeded them and, on the other hand, the long-established countryside—Rackham's 'ancient countryside'. An understanding of these differences is fundamental to a proper appreciation of the factors that determined the pattern and intensity of historic wildlife control across the country.

In the pre-enclosure era, the huge open fields around the nucleated villages, often contiguous with those of the neighbouring communities, supported a rotation of arable crops, fallows, and meadowland, which were rich in weeds, invertebrates, and flowering plants. This meant that they were important feeding places for many species of birds—not least huge flocks of winter finches—and small mammals but, except for open-ground species such as Brown Hare, Skylark, Corncrake, Quail, and Grey Partridge, they presented limited scope for supporting a wider range of breeding species. Indeed the resident vertebrate fauna of these open fields was notably species-poor. This supposition is well supported by work carried out by Pollard et al. on bird surveys in the parish of Laxton (Notts) in the early 1970s. This is the only remaining parish in England in which the ancient open three-field system of farming is still maintained and administered by the (medieval) Court Leet. Here, the historic pattern has been retained and there are no trees, hedgelines, or other relieving features in the extensive open fields. It is not surprising that Pollard's surveys found that the normal range of farmland birds, although common enough on surrounding farms, was entirely absent from the whole area of Laxton. Only open-ground species such as Lapwing, Partridge, and Skylark remained. The authors themselves extrapolated their findings to assume that the historic open field systems had indeed been relatively poor places for birds (and by extension, for mammals as well). However, it is possible that Laxton was atypical since Rackham has shown that woodland trees and limited hedgerows were more likely to occur in other areas. The situation in earlier centuries was undoubtedly better than that found by Pollard and his colleagues and the birds then present may well have included Wheatear and Stone Curlew and even possibly the occasional Great Bustard. Also it is relevant to remember that Pollard's work at Laxton took place at a time when pesticides were still widely used. Nonetheless, historically, in areas dominated by the open fields, so long as Rooks and other corvids could be kept at bay, there was perhaps little compelling reason for promulgating campaigns of vermin control. The evidence of this is discussed in Chapter 8.

Some of the earliest enclosures, that took place in the centuries before the Parliamentary Acts, were characterized by rectilinear prairie-like fields. Some of these were as much as 300 acres (120 hectares) in extent. They were the great sheep-ranching enclosures and we nowadays know to our cost, the paucity of wildlife that a monoculture of sheep pasture may support. These early enclosures were no better for wildlife than the open fields that preceded them. Indeed, wildlife probably fared worse on them than it had done previously. In both contexts, the paucity of wildlife is probably reflected in the very low levels of vermin control that are revealed in the churchwardens' accounts, as shown in Table 3.

TABLE 3. Total numbers of the species killed in three Midland counties in **all years** in existing churchwardens' accounts from C17 to C19. Nottinghamshire thus includes all records for a total of 2,050 individual years in 30 parishes; Leicestershire 4,654 years in 42 parishes; Northamptonshire 2,300 years across 29 parishes.

	Hedgehog	Wild Cat	Fox	Badger	Polecat	Bullfinch
Nottinghamshire	36	1	437	12	397	–
Leicestershire	4654	–	321	3	37	–
Northamptonshire	1554	–	490	5	717	4

Hoskins has shown that a total of some 4 million acres (1,618,777 hectares) of open field was enclosed by the Parliamentary Acts (Gonner put the figure at 4½ million), with a further 400,000 acres (161,878 hectares) or so having been achieved earlier than that. By the time that the hedgerow networks were maturing, the payment of bounties by the churchwardens was broadly being phased out anyway, with principal responsibility for wildlife management being undertaken by those with developing sporting interests on the newly enclosed lands. Consequent upon this, the records extracted from the churchwardens' accounts in parishes across the principal areas of Hanoverian enclosures (see map, p. 35) and the large open field systems that preceded them confirm that these were areas where a minimum amount of species control was normally undertaken.

So, the reservoirs of wildlife that did exist in the open field areas were to be found in the associated 'wastes'. However, we must not forget the fact that, although there were still areas of 'wastes' in virtually all counties, these declined greatly in size and in total area as the Enclosure Acts and agreements progressed. Unlike the open fields, these varied areas of uncultivated land and the residual woodlands were extremely important for the range and numbers of wildlife species that they supported. Shrubb has detailed the importance of the 'wastes' in respect of several different bird species, after 1750, ranging from harriers to Black Grouse, Stone Curlew, and Woodlark. The same principle applied to a much wider range of mammal and bird species, for these 'wastes' were the wild and natural areas in which wildlife was concentrated in ways that could not apply on the cultivated open fields. In these uncultivated areas, the core populations of numerous species defined as vermin such as Fox, Badger, Polecat, Red Kite, woodpeckers, Bullfinch, and Jay thrived. At the same time, we should recognize too the significance of the great estates with their areas of parkland, woods, and private grounds in providing further oases of wildlife.

In contrast to this are the areas of long-established countryside which are shown in Figure 4. The landscape in these counties has for centuries been characterized by a pattern of small fields with sinuous, irregular boundaries, scattered human communities, meandering lanes, a plethora of ancient wood-lands, coppices, and spinneys and hedgerows of an envious richness of diversity and age. These were—and still are, though further impoverished nowadays—the areas of the country of greatest wildlife diversity and numbers. In these areas many of the hedgerows have a far greater diversity of trees than the enclosure ones because they were very long established. They were frequently planted with a variety of native trees which served not only as field boundaries, but also as reservoirs of fuel, fruits, and other wild foods. It is this complex of features that produced an intimate countryside with greater numbers and diversity of wildlife than the enclosure lands, certainly until their hedgerows, coppices, and wild corners came to full maturity. It follows that these too were the areas in which vermin control was undertaken with zeal, where the most strenuous campaigns of parochial vermin control were prosecuted, and where large numbers of a range of species were killed (see Appendix 1).

By the seventeenth century, when extensive wildlife control really began, this 'ancient countryside' was already long established in large parts of southern Britain. Kent and eastern Essex were almost totally enclosed as were parts of Surrey and the eastern half of Suffolk. The same applied in the south-west peninsula including the majority of Somerset and parts of Dorset and the pattern was similar throughout the counties of the Marches. Thus in Cheshire, Lancashire, Durham, Devon, Cornwall, and Kent, and the counties of the Marches there were virtually no enclosures under the Parliamentary Acts since it had all been achieved long before, usually by mutual agreement. Historically, therefore, it is easy to see how the greatest problems with species regarded as pests occurred on holdings in long-enclosed countryside where mixed sub-sistence farming was the norm, wildlife populations were highest, and the actual or perceived effects of the vermin were most likely to attract attention. Table 4 shows the level of killing that took place in four diverse parishes in areas of 'ancient countryside', in a brief fifteen year period.

Even if the process of enclosure is not central to our theme, the cumulative impact that it had on wildlife, through fundamental changes wrought to the

TABLE 4. Selected species of vermin killed in fifteen years in the C17 in four parishes in 'ancient countryside'.

		Hedgehog	Wild Cat	Fox	Badger	Polecat
Tenterden (Kent)	1679–1693	1010	–	33	9	147
Morwenstow (C'wall)	1676–1690	1392	32	83	40	600
Hartland (Devon)	1657–1671	133	47	106	50	863
Bunbury (Ches)	1678–1692	3711	–	54	–	–

		Stoat	Kite	Bullfinch	Jay	Magpie	Crow*
Tenterden (Kent)	1679–1693	151	329	1230	1775	–	c.2500
Morwenstow (C'wall)	1676–1690	217	267	1033	–	–	–
Hartland (Devon)	1657–1671	7	–	–	–	–	–
Bunbury (Ches)	1678–1692	–	**	2838	–	3052	519

* Presumed to be mainly rooks. **Bunbury parish later killed 696 'kites' in eight years, 1715–22.

structure of the countryside, certainly is. Another inevitable consequence of the enclosure system was that it provided the direct conduit that led to the final demise of many of the predatory species of mammals and birds that had been targeted as vermin across the parishes of England and Wales for 300 years or more. In this respect, the act of enclosure was a critical factor leading to the slaughter and eventual local or regional extinction of a range of these species. Quite simply, the transfer of land ownership into the hands of a powerful country squirearchy meant that they now had complete control over their new lands, tenancies not withstanding. Significantly, the landowners could now indulge in the growing vogue for field sports on a level that had never been imagined before. Tapper estimated that by 1874 a quarter of Britain was held in estates of over 10,000 acres (4,000 hectares), including many in the uplands. The establishment of a country-wide network of game estates gave birth to the modern gamekeeper. For a range of species, the long era of annual attrition, albeit with little overall effect on populations in most cases, would now give way to the cul-de-sac of extinction.

The gamekeeper and his master

The taking of wild meat—the hunting of game and other wildlife for food—has always been considered a rite of passage and an essential part of British rural life. This was especially true in the medieval and post-medieval centuries. If there was insufficient feed for livestock to be kept over winter, only the breeding animals were retained and the remaining stock was therefore slaughtered in the autumn and salted down. Fresh meat in winter had to be won from the wider countryside both by the landlord in his manor and the villager in his cottage. For the villagers this requirement was vital, particularly when enclosure removed the ability for many of them to produce enough food for their families. Low-level poaching was a long-established and accepted necessity in the sixteenth and seventeenth centuries. Poachers were generally seen in a fairly benevolent light, more as Robin Hood characters seeking nothing more than a share of the wild meat as a way to even out of the inequalities of birthright. From time immemorial they had taken game with ferret, snare, net, dog, and sometimes crossbow and needed to continue their traditional rights despite the changes taking place after enclosure. They simply could not comprehend that game that had been available for anyone to hunt across the open countryside, since time immemorial, was now deemed to be the private property of a single individual; thus they continued to hunt. This of course was not how the new owners who had acquired the land through the enclosures viewed the matter. They now reserved these rights entirely for themselves. In this way, essentially by default and often through life and death necessity, the modern poacher was born.

In order to combat this illegal competition for his game it became necessary for the squire to employ men to protect his right to it. Initially such an employee would undoubtedly have come from within the local community because of the need for good local knowledge—the original poacher turned gamekeeper. It was not long, however, before the pressure on the 'keeper became greater and he was not only defending his master's game from local poachers but also from other natural predators. As Vesey-Fitzgerald suggests, since the 'keeper was housed rent-free and paid a reasonable wage he soon became divorced from the village community. The late eighteenth and early nineteenth centuries were periods of severe strife in the countryside. The penalties for poaching could be very severe; serious or repeated offences could lead to hanging or long-term deportation. This was hardly surprising since the justices themselves were drawn from the ranks of the local landowners. This had certainly been the case since 1732 when a law was passed requiring that all justices had an income of at least £100 from land. Vesey-Fitzgerald suggests that it was from thirty years or so into the parliamentary enclosures, around 1780, that the real decline of birds of prey in England can be dated. Many of the early ornithological writings support this contention. Undoubtedly a parallel decline in mammalian predators occurred from around the same date. Notwithstanding the veracity of the claim made by Vesey-Fitzgerald, the rapid habitat changes brought about by the enclosures undoubtedly had a telling effect on the populations of several species, for example harriers.

It is not certain from what date the earliest employment of gamekeepers in the modern understanding of the role originated. The earliest Game Act was passed as long ago as 1671; this restricted the rights for taking game to those with a rental income of at least £100 per annum. Tapper suggests that this franchised some 16,000 landowners. Certainly there are some fairly early records of 'keepers, for example at Ashby Folville in Leicestershire in 1699 where a payment of 1/- was made by the churchwardens 'to squire Fountin's keeper for killing a fox'. It is clear that gamekeepers were fairly widely employed by this time. In 1710, Queen Anne had passed an Act under which it was necessary for a lord of the manor to register with a Clerk of the Peace the appointment of the one gamekeeper allowed by the Act at any one time.

By the latter part of the eighteenth century the gamekeeper's role was becoming clearly established. He was employed to rear and safeguard the maximum numbers of game possible. This required that he waged unremitting warfare on any species that was either proved or suspected to prey upon, or otherwise interfere with, the interests of his game. It is easy to blame the 'keepers for the carnage that took place in the nineteenth and early twentieth centuries but of course it was the demands of the estate owners that fuelled the imperative. The gamekeeper's livelihood and job depended on producing high returns of game for his master. Failure to deliver would mean loss of his job and therefore his livelihood. The blame for the ensuing slaughter of wildlife lay firmly with landowners. Abundant manifestations of the effects of this form substantial parts of Chapters 6 and 7.

Estates were increasingly laid out to maximize the habitats for game species and by the turn of the nineteenth century and into the twentieth, many of these estates had matured and Vandervell and Coles observed that at this period the countryside of lowland Britain provided a near perfect habitat for game. At the same time, it was doubtless also ideal for a wide spectrum of other farmland wildlife, including many of the predators then widely regarded as nothing other than vermin.

By the early decades of the nineteenth century, the systematic persecution of predators and other non-predatory species in southern Britain had been carried out through payments in the parishes for at least 300 years. In a few parishes it continued for several decades beyond that time, although in a more desultory way, and mainly focused on House Sparrows. However, widespread persecution of vermin was gradually being taken over through the development of field sports and the activities of gamekeepers appointed by the shooting interests. At this time, the abundant untapped game resources in the wildernesses in northern England and especially north of the border in Scotland, had yet to be discovered by the majority of English sportsmen. Bounties for birds of prey and crows had been in place in Scotland since at least 1819 and grouse shooting had been regulated on a proper seasonal basis since as early as 1773. However, it was not until the building of rail connections to Scotland in the 1840s that wealthy Victorian Englishmen with their retinues could conveniently make the journey north and begin to exploit the enormous Highland potential for stalking, shooting, and fishing. In no time the grouse season became a prerequisite on the social calendar of the wealthy and ambitious English sportsman. Tapper relates that within two or three decades of the rail line to Edinburgh being opened the demand for grouse shooting frequently outstripped supply.

The nineteenth century and the first decade or so of the twentieth were the heyday of shooting in both lowland and upland Britain. The size of bags was often enormous and promoted fierce competition. This halcyon period for the sportsmen was not to last however and came to a sudden halt with the outbreak of the First World War. Most game management ceased with the departure to the trenches of the majority of 'keepers and a good number of their masters, many of whom did not return. After the war there were attempts to rebuild the previous structure on many estates but the situation was never to be the same again and in fact foundered further with the coming of the Second World War. By 1946, virtually all organized game shooting had ceased. Predatory birds and mammals had found some degree of respite as shown by modest recoveries in the populations such as those of Hen Harrier, Wild Cat, and Buzzard. The partial and fragmented recovery of shooting estates through the remainder of the twentieth century was slow and piecemeal. Whereas the National Census in the heyday of 1911 showed a total of 23,056 gamekeepers in England, Scotland, and Wales, Tapper estimated the number at c.3,500 in 1981. The present number, although larger again, is difficult to ascertain since not all gamekeepers are members of relevant associations and there is considerable overlap between organizations. The best estimate is about 4,500, covering the National Gamekeepers Association, the Gamekeepers Association of Scotland (c.2,000), and the British Association of Shooting and Conservation.

Human attitudes

Before examining the extent of killing of individual species over the past 500 years or so, it is relevant to consider the evolution of human attitudes towards wildlife across this long period.

The sixteenth, seventeenth, and eighteenth centuries were periods of tumultuous and violent history. Civil war and the establishment and collapse of the Commonwealth divided Britain, and even the Act of Union failed to bring an end to the threat of internal strife. It is hardly surprising that Britain from the late Middle Ages and through Tudor times was a particularly harsh and cruel society. Witches were regularly hanged or burned ('Judith Sawkyns of Aylesford

(Kent) common witch, hanged December 1656'). Torture was practised in Tudor and Stuart times and executions were relatively commonplace even for the most minor offences ('Thomas Potter, butcher of Stanstead (Kent) for stealing a sheep: hanged October 1587; Constance Gatland of Hever gave birth to a bastard male left in a ditch: hanged September 1654'). Hoskins (1953–4) reminds us that in the sixteenth century:

the majority of the population, living as they did, (had) little reserves of food or money. Death must have been as common a sight as on a battlefield. It helps to explain the horrible popular taste for cruelty and the sadistic delight in barbarous executions, a taste which the odious Henry VIII shared to the full with his subjects.

Britain, to our eyes, was a shamefully barbarous place. Cock fighting was enjoyed by all classes and bull, bear, and Badger baiting were popular recreations. Magic was widely accepted, frequently replacing reason and was generally and seriously regarded until the eighteenth century. Catholic Britain and the post-Reformation Protestant regime which followed it were heavily under the doctrines of the church. As Keith Thomas describes, religious teaching was firmly embedded at the heart of much of the thinking and many of the attitudes including, importantly for us, Man's relationship with Nature. The biblical account of the Creation was readily taken by theologians as a fundamental of belief and interpreted with literality: Man should 'have dominion over the fish of the sea and over the fowls of the air and over every living thing . . .' Thus the firmly established credo was that the world had been created for the benefit of Man and all other life should be subservient to him. His jurisdiction over other living things should be total. A clear line was drawn between Man and all other creatures. Man had rights, had a soul, he could intellectualize, reason, own land, feel pain, and comprehend the nature of God and his Creation. The other inhabitants of the natural world possessed none of these abilities and merely existed, subsisted, and procreated. Animals were here to be employed as beasts of toil, as food, for sport, for vivisection, or whatever other requirement might be designed. Certainly, the line drawn between Man and beasts gave clear justification for the elimination as vermin of any creatures that were thought to compete in any way with his interests. Few wild creatures, save those taken for food (even 'four and twenty Blackbirds baked in a pie') were seen as beneficial and could therefore understandably be hunted, persecuted, and eliminated. Furthermore, and importantly, there was very little consideration that one could be cruel to animals; after all they were deemed to be incapable of feelings. Even domestic stock was sometimes appallingly treated. Thomas relates how domestic fowl were at times nailed to the floor by their feet, in order to fatten them, kept in the dark, blinded, or had their legs cut off in the hideous belief that it increased the tenderness of the meat.

Against this sort of background, the wholesale slaughter of undesired wildlife by any or all means was of little consequence and must have hardly impinged on the conscience of rural inhabitants, inured by the strife of continual hardship and the fight for subsistence. It would not only have been seen as a need but also, certainly in the earlier years, as a perfect right supported by the teachings of the scriptures.

However, even in those dark days of inhumanity, there were a few beacon voices expressing a new interest in the creatures and plants of the countryside. Even if they did not directly advocate respect or consideration for wildlife, they established the first real steps in improving knowledge of nature and thereby sowed the first seeds of a better understanding and enlightenment. William Turner, born in Morpeth in 1510 a year after Henry VIII's accession, is widely regarded as the father of British botany and ornithology. He was unique in his time, an active field naturalist, learning much from fowlers and other rural folk, and his writings began to point the first tentative ways towards an alternative attitude to the animal kingdom. Other luminaries followed in the next century: John Ray (born 1627) one of whose works lauded *The Wisdom of God in the Works of his Creation*; Francis Willughby (born 1635) whose *Ornithologia* is revered even today; Edward Lhuyd the Welsh botanist; Thomas Johnson another pioneering plant hunter and an amender of Gerald's *Herbal*. In Scotland, naturalists such as Robert Sibbald (1641–1722) and, somewhat later, John Lightfoot, who wrote the first book on Scottish flora in 1778, began to have an influence on thinking there. The views of all these men, among others, began to spread and from the latter part of the seventeenth century these and many other lesser-known naturalists started to debunk medieval beliefs such as magic and those pertaining to fabulous creatures. This period also saw the first attempts to produce county natural histories, e.g. Robert Plot's *Natural History of Oxfordshire* (1677) and *Natural History of Staffordshire* (1686) and marked the beginnings of a clear separation between the attitudes and erroneous popular beliefs about wildlife and the more considered and advised views of at least some of the educated classes.

As the following chapters show, the level of killing promoted by the parishes was at its zenith in the seventeenth and eighteenth centuries. In some counties, the numbers of birds and mammals slaughtered in this period were enormous. However, amongst all this killing the attitude to wildlife had begun to soften by the beginning of the latter century. Although the numbers killed remained high at least we can persuade ourselves that with the wider availability of guns, increasing numbers were removed in a more humane manner. There are many payments by churchwardens for powder and shot. The evolving trend towards a better understanding of the wide spectrum of the natural world and Man's place in it was emphasized by naturalists such as John Hill (his *Natural History* was published in 1751), Thomas Pennant (famous for his several tours and commentaries around the British Isles and author of *British Zoology*), and Gilbert White the Hampshire clergyman/naturalist. Even the eccentric clergyman William Gilpin (1724–1804) with his idealistic view of the picturesque, had a wide impact on public perceptions at the time. Interest in the nature of wildlife itself was gradually developing and natural history became one of the fashionable amateur pastimes for more of the middle classes. The tide of moral attitudes to wildlife was slowly turning and by the end of the eighteenth century there were the tentative beginnings of a clear separation between the long-held views of wildlife and those of the newly-informed classes. Nature could legitimately be studied for its own sake. At the same time, but more slowly, the welfare of animals became a matter of increasing concern, although the predominant philosophy still remained that the rest of nature existed for the benefit and use of humankind.

During the nineteenth century there was a further change in attitudes. Game shooting had existed for 200 years or so but in this century there was a rapid evolution in shotgun technology and, coinciding with the new enclosures, there was an upsurge in shooting. At this time interest in wildlife focused more and more strongly on preservation of selected game species and concomitant control of competing vermin and predators to meet the sporting aspirations of land-owning gentry. This reached its zenith in the latter half of the nineteenth century and was accompanied by a renewed drive to control those species that impacted on the aim of producing the largest bags possible for the Victorian sportsmen. At the same time, there was a deluge of publications cataloguing, describing, and researching our wildlife—a flood of county avifaunas and natural history accounts and the introduction of journals such as *The Field* and *The Zoologist*. Despite this new interest, even as late as the second half of the nineteenth century, there were still accounts of such practices as the regular taking of Kittiwakes for the millinery trade at Bempton on the Yorkshire coast. After capture birds had their wings cut off and were then thrown alive into the sea. As Sir Alfred Newton—pioneer of bird protection—said of ladies thereby adorned, 'She wears a murderer's brand upon her head'. Such activities as this and other aspects of the millinery trade were behind the passing of the first Protection of Birds Acts (Sea Birds Protection Act 1869 which protected thirty-three seabird species during their nesting season) and the formation of conservation bodies such as The Royal Society for the Protection of Birds. The Royal Society for the Prevention of Cruelty to Animals was established as early as 1824 because of concern about the treatment of both wild and domestic animals. Attitudes may have changed and heralded a more sympathetic understanding of our relationship with the natural world, but this was by no means universal. The nineteenth century was characterized by wholesale war on predatory birds and mammals and the taking of enormous numbers of songbirds such as Skylarks, Wheatears, and Goldfinches, both for the table and for the cage bird market. It was also an era cursed with a destructive vogue for the collection of birds' eggs and the display of mounted specimens of any and all of our native mammals, birds of prey and others. This nineteenth-century phenomenon alone had a significant effect by decreasing even further, the numbers of many of our rarer species.

The first decade of the twentieth century continued the lust for large shooting bags and the accompanying assault on a wide range of competing species. As mentioned above, it came to an abrupt halt with the outbreak of the First World War. The post-war decades saw a dramatic change in public perceptions of wild-life and indeed of the countryside itself. A statutory conservation body, the Nature Conservancy, was set up in 1949 and a tidal wave of initiatives by them and a new generation of voluntary wildlife bodies began to establish a nation-wide system of nature reserves and other protected areas. The focus was sharp-ened because of a range of serious post-war environmental threats—agricultural mechanization and intensification, rapid urban and industrial developments, industrial pollution, widespread use of chemicals, etc. and their impact on wild-life. Stimulated by television and other media, public concern about these issues grew as the years passed. During the twentieth century, a large number of laws were passed to protect a wide range of wildlife species—birds, mammals, invertebrates, and marine life—and the habitats on which they depend. In add-ition, there was less public tolerance for the persecution and illegal killing of protected birds and mammals, which was still taking place. Legislation was strengthened and the range of legitimate control methods for different vermin species was also restricted. The tide of public feeling reached its controversial climax with the passing of the Hunting with Dogs Act in 2005. Traditional Fox hunting as we had known it was at an end. Although this Act was welcomed in some quarters it is important to remember that it was passed on the basis of welfare issues rather than for the conservation of species.

3

To kill a Rat or catch a Kite: methods of control

HENRY VIII's Act of 1532 was specifically aimed at reducing the populations of Rooks, crows, and 'Choughs' and in fulfilment of this, required that:

Every One shall do his best to destroy Crows etc upon Pain of Amerciament. Every Town, Hamlet of more than ten dwellings (is to) provide and maintain Crow-nets during ten years. The inhabitants shall during ten years assemble and take order to destroy Crows, Rooks etc.

Thus at the very beginning of the statutory process of vermin control, initially focused exclusively on the corvid family, the method of taking the birds was clearly prescribed. Villagers authorized to take crows on other's land were to be paid at the rate of 2*d*. per dozen. There is little doubt that the standard method of netting was an early form of clap net used at a regular site ('scrape') baited with corn. The net, laid flat on the ground was jerked over the baited scrape by a taut cord, once sufficient birds were feeding there.

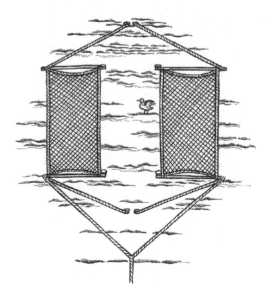

Figure 6. Mascall's clap net
for catching crows, etc. (redrawn).

Mascall, in his classic 1590 book on trapping methods, may have been the first to illustrate this device although the technique in its simplest form is doubtless almost as old as time itself. He also illustrated and described other fiendish and ingenious devices recommended for taking different species of vermin. These were invariably referred to as 'engines' a word deriving from the old French word *engin*, meaning engine or mechanical device. Several of Mascall's traps are illustrated below.

The Lay trappe to ſet about corne fields, or orchards.

The hoope nette for the Buzard, ſet againſt ſome buſh in a plaine or open place.

The kragge hooke.

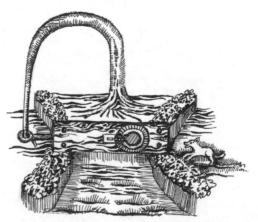

This engines is called a fore trappe or foote trappe, because it taketh all by the foote.

Figure 7. Some of Mascall's 'engines': devices for specific types of vermin (redrawn).

In 1678, Willughby offered an innovative method for controlling Rooks in Spring, the season when the birds were pulling up the young corn seedlings:

Take some thick brown paper and divide it into 8 parts and make them like sugar loaves (*i.e.* cone-shaped). Then lime the inside of the paper a very little. Then put some corn in them and lay 50 or 60 up and down the ground as much as you can, in the early morning before they come to feed. Then stand at a good distance and you will see some excellent sport. For as soon as the Rook or Crow comes to pick at the corn, it (the paper) will hang upon his head and he will immediately fly bolt upright so high that he shall seem like a small bird and when he is spent, come tumbling down as if were shot in the air.

He also offered a refinement of the same system for taking Starlings—dubious though its efficacy may seem to us:

Take a small string a yard or so long, bind it to the tail of a Stare having first carefully limed it all over excepting the palm next to the bird. Having found a flock of Stares come as near as possible, let (your bird) go to her fellows which as soon as you show yourself to them will presently take wing. Thrusting herself in the middle of her fellows she will entangle many of them and so, not being able to fly, they will afford a pleasant spectacle in tumbling down to the ground where you must be ready with a brush or besom to strike them down.

Bird lime was an important constituent in many of the techniques for catching birds and there were numerous variations for making it, of which the following—with variants—was a frequent recipe:

Take at Midsummer of the Bark of Holly and boil it in running water till the grey and white bark rise from the green: which will take a whole day or better. Then take it from the fire and after the water is very well drained, separate from it the barks. Take all the green and lay it on a moist floor, as in some low vault or cellar, and cover it all over with a good thickness of Docks, Hemlock and Thistles and so let it lie for the space of ten or twelve days, in which time it will rot and turn to flimsy matter. Then pound it in a mortar till it come to be one uniform substance or paste. Which done carry it to a swift running stream and wash it exceedingly. Then put it in a close earthen pot and let it stand for divers days, not omitting to skum it if any foulness arises, and when no more will arise, put it in a clean vessel, and cover it close, and keep it for use.

Then of course it is a matter of putting the bird-lime to use:

To take Bullfinch or other small birds. Your lime bush must be the main bough of any bushy tree, whose twigs are long and smooth without prick, knots or other roughness or crookedness. Having prik't and trim'd it, lime every twig and branch from the top down within four fingers or thereabouts of the bottom. Dabble not your lime too thick nor leave any part bare. Your bush thus prepared, carry it forth into the fields where the haunts of the small birds are, and place it as close as you can to any of these haunts. You may very near it have some close covert to lie concealed in and there chirp like a Sparrow, or call with a note like a Bullfinch (as cocks do when they miss the hens), altering your note according to your fancy, but continually calling in one note or other. And when you see them light upon your bush let them alone and move not till you see them fatally entangled. Neither shall you stir for a single bird or two, but stay till many be entangled.

Among the small birds not even Kingfishers were spared the attention of the bird limers. In his book in 1705, Conyers urged that the regular haunts of the Kingfisher, roundly accused of taking valuable fish eggs and fingerlings, should be studied to determine its favourite perches: 'Mark where he haunts and lime some of the twigs and he'll come and settle there in a small time or as soon as he has catched his fish'. Even dead Kingfishers could be put to use. W. W. (see references) asserted that, 'This bird, being dead, if he be hanged up by the bill with a thread in your house where no wind bloweth, his breast will always hang against the winde. Whereby ye may know perfectly in what quarter the winde is at all times, both day and night.'

Other piscivorous creatures were pursued with equal zeal and ingenuity as Willughby described:

One heron that haunts a pond in a year shall destroy one thousand store carp; nay fifteen hundred in half a year. Now the best way to take this great enemy of the fish is this. Get three or four small (live) Roaches or Dace and, having a strong hook with a wire to it, draw the wire just inside the skin of the fish beginning beside the gills and running it to the tail and then the fish will lie alive for four or five days. Then having a strong line made of silk or wire about two and a half yards long tied round a stone of about a pound in weight and lay three or four of these hooks and in two or three days you shall not fail to have him if he comes to your pond. Colour the line dark green for he is a very subtle bird.

The fish-eating Otter fared no better than these birds. Robert Smith in 1768 recommended the use of a strong steel trap placed in mud under the water at a place where the Otter was known to emerge onto land. Indeed, evidence of this technique was found when the National Trust cleared a decoy pond on the Gower, in South Wales, and unearthed precisely this device. Gin traps had been fixed to submerged logs and the Trust was told by an old estate worker that they had caught many Otters in this way up to the 1920s.

In earlier centuries, Kites and Buzzards were always prime targets and there were various devices, some credible and others bizarre, for entrapping them. Mascall described several methods, among which his spring trap is certainly elaborate. Illustrated below and baited with half a coney, it was specifically devised for carrion-feeding birds such as Buzzard and Kite.

'How to take Crows, Pies, Gleads etc. with lime twigs,' Willughby again. 'Stick up lime twigs on the carcass of a dead horse, newly stript, or any other carrion, so soon as these birds have found it. Let them be very small and not too thick set less they see them and take distaste.'

Robert Smith advocated a different way of:

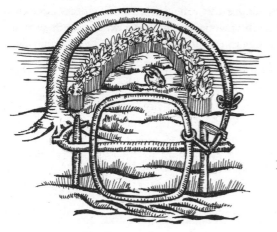

Figure 8. Mascall's spring trap for
Buzzards and Kites.

destroying noisome and ravenous fowl, as Ravens, Kites and Buzzards. Take a pretty
quantity of Nux Vomica* and dissolve it in wine vinegar. Then take the garbage of any
Fowl, and all besmear them over with your solution of Nux Vomica and cast them forth
where such noisome birds haunt: and watching the birds in a convenient place, you shall
see that after swallowing a bit or two, any such fowl will presently grow dizzy, reeling and
tumbling up and down, till at last it falls into a dead swoon. Others take pretty big
gobbets of raw lean flesh, as beef, mutton etc and making therein secret little holes, put
in them small pieces of Nux Vomica and close them up again.

William Blundell of Crosby (Lancs), at the end of the eighteenth century,
showed that you could take a Kite 'easily with a pigeon and lime', but he also
claimed the improbable use of a Kite in helping to control crows:

Take a Kite and a Carrion Crow and tie them down in the stubble. With sufficient liberty,
they will fight and cry in a strange manner, upon which there will come immediately great
flocks of crows from all parts, which, striking freely at the Kite will many of them be taken
in the lime twigs that must be placed round in the stubble for that reason. Remember that
you tie up one foot of the Kite to make the battle more even.

Rats and mice afforded immense opportunity for inventive methods of control
and although the majority were on the lines of variations on simple, baited
drop traps, several books mention more interesting ways of eliminating or discouraging them. A Scottish remedy along the following lines in the early nineteenth century was fairly traditional: a little lard and sugar was mixed with some
browned oatmeal and placed as bait. After several days a larger quantity was
mixed, to which was added ½ oz of powder of arsenic and the same amount of
sweet mercury. The results presumably spoke for themselves.

* Nux vomica is the seed from an East Indian tree, from which the poison strychnine is made.

Conyers had a novel way of luring mice out into the open. 'Put a few mice in a deep earthenware or copper pot on the fire. When it grows hot the mice start to jump about and chirp and all others in the house come about them.'

The same author applied himself to recommended methods of ridding areas of Moles. 'Take a head or two of Garlick or Onyon or Leek and put it in their holes and they will run out as if amazed and so you may with a spear or a dog take them. Approved.' Alternatively, 'Take the dregs of oyle or juice of wild cucumber and pour it into their holes and it kills them. Approved.' A more subtle method involved playing somewhat unfairly on the male Mole's sexual proclivities. 'In gendering time, if you lead or draw a bitch Mole on a string along the ground, the buck will grice her and so you may catch them in a pot set in the ground'.

Feral cats have long been regarded as nuisance animals and have been killed consistently over the ages (not least in great numbers on many nineteenth-century shooting estates in Scotland and England). It is interesting, though not particularly surprising, that even 400 years ago there was clear distinction between the genuine Wild Cat and the feral tabby. In southern England, Wild Cats were traditionally caught in box traps/hutch traps with drop doors at both ends and a baited trigger device in the middle. According to Robert Brown in 1759, these traps were sometimes scattered with Valerian powder or Cat Thyme which all cats love to roll in, but more regularly they were baited with fish remains. Frequently such traps were placed on a plank over a stream, the more readily to drown the captured animal. In *Nature with a Camera*, the Kearton brothers describe a sophisticated stone tunnel trap up to six feet long and twelve inches high baited with a Brown Trout suspended within: 'no cat can resist a Trout'. In Scotland too 'drowning sets'—baited spring traps set on little promontories or islands in streams and firmly anchored—were frequently used.

Another unique device, but similar to that described by the Keartons, is a granite tunnel trap, a number of which that have been found around the old Rabbit warrens in the upper Plym valley on south-west Dartmoor. These probably date, at the earliest, from 1700 and were presumably aimed at Stoats and Polecats. As the illustration below shows these carefully constructed, immovably heavy structures must have been laboriously crafted as rectangular tunnels (some of the roof stones are almost too heavy to be moved by one man!).

They were situated around the warren where guide walls directed prospecting predators into the openings of the traps. Details of the triggering device within the tunnel have not survived, but it operated to drop a slate down grooves in the side stones at either end, once the intruder was inside. Thus the traps captured but did not kill. Many of the traps had an unusual opening in one of the side

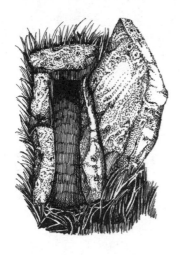

Figure 9. A granite vermin trap, *c*.1700, from Dartmoor. Redrawn from Cook (1964) with permission of the author and the Devon Association.

walls but the reason or purpose of this is not understood unless it provided the means for extracting the victim.

A major development in the mid 1700s was the introduction of the steel gin trap (the word again originating from the French '*engin*'). This, together with the gradual evolution of guns and their equally gradual availability for game-keepers as the century advanced, marked important turning points in the method available for the control of vermin. The somewhat fanciful devices of sprung saplings, etc. promoted by Mascall and others, were soon items of the past. The new steel traps came in a variety of forms and sizes, specific to different needs. All were mechanical traps operated by a triggered metal spring and designed to hold the victim by the leg in toothed jaws until the operator returned to put it down. The most familiar was the gin itself illustrated below which was very widely used, although until 1880 it was legally restricted to those employed on game estates. After that, the Ground Game Act broadened its availability so that farmers and others were able to deploy it to combat the rising tide of Rabbits. Slightly smaller versions were manufactured for use against ground predators such as rats, Polecats, Stoats, and Weasels. A circular variety for use above ground, known appropriately as a pole trap was specifically designed for trapping birds, especially birds of prey. Fixed by chain to a pole or other regularly-used eminence, it caught the bird by the leg, fell off the post, and kept the bird hanging there until disposed of; some of these traps had smooth, curved jaws to avoid too much damage to the leg if the intended victim was to be taken for falconry, etc.

The smallest variety of pole traps were the ones specifically produced for Kingfishers, small traps with jaws no larger than 2 inches. At the other end of the scale were the appalling man-traps, precisely the same design and used with

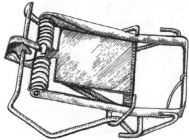

Figure 10. Gin trap (above, left) and Fenn trap.

impunity to catch poachers and burglars. These man-traps were finally outlawed in 1827 except that their use was still permitted in houses between the hours of sunset and sunrise. Pole traps—specifically the setting of a trap in an elevated position—were made illegal in 1904 but it was not until 1958 that the gin itself was removed from use in England and Wales (a decade or so later in Scotland) on the basis of the unarguable cruelty caused by its leg-trap system. Many old gins still hang disused in the outbuildings of farms or forgotten in the sheds of country estates.

The development of firearms has been another major factor in the control of vermin. The very earliest firearms were in existence from the middle of the sixteenth century and although there was some use of them for the limited shooting of game, it was many more years before they became generally available for controlling vermin. In the sixteenth century long-barrelled, flint-lock guns were developed, which were a marked improvement over the previous, more primitive hail-shot firearms. Although these long, muzzle-loading pieces were slow to recharge and sometimes risky to reload when hot, they remained essentially unchanged for the next 150 years or so. It was not until the turn of the nineteenth century that much improved techniques evolved to furnish game-keepers, as well as their masters, with much more efficient weapons. Shorter, more manageable barrels were introduced in the 1820s, to be followed by per-cussion caps replacing flint locks ten years later and by 1860 muzzle loading at last gave way to breach loading and the introduction of cartridges. In effect the modern sporting gun was thus developed and has changed little to the present day. These nineteenth-century developments, producing much faster and more efficient weapons, evolved at precisely the time when the greatest assaults on wild-life throughout Britain were being made and were therefore one of the principal instruments for achieving much of the carnage that took place since then.

So it was, for a hundred years or more, from the late eighteenth century, that the war against those native creatures perceived as vermin by farmer, small-holder, or gamekeeper, could be prosecuted with the triple weapons of gun, trap, and poison. With these means at their disposal the nineteenth and early years of the twentieth centuries saw the catastrophic demise of many of our fine native birds and mammals.

Modern vermin control falls under several distinct disciplines. Rats and mice in domestic properties, farm buildings, and industrial premises are usually controlled nowadays through the use of a wide range of pelleted rodenticides or dressed baits as well as the time-tested and familiar proprietary break-back traps. Moles, still persecuted to the extent that they have been for the past 400 years or so, are controlled by traps placed in the runs or by the use of poisoned baits (worms) similarly entered into the runs. Strychnine, the most deadly and dangerous of all poisons has been legally obtainable only under tightly controlled licence for exclusive use against Moles underground. Despite these requirements it has frequently occurred as the toxic agent on illegal meat baits laid in the open. However, years of public concern about its use and misuse have eventually resulted in its total withdrawal under European Directive in 2006.

The narcotic chemical alphachloralose is available, again under strict licence (but has been regularly abused), as a means of controlling pest levels of species such as urban pigeons or occasionally 'plague' numbers of roof-nesting gulls in seaside towns. In another form, professional operators can use it as a rodenticide, again under licence. It has also been used in past decades as a wildlife conservation tool to reduce numbers of gulls in breeding colonies where sheer numbers have impacted on more vulnerable species or fragile habitats.

Now that the legal use of poisons is no longer an option, the gamekeeper's armoury in controlling competing species on game estates comprises two time-honoured methods, shooting and trapping. His main enemies are Stoats, Foxes, and corvids—most notably Carrion/Hooded Crows and Magpies. The modern Larsen trap was developed primarily to reduce the illegal use of poisoned eggs and has proved a very efficient method of catching meaningful numbers of crows and Magpies. Otherwise opportunistic shooting of the birds or their nests is widely employed. Stoats (and non-target Weasels as 'by-catch') are traditionally caught in baited spring traps set in natural or artificial tunnels. Almost invariably these are Fenn or Springer traps (illustrated on p. 58) which kill outright. Under the Spring Traps Approval Order of 1995, these traps can only be used legally in covered situations. Unlike the gin traps, they normally kill when two powerful bars snap together on release, breaking the spine. Tapper (1992) quotes 100 such traps per 1,000 acres on a shooting estate as a normal expectation as shown in Figure 10. It is worth making the point that increasing numbers of Pheasants and Partridges are reared in captivity, and then released, therefore reducing the need for such intensive predator control.

The options available for Fox control have been considerably lessened through the latter half of the twentieth century by the increased restrictions imposed by legislation. After the banning of gin traps, the use of Cymag (hydrogen cyanide gas) was a popular form of control at earths and permitted since 1947, but subsequently removed again under the Food and Environment Protection Act in 1985. Similarly, self-locking wire snares (those which tighten as the animal struggles but do not release as it relaxes) finally became illegal through the Wildlife and Countryside Act in 1981, while free-running snares are still legal. With the introduction of the ban on hunting with dogs in Scotland (2002) and England and Wales (2005), individual Fox control now principally relies on a combination of snaring, reduced hunting, and night shooting with a spot light and high-powered rifle.

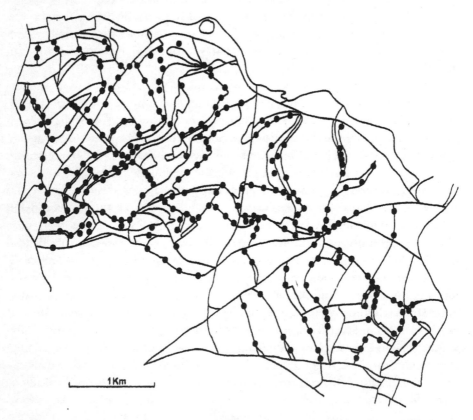

Figure 11. A network of tunnel sites containing Fenn traps on a 3,000 acre shoot in the south of England. Reproduced from Tapper (1992) with the author's permission.

4

Killing in Scotland

IN considering the extent of Man's deliberate attempts to eliminate many species of our wildlife, no chapter of that story is more firmly etched in the national consciousness than the appalling destruction that was carried out in Scotland across relatively recent generations. The killing of some of the larger predators had been going on since the seventeenth century, but the wholesale persecution of a wider range of birds and mammals started no further back than 200 years or so, some 300 years after serious campaigns in England and Wales. Because the slaughter in Scotland occurred on such a scale, took place in the more recent past, and resulted in the loss of some species, it is relevant to examine it first, before considering the much longer history of organized killing in England and Wales.

Tracing the history of vermin control in Scotland provides a different challenge to that in England and Wales. To start with, the Tudor Acts, which marked the beginning of a structured approach to vermin control in the south, did not apply in Scotland. The country was not part of the Union for a further 175 years and therefore, at that time, not subject to the statutes of Westminster. As a result, whereas English and Welsh parish records are a gold mine of early vermin records, nothing similar exists for the equivalent centuries in Scotland. The Tudor Acts of Henry VIII and Elizabeth I were directed towards the reduction or elimination of the birds and mammals that were perceived to be in conflict with the interests of successful agriculture. The imperatives that drove the subsequent campaigns of persecution in England and Wales clearly did not apply to the same extent in Scotland. Several of the species that were targeted in England under the Acts—e.g. Bullfinch, woodpeckers, Hedgehog—would never have been of great consequence in Scotland anyway. Paradoxically, there was official bird protection in Scotland which stretched back to the twelfth and thirteenth centuries, although at that time it was primarily concerned with the protection of eyries of Goshawk, Sparrowhawk, and falcons. Baxter and Rintoul have pointed out that even when grants of estate lands were made, the owners often reserved the rights on the eyries therein.

However, in 1424, 128 years before Henry VIII's Act in England and Wales, James I of Scotland, in the first year of his reign, passed an Act aimed specifically at Rooks. The wording was rather strange and implied that people should allow the birds to nest so that they could then be killed:

Of rooks that build in churchyards and orchards.

Item, it is ordained that since men consider that rooks building in churchyards and orchards do great harm upon corn, that those to whom such trees pertain (should) let them build (but) not allow their birds fly away under any circumstances; and where it may be found that they build and those birds fly away, and the nest is found at Beltane, the tree shall be forfeit to the king, unless they are redeemed from him by those to whom they pertain (and 5/- to the king's unlaw).*

Thirty-three years later, in 1457, his son James II enacted stronger legislation that provided for the destruction of a wider range of specified winged vermin.

Item, rooks crows and other fowls of plunder like eagles buzzards kites and hawks the which destroy the corn and wild fowls such as partridges plovers and others. And as to the rooks and crows bigging in orchards kirks gardens or other places it is seen expedient that they that such trees pertain to let them nest and destroy them with all their power and in no way that the birds fly away. And where it is proven that they roost and the birds be flown and the nests found in the trees at Beltane the trees shall be forfeited to the king except if they be redeemed again. And that they own the said trees—for their part—5 shillings of fine to the king. And that the said fowles of plunder be utterly destroyed by all manner of men and all means and manner of ways that may be appropriate thereto for the slaughter of them shall cause great multitude of divers kinds of wild fowl for man's sustenance.†

Sadly, nothing is known about whether these Acts were enforced or were ever effective. The suspicion is that they had little effect, even though they may possibly have marked the beginning of the reduction of some of the larger raptors—eagles, Red Kite, and Raven—in the lowlands. However, this is supposition and before the nineteenth century we only have scraps of information to rely on. Nonetheless, it is known that as long ago as the seventeenth century, some of the larger predators were already being killed. A letter from Sir John Campbell of Glenorchy to his son in 1673 advised him on better methods of dealing with 'eagills and foxis': 'I intreat you to send for a pound or two of unbeaten arsenic which is the best sort of poyson to destroy them which I know by my own experience'. The Old Statistical Account, written by ministers in parishes throughout Scotland between 1791 and 1799, included among the many recommended headings for their reports, a request for summaries of notable 'quadrupeds and birds' that characterized their parishes. However, there was no mention of vermin or vermin control and this omission seems to lend

* Modernized translation by Roland Tanner.
† Modernized translation by Prof. Robert Dodgshon.

weight to the impression that these issues were not matters of general importance at that time. An exception to this was the persecution of species such as Sea
Eagle that had been practised in some areas, e.g. Orkney, since the seventeenth
century. Nonetheless, the references to birds or mammals in the Old Statistical
Accounts occur only incidentally in the form of statements of their presence and
(sometimes) abundance.

There are other disparate sources that occasionally add colour to the picture.
For example, in 1759, the Commissioners of Supply in the Kintyre District of
Argyll formed a committee to produce a plan for destroying Foxes and eagles
and two years later prosecuted any of those small heritors who had failed to pay
their required levy towards the fox-hunter's wages. The fox-hunters had wider
responsibilities than those their title suggested and were also deployed to destroy
other species such as eagles, a practice that continued in this area until at least
1812. By this time, the Argyll District Road Trustees had taken over the
responsibility from the Commissioners and Allan MacIntyre was paid £2.7s.4d.
in 1793 for 'killing ravenous birds' and £1.19s.7d. five years later for the same
annual task. Parallel schemes operated in Sutherland (and probably elsewhere)
where in one year alone, 1787, payments were made for 330 Foxes plus 115
cubs and 31 eagles. So, there is no doubt that vermin control, albeit with a
limited range of species, was being practised in different parts of Scotland fairly
soon after the arrival of extensive sheep ranching.

A short time before this Alexander Wight, writing around 1778, recorded
that:

Mr Farquharson (of Invercauld) promoted a plan for destroying foxes, eagles and other
ravenous animals. A sum is raised by subscription for giving a premium of half a guinea for
an eagle, the same for a fox, five shillings for a polecat and as much for a wild cat, half a
crown for a hawk, a shilling for a kite as much for as a raven and sixpence for a hooded
crow. These premiums would by this time have cleared the braes of Mar, but for an influx
from neighbouring places. They, however, have produced an effect still more advanta-
geous for the public. There are at present in the braes of Mar above a hundred stout men
who can enter the lists with any American rifleman for hitting a mark.

(This was the time of the American War of Independence!)

In his *Report on the Hebrides* (1764 and 1771), John Walker said that on Mull,
eagles were a pest of sheep farming but that Foxes were much worse. He also
extended his local tirade against Foxes to the Highlands in general which, to a
lesser extent, also included eagles. It is interesting to note that Foxes were
eventually exterminated on Mull. Thomas Pennant, in his tours of Scotland in
1769 and 1772, recorded his observations of wildlife and described some of the
earliest measures of game preservation that were also under way then. He found
that the widespread destruction of birds of prey was encouraged and that a

bounty of half a crown (2/6) was given for the head of an eagle and a shilling for a 'hawk' and a Hooded Crow. Bounties and rewards of this nature were frequent, one might almost say habitual in northern Scotland, for the taking of vermin species such as these. Examples abound in the early nineteenth century and the following is typical of many others:

Rewards and premiums offered by the United Association of Noblemen, gentlemen and farmers of the counties of Sutherland and Caithness for the protection of property

Head and talons of each full-grown eagle killed in the county of Sutherland or on the estates of Langwell and Sandside in Caithness	10/-
Face and ear of an old Fox as above	£1
Face and ears of cub as above, including all found within the belly of the mother	7/6
Head and talons of each young eagle	5/-
For each egg of an eagle	2/6
Face and ears of Marten, Polecat or Wild Cat	1/-
Head and talons of a Raven	1/6
Head and talons of hawk, crow or Magpie	2*d.*

When serious vermin control did start in Scotland it was almost with a breathtaking suddenness. The initial stimulus was the rapid expansion of sheep farming. Soon after the second Jacobite rebellion and in part stimulated by the ensuing land forfeitures, flockmasters in the Southern Uplands saw the chance to move north and the great colonization of the Highlands of Scotland by sheep was under way. At the same time many Scottish lairds realized that money could be made by leasing their land to sheep farmers from the Lowlands and England. Thus began the infamous period during which tenant crofters were systematically evicted to make way for the sheep, the so-called Highland Clearances. By 1790, Argyll and Perthshire had been colonized, the first flocks had arrived in Wester Ross, and soon after the turn of the century even Caithness and Sutherland were populated by sheep.

At the same time as the land was cleared for 'the coming of the sheep' widespread persecution of predatory birds and mammals began in earnest. There are several references in the New Statistical Account (see below) and elsewhere to the hatred that was immediately engendered by the depredations on lambs inflicted by three top predators, eagles (there was no immediate differentiation between Sea Eagle and Golden Eagle), Fox, and Raven. It signalled the first signs of widescale persecution that became evident before the end of the century. Predatory birds and mammals had been given notice and their future was bleak.

During this period, these same predators also began to suffer persecution for another reason. There was an increasing interest in the commercial value of game on Scottish estates and once commercial interest became a factor the primary role of the gamekeeper changed. Up until then, the taking of game—deer, grouse, salmon—had been relaxed and low intensity. Osgood Mackenzie, who had a family estate at Gairloch, illustrated the attitudes that had prevailed before the arrival of sheep and the establishment of serious game management. He wrote concerning the period before 1750:

There was so much vermin in those days but the so-called gamekeepers were in reality only game-*killers*, and vermin trappers were only just then being started. In these times all the lairds had was a hunter who provided their big houses with venison and other game.

As Smout has pointed out in *Nature Contested*, before 1800 or so, visiting sportsmen were able to shoot or fish whereever they wanted and take what they could, merely by asking permission of the landowner. An Act of 1831 removed the requirement of birth and estate to permit the killing of game and thereafter any authorized persons could shoot, provided they were granted permission by the landowner. Many Highland estates came on to the market around the same time and were often bought with 'new' money, by men from the south. The potential for shifting the emphasis from sheep farming to game estate, with the prospect of lucrative profits from sporting rights—deer, game, and angling—was new and exciting. The situation was changing fast. Although the Old Statistical Account gave little hint of persecution, the New Account written between *c*.1832 and 1840, only forty years after the original one, contains numerous references to the fact that some species perceived as vermin were by then already showing marked declines. At Abercorn (West Lothian), for example, the Account recorded that 'a war of extermination is waged against crows, magpies, hawks and owls'. The genie's bottle was uncorked. The subsequent records of huge numbers of vermin killed in the nineteenth and early twentieth centuries in the name of sheep rearing and game preservation would account for the demise of so many Scottish species.

Thus, the second major difference between the sources of records in Scotland and those in England and Wales becomes obvious. In Scotland meticulous vermin records were kept on many of the new sporting estates up until the twentieth century. The majority have been lost or destroyed or are unavailable for a variety of reasons (e.g. the huge volume of uncatalogued material in estate archives). Those that do exist contain graphic evidence of the colossal levels of killing that took place in the name of sheep husbandry and, in particular, game preservation.

Man's effects on landscape change

Whilst direct persecution was the main reason for the decimation of so many species in Scotland, habitat loss and land use change also indirectly reduced 'vermin' numbers. In southern Britain, as we have seen in Chapter 2, the nature of the landscape, varying patterns of land use, and agricultural systems in different parts of the country had a major bearing on the species of vermin that were targeted and the intensity with which that control was carried out.

Mammals such as Pine Marten and Wild Cat are primarily forest animals and, although both can thrive in more open habitats, they are certainly localized in relation to the distribution of woodland. Woodland cover is also important for several of the predatory birds and corvids that featured on every vermin list. In Scotland most of the post-glacial woodland cover had been removed in the distant past, initially through climate deterioration and later by millennia of grazing flocks. Smout has suggested that by 1500 AD no more than 10–15% woodland cover remained and that this was further reduced to no more than 5–6% (including plantations) by the end of the nineteenth century.

The significant effect that the open field system had on wildlife populations, and consequently the pattern of vermin control in England, was not reflected as strongly in Scotland. On the fertile soils of the lowlands, runrigs which, as Shrubb has shown, were dying out by the end of the eighteenth century, were on a far smaller scale than the equivalent open fields in England. Nonetheless, the infield/outfield system in which the rigs were placed produced a landscape more devoid of hedgerow trees and shrubs than anywhere in England. There was no organized or mandatory system of enclosure as there had been in England; the right to enclose land in Scotland was invariably the prerogative of individual landowners and was therefore undertaken by them as they pleased. Turner has shown that the origins of Scottish enclosure dated back to the late years of the seventeenth century. However, the progressive enclosure of agricultural land in the lowlands occurred principally in the years following the 1745 Jacobite rebellion, but was still incomplete by 1800. The rate and scale of agricultural improvement that followed in the second half of that century was remarkably rapid and involved the draining of much wetland (the famous Billie Mire in Berwickshire was a classic example), removal of scrub, and the small-scale establishment of patterns of enclosed fields. Even if the scale of land 'improvement' in Scotland was less than that in England, the resultant changes in habitats inevitably impacted on the populations of a wide range of species and must have had consequences for the control of vermin. Unfortunately, the sparsity of eighteenth-century vermin records in Scotland means that we do not know what the effects were.

The development of Scottish sporting estates

The concept of an estate managed wholly or substantially for its sporting potential was unknown before the beginning of the nineteenth century. In the eighteenth century, Scottish estate owners found their roles as clan leaders greatly reduced and many decided that part of the year was better spent enjoying the pleasures of social life in London. Towards the end of that century they also began to reap the benefits of high rents from sheep farming. Sheep grazing at moderate levels, together with associated muir burn, can enhance the quality of heather-dominated moorland which is the prime habitat for Black Game and Red Grouse. Thus, moderating the number of sheep kept on moorland could open the door for the development of grouse shooting.

The lairds were not slow to recognize the developing potential of their game resource, nor the gathering interest in sporting activities of rich industrialists and pleasure-seeking sportsmen in England. At the beginning of the nineteenth century the main problem was actually getting there. Scotland, in particular the Highlands, was still a great distance away and the journey to reach the moors from London was tedious and uncomfortable. Passenger coaches had run between London and Edinburgh as early as 1658, but the journey took three weeks! Mail coaches, which took four passengers inside and three outside, were introduced in 1784. This was obviously an improvement but the journey still lasted several days and was only for the determined and dedicated. Despite this, there were plenty of pleasure-seeking sportsmen prepared to make the journey and to pay handsomely for the outstanding game shooting, deer stalking, or fishing that was to be enjoyed.

At the same time the terms of employment and role of the gamekeeper changed from that described by Osgood Mackenzie in the previous century; now his overriding priority was the eradication of any winged or four-footed predators that might compete for the native stock of game birds or fish. Thus it was not only the terrestrial predators that were targets for trap and gun but also aquatic species—Otter, Osprey, Cormorant, and even Dipper and Kingfisher. The deer forests in the north and west were exceptions. As long as deer stalking was the principal aim there was no particular need for vermin control because deer had no wild predators, except for eagles occasionally taking a young fawn. In fact, as long as those moors remained exclusively for deer stalking, predators were reasonably welcomed since they predated grouse whose annoying alarm calls could alert the deer prematurely during stalking. It was only when the deer forests were opened for wider sporting opportunities, from the 1840s onwards, often with sheep being reduced or removed, that heavy persecution of a wide range of predators became the norm. Fluctuating sheep prices helped persuade landowners to bolster their incomes by letting grouse shooting. In the 1800s rents for such shootings were usually based on a value of 5/- per brace. By 1841, Prebble maintained that there were already ninety Highland estates with rental incomes from shooting tenants of at least £125 a month. Whereas there were 6 deer forests in 1811, the number had risen to 40 by 1842 and 117 (possibly more) by 1895, covering some 2.5 million acres (1,012,000 hectares) in the Highlands.

As an example of this shift in upland management, by 1880 Octavius Smith and his son had cleared sheep off 11,200 acres (4532 hectares) of deer forest in Morvern (Argyll). Besides markedly improving the number of stags shot and increasing the numbers of grouse, they encouraged the preservation of all game by the payment of vermin money to the 'keepers. From 1872 the rate was 6d. for birds' heads and eggs (mainly Hooded Crows, but also 'gledes' and 'hawks'), £1 for each vixen, 10/- for a dog Fox, and 5/- for cubs. Between 1872 and 1879 his annual vermin totals averaged 118 heads, 38 eggs, 3 vixens, 2 dog Foxes, and 9 cubs.

For the southern sportsman the real breakthrough came in the middle of the nineteenth century. The opening of the railway to Edinburgh in 1843 meant that the Scottish capital could then be reached in ten hours. Initially, horse-drawn coaches continued the journey from there northwards as far as Inverness, until the rail connection was eventually completed in 1863. The principal grouse moors of Perthshire and Aberdeenshire suddenly became as readily accessible as the Southern Uplands and the Pennines had been previously. The other significant development was the great improvement in sporting guns, described in the previous chapter. In the 1830s, flint-lock ignition was superseded by the development of percussion caps and by the 1860s breach loading and the introduction of cartridges replaced the slow and dangerous muzzle-loading process. These improvements had important implications for both the sportsman and the gamekeeper. Birds could now be more easily shot on the wing instead of being walked up and shot on the ground and the gamekeeper had a far more efficient weapon with which to deal with vermin. Grouse shooting reached its peak in the 1880s and 1890s. The migration of Victorian sportsmen and their retinues to the rivers and moors of Scotland every autumn became an important part of the social calendar for the wealthy classes.

Wanton slaughter by the English 'sportsmen'

One of the most shameful elements in the nineteenth-century destruction and extinction of Scottish wildlife was the part played by 'sportsmen' and collectors, both Scottish and English. Their aim was not only to participate in the recreational shooting of game but also to shoot or collect whatever species they could, either for fun or for profit. It is easy to point fingers at gamekeepers for the carnage they inflicted, but they were only carrying out what they were paid to do and what their masters demanded. The lairds themselves saw nothing immoral, shameful, and certainly not illegal, in what they required of their gamekeepers. Vermin were considered to be an abomination in the context of maintaining successful game stocks and had to be eliminated. On the other hand, a handful of self-indulgent English 'sportsmen' and collectors who went to Scotland to exploit its wildlife for their own entertainment, and knowingly killed the last individuals within a species, were guilty of wildlife genocide.

One of the most infamous was Charles St John. He was born in Sussex in 1809, grandson of the second Viscount Bolingbroke. He developed an early passion for wildlife and field sports in his native countryside. After a brief two-year period of employment in the Treasury, the generosity of an aunt allowed him to indulge his sporting interests full time and still enjoy London society. He could ride 40 miles out from London to shoot Blackcock and return the same day. His cousin Bolingbroke gave him the use of a small property at Oykell in Sutherland from which he began a lifelong love affair with the wild places of the Highlands and their wildlife. He had the foresight to marry the daughter of a rich Newcastle banker who was happy to see her fortune used to share and further St John's passions in northern Scotland. They lived in several houses in the Highlands and he spent the majority of his time in the field. On one hand he was a very knowledgeable and experienced naturalist and a competent and entertaining writer; on the other he was a hypocritical man who hid his wanton killing behind crocodile tears and pretensions of moral respectability. He had an insatiable appetite for killing and was responsible, among many other despicable acts, for the final elimination of the Osprey in Sutherland. He was equally hypocritical too about the loss of the Red Kite:

That beautiful bird the Kite is now very rare in this country. Occasionally I have seen one wheeling and soaring at an immense height; but the English 'keepers and traps have nearly extirpated this bird, as no greater enemy or more destructive a foe to young grouse can exist. In consequence of her greedy disposition, the Kite is very easily trapped. From her habit of following the course of streams and hunting along the shores of the loch in search of dead fish or drowned animals of any kind, one of the most successful ways of trapping the Kite is to peg down the entrails of some animal in the shallow part of the water and then to place the trap either on the shore immediately adjoining; or, as is often done, to form a small artificial promontory close to the bait and to set the trap on this. The garbage catches the sharp eye of the bird as she soars at a great height above it and the clever trapper seldom fails in catching her in this manner.

Edward Booth was another man of independent means from the south of England. He was born in Buckinghamshire in 1840 of wealthy parents and was

educated privately before going to Cambridge. However, his time spent
indulging his interests in the countryside in preference to studying resulted in
him being sent down. Despite this temporary setback his parents provided him
with a considerable income which he used to indulge lavishly his passion in
collecting birds. When his home in Brighton became too small to accommodate
his growing collection of stuffed specimens, he merely built a museum in the
garden. His immodest ambition was to obtain specimens of every bird occurring
in Britain 'in all their various stages and forms'. In this he failed by the time of his
early death at the age of 50. By then, however, he had succeeded in preparing
308 display cases showing 236 bird species that to this day still form the distasteful centrepiece of the Booth Museum in the original building in Dyke Road,
Brighton. Booth's further contribution to posterity was his *Rough Notes on the
Birds Observed during 25 Years of Shooting and Collecting in the British Isles*. He
spent many years in the Highlands, attired in his trademark bowler hat, an
obsessive alcoholic who was paranoid about other collectors. He slaughtered
many birds of prey and Watson describes how he plundered Hen Harrier sites,
on more than one occasion waiting hours for the return of the surviving adult
after he had shot its partner and despatched the nestlings.

Booth remains infamous for numerable acts of this nature, not least for his
elimination of the last Kite in Rothiemurchus. He must have known that this
was the last pair in Speyside and almost one of the last in Britain, but that did not
deter him. He described how he hid near the nest to await the return of the
birds:

I could plainly see his shadow thrown through the upper branches of the tree before he
came in view; as there was an open space round the nest, he afforded the easiest possible
shot and fell as dead as a stone at my feet. The female, who was at that time at great
height, immediately sailed away to the north without turning round to see what had
happened to her mate and young.

Booth was not so forthcoming in writing about his subsequent action. However
it is known that he then climbed the tree, took the young one from the nest and
reared it until it was full size. He then killed it and mounted it in a glass case to
add to his ill-gotten collection. In another instance in 1877, Booth shot an
Osprey off the nest, shattering both wings but not killing it. He recovered the
bird from the loch, tied it beak shut, bound its legs together and took it with
him.

Not all the perpetrators of merciless wildlife slaughter were from south of
the Border. John Colquhoun was as heartless an individual as any. In his book
The Moor and Loch written in 1840 he devoted a whole chapter to the different
methods of trapping and poisoning. He gave details of how to set traps, half
a dozen at a time, around bait for Fox or Marten, with refinements of this

technique for Otters. He was responsible for killing the last pair of Ospreys on Loch Lomond.

Throughout the nineteenth century and on into the twentieth, Scottish birds' nests were also heavily plundered by English egg collectors. The rarer a species became, the greater the desire to obtain its eggs. The list of such collectors is enormous (see *The Egg Collectors of Great Britain and Ireland* by Cole and Trobe)—Selby, Wilson, Jardine, Milner—but this is not the place to enumerate them all. In many cases they were assisted by 'keepers or others who would in effect act as agents for them and make a few pounds on the side. The Dunbar brothers were a case in point, collecting regularly for oologists such as John Wooley and John Hancock. One of the brothers, Lewis Dunbar, operated in the Morayshire area and William worked mainly in Sutherland, although it was he in fact who took the last Osprey eggs from the Loch an Eilein nest (Speyside). William was also a visionary, as Eden described him, who foresaw the potential of sporting in the Highlands and persuaded owners to build access roads, lodges, kennels, and 'keepers cottages in Caithness and Sutherland.

The Dumfries Fur Market

A tantalizing glimpse of Man's effect in earlier centuries on the fur-bearing mammals of Scotland is given through our frustratingly incomplete knowledge of the trading in skins and furs. However, both Robert Service, in an article in *The Scottish Naturalist* in 1891, and James Ritchie in his 1920 book (which relies heavily on Service's data), provide sufficient information to enable us to gauge the extent of the trade, at least in the nineteenth century. This summary draws substantially from their accounts together with extracts from the *Dumfries Courier* 1816–74.

In medieval times, Scotland had a reputation throughout Europe for the quantity and quality of its animal skins. By the sixteenth century written accounts testify to the economic importance of a thriving market in skins, for people as far north as the islands of Orkney. The furs of Marten, Stoat (especially in winter ermine), Beaver, and Fox were listed as important items of trade in Inverness and doubtless the same applied to other areas were records to exist.

Various minor fur fairs were held at country towns in Scotland but by far the most significant was the annual Dumfries Fur Fair. The origins of this important market are, sadly, lost in the unrecorded mists of time. The popular wisdom is that by the beginning of the nineteenth century it was already long established; for several centuries according to some claims. Certainly, its well-established status by 1816 as the most important fur market in Britain is apparent from the breadth of the area from which the skins were brought in, and the numbers of furriers and their agents who came from distant centres. The market was held in the open street as part of the Candlemas Horse Fair in the third week of February, at the season when winter pelages were at their best. No record has been found to testify to the numbers of skins that were traded in the eighteenth century or earlier and the most complete summary is that compiled by Service and reproduced below.

STATISTICS OF DUMFRIES FUR MARKET, *Formerly held annually in February.*

Date.	Hareskins. No. Exposed.	Price p. Furrier's dozen.	Rabbit Skins. No. Exposed.	Price p. Furrier's dozen.	Foumart Skins. No. Exposed.	Price p. Furrier's dozen.	Otter Skins. No. Exposed.	Price each Skin.	Various Skins.
1816		16s							
1819		12s				15s		11s	
1820		12s							
1821		16s		8s to 9s					
1822	48,000	16s to 17s		14s					
1823	50,000	14s to 15s							
1824	"less than usual"	12s		6s					
1825	60,000	14s to 15s		4s 6d to 5s 6d					
1826		12s		5s to 5s 6d			18s to 21s	7s to 7s 6d	
1827	48,000	12s		3s 6d to 4s			16s		
1828	38,400	12s to 14s	18,000	4s 6d					
1829	40,000	14s 6d		3s to 5s	400	"few"	16s to 18s	8s to 10s	
1830	10,000	12s	4000	3s to 4s		18s	50 { "fewer than last year" }	8s to 10s	
1831	10,000	12s	2500	4s	600		226		
1832		12s		5s		18s			6 Badgers 2 Foxes, 36 Cats.
1833		11s 6d		5s to 5s 6d	{ "a drug in the market" }	14s	"few"	10s	
1834	13,258	13s	4667	5s		12s	"limited"		
1835	18,000	11s		3s to 4s	"below average"	14s to 15s	"one or two"		
1836		7s		2s to 3s 6d		12s to 13s	"two or three"		
1837	8000	6s & 6d to 7s			"almost none"	15s	"a few"		
1838	10,000	5s to 6s		1s to 1s 3d	"scarce"	14s	"scarce"		
1839	4800	10s 6d		1s 6d	"few"		"few"		
1840	10,000	10s	16,000	1s 6d	"considerable numbers"	24s to 28s	"stock small"	12s to 13s	"Badgers 5s to 6s each, stock small."
1841	20,000		7500	1s 6d		18s		12s	
1842	23,000	9s 6d to 10s 6d		1s 3d to 1s 6d			"average prices"		
1843	20,000	5s to 5s 6d		1s 3d to 1s 6d		12s		6s to 9s	
1844	18,000	5s 6d to 6s 6d		1s 9d to 2s		12s		10s	
1845	23,000	5s 6d to 6s	22,000	2s to 2s 6d	120	20s			
1846		2s to 2s 6d		1s to 1s 3d					
1847	4000	1s 3d to 1s 4d		6d to 8d	"small number	12s	"no otters"		
1848	"The once extensive fur	tensive fur	market has	dwindled a	way to nothing."				
1849	600	1s 6d							
1850	5600	4s		3s					
1851	10,000	3s to 3s 6d	10,000	1s 10d to 2s		18s		7s 6d	
1852	10,000	4s	10,000	1s 8d to 2s		26s to 30s		8s to 10s	
1853	16,000	5s 3d to 5s 6d	10,000	3s 3d		28s to 30s		8s to 10s	
1854	37,000	4s 6d	35,000	2s 6d.. to 3s 10d	"getting scarce"	30s		8s to 10s	
1855	35,000	3s	35,000	2s	do.	24s to 26s		5s to 6s	Foxes 9d each; Cats 2s p. doz.
1856	40,000	5s to 5s 6d	50,000	3s 6d to 3s 9d	240	30s to 36s		8s to 10s	,, 1s ,, ,, 3s ,,
1857	50,000	6s to 7s	70,000	4s 3d to 4s 4d	"rather scarce"	42s to 45s	12	6s to 7s	,, 2s 6d ,, ,, 4s ,,
1858	45,000	3s	60,000	2s	"very scarce"	18s	6	8s to 10s	
1859	65,000	7s	75,000	4s to 4s 3d	168	24s to 30s	"very scarce"	8s to 10s	
1860	70,000	6s to 6s 6d	100,000	3s to 3s 3d	"becoming rare"	24s to 30s		7s to 9s	
1861	50,000	6s to 6s 3d	75,000	3s 3d to 3s 6d	"no great number"	24s to 33s		8s to 10s	
1862	45,000	4s 3d to 4s 6d		2s 4d to 2s 7d	3s 9d	24s to 33s	36	8s to 10s	
1863		5s 6d to 5s 9d		3s 9d		30s to 30s 6d		8s to 10s	
1864		6s		3s 9d to 3s 10d		30s to 30s 6d		9s to 10s	
1865		5s 3d to 5s 6d		3s to 3s 3d	12	36s	"a few"	3s to 6s	
1866		5s 4d to 5s 6d		3s 1d		42s	6	9s to 10s	
1867		5s 6d to		3s 3d to 4s		24s to 36s		8s to 11s	
1868		5s 6d		3s	"No foumart,	otter, or fox	skins on offer."		
1869		5s		3s	Do.	do.	do.		
1870		4s to 4s 6d		2s to 2s 3d	Do.				
1871	45,000*	4s 6d	200,000*	2s 3d to 2s 4d					
1872					"No foumart	skins or otters offered now-a-days."			* Quantities sold by dealers during the entire winter.
1873		5s 9d		3s 8d	Do.	do.	do.	do.	
1874	180,000*	5s		2s 6d					

Figure 12. Service's table of skins sold at Dumfries Fur Market.
Courtesy of Dumfries and Galloway Libraries.

As can be seen from the table, the majority of the skins offered for sale were Brown Hare (peaking at 70,000 in 1860) and Rabbit. The 1874 figure of 180,000 Hares is thought to be either a misprint or a cumulative total with Rabbits. Most of these furs were exported to Europe, but in this same year a petition was entered to Parliament to prohibit such a lucrative export in favour of retaining the furs for the home-grown hat industry, which was suffering a lack of sufficient materials. British furs were regarded as superior to Continental ones and British-made top hats commanded a fine price overseas.

Apart from these two principal furs, there was a ready market for Otter and Polecat (Foumart). Otter skins were fetching as much as 30/- each around 1800 although through the remainder of the century the price was generally much lower, between 3/- and a high of 15/-, governed by supply and demand. Large numbers of Foumart (Polecat) skins passed through the market too, even eliciting the comment in 1832 that they were 'like a drug on the market'. Small numbers of Badger, Fox, and Feral Cat skins were occasionally traded but the most obvious omission is Pine Marten (Mertrick) whose fur was so highly esteemed. As discussed earlier, the likelihood is that inroads into its population in southern counties of Scotland in previous centuries were sufficiently serious that, by the time the Dumfries Fur Market records first occur, it had already been effectively eliminated. However, contrary to this suggestion, Ritchie maintained that it was still common as far south as Kirkcudbright until the late 1790s.

Skins flowed into Dumfries from all the southern counties from Ayrshire and Kirkcudbrightshire to Lanark, and as far east as Roxborough, but also south of the Border from Cumberland and Northumberland. The furriers' agents came from even farther afield and through them most skins went south to London and many of the towns and cities in northern England from Berwick to Manchester and Penrith to Sunderland. A smaller number were destined for Scottish centres such as Aberdeen, Edinburgh, and Glasgow.

Despite its long history and indisputable importance, by the middle of the nineteenth century the market was clearly in decline. There were several reasons for this apart from the evident reduction in the availability of skins. From around 1830, as Service's table shows, there were declining supplies of Otter and Polecat furs and from 1870 there were none on offer, up to the final demise of the fair as a street market in 1874. However, other factors also contributed to its decline. Arctic furs from companies such as Hudson Bay became more readily available and were of high quality and for top hats silk began to replace Hare and Rabbit fur. In addition, the opening of steamship routes from small ports on the south-west coast of Scotland to English ports, and later the development of railway communications to the south, meant that supplies of skins could readily be transported at any time during the winter months without the necessity of an annual market. Many agents now bought and collected directly from the farms, thereby bypassing the middleman in the market. The annual market eventually became irrelevant, although the trade, declining though it was, continued a little longer in a different form.

The effect of the long-running demand for Scottish furs on populations of these mammals in southern Scotland, and possibly northern Cumberland, is clear enough. The market shows the rapid decline in the availability of Otter and Polecat as supplies dried up. Marten had already effectively gone by 1800 and even Badgers, according to Service (see p. 231), were so rare in Dumfriesshire that the presence of one near Dumfries town in 1887 merited particular mention.

The level of killing

The concerted campaign of 'vermin' destruction that peaked in Scotland in the nineteenth century was unrivalled in its intensity and determination. In terms of scale, there was no parallel with the situation in England. Centuries of habitat loss south of the Border, together with general persecution on the parish basis had already drastically reduced the status of most of the species that had now become prime targets in Scotland.

The opening of the railway in 1843 was associated with a dramatic increase in the numbers of sportsmen travelling to take advantage of the wealth of game in Scottish waters and on the moorlands. However, the escalation in vermin per-secution had begun before this and it was in the middle years of the century, roughly from the 1830s to the 1860s, that the huge numbers of kills were achieved. There were 608 gamekeepers in Scotland in 1836; this figure had increased to 774 by 1853, and 1,050 in 1868. There are disappointingly few existing lists of estate vermin records from the first half of the century, but sufficient to show that there must have been extraordinary levels of killing. The figures in Table 5 from different parts of Scotland illustrate the appalling toll of wildlife that was taken across this period. A mere sixty-one individual years are involved in the sample figures for these six estates.

Perhaps the most infamous set of published records is that for the Glengarry (Inv'ness) estate which have been quoted many times. However, they are included here in full to illustrate a level of killing that must have been repeated many times on other Scottish estates in the mid nineteenth century. The area in question is some 16,000 acres in the parishes of Kilmonivaig, Kilmalie, and Glenelg.

Glengarry Estate, four years 1837–40

Fox 11
Wild cat 198
Marten cat 246
Pole cats 106
Stoats and Weasels 301
Badgers 67
Otters 48
House cats 78
White-tailed sea eagles 27
Golden eagle 15
Ospreys 18
Blue hawks 98
Orange-legged falcons 7
Hobby hawks 11
Kites (salmon-tailed gleds) 275
Marsh harriers 5

Goshawks 63
Common buzzards 285
Rough-legged buzzards 371
Honey buzzards 3
Kestrels 462
Merlin hawks 78
Hen harriers 63
Jer falcons 6
Ash-coloured hawks 9
Hooded crows 1431
Ravens 475
Horned owls 35
Fern owls 71
Golden owls 14
Magpies 2

TABLE 5. Random vermin totals from six Scottish estates in years up to 1868. Note the brief time spans to which these totals apply. Langwell figures by courtesy of the Duke of Portland. Remaining data courtesy of National Archives of Scotland.

		Polecat	Weasel*	Pine Marten	Otter	Wild Cat	Fox	eagle
Taymouth	1782–97	151	95	50		15		
Duniva	1809			15				
Buccleuch	1819–27	364	2526				19	
Langwell and Sandside	1819–26			1143	7		547	295
Assynt	1848–52	11	69	45		52	53	32
Langwell	six months only in 1848	37		1		25	1	
Langwell	half years only 1858–68				3		5	
Loch Naw	1853–68	65	316				57	

		'hawk'	Hen Harrier	Kite	Crow	Magpie	Raven
Taymouth	1782–97						
Duniva	1809	21		30		25	9
Buccleuch	1819–27	572	42	58	4049	1450	47
Langwell and Sandside	1819–26	1115			2647		1962
Assynt	1848–52	84			235		107
Langwell	six months only in 1848						
Langwell	half years only 1858–68	60	32				7
Loch Naw	1853–68	238				324	4

*There was frequently no differentiation between Weasel and Stoat and both were frequently included under the former species.

The identification of some of these Glengarry species may need to be treated with reserve. The alleged number of Rough-legged Buzzards is difficult to accept. The 98 Blue Hawks are presumably Sparrowhawks or Peregrines. Ash-coloured Hawks were probably male Hen Harriers.

In the latter half of the nineteenth century, there were in the order of 650+ upland grouse moors with an average size of c.10,000 acres (4,050 hectares). A large number of these, especially in the west of the country have subsequently been swallowed up by afforestation (the number of grouse moors at the end of the twentieth century was about 486). We can never know, and can only imagine, the full scale of the killing that took place on those moors in the name of game preservation. How many estates were killing at the levels that were achieved in only four years on Glengarry? What may have been the totals of birds of prey, Pine Martens, Wild Cats, Polecats, and other predators slaughtered in fifty years or more on 650+ upland estates? In a way it is perhaps better that we can never know.

In 1902, the Scottish naturalist John Harvie-Brown wrote to most of the Highland estates from Perthshire and Argyll northwards to request vermin totals from the 'keepers, for incorporation in his regional natural histories. The results submitted to him from more than seventy estates covered the last decade of the previous century and occasionally the decade prior to that also. They are interesting as confirmation that the populations of many of the target species had by then been severely reduced, with the result that the totals reported to Harvie-Brown overall were shadows of those that had been achieved earlier. The real devastation of Scotland's most vulnerable species had taken place through the middle of the century, so that thirty or forty years later it was more a question of mopping up the remainder.

Harvie-Brown's returns showed continuing heavy control of Hooded Crows and Magpies, and still high numbers of Ravens. Foxes too were universally targeted and the all-embracing heading 'hawks' featured on almost every estate in substantial numbers, e.g. 2,590 on Atholl 1894–1903. Other than Peregrines (listed on twenty-four of the returns), Buzzards (specified on nine returns), and eagles, no other birds of prey are specified except for two cases of Kestrels and one of Merlin. Hen Harrier was not mentioned once. By this latter part of the century the number of eagles killed had fallen dramatically, simply because the birds themselves were then so scarce. Eight Sea Eagles were killed on Rum in 1886 but only occasional Golden Eagles elsewhere. While huge numbers of Stoats and Weasels were killed almost everywhere (e.g. 9,849 on one Perthshire estate in eleven years), the geographical pattern of returns for Wild Cat and the two rarer mustelids, Polecat and Pine Marten is revealing, since almost every record comes from the far west or far north. There was a substantial figure of forty-one Pine Martens killed on four Sutherland shootings; other reports were few and far between by this time with the major exception in Harvie-Brown's records of a large kill of fifty-six in Perthshire.

On the basis of Harvie-Brown's figures, at the end of the nineteenth century the Wild Cat was still present in good numbers in western districts, whereas there were no records from farther east. Several estates in Wester Ross and west Inverness-shire were still killing considerable numbers—Inverate, Kishorn, Arisaig, Morar, Torridon. At the same time there was a consistently heavy toll taken on Feral Cats ('house cats') in many areas; for example 1,647 taken by gamekeepers on Lewis in sixteen years and an alleged 4,042 on a Perthshire estate in eleven years!

TABLE 6. Vermin records from 15 out of c.70 Highland estates from surveys carried out by Harvie-Brown. By courtesy of the National Museum of Scotland.

		House Cat	Wild Cat	Pine Marten	Weasel/ Stoat	Polecat	Otter	Fox	Hooded Crow	Raven	'hawk'	eagle
Lewis	1876–85	287	–	–	–	–	95	–	698	637	443	30
Lewis	1887–1902	1360	–	–	–	–	–	–	2539	2251	982	–
Un-named, Perthshire	1891–1901	4042	–	56	9849	8	26	1239	2517	576	2517	37
Atholl	1894–1903	–	–	–	7198	–	–	1425	4009	–	2590	–
Garrogie	1893–1902	–	1	1	41	2	3	182	72	18	96	8
Balmacaan	1894–1902	586	–	–	1313	–	–	202	279	20	808	–
Inverinate	1874–83	–	51	–	230	57	2	25	363	84	172	–
Tulloch Brae	1893–1902	–	–	–	1400	–	–	3	80	–	135	–
Glen Kyllachy	1891–1901	–	–	–	494	–	–	160	103	22	108	–
Glenborrodale	1862–81	506	–	–	345	46	84	123	2111	107	330	–
North Morar	1879–88	–	3	2	238	28	68	189	1249	81	184	–
Arisaig Forest	1880–89	–	12	–	669	34	30	39	485	34	153	3
Appin	1880–89	–	34	9	136	6	15	27	239	23	84	–
Inverewe	1897–1902	–	4	–	201	–	3	54	64	27	72	2
Inchnadamph	1880–99	–	16	7	62	25	–	248	873	240	158	–

N.B. 'Hawks' were usually not identified in the 'keepers's returns but, in the above lists, included one or two specific mentions of Buzzard and Peregrine. Rats, Magpies, Jays, Jackdaws, and Badgers were all killed on a few estates, sometimes in large numbers (2,783 Jays on the Perthshire estate); 473 (!) owls were killed on Balmacaan.

If Harvie-Brown's survey had been a few decades earlier, the figures they revealed would probably have been staggering (cf. Glengarry). Nonetheless, a sample of eleven species from fifteen of his estate returns shown in Table 6, gives a clear impression of the level of slaughter that was still taking place in the Highlands at the end of the nineteenth century.

The above table indicates the level of persecution of predators that was taking place up to the earliest years of the twentieth century. This is not to suggest that such killing ceased then, for it certainly did not, and it continued for the immediate decades thereafter, despite the interruptions and consequent reductions in activity caused by the two World Wars. Since then, and regardless of increasing protective legislation, illegal persecution has continued to take a heavy toll on wildlife in Scotland. The upland areas of Scotland continue to this day to produce the worst annual catalogues of illegal killing of protected species anywhere in Britain.

5

In on the Act—searching the record

In England and Wales, long before the establishment of the large game estates, dramatic changes to the landscape through the removal of forest cover, drainage of wetlands, and conversion of land to agriculture had already removed huge areas of natural habitat for many species. Mammals such as Pine Marten and Wild Cat, and birds including harriers and eagles had already been pushed back into their final refuges. We have already considered the impact that the fur trade had on a range of fur-bearing mammals. It is necessary now to concentrate on the third major factor, that of deliberate persecution, to establish the legal framework that was put in place in the sixteenth century for statutory control of these 'vermin', and to examine the processes of implementation of those laws through the parishes.

The basic aim of the Tudor Vermin Acts was the elimination of the relevant species regarded as vermin. Although this was never likely to be attainable, in parts of the country the effects of these Acts were certainly considerable, particularly with ecologically vulnerable predators such as Pine Marten and Wild Cat. In other instances even the regular killing of vast numbers of smaller species such as Hedgehogs, House Sparrows, and others had negligible effects on the overall populations. The introduction of the Tudor Vermin Acts, at the very time when the demand for fur had declined, does raise the question as to whether the ensuing persecution of the same mammals as vermin actually prevented moderate recoveries of some of the rarer species that might otherwise have taken place.

Nonetheless, the ultimate impact that 'keepered estates had in the nineteenth century must not be diminished. The figures from the Glengarry estate in Inverness-shire for the four years 1837–40, quoted in the previous chapter, illustrate graphically the levels of slaughter that were perpetrated without a second thought. However, the full story begins far back in the middle of the sixteenth century in the dynasty of the Tudors in England and Wales.

As a result of the succession of poor harvests and social privation of the early 1500s, and notwithstanding the fact that harvests in the early 1530s were more bountiful, in 1532 Henry VIII passed 'An Acte made and ordeyned to dystroye Choughes [i.e. Jackdaws, see p. 150], Crowes, and Rokes'. It was clearly focused on attempts to protect the grain harvest:

for as much as innumerable numbers of Rookes, Crowes and Choughes do daily consume a wonderful and marvellous great quantituy of corn and grain of all kinds . . . as well in the sowing . . . as also at the ripening and kernelling . . . and over that a marvellous destruction and decay of the covertures of thatched houses, barns, ricks and such like.

By this Act, local communities were required to provide nets for catching these birds and to meet annually to review the work and decide how to succeed in killing all young. This was the first of a series of Tudor Acts legislated by Henry and his daughter Elizabeth, and which were the foundations that defined a statutory basis for the control of perceived species of vermin across England and Wales in succeeding centuries.

The 1532 Act was a reflection of the fear that multitudes of corvids were threatening the very basis of agriculture and therefore needed serious reduction. In this respect, as we well know, the Act failed abysmally. However, it was draconian in its intent. It made it obligatory on owners of land in all parishes and every settlement of more than ten households

to doo and cause to be don as moche as in hym or in theym reasonably shall or may be to kill and utterly distroye all manner of Choughes, Crowes and Rookes comyng, abyding, bredying or hauntyng (their property) upon peyne of grevous amerciament to be levied by distresse of the goodes and catalles of the Offendours.

Each community was required to furnish itself with an appropriate crow net and a shrape baited with chaff—failure to do so rendering the inhabitants liable to a fine of ten shillings—and to maintain and use these for the ten-year period for which the Act ran. Twopence for every dozen of old crows, etc. was to be paid by the owners and tenants of the manor, or of other lands. Interestingly, this Act, unlike subsequent ones that were the responsibility of the parishes, was enforced through the manorial courts. The parish net and its accoutrements therefore had to be presented to the steward of the Court Leet every year to substantiate their existence and proper working order. For this ten-year period, owners and tenants of farmland had to meet annually with a steward appointed by the court to agree the optimum methods possible to achieve the destruction of 'of all the yonge brede of Choughes, Crowes and Rookes for that yere'. A community in default of this requirement was subject to a penalty of twenty shillings.

As Charles Oldham pointed out as long ago as 1930, the Act sounds drastic and far-reaching but, as he admitted, there is only scant evidence as to its effective or widespread implementation. There was little of the nation-wide administrative network that was needed to ensure its uptake across the country-side, with poor communications and a very small and widely dispersed rural population. Diktats could be issued from Parliament and the king but their implementation and the organization and administration of communities to which they applied were at the whim of the manorial courts. Added to this, much of the northern, western, and south-eastern parts of the country were relatively heavily wooded, making any achievement of the aim to eliminate these members of the crow family no more than a pipe dream. There is plenty of evidence scattered through the parish records of the provision of crow nets in the next two centuries and occasionally beyond, but very few records of the results of netting. There is occasional evidence that other organized vermin control was undertaken, for example the payment of 4/8*d*. for the provision of a Fox net at Woodbury in Devon in 1560–1. However, suspicion remains that the implementation was not rigorous although there is occasional proof that defaulting parishes were sometimes brought to book. The archives of the Court Leet at Leominster for 1566 record that 'They present the Churchwardens of this towne to have incurred the penalty of the Statute in that case made and provided for not keeping of such nets as whereby crowes and such other vermine might be destroyed, which devoure and spoyle corne to the greate prejudice of many of the inhabitants within the Borough'. The Rev. G. F. Townsend in his *History of Leominster* records that in earlier years (i.e. after the enactment of Henry's 1532 legislation) a large net for this purpose was suspended from the western tower of the church. How it may have operated leaves much to the imagination.

The second half of the sixteenth century saw the onset of one of the most severe phases of the Little Ice Age and a succession of long and bitter winters, the first of which was in 1664–5. It was a time of particular hardship made much worse by a series of bad harvests, famine, epidemics, exploding food prices, and a rapidly expanding population. Elizabeth's response to this situation was much stronger legislation passed in 1566. This was a far more important Act and marked a defining point in the attitudes to a wide range of birds and mammals that were hereafter to be branded officially as undesirable vermin. The effects of this Act continued to be felt in succeeding generations and it can be argued that its legacy is manifest to the present day. Many of the named species are still legally controlled as pests. The Act made it a requirement for all parishes to raise a levy from landowners, farmers, and tenants, in proportion to their land holding. This was to provide the means, separate from the church funds themselves, out of which bounties were to be paid to parishioners, at stipulated rates, for the killing of a wide range of vermin. Whereas her father's Act was clearly directed at avian pests of grain crops, Elizabeth's Act was strangely mis-named as it contained a wide list of species, none of which, with the exception of members of the crow family, mice, and rats, can remotely be classified as graminivorous. Entitled 'An Acte for the Preservation of Grayne', it contains a long list of mammals and birds which, by stretching the imagination, might be deemed to impact on Man's interests in agricultural or almost any other field. It is significant—certainly in terms of numbers killed—that the Bullfinch (Bullfinch control legislation in the twentieth century was nothing new!) was specifically singled out among a catchall for other small passerines. Kingfisher, assumed to be serious predators on fish fingerlings, earned its place on the list and woodpeckers were included for less obvious reasons that are explored on p. 140. The Act included every one of our native mustelids, rats and mice, Fox, Wild Cat, and Mole together with a full list of corvids, Starling, many birds of prey, and, slightly incongruously, Cormorant and Shag. It is this list of the native species in this Act that defines those that are the subject of this book.

Elizabeth subsequently renewed the legislation in 1572 and 1598 and this Act was critically important in so far as it initiated the serious and intensive campaign of vermin control throughout England and Wales. The Act was not repealed until 1863.

An Acte for the preservation of Grayne

The heads of any old Crowes, Choughs (*viz Jackdaw*), Pyes, or Rookes, for the heades of every three of them one penny and for heades of every six young Crowes, Choughs, Pyes or Rookes, one penny; and for every six egges of them unbroken one penny: and like wise for every twelve Stares (*Starlings*) Heades one penny; for everie Head of Martyn Hawkes, Furskytte (*Stoat*), Moldekytte (*Weasel*), Busarde, Schagge, Carmarante, or Ryngtale (*harrier*), two pence; and for every two egges of them one penney; and for every Iron (*Sea Eagle*) or Ospreyes Head Fower pence; for the Head of every Woodwall (*woodpecker*), Pye, Jaye, Raven, Kyte, one penney; for the Head of every Byrde which is called the Kings Fyssher; one peny; for the Heade of every Bulfynche or other Byrde that devoureth the blowth of Fruite, one peny; for the Heades of everie Fox or Gray (*Badger*) twelve pence; and for the Heades of every Fitchou, Polcatte, Wessel, Stote, Fayre bade or Wilde Catte, one peny; for the Heades of every Otter or Hedgehog, two pence and for the Heades of every three rattes or twelve Myse, one penney; for the Heades of everie Moldewarpe or Wante (*Mole*) one halfpenney.

This administration of the new Act was the direct responsibility of the parish officers, not of the Court Leet, as was the case with the earlier Act. A committee of two churchwardens and six other parishioners was required in every parish, whose duty it was to select two 'honest and substantial persons' annually, to act as distributers of the fund. Because the bounty money was provided under a separate assessment, and not as part of the general church fund, the churchwardens were not normally directly involved in accounting for the receipts or payments of the vermin money. This means that, sadly, there are very few existing records of the results of this important Act in the decades of the sixteenth century immediately following its implementation.

What evidence there is, suggests that the take up, piecemeal though it was, was certainly considerably better than had been the case with the 1532 Act. Clearly, in those parishes that applied the law, the distributers went about their business and fulfilled the requirement to report monthly to the churchwardens, although tantalizingly few records of these earliest transactions exist. At Melton Mowbray (Leics), the Act was certainly being implemented and John Sawell was paid iijd (*viz* 3*d*.) 'for kylling off rats according to ye quenes majesties statute'. At Ludlow (Salop) in 1569, mouse, crow, and 'chough' payments were actually disbursed from the main church funds and Minchinhampton (Glos) the same year and Kirton (Lincs) two years later have similar entries.

Records such as these and a few others are traceable only because they were, unusually, made from the general church funds administered and accounted for by the churchwardens. It is evident that the passing of the legislation provoked an increase in the killing of some species. At Braunton (Devon) there was an upsurge in the number of payments for Badgers and Foxes with an increase in Foxes too at Tavistock. Also in the same county, the church accounts at Crediton record the receipt of 15/2 'as money collected . . . towards the payment of vermyn, according to the statute' with disbursements of £3 'unto divers and sundry person for the killing of vermyn'. The enthusiasm at Crediton did not last long, however, for 1567 was the only year in which payments were made for vermin.

Even in these early years there were already inconsistencies in the ways in which the Act was being interpreted and applied. The fact remains that the vast majority of the sixteenth century record is lost simply because it did not form a part of the official church record but was kept separately. The most complete example from this time is the record of Edward Wylley who was a distributor under the terms of the Act in the Hertfordshire parish of Bishop's Stortford, quoted by Cox and subsequently by Oldham and others, and reproduced below.

Edward Wylley, 'collectore of all manner of vermayne' whose 'Accounte and Recoynge' includes both receipts and payments for the period 12 April 1569 to 12 April 1571. His receipts totalled lijs, vii (i.e. 52 shillings, 7*d*.). In these two years he paid out to unnamed parishioners for 141 Hedgehogs, 53 Moles, 6 Weasels, 202 crows' eggs, 128 Pies' eggs, 18 young crows, 80 Rats, 18 crows, 2 Bullfinches, 5 hawks, 24 Starlings, 5 Kingfishers, 1 Polecat, 1,426 mice, and 118 heads of crows, hawks, and cadows (i.e. Jackdaws).

In most cases, it is not until the second or third decades of the seventeenth century that vermin payments start to appear in the churchwardens' accounts, and we begin to get a measure of the killing that was taking place. Whether or not the levels of killing that were then evident in parishes across the country had occurred, unrecorded, in the preceding decades, we cannot tell. It is quite possible that, with some relief from the earlier disastrous harvests, the preliminary years of the seventeenth century saw a growing unpopularity among landowners for the raising of yet another burdensome tax and that persecution was at a low level for that reason. Furthermore, the lack of evidence could reflect the somewhat unpopular arrangements required for implementing the Act, leading to local reappraisal of its priority, and its abandonment. We simply do not know how widespread or intense vermin control was in the critical fifty years or so after the passing of the 1566 Act.

Although records for those years are very sparse, it is clear that not all parishes implemented the Act in any case. While the figures vary considerably from county to county, evidence from the seventeenth and eighteenth centuries shows that over 50% of parishes overall were then making payments for vermin. Furthermore, what is clear from the abundant evidence from those years is that even if Elizabeth's Act itself fell into early disuse, its purposes were reincarnated with colossal zeal and enthusiasm a little later in the seventeenth and eighteenth centuries. In many areas of the country in these two centuries—and in a good number of cases up into the nineteenth—vermin payments were by then being made directly through church funds and thus recorded in the churchwardens' accounts where they have provided the core of the historical evidence.

Individual payments for a given species frequently varied from one parish to another and, not infrequently, within a parish from year to year, or even seasonally. Every parish had its own pattern of approach (or not) independent of its neighbours and evidence of inter-parish co-ordination was very rare. The Acts sometimes appeared to serve as an open-ended licence to kill any creature that particularly offended the inhabitants; snakes, for example, were heavily persecuted in some parishes. Bats often suffered the same fate. Not infrequently special short-term campaigns were initiated supported by enhanced payments. In 1756, the parishioners of Otterton (Devon) decreed that there should be a premium for killing birds of prey for the following two months 'with this alter-ation that for every Kitt and Hoak to be killed 4d for each to be paid' (normal payment was 2d.). In the same county, a meeting of parishioners at East Budleigh in June 1802 decided that 'It was this day agreed to pay double the price for killing small birds and others . . . from Michaelmas to Lady Day in every year'. Sometimes the vermin was displayed publicly and nailed to the churchyard gate: 'St Michael's Church, St Albans 1637: Item. For a stoate & a heade for ye church yard gate . . . 1s'.

All this is not to say, of course, that some vermin were not controlled before the sixteenth century because they most certainly were. Long before this Act, as the historical record shows, churchwardens around the country had been involved in the expense of trying to keep their churches free from bats, Starlings, Jack-daws, and owls. What the Tudor Vermin Acts did was to signal the beginning of a more concentrated drive to keep a much wider range of species under control in the general countryside. Although clearly ignored in some parishes, it became a campaign pursued with missionary zeal in others, most notably in the seventeenth and eighteenth centuries and was thereafter continued with increasing purpose on many of the nineteenth and twentieth century game estates.

The numbers slaughtered in some parishes in the seventeenth and eighteenth centuries were impressive. How many of us realize, for example, that the inhabitants of one rural parish in Cheshire killed over 6,600 Bullfinches in thirty-six years with as many as 452 in one year alone (1676) while a few years later the same parish disposed of 696 Kites in eight years? Or that in Dorset 3,344 Hedgehogs were killed in Sherborne parish in 137 years up to 1799 (see below)? There are many such parishes across England where both the range of species targeted was wide and the numbers killed impressive but not that many that could compete with somewhere like Sherborne for sheer volume.

TABLE 7. Vermin killed at Sherborne, Dorset, 1662–1799.

	Fox	Hedgehog	Badger	Otter	Polecat	Stoat
Sherborne 1662–1799	772	3344	280	77	693	1940
	Marten	'Rat'	Kite	Jay	Rook	Sparrow
Sherborne 1662–1799	68	135890	4	436	3036 doz	8379 doz

Thus it can be seen that before the game estate owners of the nineteenth century and their gamekeepers had any chance of delivering the final *coup de grâce*, intensive control of many species had already begun in some areas. The effect this may have had on populations of the species involved is discussed later.

The parish and its officers

Because the data in old parish records are such a central part of the examination of the history of the management of British wildlife, it is relevant to explore a little of their background and the role played by the different officers appointed to administer the various parish functions. In this way, the substantial part that vermin payments assumed in many parishes can be seen in the wider social context of the times.

The distant origins of our parishes have roots deep in local agricultural units, reaching back into the Dark Ages. The pattern and confirmation of parish boundaries evolved gradually thereafter under the Anglo-Saxons and later the Normans. They were, to quote Anthea Jones, 'the boundaries of their farming world, with pasture, meadow, arable fields and woods all comprised within them'. They defined the limits of the land worked and otherwise used by the individual nucleated villages and townships. By the time of the Norman Conquest the parish network was well established and completed by them between 1150 and 1250.

The parish system established a stability and efficiency which has been one of its hallmarks ever since. In the sixteenth century, it developed as a unit of secular government, organized on a statutory basis and this system of 'parish government' lasted until the nineteenth century. The system itself was stable, albeit its constituent parts have evolved and changed over the centuries to match the needs of growing or shifting populations. For example, soon after the Restoration of the Monarchy in 1660, an Act was passed that enabled the division of parishes. This occurred principally in those districts where it could be shown that the proposed new parish was substantially founded on an pre-existing township as determined at the time of the Elizabethan Poor Law in 1601; in practice this usually meant that an area could seek to secede from the mother parish if it could demonstrate that up until then it had supported a constable of its own.

The sizes of individual parishes were—as they still are—enormously variable. The main determinant in rural areas has always been the fertility of the parish land. Where land is good the parish size is small, and where conditions are harsh and the land less productive, the area of a single parish is much larger. For these reasons there has always been a huge size discrepancy between parishes in the south of England and many of those in the north. By 1810, the average area of parishes in the south varied between three square miles in East Anglia and eight in Devon and Cornwall. In the north, the average size averaged sixteen square miles in Cheshire and as much as twenty-four in Cumberland and Westmorland and seventy in the western half of Northumberland. Many of these huge northern parishes contained a number of chapelries, subservient to the mother church. The largest parish in England was Simonburn in Northumberland, with one rector, one church, and an area of 249 square miles! Sadly at Simonburn no parish records exist until 1787 after which only a handful of vermin payments were made for Foxes and one or two Polecats. These differences in parish size, however, need to be borne in mind when considering the levels of wildlife killing that took place from parish to parish.

With the rapid growth of population and the coming of the Industrial Revolution in the second half of the eighteenth century, there were many more divisions of the original parishes, especially in the newly burgeoning industrial areas of the north. Halifax is an example often quoted. Before the Industrial Revolution it was a huge parish of some 118 square miles, at its widest some 15 miles long and 13 across. It included 23 separate townships but was subsequently broken down into a similar number of individual modern parishes, in addition to the numerous ones now in the town itself. In Lancashire, the parish of Whalley, even up to the nineteenth century, extended to some 30 miles by 15, included 50 townships, and had an area of 170 square miles. Manchester was another example in the same area; by Act of Parliament in 1850 it was divided to create 101 rectories in the old parish. The division of some large parishes happened earlier than this, however, and by 1844, according to Tate, 5,355 townships and chapelries up and down the country had already become independent parishes. In 1600—the early years of my searches—there were fewer than 9,000 parishes in England and Wales; the figure now is around 12,000.

The affairs of the parish, from at least as far back as the fourteenth century in some cases, were entrusted to a vestry committee. At a time in the sixteenth century when the manorial courts were starting to crumble, the vestry committee evolved as the obvious successor for the management of the ecclesiastical business of the parish. The vestry was the committee that had the primary responsibility of maintenance and repair of the church, the safeguarding of its treasures, and the imposition of a church rate to fund the necessary works. There was no specific point in time when transfer or merging of responsibility with manorial courts took place; the process evolved across the parishes and counties, as need and circumstance demanded, and often the manorial courts and the vestry committees existed side by side for decades. In terms of the whole operation for the control of vermin and payment of bounties—or deciding not to undertake any—after 1566 the vestry had an omnipotent role. The financial outlay disbursed by some parishes for the purposes of vermin control in the seventeenth and eighteenth centuries sometimes seems wildly disproportionate to the other social priorities of the parish. Four pence given by the church-wardens for a Hedgehog's head is difficult to relate to accompanying payments of twopence handed out to a maimed sailor or a soldier having had his tongue cut out by the Turks.

Tudor legislation considerably expanded the responsibilities that were devolved to the parishes so that as well as carrying the accountability for ecclesiastical affairs and the maintenance of the church and its demesne, the vestry was soon submerged in an additional plethora of civil tasks. Gradually parishes took over wider and wider civil responsibilities. They assumed accountability for funding the provision of arms, the supporting of maimed seamen and soldiers, highway maintenance, disbursing the poor rates, appointment of constables, haywards, and fieldmasters, setting of stinting levels, maintenance of stocks, pinfolds, and of course among it all, the raising of rates for the payment of bounties for the killing of vermin. In these ways the parishes became the ultimate units of local government, the birthplaces of our liberty, and the genuine cradles of democracy. The community itself was the architect and deliverer of local governance wherein householders served their turns in one administrative post or another for one year—sometimes more—and then retreated again to their original destinies, wiser, more experienced, and probably very relieved, persons.

Of the host of officials appointed to carry out these functions, the church-wardens were the most important. This 'ancient and honourable' office dates back many centuries and there were certainly appointments to these offices through the Council of London as early as 1127 and probably considerably earlier. Usually there were two wardens appointed each year for most parishes, one nominated by the incumbent and the other by the vestry committee. Some of the larger parishes opted for four wardens and at Kendal in Westmorland, a huge parish with many satellite chapelries, they actually appointed twelve each year. The churchwardens and other officers were elected annually at an Easter meeting of the vestry and any householder was liable to be called to serve in one parish office or another, but the churchwarden appointments were not by any means always popular with the appointees, despite the fact that they carried more status than the other parish offices. The posts were quite onerous and individuals were elected either on the basis of 'Buggin's turn' or because they had the desirable attribute of being literate. However, many of the church-wardens did not have the necessary literary skills to compile the accounts them-selves, as shown by the fact that they sometimes signed the accounts by mark. In these cases another parishioner took on the task of transcribing into the parish record from the 'warden's notes. We should probably not be surprised that to avoid offending their dignity, exemptions to churchwardens' duty were allowed to peers of the realm, MPs, military officers, and attorneys. Otherwise, for lesser mortals to refuse the appointment was serious and could result in substantial fines. At Mere (Wilts) the level of fine was 13/4 and at Spelsbury (Oxon) two bushels of malt. The churchwardens' accounts were rendered either quarterly or annually to the vestry committee and were by no means formalities. Church-wardens were sometimes capped as to the amount they could disburse for vermin or other purposes, and were certainly directed as to what species of vermin and what levels of payment for them would be applied. Such decisions were the prerogative of the vestry. Not infrequently churchwardens were chastised and sometimes even fined for profligate spending.

Searching the record: implementing the Acts

Parish registers were first instigated during Henry VIII's reign in 1538, at the time of his conflict with Rome, the dissolution of the monasteries, and the establishment of a State Church, separated from Rome. Initially the church-wardens' accounts were not included as part of the statutory requirement for the registering of births and deaths although many were already being kept and some still exist, even from the previous century.

These historical churchwardens' accounts are gold mines of information about the variety and numbers of vermin that were killed between the sixteenth and nineteenth centuries. In some cases the amounts paid out for the killing of a wide range of species provide us with a wonderful catalogue of local wildlife, but at other times seem disproportionate to the human needs of the parishioners. Without doubt the churchwardens' accounts (together with those of the constable and the overseer of the poor) are the greatest composite records of our social history that exist. The church was the core of community life in these times and the combined parish records of the vestry, the constable, overseer of the poor, churchwardens, and surveyors of the highway paint the most graphic picture of the life of ordinary people in their local communities. They encompass burning social issues of the day, of poverty, taxing, punishment, bastardy, insanity, welfare of maimed soldiers and seamen, upkeep of the church and its graveyard, and countless other aspects of local life. And among it all, often incongruous in comparison with social payments made, is the continuing battle against the creatures sharing the countryside with the human population. The reproduced page from Cranborne (Dorset; p. 90) parish below is a typical example of the type of record that exists.

These invaluable records are commentaries on life of the times and the issues that featured as major aspects of parish affairs. Heavy expenses were incurred for example in connection with church bells in every parish. Ropes, wheels, oil (oyle), rehanging, and paying for ringers on a host of different occasions are subjects that constantly appear. They record the history of passing events such as coronations, victories, royal births, gunpowder plot (annually), and other like occasions, and the period of most intensive vermin control in the seventeenth and eighteenth centuries was taking place across one of the most tumultuous periods of our history. The following table gives a snapshot of the immense variety of topics covered by the churchwardens up and down the country.

TABLE 8A. A typical range of payments made by churchwardens in C16 to C19.

Preston (Leics)	1626	"To Thos Dalby for whipping the dogges*............6d"
Alderley (Ches)	1724	"Given to a man whose tongue was cut out by Turks....6d"
Claines (Worcs)	1805	13 Nov "Ringing for Nelson's victory...............2/6"
Corbridge (N'humb)	1692	"For 1 gled and 1 fulmard ....6d"
Sherborne (Dorset)	1693	"Taking down and burying the quarters.............1/-"
Kirby Wharfe (Yorks)	1697	"To two men that lost all by fire ....6d"
Glaston (Leics)	1737	"for repairing the pinfold wall" ....1/6"
Knockholt (Kent)	1749	"for mending the shingles ....2/2"
Barnes (Surrey)	1712	"gave to a man and a woman and 12 children..........1/"
Oxted (Surrey)	1711	"to 2 maymd soldiers 2d; for 2 hedgehog heads ....8d"

* A parish dog whipper was employed in most parishes to control or expel the hordes of dogs from church services. An example of an actual whip is hanging in the church at Baslow (Derbys).

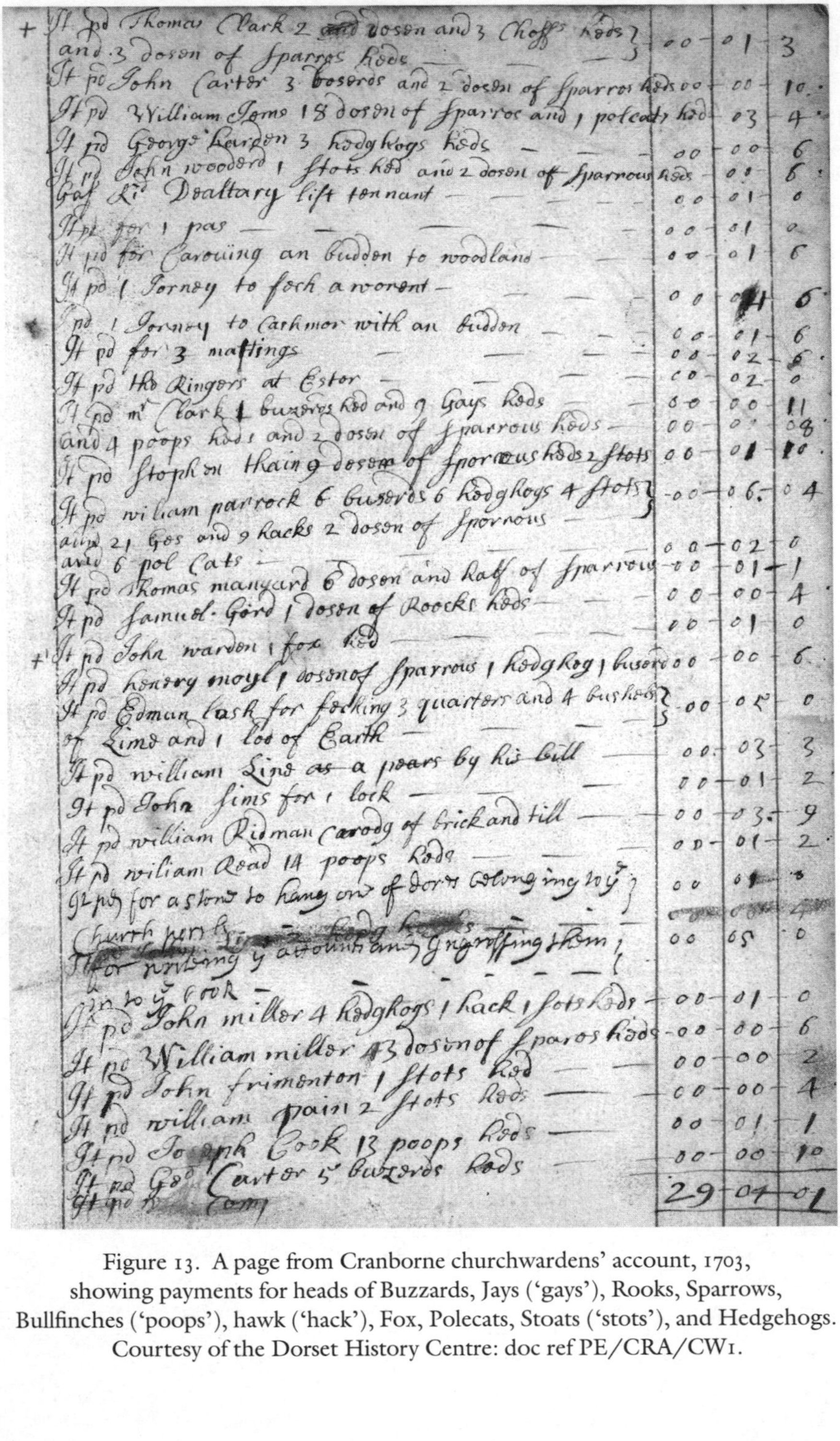

Figure 13. A page from Cranborne churchwardens' account, 1703,
showing payments for heads of Buzzards, Jays ('gays'), Rooks, Sparrows,
Bullfinches ('poops'), hawk ('hack'), Fox, Polecats, Stoats ('stots'), and Hedgehogs.
Courtesy of the Dorset History Centre: doc ref PE/CRA/CW1.

Other entries one simply finds more amusing or enigmatic but they give further insights into the vagaries and vicissitudes of post medieval life, for example:

TABLE 8B. Miscellaneous selection of items paid for by churchwardens.

Peopleton (Worcs)	1692	"Given to a great-belly'd woman . . . . .1/6"
Betws Gwerfil Goch (Mer)	1731	"For whipping a vagabond . . . . .1/-"
Ossington (Notts)	1754	"watching a strouling man . . . . .1/-"
Blythe (Notts)	1714	"pd for ye ale wh ye scaffold was build . . . . .4d"
Everton (Notts)	1835	"Retford to get a summons for men playing football. .2/6d"
Newnham (Glos)	1740	"spent with Rimmington's maid . . . . .1/2d"
Heslington (Yorks)	1749	"spent with a fresh parson . . . . .6d"
Drewsteignton (Devon)	1663	"pd to two men when Penrudorke was put to death . .£1"
Kirby Malzeard (Yorks)	1591	"*Item* bearing horse dung to the bell casting . . . .£1"

These parish accounts give endless evidence of the terrible hardship of life for many of the citizens, both rural and urban in the seventeenth and eighteenth centuries. Countless payments were made to itinerants, vagabonds, and maimed militia men in parishes throughout the land and one gets occasional glimpses of the more mundane hardships:

Warter (Yorks) 1776: 'Pd to Margt Butler for her & children gathering 83 tons of stones at 8d per ton for ye Highways. To assist her in bringing up her children . . . £2 15s 4d'.

Searching the oldest records is particularly slow and often difficult. At one extreme the script can be copperplate, beautifully inscribed, and a pleasure to read; at the other extreme one can almost feel the excruciating effort of the press-ganged 'warden in forming his words, leaving a legacy for us 300 years or so later that borders on the illegible. There are other problems. Records are often incomplete with years missing or badly damaged or fragmented pages, and often very faded script. Some of the earliest are in Latin and others in Welsh. Another hazard is associated with the fact that the vestry meetings at which the accounts were considered were often generously assisted with liberal amounts of ale, sometimes to the evident detriment of pages of the accounts. It is easy to smile at some of the difficulties such 'wardens experienced as seen through some of their spelling, many of them accurately phonetic, for example whisuntyde, wisundy, Asakrement at Crismus, gale (for jail), out of pockitt, bread and whine, soulgers and saylers, artikills, procklymacion, cutton ye ivy, cyling vermin, and the well-known Wiltshire town of Chipnum. Occasionally one even clearly 'hears' dialectal phonetics as in 'communion brade' in Norfolk! Amusing they may be, but the phonetics are easy to read and still perfectly identifiable in much of our own slack speech 300 years later.

As we shall see in Chapter 8, there were clearly different priorities put on various species of vermin in different areas. Notwithstanding this, the selected focus of target species for which the churchwardens were prepared to pay was sometimes very narrow. Time and again in hundreds of parishes Foxes, Hedgehogs, or House Sparrows dominated, often to the exclusion of other species. There were frequently totally different approaches in adjacent parishes where a much wider range of species applied. For example, in Westmorland large numbers of a wide range of vermin were killed over an extended period between 1688 and 1812 in Kendal parish, whereas next door at Hawkshead the focus from 1612 to 1797 was exclusively on Ravens with only a very occasional Fox to vary the record. Again in the nearby parish of Beetham, it was Badgers and Foxes that were targeted with only a brief spate of eight or nine years around 1670 when other mammals were added to the list. There are innumerable other such enigmas. The fact remains that for whatever reasons many parishes did not pay any bounties at all and others only produced payments for very occasional Fox, Hedgehog, or other species (see Appendix 1).

It is accepted that in many of the rural areas the enforcement of statutes was often ineffective and the more remote the area, the more likely this was to have been the case 300 years or more ago. There are occasional records of action being taken against individual parishes that defaulted in their application to vermin control. The most famous of these involved Worfield parish (Salop) where in 1575 it is recorded, 'It'm amersed by the commysoners at Bridgnorth for not destroyinge foules and vermynt accordinge to the Statute in that behalf.' The result of this chastisement was certainly dramatic, for the following year they launched into a frenzy of killing. However, it was short and sweet and within a couple of years they lapsed back to their previous casual killing of the odd Fox until, at the end of the seventeenth century, they developed a sudden lust for killing hundreds of Hedgehogs. By the same token the absence of bounty payments in any particular parish does not necessarily imply that no killing was taking place. For example Rats and Moles are not mentioned in nearly as many parishes as one would expect for the simple reason that independent freelance operators, paid directly by landowners, frequently dealt with both species. As mentioned above, some records are clearly hidden in the documents remaining in the parishes, and others are sometimes to be found in the overseers' or constables' accounts and a close examination of old manorial records may well show that in some areas vermin control was also prosecuted through that route.

The clear picture emerging from an examination of the parish records is that the decision as to which vermin, if any, were to be allowed for payment in a particular parish was determined by the vestry committee, and not by the prescriptions of the original statute. Parishes themselves decided what to kill and what payments to make for targeted species. Thus the vestry committee at Piddlehinton (Dorset) recorded on 7 April 1740, 'We do agree no more to pay for stoats' heads, pole cat heads, sparrows heads'. In Great Budworth (Ches) in 1703, the vestry announced that 'churchwardens for the time to come shall not pay any moneys out of the Parish Purse for any Crow Heds, ffox Heds or urchen (*i.e. Hedgehog*) Heds'.

The haphazard way in which vermin control was exercised from parish to parish defines one of its great weaknesses, and thereby the major shortcoming of the Act is revealed. Because there was no co-ordination between parishes there was no consistency between what was being targeted in one parish and what happened in the neighbouring ones. There are innumerable examples of this from almost every county. What could be the real effectiveness if one parish had a major, long-term assault, for example, on Kite or Hedgehog when none of four or five contiguous parishes was concerned with the same species? Wildlife does not operate to parish boundaries! It is small wonder that somewhere like Much Cowarne (Hfds) or Cheddar (Som) could go on killing high numbers of a dozen or so different species year after year when none of the neighbours was paying any attention to them.

There are endless examples of high levels of kills being carried out for years on end with no apparent reduction in numbers over the passage of time. House Sparrows are a classic example of this, as outlined in Chapter 6, but there are graphic examples from other species as well. In Tenterden (Kent), Jays were killed at an average of 193 a year over 9 years and at Rostherne (Ches) a 24-year average of Hedgehogs was 170 per annum. Lezant (C'wall) killed an average of 32 Polecats annually over 86 years and at Dent in Yorkshire (now W'land), Ravens were systematically removed at the rate of some 22 a year—sometimes as many as 58 a year—for more than 20 years. In all these instances, a perfect species vacuum was achieved each year. This resulted in an influx from adjacent parishes which then became the following year's kill: useful as income for the parishioners who benefited from the ongoing bounties, but of negligible effect in reducing populations or safeguarding crops or stock.

A general conclusion can be drawn that the records overall show that during the period of maximum persecution through the parish system, populations of most species remained fairly stable, despite or because of the disparate nature of the parish killing. There are exceptions of course and these are highlighted when the individual species accounts are examined.

A more difficult issue arose for the vestry if protected species such as deer were involved in creating problems. The vestry committee at Branston (Leics) in 1688 took steps to combat a pest problem outside the normal scope of vermin control but one that was doubtless a familiar, if unspoken, problem elsewhere also:

Memorandum that it is covenanted and agreed upon betwixt the inhabitants that have land in the field on the one hand and John Sumner the ygr on the other and the said John Sumner doeth hereby engage himself to use his best endeavour both by day and by night to preserve the peas and other corn to be sown upon longlands this spring from being destroyed by deer as also to take care and have an eye upon getters of peas without leave being first obtained of the owners; and this from the time of the first sowing till they be juned; & the inhabitants engage to pay him for said labour & pains 50 sh, the one half at May Day next, the other half at Michaelmas—2s 6d earnest paid over the above.

Furthermore the bounty system—as with similar ones in more modern times—was clearly open to abuse. Payments were normally made on the express stipulation that victims or their heads were actually taken in that parish. In Devon, the East Budleigh vestry committee met on 24 March 1788 and emphasized that '(all vermin) shall be killed and destroyed within the aforesaid parish' and at Otterton they even insisted that the recipients of bounties declared on oath that the vermin had been taken locally.

In many instances we can surmise that parish boundaries counted for little if the incentive of enticing payments existed in one parish and a ready supply of the target vermin existed next door where no bounties were on offer. Otherwise how could it be that in a tiny parish like Lezant (C'wall) they could go on killing between twenty and seventy 'kites' (aka Kites and Buzzards?) each year over a period of more than thirty years? The records of vestry minutes sometimes confirm this fact. At Youlgreave (Derbys), the inhabitants determined that no more vermin payments should be made because 'by reason ye parish hath been grossly abus'd and impos'd upon in this respect' and the parishioners of Flint in North Wales decided in 1712 that there should be no more vermin payments because of such abuse. Similarly, the vestry committee at St Stephens, Saltash (Devon) recorded at Easter 1780:

. . . 4th Feb paid Sam Frost for a Fox 10s–0d. It's thought the charge for killing this fox was a cheat in this parish for they were hunting and by all likelihood got a dead fox in a bag and protested that they catched the fox in a bramble bush without stering. The churchwardens endeavoured to find out the vilany but not proved it sufficient to punnich—therefore in future let no churchwarden pay for a fox until the following Easter.

At Clifton in Westmorland (now part of Cumbria) the Easter vestry was obviously suspicious of malpractice in the same respect and at its meeting in 1755 it decreed that:

Being Easter Monday it is this day ordered and agreed by the four (i.e. the wardens) and twenty other inhabitants there present that hereafter no money shall be paid for killing foxes or cubs unless the Heads of such be brought immediately after such killing (which must be in this parish) and Delivered to Walter Cowperthwaite in this town which must by him or his son be broke into pieces.

Those not on the list?

This book focuses on those native species that were identified as pests in the Tudor Acts of the sixteenth century. At the same time, we should remind ourselves that at different stages in the recent past, there have been large kills of other species that have been considered as pests for one reason or another; Rabbit and Red Squirrel are obvious examples. Also there are several species which do not appear on the Tudor lists, but which we might have expected to find there, even 400 years ago.

Owls are not specifically mentioned in the 1566 statute, but appear on a number of the parish accounts, most frequently because of a need to remove them from within the church. Usually these were probably Barn Owls, the balance of nuisance in the church buildings presumably outweighing the unquestioned good they did in helping to control rodents. (Owls feature more prominently in nineteenth century gamekeepers' records, perceived as enemies of game rearing, and although it is rare for the species of owl to be identified in the 'keepers vermin records, most species were doubtless victims at different times. 'Fern owls' are often mentioned, particularly in Scotland. This is an old name for Nightjar—not an owl at all—but, confusingly, the name also applied to Short-eared Owl so that there remains uncertainty as to how many of either species were killed on upland estates. The toll was sometimes heavy, as witness the seventy-one included on the Glengarry (Inv'ness) vermin list.)

Bats were frequently targeted in and around churches. Presumably their crimes were more 'nuisance-by-presence' than any serious pestilential acts, other than perhaps leaving pellets and droppings on the pews. At Cranfield (Beds) between 1820 and 1830 more than 450 were killed. Snakes, too, were automatic targets in some parishes. Nominally Adders (there were Viper catchers in London), Grass Snakes, and probably Slow-worms doubtless fell victim. Keith Thomas affirmed that Slow-worms and Grass Snakes were indiscriminately and erroneously persecuted as venomous reptiles. One or two examples of excessive killing are given in Chapter 8 but in other parts of the country too, Adders were taken in numbers. Everton parish (Beds) killed 204 in a short time and at Crosby (Lancs) it was claimed that 72 were taken in 2 hours in 1708 and 112 in June 1711 together with various others at later dates. In at least one area of Sussex, farm children were paid 6*d.* each for Adders in the 1860s, because the creatures were held responsible for occasionally causing the death of sheep by biting them on the muzzle, the subsequent swelling then suffocating them!

For many people it is surprising to find the Red Squirrel regarded as vermin, in any era. However, it has had a chequered history in Britain, having suffered badly from deforestation, severe winter weather, and epidemic diseases, even before the arrival of the larger Grey Squirrel from North America. In times of abundance it was regarded as a serious problem in regenerating woodlands and plantations, in much the same way as the Grey Squirrel is abhorred at present. Shorten recorded that control was initiated in the New Forest in 1880 when up to 2,200 Red Squirrels were killed annually. Even in Cornwall a Squirrel club was formed around 1910 for the same purpose. In Scotland, surprisingly, it was reckoned to be on the verge of extinction in the Highlands in the seventeenth century and the New Statistical Account suggested that they were extinct throughout by 1842. Whether or not this is true, there were numerous re-introductions in the nineteenth century and the animal prospered greatly thereafter. As a result, it rapidly became seen as a forest pest and was shot in enormous numbers. The Highland Squirrel Club was established in 1903 and was responsible for killing some 82,000 Red Squirrels on thirty or forty Highland estates in the first thirty years. The price paid for tails varied from 3*d*. to 4*d*. Before that, the Strathspey estate alone killed 13,875 in the nine years from 1881. In England, some of the Rat and Sparrow clubs also killed Squirrels and there are one or two rare entries in the churchwardens' accounts, e.g. one Red Squirrel at Meppershall (Beds) in 1714. Steele Elliott asked an old Bedfordshire gamekeeper why he was killing Squirrels: what harm did they do? 'It isn't that they do any harm, but what good do they do?'

The Brown Hare is now on the UK Red Data list of endangered species. It was not always so; in fact, on the contrary. For many hundreds of years it has been a valued animal of the chase, and up until the Ground Game Act of 1880, which allowed killing all year round to protect crops, it was an extremely abundant animal. Its numbers declined thereafter, although it was still regarded as a severe agricultural pest in the early half of the last century when huge numbers were shot of necessity, although many found it a distasteful job. The Lockinge estate at Sherborne in the Cotswolds organized Hare shoots which killed up to 600 in a day and there are other records of as many as 400 or more being shot in a day on estates in southern and eastern England in the 1930s.

Small songbirds were not necessarily exempt from the parish assassins. 'Nopps'—normally referring to titmice—occur in the records of various southern parishes, particularly in Devon where Sidbury, East Budleigh, Dartington, Exeter St Thomas, and Modbury all killed them in numbers, as did Dursley (Glos). Gilbert White at Selborne (Hants) reported how they could be caught on suet in mousetraps. At Cotleigh (Devon) the churchwardens even paid for 'thrushes' in 1832–4 with differential payments for old and young. At Foulden (Norfolk) Linnets were specifically mentioned.

In the original context of justifying the destruction of vermin that the Tudor monarchs perceived to be a threat to 'the preservation of grayne', it is interesting to consider what other species might have been included, but are absent from their list. One obvious bird in that category is the Woodpigeon. Since nowadays it is recognized as an agricultural pest, it might seem surprising that it is not on the sixteenth century lists; however, there is good explanation for the Woodpigeon's absence. Until the seventeenth century, it was not a particularly common bird and had remained a widely scattered inhabitant of deciduous woods. It was only as new agricultural cropping systems were developed that Woodpigeons started to find alternative feeding opportunities on open agricultural land. Foremost among these were turnips and clovers, which were introduced as key crops in new systems of rotation, famously promoted and encouraged by 'Turnip' Townsend, among others, from the 1730s onwards. Writing in 1780, Gilbert White recounted the explosion of Woodpigeon numbers following 'the vast increase in turnips'.

In Scotland, as elsewhere, numbers burgeoned in the nineteenth century and reached pest proportions in many areas. E. L. Jones records how there were severe problems in arable areas such as East Lothian and Selkirkshire, where the bird had previously been rare. The problem was so severe that by 1862 the United East Lothian Agricultural Society was paying 1d. a head and accounted for 130,440 Woodpigeons between December 1862 and June 1870. More recently, as Murton pointed out, with the removal of so much of our woodland, especially in the main cereal areas of south and east England, the Woodpigeon has become intimately associated with arable farming, thriving even in areas with only residual tree cover. They can devastate crops of peas and do considerable damage to standing corn in summer. In winter they feed on stubbles, root crops, and clover in pastures and leys. From 1954, a 50% subsidy was given for cartridges and this resulted in large-scale organized shoots in autumn and winter although these were short lived as they clearly had little impact on population levels and merely hastened the normal winter mortality rate. Numbers killed were often large. Gladstone quotes a whole-county shoot on one day, in Devon in 1917, which accounted for over 25,000 birds.

One other point to make about the Woodpigeon is that, far from being seen simply as a pest, country people regarded it as a useful item of food and it has long been exploited for that purpose. The practice of tying the squabs into the nest by their legs as they continued to fatten, thus preventing them from flying before they were ready for the pot, remains a part of rural folklore. Whereas the squire in his manor had his pigeon meat in the purpose-built dovecote, the rural peasant secured his opportunistically from the wider countryside, mainly in the months of late summer and early autumn.

There are one or two other species that we might have expected to find on the Tudor lists. The Great Black-backed Gull is a large and powerful bird with a bad reputation as a lamb killer in some coastal counties. Archaeological records of its existence in South Wales go back as far as 9,000 years and it must have found easy pickings in the lambing flocks in spring and the free-range poultry. Harrison points out that by the beginning of the nineteenth century, it was heavily persecuted as a lamb killer and a possible predator on game stocks. Nonetheless, it does not feature in any parish accounts in earlier centuries which probably indicates that it was not regarded as a problem at the time, or that it was scarcer than it is now. In Scotland, the Great Black-backed Gulls (known as 'blacknebs') were heavily persecuted by some of the nineteenth-century gamekeepers, e.g. on Islay and on the Buccleuch estates.

A similar absentee from the list was the Great Crested Grebe (later shockingly exploited for its plumes). Because of the importance of fish to people in previous centuries, and the fact that species as unlikely as Kingfisher and Dipper were targeted, it is a little surprising that it escaped persecution. However, it was not a very numerous species, especially in the west, and suffered notable set-backs, for example at the time of the Little Ice Age. It did not occur in Scotland at all until 1877. The Grey Heron may also appear a surprising absentee from the Tudor inventory since most other fish-eating birds and mammals were included. After all, it has always been recognized as the archetypal avian piscivore and plunderer of fishponds. The answer of course is that the Heron was esteemed as a quarry for falconry and the laws of the land ensured that they were reserved for those privileged to hunt them. From medieval times the bird was protected for this purpose. The last club entering falcons to Herons in Britain, at Didlington in Norfolk, was still operating up to 1838. In more recent times, with the expansion of artificial fish rearing on fish farms, Herons have been less fortunate, despite modern protective legislation, and have suffered much from illegal control. In the statute of Elizabeth in 1566, the term Iron is occasionally misinterpreted as meaning Heron but this is erroneous as it is the old English name for 'eagle', and, more precisely, a male Sea Eagle. Thus 'Heron' was certainly not included in the original Acts.

6

Birds—individual species accounts

THIS chapter details the levels of persecution that individual species of birds listed in the Tudor Vermin Acts have endured over the centuries, up to recent times, and identifies the effect that this persecution has had on their status. In some cases, Man's determination has successfully eradicated species (Sea Eagle, Goshawk) or has reduced them to the merest fragments of their former numbers and distribution (Red Kite, Chough). In other cases, intensive killing over great expanses of time has had virtually no effect (House Sparrow, Jay). One factor that stands out from examination of the historical record, as represented by the churchwardens' accounts, is the difference between the number of birds on the Tudor lists (20–1) and the amount of control that was exercised against them, compared with that meted out to the smaller number of listed mammals (11). With the exception of a few geographical areas, the heavy emphasis was always on the mammals, as can be seen clearly in Appendix 1.

Cormorant and Shag

These two similar and closely related species have always been subject to a certain amount of confusion. Both are marine birds feeding on fish that they catch by surface diving and pursuing underwater. Both are also predominantly birds of rocky coastlines, breeding on cliffs, in sea caves, or amongst boulders. However, there are important differences in their feeding habits that are of consequence in relation to their persecution by Man. The Shag is exclusively marine, feeding on sand eel species, Sprat, young Herring, gadoids, and other free-swimming species. It therefore feeds in deeper offshore waters than the Cormorant which is typically found in muddy/sandy estuaries, inlets, and shallow inshore waters up to 9–10 metres deep, where it feeds mainly on bottom-dwelling species such as Dab, Flounder, and Plaice together with a lesser number of gadoids, blennies, and other free-swimming species. However, unlike the Shag, it is not exclusively marine and is frequently found on inland rivers and open waters. It is here that it comes into immediate conflict with freshwater fishing interests, both commercial and recreational, and always has done.

Fishermen have long detested Cormorants, both inland and on the coast. As long ago as 1584 Harrison (in Raine 1852) described them as 'being full of gluttony' and 300 years later fisherman in north-east England were still demanding that they should all be shot. Similar sentiments were expressed in many other inland and coastal areas where Cormorants were numerous, for example on the River Eden in Cumberland where they were regularly regarded as a pest.

It is predictable that these species (although the Shag is irrelevant in this respect) attracted attention from the Tudor legislators because the Cormorant was widely encountered inland throughout the year and formerly bred at many inland sites. Gardner-Medwin cites tree-nesting in Norfolk as long ago as 1540, and Lord David Stuart recorded breeding on freshwater lochs in Wigtownshire since before 1663. Wallis was clearly familiar with the bird inland in Northumberland in the eighteenth century. Both species earned their place on the 1566 Act ('for the Preservation of Grayne'!) although it was probably confusion alone that led to the Shag being included; it is only a rare vagrant away from the open sea and can have been of negligible concern to Tudor interests. Despite being listed in the Tudor Act of 1566, only two references to bounties for Cormorants have been found in churchwardens' accounts and it clear that they did not rate highly in the priorities even of coastal parishes. In view of the high levels of persecution of other species in Devon and Cornwall we might have expected some evidence of Cormorant/Shag killing in the old parish records, but none has been found. The only two payments found in any of the churchwardens' accounts are for two Cormorants at Bedlington (N'humb) in 1708 and one at Llanfiangell y Traethau (Mer) in 1699. Perhaps some idea of the difficulty or lack of priority in securing these birds in those distant days can be gleaned from the fact that the Merioneth bird—doubtless from the now famous inland colony at Craig yr Aderyn (Bird Rock)—commanded the princely price of 1/-.

Thus, with the absence of further evidence from past centuries, it is to more recent history that we must turn to seek evidence of intensive killing. Even then the records are sparse although it is clear from various accounts of the Cormorant in early county avifaunas and elsewhere, that the birds were generally persecuted, especially inland. In this respect, the development of effective guns in the eighteenth century undoubtedly had a major part to play in their decline. Bolam, for example, writing in 1912, claimed that it had been more common before the use of firearms became widespread. However, it is not until the twentieth century that we can find firm evidence of the heavy local persecution to which both species have been subjected.

On inland waters Cormorants are regarded by anglers as serious pests on fish stocks. Here, their principal diet consists of Brown Trout, young Salmon, Perch, Roach, and Eels, although they are opportunistic, reflecting availability, and will take what other species they can find. Mills (1965) showed that in Scotland Cormorant predation probably had little detrimental effect on young Salmon stocks, contrary to what had been widely assumed and he even suggested that the Cormorants' consumption of coarse fish may be beneficial to Salmon stocks. He thought that Brown Trout stocks were most at risk and that therefore, for these fish, there may be genuine concern. He concluded that the bounty schemes that were operated at that time by River Boards in England and Wales and Fishery Boards in Scotland served no useful purpose. By the 1960s, several of the Scottish Boards had already ceased payments, particularly when they became aware of widespread abuses of the system.

Because both species are predominantly birds of the western seaboard, it is on these coasts that measures of control are most likely to be undertaken in the name of fishery protection. However, there is also one important breeding site in north-east England; in Northumberland Bolam recorded that persecution was at a high level, in the nineteenth century, through shooting and egg destruction at the colony on the Farne Islands, and seasonal shooting on the nearby River Tweed.

Anne Wilson (in prep.) has carried out detailed research on the history of Cormorants on the Farnes from which the following account is taken. Persecution in the nineteenth and twentieth centuries was regularly at a high level involving eggs, young, and adults. The Tweed Commission paid bounties of 5/- per head for Cormorants up to 1920 and thereafter 3/6 (after which the numbers killed soared!) until the bounties were eventually withdrawn in 1966. At the same time they paid 2/6 for 'small Cormorants' (*viz* Shags). Bolam recorded the annual totals of 'vermin' killed on the Tweed and its tributaries up to 1930 as shown in Table 9.

Killing continued after this and out of a total of 1,938 Cormorants ringed on the Farnes between 1952 and 1971 that were subsequently recovered, 205 had been shot. In many of the years throughout this time there was also repeated destruction of nests and young on the islands.

TABLE 9. Piscivorous birds killed on River Tweed 1911–20 and 1921–30.

	1911–1920	1921–1930
Cormorant	389	746
Shag	0	249
Goosander	0	243

In Wales, where there are many long-established coastal colonies—five have well over 100 pairs—and one famous inland one, the historical record documenting any persecution is almost non-existent. Thus it is to the south-west peninsular counties of Devon and Cornwall that we must turn to assess the toll that has been taken on either species in the twentieth century.

Fairly comprehensive minutes exist of the committees of the individual River Boards in south Devon. Eight of these Boards were set up by Act of Parliament in 1923. From the earliest years of that century, there was constant pressure from inshore fishermen, netsmen, riparian owners, and bodies such as the Salmon and Trout Association to reduce the populations not only of Cormorants and Shags but also Grey Heron and Black-headed Gull. In 1929, aspersions were even cast at Mute Swans that were allegedly 'becoming too numerous' according to bailiffs on the rivers Avon and Erme. Representations were made to the Ministry Inspector at Plymouth to ascertain whether or not they could legally be controlled. Lack of further mention seems to suggest the nature of the reply.

Records of the Boards' decisions and policies with regard to Cormorants and Shags, together with some account of numbers killed, exist for the rivers Avon, Erme, Axe, and Exe from the 1920s onwards. Payments varied between 1/- and 2/6 per head but were usually 2/- unless there were special short-term campaigns such as the 'Cormorant weeks' on the Axe each year in the 1930s when higher bounties were payable. In 1933, the level was raised to 5/- for those killed on the river and 2/6 for those taken seaward—an oddly pointless differential since the same individuals were likely to be involved in either place. In the same year, local fishermen commended the Axe Fishery Board in writing, for its efforts of control. Unfortunately the minutes of these Boards do not contain many figures for the numbers of Cormorants killed each year. Sparse records for the Avon/Erme and the Axe in the 1920s only indicate c.10 birds per year but the record is incomplete and on the Exe no figures at all are mentioned although in 1949 the sum of £21 was paid out. Different rates were paid on that river, 1/6 for Cormorants from Exmouth seawards and 2/6 for birds claimed upstream of Exmouth.

It is on the River Dart that the longest and most detailed sequence of data exists, from 1903 to 1942 (Table 10 below). The contrast between this river and the others, in addition to the completeness of the figures, is that it was not until 1942 that the word Cormorant is mentioned anywhere in the Board's minutes. On the Dart it was all about Shags. The implication is that the pressure here was principally from the local coastal fishermen and the considerable numbers of birds killed were taken in the estuary, at nearby roosts, at nest sites, and in the inshore waters. Of course, there was not necessarily any requirement to distinguish between the two species for the sake of bounties, and undoubtedly both were taken and simply referred to in the minutes by the name of the predominant one. Tony Soper, who lived on the estuary for several years, confirms his belief that the majority were undoubtedly Shags, although any reference to upstream birds would clearly have involved Cormorants. Here, with an echo of earlier times, one of the bailiffs, J. H. Collings, made a handsome income each year, since he was responsible for most of the birds shot.

TABLE 10. Numbers of Cormorants/Shags for which bounty payments were made on the River Dart 1903–32. Figures are missing for 1908–10 and 1920. Some payments continued up to the 1940s (e.g. 36 'Cormorants' in 1942) but the record for those years is fragmentary.

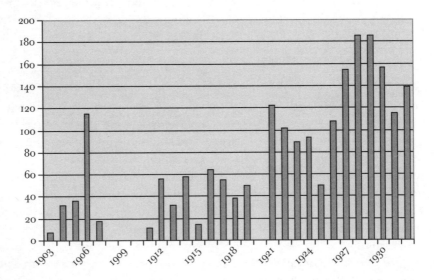

In Cornwall there was also heavy twentieth-century predation of Cormorants and Shags. In this respect, Lambert researched the papers of the Cornish Sea Fisheries Committee and published his findings in *British Birds* in 2003;

the following account is a synopsis of his results. In 1910, the Sea Fisheries Committee, spurred on by local fishermen from Newlyn and elsewhere, decided to focus its control of piscivorous birds on Cormorants and Shags, ignoring a long-held concern that was expressed about the effect on inshore fisheries of large numbers of gulls. The Committee obtained an exclusion order from the Protection of Birds Acts from the County Council and offered 1/- a head for either species taken outside the nesting season. Bounties were readily taken up, and between 1911 and 1915, 4,200 heads were submitted. Between 1925 and 1929, a further 6,739 birds were killed (bounties had been suspended during the First World War and not reinstated until 1925). As Lambert points out these figures are certainly minima, as an unknown number of birds were doubtless shot but not recovered to claim bounty.

Although these are high numbers, it is only a part of the picture in Cornwall because on Scilly the Tresco estate under Major Dorrien-Smith killed Cormorants with enthusiasm from 1920. Ignoring any mainland condition that banned control during the nesting season, Dorrien-Smith had concentrated on nest and egg destruction, shooting birds on the nest and continuing control throughout the year. By 1926, he claimed to have killed some 6,000 birds—around 1,000 per year—the vast proportion of which were undoubtedly Shags (there are relatively few Cormorants on Scilly). The perceived effects of all this control on juvenile fish stocks around the mainland coast or Scilly is not recorded, although the fishermen expressed themselves satisfied and claimed improved results. As late as 1946 the subject arose one last time on Scilly when the Ministry of Agriculture and Fisheries eventually agreed a 'one-off' grant of £15 for control of Shags, but no figures remain to tell us what the take up or results may have been.

Although both species are now protected under the Wildlife and Countryside Act 1981 licences have been given in past years to control the Cormorant 'to prevent serious damage'. However, in 2004 the Department of Environment, Food and Rural Affairs in England removed the requirement to prove serious damage: the effect of this change is evident in Table 11.

It is well known that in China captive birds of the *sinensis* race of the Cormorant are used to catch fish for their owners. What is not widely recognized about Man's relationship with the Cormorant in Britain is that the bird's supreme fishing abilities were at one time put to similar use here. Charles I had his own Master of Cormorants and Willughby, writing in the 1670s, relates how 'they were hoodwinked in the manner of falcons, till they were let off to fish and a leather thong was tied round the lower part of their necks to prevent them swallowing the fish'. Morris claimed that he had watched tame Cormorants operating in this way in the Bridlington area.

TABLE 11. Licences issued for killing of Cormorants 1999–2005. Note the increase in England following the Government's revision of licence requirements in 2004.

Season	Number of licences granted	Number of birds licensed to be shot	Numbers shot
England			
2001–2	99	570	189
2002–3	120	603	273
2003–4	146	828	499
2004–5	331	1996	1258
2005–6	355	2302	?
Wales			
2001–2	1	?	?
2002–3	0	0	0
2003–4	2	9	9
2004–5	9	28	21
Scotland			
1999–2005	110	?	650

Osprey

Few terrestrial birds have a wider global distribution than the Osprey. In many European countries however, it has been dramatically reduced or exterminated over the past two centuries. Britain is no exception to that, for the bird, formerly widespread, was apparently exterminated early in the last century. Its last stronghold was in the vastness of the Scottish Highlands and the plundering it suffered there, leading to its inevitable demise, is well documented. It is one of the most disgraceful episodes in the extermination of our native species. Farther south, the Osprey provides another example of a species that disappeared with little evidence left for us to trace its going. There are enough records from the sixteenth and seventeenth centuries to illustrate the fact that it was a well distributed bird throughout England. Roy Dennis (*in litt*), who has traced existing records, quotes Peele, Harrison, and Caius all of whom testified to its abundance in sixteenth century England. Caius specifically mentioned coastal areas and Harrison wrote of it breeding in parks and woods 'whereby the keepers of the same do reap in breeding time no small commodity, for so soon as the young are hatched they tie them to the butt ends of sundry trees, where the old ones finding them do never cease to bring fish unto them, which the keepers take and eat from them'. Man proving himself to be as resourceful as ever. The fate of the hungry young Ospreys is not on record. We can only guess what happened when their usefulness was exhausted! It is likely that the last breeding pair of Ospreys in southern England was at Monksilver in Somerset in 1847. Further north Macpherson claimed that they ceased to breed in Westmorland as early as the latter years of the previous century. There are various scattered records from other English counties, predominantly coastal ones, up to the middle of the nineteenth century. Wales provides no written record of breeding—and a degree of confusion with the fish-eating Sea Eagle—although Ospreys patently did breed there. To add credence to the Welsh claim, the coat of arms of the modern City and County of Swansea has on its crest an Osprey, the origins of which apparently go back as far as 1316. Erroneously this particular bird is clutching a fish in its beak and not its foot!

The reasons why the Osprey was so ruthlessly persecuted in southern Britain are not difficult to surmise. As with any large bird of prey, it was viewed with suspicion, but since it lived exclusively on a diet of fish it was doubly vulnerable. In Roman Catholic Britain of the Middle Ages and in the pre-Reformation era, Friday fish was obligatory in place of meat and the enormous number of fish ponds which were constructed and maintained for the purpose of supplying that need attest to their great importance. The Ospreys which have returned to breed in Britain in recent years have demonstrated the readiness with which they will take advantage of convenient sources of food in fish farms, etc. There can be no doubt that in former times they took similar advantage of the medieval fish ponds and in doing so effectively sealed their fate. 'Ospreys fished every day, the monks only once a week'.

It cannot be proved, but it seems extremely likely, as Dennis has suggested, that Ospreys had been severely reduced, at least from inland waters, before the time of the Tudor Acts. They are clearly listed in those Acts although there is no mention of them in any of the 1,579 parish records that I examined. With a princely price of four pence on their heads in the sixteenth century they would surely have appeared here and there had they been more numerous than individuals passing through on seasonal migration. Their inclusion on the Tudor lists may thus have been precautionary and more in hope than expectation, reflecting the knowledge of their habits and their former status. The only possible references that I found occasionally in the parish records was to 'Bald Buzzard' which was a colloquial name used for Osprey, Marsh Harrier, and also at times, Red Kite and even Buzzard. Because of the confusion I have disregarded those few records. (It is worth noting that the French name for the Osprey is '*balbuzard*' or '*balbuzard pecheur*'). Morton, in his *Natural History of Northamptonshire* in 1712, is one writer who referred specifically to the Osprey by the name Bald Buzzard saying that it was uncommon then, but was some-times taken in traps in the wildfowl decoys 'where it is very mischievous'. Vesey-Fitzgerald emphasized how it was disliked by gamekeepers and hated by water bailiffs in the nineteenth century and was therefore eliminated at every opportunity. Glengarry was only one Highland estate amongst many where, as an example of the intensity of persecution, eigtheen were shot on that estate in only four years, 1837–40. It was a relatively easy bird to take, both at the nest and because of its persistent use of the same perch—a fact remarked on by Mascall in Hampshire as long ago as 1570 when he recommended that one should 'watch where he takes his fish and wait there with your gun'.

If the Osprey's elimination in England was achieved with only fragmentary remaining evidence of its demise, the same is certainly not true in Scotland. The bird may well have almost disappeared from the lowland counties and the Central Lowlands around the time of its extinction in England (mid nineteenth century). At the same time it must have gone even from the lower-lying, richer farmland areas in counties such as Morayshire. In the latter county, the presence of the monastery and its extensive fishponds at Elgin in medieval times may have had relevance. In areas in southern Scotland, Ospreys were also exterminated before the written records began, although the last few probably held on until *c.*1860. Interestingly, the Buccleuch vermin records from seven estates there in the early half of the century, that were extensive in the range of species killed, contain no Ospreys, neither do the Lochnaw records at Stranraer between 1853 and 1868. Gray and Anderson and Robert Service all believed that they had been eliminated from their last sites in the south-west by 1860. In the Highlands, the Osprey maintained a presence well into the nineteenth century, despite intense persecution from the late eighteenth century onwards. In the earlier years, after the arrival of the great sheep flocks, Ospreys were not specific-ally harassed in the Highlands in the same way as eagles, because they were no threat to the sheep. Baxter and Rintoul listed a catalogue of records in northern Scotland that confirmed its former distribution, at least in the first half of the eighteenth century. Sir William Jardine, for example, is quoted as claiming that there was a pair or two on most Highland lochs in the 1830s. After an interval of forty years or so, Gray commented that it was, by then, the rarest of birds in Scotland except for the Red Kite and Goshawk. Although the written record of the Osprey's persecution through the middle years of the nineteenth century is negligible, the severity of persecution and the devastation of its numbers across that period is illustrated by the changing nature of the written accounts. Instead of comments on widespread distribution, etc. in the second half of the century ornithological notes refer more and more just to individual occurrences. Harvie-Brown recorded several sites in Inverness-shire, Lewis Dunbar claimed to have found 'two old nests by the River Nethy in 1850', 'Ospreys bred at Abernethy until recently' according to the Rev. Forsyth, and so on. Harvie-Brown believed that Ospreys were extinct in the far north-west as early as 1860.

A sickening cynicism accompanied much of the war that was waged by game-keepers and bailiffs and others. As the birds became rarer, the remaining pairs were annual targets for egg collectors and 'sportsmen' to display as trophies or simply to satisfy a lust for killing. The famous eyrie on the chimney of a ruin on Inch Galbraith in Loch Lomond was robbed almost annually and the pair there was eventually destroyed by the infamous John Colquhoun. He shot the female, then put a trap in the nest and caught the male within three hours. Charles St John's hypocrisy was almost beyond belief. In his Tour of Sutherland he mused as to 'why the poor Osprey should be persecuted I know not as it is quite harmless'! Despite such words his own lust for killing knew no bounds. Three miles from Scourie in Sutherland he shot a female off her nest and took the two eggs. He then lamented the evident distress of the male, saying that he was remorseful that he had shot its mate. Despite this he was later told that the male had found another mate and so returned the next year and robbed the nest again. At another Sutherland site he failed to shoot the adults but took the young and then shot the male at a further nest, missed the female, but took the three eggs. The Sutherland birds were virtually eliminated at the hands of St John and his henchman William Dunbar, the final eggs and adult skins probably being destined for patrons from the south.

Such examples as these exemplify the manner in which the Osprey was driven to extinction. No species could withstand the relentless level of persecution to which it was subjected by so many sportsmen, egg collectors, bailiffs, and game-keepers. A mere handful of pairs survived tentatively in Perthshire, Cromarty, and Inverness-shire into the first few years of the twentieth century. Despite the efforts of the Grant lairds, the famous nest on the old ruined castle in the Loch an Eilein in Rothiemurchus was robbed of eggs, year after year until 1899, by a succession of collectors, including the same William Dunbar who swam to the site at night on at least one occasion. One bird returned annually until 1902 when that too disappeared, fate unknown. A pair nested at Loch Arkaig up to 1908, but despite protection by Cameron of Locheil it had no long-term success. At Loch Loyne on Glengarry estate a pair was probably nesting until 1913 but after that only one pair survived in west Inverness until the final nesting in 1916 at Loch Loyne. After that date the breeding Osprey had seemingly finally vanished from Britain. Notwithstanding this, Ospreys continued to be recorded as passage migrants in Scotland, England, and Wales in most years. However it seems that they may not all have been passage migrants. A recent re-examination of data by Dennis from the early part of the twentieth century, strongly suggests that there was breeding taking place in Invernessshire in the 1930s. This was well before the celebrated discovery of nesting at Loch Garten in 1954; in fact Dennis has now shown that breeding was taking place there at least as early as 1947. Despite these revelations, the Osprey became another species, formerly common and numerous, that was effectively wiped off the map of Britain by a ruthless campaign to eliminate it. William Dunbar, in a letter to the egg collector John Woolley wrote, 'I am afraid that Mr St John, yourself and your humble servant have finally done for the Ospreys'.

Sea Eagle—Erne

This huge eagle, the largest bird of prey in Britain, was at one time a relatively numerous and widespread native species until it was completely exterminated by Man, the last native pair having been eliminated in Scotland by 1916. This magnificent bird had been subject to long-term persecution of varying intensity stretching back at least 500 years and probably for much of that millennium. Dennis (pers com) has postulated that, like the Osprey, its early extinction from lowland Britain was due to persecution in the Middle Ages associated with its indisputable predation on fish ponds. Although its stronghold has always been regarded as the rugged western seaboard, it is a bird that is equally at home along low coastlines and inland where wetlands provide fish and other aquatic prey. Accordingly, it was very widely distributed in Britain and bred at suitable sites both inland and coastally, from its northern stronghold in the Shetlands south to the chalk cliffs of the southern coast of England. Its extensive distribution is confirmed by archaeological evidence and early Saxon literature sources. Love, in his monograph on the species, suggests that the decline in the Sea Eagle's fortunes began first with the gradual draining of English wetlands such as the Somerset Levels and the Fens, most notably in the seventeenth century. As direct persecution increased, the birds were lost first of all from their remaining inland sites, although the sparse records that exist for southern Britain suggest that the process was slow, at least until the destruction of the final pairs in the last decade or so of the nineteenth century. Yarrell recounts them nesting on Culver cliff on the Isle of Wight until then, and individual pairs appeared to hang on on Lundy and at a site near Plymouth on the south coast of Devon until around the same time.

Apart from these one or two records and the Lakeland story outlined below, the pattern of disappearance in England and Wales can only be surmised. Plot recorded the killing of an eagle in Staffordshire prior to 1686 which may well have been a Sea Eagle. In 1514, well before the inception of the Tudor Acts, there is an entry in the Worfield (Salop) churchwardens' accounts 'to William Hichecox for an yron iij' (*viz* 3*d*.). In Wales there are no written records of proof that this eagle bred, although it clearly did so. To confirm this it is now known, through the existence of a pair of mounted Sea Eagles held on a Gower estate, that this species was still breeding in Cwm Madoc, Margam (Glam) in 1822. Here the male was shot at the tree nest, but the female survived, only to meet the same fate the following year (other individual birds were still recorded in the vicinity up to 1848). The only other Welsh record was mentioned by Hale (in Love 1983 and pers com) who was told, by a well-known egg collector, of men climbing to a nest near Nefyn on Lleyn around 1880. Although the evidence is circumstantial and the date a very late one, it was in all probability Sea Eagles.

The Lake District is the only area of England where a written record of the persecution of the Erne exists, which is reproduced below. This eagle was specifically included in the 1566 Act but apart from the evidence from the Lake District, there is no record of bounties being paid elsewhere. Although the whereabouts of the original document is not known, a transcript of the Crosthwaite (Cumb) churchwardens' accounts is still to be found in the church and provides a striking picture of the eighteenth-century persecution of breeding Sea Eagles in Borrowdale. The birds were persecuted time after time at traditional Sea Eagle nest sites through the eighteenth century, with adults repeatedly killed and eggs and young taken. It is impressive that, as fast as an adult bird was killed, the survivor appears to have had no difficulty in recruiting a new mate, presumably from western Scotland or Ireland.

1713 John Jackson an old eagle 1/-
      Edward Birket a young eagle 6d
1719 Miles Wilson an old eagle 1/-
      John Jackson of Amboth an old eagle 1/-*

1731   Thomas Raven 2 young eagles 1/-
        Thomas Birket a young eagle 6d
1736   John Youdall a young eagle 6d and an old fox 3/4
1741   John Braithwaite a young eagle 6d
1743   John Harris an old eagle 1/-
1744   John Birket an old eagle 1/-
1745   Joseph Harris an old eagle 1/-
1747   Hugh Workman a young eagle 1/-
1749   James Bowes' man an old eagle 1/-
1750   James Bowes 2 young eagles 1/-
1752   William Wane an old eagle 2/-
        Isaac Gateskel 2 young eagles 2/-
1755   Isaac Gateskel a young eagle 6d
1756   anon 2 young eagles 1/-
1757   anon 1 eagle 1/-
1759   for eagles 4/-
1760   an eagle 1/-
1762   2 eagles 1/-
1763   an eagle 1/-
1765   'sundry eagles *et al* 4/-
1774   at least 1 eagle
1776   at least 1 eagle
1778   at least 1 eagle

The respective payments made for Fox and eagle in 1736 are interesting but by no means unique. Why the high payment in 1752 was made is not clear.
* Amboth is a wild area of peat bog between Borrowdale and Thirlmere.
The young eaglets were regularly sold to ready buyers for 'high prices' according to MacPherson.

A 'long strong rope' was kept in Borrowdale specifically for use at eagle sites and was also available for loan to neighbouring parishes—Buttermere, Eskdale, Langdale et al. Unfortunately no payments of eagle bounties have been found in the records of these neighbouring sites. Known Sea Eagle sites were on Buck Crag in Martindale on the south shore of Ullswater (the village of the same name was drowned when Haweswater reservoir was created in 1936), Wallow Crag, Haweswater, Eagle Crag in Langstrath, and Birkness Combe in Buttermere. John Aubrey, writing to John Ray in 1692, recounted that the Erne bred annually on Wallow Crag. The birds' presence there was reconfirmed more than a century later when a farmer was lowered to the site to take the single eaglet and counted the remains of thirty-five fish around the nest. In the parish of Barton, just to the east of Crossthwaite, William Lancaster was paid a shilling for taking an eagle in 1736, and another eagle was paid for there in 1750. A little further east, in Bampton parish, a bounty of 1/- was paid for an eagle as late as

1796 although there is no evidence as to which species was involved, nor indeed as to whether it was a breeding bird. Neither of these records appears in previous literature and both were found in the relevant parish archives.

Lakeland was the last refuge of the Sea Eagle in southern Britain but its great stronghold was always Scotland. Here it was plentiful up to the eighteenth century both among the numerous inland waters and, particularly, on the rugged western coasts and offshore islands, including Orkney and Shetland. It must also have been extremely numerous in such areas, reflecting the numbers that can be seen to this day on the similar wild coasts of northern Norway.

Its decline and eventual extirpation by the time of the First World War, was entirely at the hand of Man. It shares, together with the Osprey, the distinction of being the only species of bird or mammal on the original Tudor Vermin Lists—decimated though many of the others have been—to be totally eliminated in Britain. The Goshawk, which was also exterminated, was not specifically named in the Tudor Act. Love suggests that persecution of Sea Eagles had taken place for many centuries, but at a fairly low intensity, until the arrival of sheep flocks in the Highlands and later the development of game preservation and the employment of gamekeepers.

Persecution in Scotland was encouraged by bounty payments for the Erne going back at least to the early seventeenth century. A local Act was introduced in Orkney in 1625 that, regardless of who killed an Erne, promised payment of 8*d*. for every cottage in the parish, with the exception of those without sheep, and 20/- for anyone who destroyed an eagle's nest. In 1774, Pennant recorded that 'these birds are proscribed, half a crown being given for an eagle, a shilling for a hawk or a Hooded Crow'. The Old Statistical Account records that in Orkney the rate had been settled at 5/- a head by the 1790s, later in 1806 reduced to 3/6, and then abandoned in 1835. At one time, the small island of Hoy alone supported three pairs of the birds. The Seaforth estates offered bounties and paid a premium of 7/6 to John MacLeod for three eagles killed in the Forest of Lewis in 1791 and 2/6 to another islander for two young eaglets the same year. At the same time bounties were also being paid at Glenorchy and Inishail (parts of the Breadalbane estate in Argyll). Skye was always a great stronghold 'with eyries on most headlands'. During the 1860s, Gray reported that a 'keeper there had shot 57 on one estate and another correspondent informed him of 62 others that had been killed on the island'. On Rum five were killed in one day in 1825 and the gamekeeper there shot and trapped another eight in 1866. It was not surprising that by 1892 it was regarded as very rare there.

Throughout Scotland, the White-tailed Eagle was slaughtered remorselessly through the nineteenth century as documented and lamented by many writers.

Charles St John maintained that it was still more numerous than the Golden
Eagle by 1849 and ten years earlier Macgillivray observed that it was still fairly
numerous in the Western Islands. Ritchie, writing in 1920, deplored the carnage
and suspected that if it had not already been extirpated (which in fact it had) it
would be gone shortly.

Love plotted the increasingly rapid decline of numbers from the 1840s to the
removal of the last mainland nest in 1911 and the last island one on Skye in
1916. He has given a full account of the demise of the species throughout
Scotland, the detail of which need not be repeated here. In summary, however,
the birds had probably gone from south-west Scotland by the 1840s (see Gray)
although in other parts of southern Scotland occasional pairs lingered on at
inland sites until the mid 1860s. Even on remote island sites, such as the mighty
cliff of Conachair on St Kilda, and on Fair Isle, the cragsmen had eliminated
isolated pairs by 1830. MacGillivray, in 1836, lamented that 'they daily become
more limited but are still pretty numerous on the islands'. By the 1860s, Love
showed that even some of the other remote sites were being extinguished—
Glencoe, Hebridean sites on Barra and the Uists, and Unst in Shetland. Elsewhere on Shetland, however, in 1874 Saxby believed there had been 'little
diminution in numbers over the past 16–18 years'. The following two decades
saw more extinctions at sites as widely distributed as Orkney, Rannoch, the
Small Isles, Mull, and Harris. However, by the end of the century, remnant pairs
were only found at two or three Shetland sites together with isolated pairs on
Rum, Shiants, and the Outer Hebrides. Beyond this, and the final recorded
nesting on Skye in 1916, the Sea Eagle was extinct in Britain.

The Sea Eagle has a catholic diet comprising fish, mammals, sea birds, and
carrion. Its conflict with Man's interests can be confined to the first two items.
Presumably its coastal fishing habits have never been of concern. However,
on inland waters where it took Pike and other available species, it fell into the
same category as Osprey, Cormorant, Dipper, and Kingfisher (q.v.). It was perceived, or assumed, to compete with Man's own interest in wild fish stocks or
stew ponds. It was therefore deemed undesirable and deserving of removal
whenever possible. Another charge against it, and certainly the one that drove
the determined onslaught against it in the nineteenth century, was the taking of
lambs. In the Lake District James Clarke, a legendary local naturalist, writing
in 1787 alluded to the presence of seven lamb carcasses at the Wallow Crag
nest when it was robbed. The poet Thomas Gray, visiting the Lakes in 1769,
wrote in his journal that 'all the dale (Borrowdale) are up in arms . . . for they
lose abundance of lambs yearly . . .'. MacPherson writing with prescient hind-
sight a hundred years after the last pair had nested there, considered the birds 'so
destructive to the lambs that their extermination became absolutely necessary'.
Charles Dixon (1888) lamented that 'persecution has driven it from the

precipitous coasts and freshwater lakes of England but in the remote Highlands it still survives and a pair may generally be met with on most of the inland lochs or on the bold headlands of this rockbound land'.

The die had been cast, however, by the time of Dixon's lamentations and those of Woolley, for the species' fate was already sealed. As the sheep flock in the Highlands and Islands increased in the eighteenth century, powerful antipathy towards the Sea Eagle (and the Golden Eagle) as lamb killers was widespread and became the driving force in attempts to extirpate them. Despite the execrations against the Sea Eagle for this reason, it seems to be a case of 'giving a bird a bad name and it sticks', whether or not it is justified. All the evidence (and again Love has analysed all the information available to him) demonstrates that it is only a small number of individuals or pairs that regularly predate lambs. Even then, many of those taken can be shown to have been dead already. Sea Eagles are considerable carrion feeders, regularly scavenging on shorelines and inland, so, in reality, their conflict with Man is minimal. In respect of their feeding habits they were particularly vulnerable to poisoned baits.

The levels of killing at the height in the second half of the nineteenth century were sometimes horrifying and are a testimony to the number of Sea Eagles that had populated Scotland. In Caithness, where a landowner offered 10/- for adults, 5/- for young, and 2/6 for eggs, 295 eagles (both species) plus 60 eggs and young were killed in only 7 years between 1820 and 1826. On another estate in Sutherland a year or two later, where many pairs nested around the numerous lochs, a further 171 plus 53 young were killed in 3 years. At Glengarry, 1837–40, 27 were taken. The 60 'eagles' killed by one keeper on Skye were almost all Sea Eagles. On Lewis, between 1871 and 1885, 32 eagles were killed and although the species were not confirmed it is probable that the majority were Sea Eagles. Harvie-Brown's research showed a scatter of individual eagle kills in the last years of the century from Beauly in the east to Arisaig, Rum, and Inverewe in the west, but by this time the numbers available for killing were evidently few and far between. The Sea Eagle has been a remarkably easy bird to kill and as such has hastened its own demise. It is relatively tame, nests in obvious places, defends its nest against intruders (not disappearing into the distance as the Golden Eagle does), and comes readily to carrion. It was even taken by hand in some places by an operator in a hidden dugout alongside bait!

As the bird became rarer, the final insult was the ruthless attention paid to the birds by unscrupulous egg collectors. From the mid nineteenth century until the final extinction, nests were regularly robbed. Again Love analysed all the data he could find relating to stolen clutches and identified fifty-one that had been taken between 1830 and 1901 when the notorious egg collector Jourdain took the last clutch in Sutherland. The majestic Erne, the White-tailed Sea Eagle, had finally been eliminated.

Golden Eagle

The Golden Eagle does not appear among the many species on the Tudor vermin lists that form the bases of these accounts. The reason for this absence is presumably because it had long been lost from lowland Britain and thus did not even justify consideration. It is, of course, a native bird and is included here simply because, particularly in Scotland, the nineteenth-century destruction of both eagle species is inextricably interwoven. On many of the Scottish records of vermin kills no distinction is made between the two species.

Although, understandably, we regard the Golden Eagle in Britain as a bird of mountain areas, it was not always the case, for it is equally at home in lowlands when left undisturbed. There is certainly no reason to believe that it did not occur throughout southern Britain in the distant past. There is even a report of a nest in East Sussex as late as 1750, not dismissed by reputable ornithologists at the time, but looked at askance nowadays. More traditionally, it is regarded as having occurred north of a line between Derbyshire and North Wales. John Ray found an eyrie in the Derwent valley in Derbyshire in 1668 and John Leland recorded it nesting on the cliffs below Dinas Bran near Llangollen (Denb) in 1538. Elsewhere in North Wales its last great stronghold was always Snowdonia, where Ray and Willughby both recorded it nesting in 1656 and 1662 respectively. Forrest maintained that it was still to be found in the mountains of Snowdonia c.1800. Macpherson believed there was abundant evidence of breeding in central and western Lakeland in the seventeenth century and that it persisted through the next century with the last birds being eliminated by 1803.

In Scotland, where the Golden Eagle was very widely distributed up to the eighteenth century, its range overlapped with that of the Sea Eagle, certainly at inland sites. Although James II had urged the killing of eagles as early as 1457, the real pressure began with the expansion of the sheep flocks from the second half of the eighteenth century. The Golden Eagle, together with the larger Sea Eagle, was implicated as a lamb thief in the minds of shepherds, despite the fact that it has never been as culpable as the larger bird in the taking of lambs.

The two species have distinctly different feeding regimens. Colquhoun described both species nesting in proximity at Loch Baa on Rannoch Moor and he watched the Golden Eagle typically depart to hunt the high hills for hare and grouse, while the other kept to the low ground and watersides. However, no such simplistic distinctions prevented indiscriminate attrition.

Baxter and Rintoul have shown clearly how the numbers of Golden Eagles were seriously reduced in Scotland between the dates of the Old and New Statistical accounts, although there were still pairs in the Borders as well as in their Highland and Island strongholds further north. Much of the persecution in the earlier decades was at the hands of shepherds with their recently arrived sheep flocks and many traditional eyries were already deserted. By 1850, the last pairs had gone from the south-west counties and from most of Ayrshire a few years later. On the Hebridean islands the story was the same. On Jura, where seven pairs originally bred regularly, fifty-plus were killed in six years and it was extinct by 1887. According to Graham, shepherds had greatly reduced its number on Iona and Mull by 1890 and while it still held its own on the Outer Hebrides, Macgillivray claimed that 'vast numbers' had been destroyed by shepherds up to 1830. On the larger islands of Lewis and the Uists, it was never completely eliminated. Writing of the northern counties of the mainland in 1888, Colquhoun said that shepherds did not bother particularly with the old birds but regularly harvested eggs and young which fetched good prices and a ready market from collectors from England. The Golden Eagle was hated more by the grouse moor owners than by those with deer forests. Colquhoun's story also illustrates the fact that in that century—and extending into the next—there was a great demand for the eggs (at least twenty-five clutches were taken in 1980–4 alone) and mounted specimens of this bird, and that the rarer it became, the greater the desire to collect eggs and skins.

As mentioned earlier, the historical evidence for numbers of eagles on Scottish vermin lists frequently fails to differentiate between the two species so that we have little accurate knowledge of the numbers that were destroyed in different areas over time. The Glengarry records from 1837–40 are one exception where 15 Golden Eagles are specifically listed together with 27 Sea Eagles. In addition, we do not know what the population of Golden Eagles was in times past. A survey organized by the Nature Conservancy Council and RSPB in 1982–3 showed that there were then 424 pairs with another 87 single birds holding territory. A repeat survey in 2003 produced 435 pairs.

It is indisputable that the persecution of Golden Eagles over recent centuries in Scotland has been relentless and that this has continued since the extinction of the Sea Eagle in 1916. Persecution is still most severe on grouse moors in the east of Scotland where it is at risk of jeopardising the viability of local populations, but is less so on deer forests where they are little molested and breed more successfully. Nonetheless it is surprising that the Golden Eagle in Britain did not eventually follow the same route to extinction as the Sea Eagle. Persecution still takes place and an indication of the current level of illegal killing is shown in Chapter 10.

Red Kite

> Ah could I see a spinney nigh,
> A paddock riding in the sky
> Above the oaks, in easy sail
> On stilly wings and forked tail
>
> John Clare (1793–1864)

We gain the first accurate picture of the Red Kite's historical status in Britain during the Middle Ages. It is clear that at this time the Red Kite was an extremely numerous species over much of the country, in both towns and rural areas. In urban areas it achieved a status, protected by Royal Decree, together with the Raven, as an indispensable scavenger in the foul and insanitary filth of unpaved streets and choked watercourses— the breeding ground of plagues such as the Black Death that first struck Britain in 1348. In London, clouds of Kites filled the skies as witnessed by visitors such as Baron von Rozmital in 1465, who also pointed out that it was then a capital offence to kill either Kite or Raven. It is a safe assumption that it was as numerous in the other major towns—Norwich, York, Bristol, etc. A century later Shakespeare alluded to London as 'the city of Crows and Kites' and Carolus Clusius, a French botanist, believed it to be as numerous there as its counterpart, the Black Kite, was (and still is) in the streets and waterways of cities such as Cairo—prodigious numbers indeed. There is no doubt that the Middle Ages represented the zenith of the Kite's fortunes in Britain. At this time it was almost certainly the most numerous bird of prey throughout the land.

It is interesting that in the fifteenth century when protection was being afforded to the species in England, at least in the major towns, in Scotland it was the opposite. The statute of James II in 1457 urged that Kites should be destroyed whenever possible. Sadly, no record exists as to whether or not the Act had any effect or was even implemented with any seriousness. The castigation of the Red Kite was undoubtedly a reflection of the fact that in rural areas the bird was never popular, since it was regarded, justifiably, as a thief of farmyard poultry and young rabbits (highly valued as human food resources in managed warrens). Willughby wrote of the Kite in 1678 'They are very noisom to tame birds, especially Chicken, Ducklings and Goslings for which cause our good house-wives are very angry with them and of all birds, hate and curse them most'.

> And other losses to the dames recite,
> Of chick and duck and gosling gone astray,
> All falling prey to the swooping kite.
>
> (Clare: Village Minstrel)

> Voracious, bold, to rapine prone,
> Who knew no int'rest but their own;
> Who, hov'ring o'er the farmer's yard,
> Nor pigeon, chick, nor duckling spar'd.
>
> (Moore: Eagle and Birds)

The Kite was certainly a detested bird throughout rural Britain and the church-wardens' accounts testify to the numbers that were killed in the seventeenth and eighteenth centuries in parts of England. In the somewhat fragmentary church records that survive in Wales, there is little evidence of payments for Kites. The only records that have come to light are several in Monmouthshire, in the second half of the eighteenth century.

Thus, it is beyond dispute that, historically, the Red Kite was distributed throughout most of Great Britain and was very numerous. It is equally clear that the Kite was universally disliked by rural smallholders and henwives, as we have seen above. With these two thoughts in mind the remarkably localized pattern of persecution that occurred in England is perplexing, certainly as represented by bounty payments through the churchwardens from the sixteenth to early nine-teenth centuries. The map in Figure 14 shows that there were twenty-eight English counties in which I did not find one record of payment for a Kite in that long period. However, it must be remembered that the historical records for that period no longer exist in the majority of parishes; nonetheless it would be a remarkable coincidence if the ones that I have examined in those counties just happen to exclude all those which had records of Red Kite bounties. Clare in Northamptonshire, Robert Bloomfield in Suffolk—'where the kite brooding unmolested flies'—and Charles Kingsley writing of 'kite beyond kite as far as the eye could see' over Whittlesey Mere in Huntingdonshire all testify to the birds' ubiquitous presence in some of the very areas where bounties might have been expected. So, it remains an intriguing enigma that in those counties it was abundant and widely despised, but not apparently persecuted through the normal reward system of parish funds. Only at Over (Cambs), where 103 heads were paid for between 1709 and 1722, can records of bounties for Kites be traced.

In contrast to the absence of churchwardens' payments for Red Kites in most of Wales and in the twenty-eight English counties mentioned above, there were some quite astonishing levels of killing elsewhere and some protracted

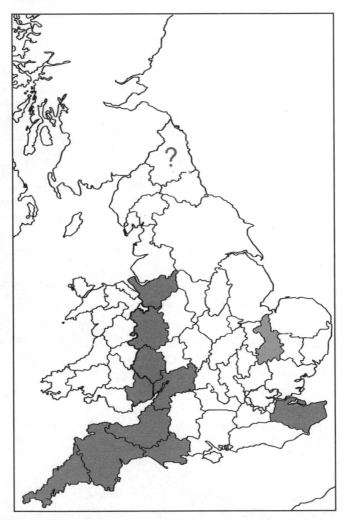

Figure 14. Map showing the counties in which churchwardens' bounties were paid for Red Kites from late C17 to early C19. By far the highest totals were in Devon and Cornwall (see pp. 121–2). In Northumberland, numbers of 'gleads' are referred to but the identification of them is uncertain.

campaigns. These were specifically restricted to the counties of the south-west and the Marches, as indicated on the map. Devon and Cornwall were far and away the most prolific counties both in terms of the totals of Kites killed and the number of parishes involved. In Devon, twenty-one out of the eighty parishes that I searched killed Kites, and in Cornwall, it was twenty-eight out of forty-five. Somerset, Dorset, and Gloucestershire and Herefordshire were areas of fairly widespread killing but with lower numbers. The situation in Cheshire is interesting. Here, only three parishes record payments for Kites but the numbers involved were impressive. Totals are shown in Table 12, within which Bunbury

TABLE 12. Totals of 'kite' heads paid for by churchwardens C17 to C19 in counties where kites were notably targeted. Note that in *all* instances the parish record is incomplete and therefore represents only a part of a fuller picture. For example, the figure given for Stoodleigh above cannot take into account the fact that in a further sixteen years bounties were given for 'kites, hedgehogs and jays' without specifying numbers. In many other cases, the existing record is only for a relatively brief period of years. Also only a small number of parish records exist in most counties. The actual totals in these counties were presumably substantially higher.

	No. of Years	Within the Period	Total kites
CORNWALL			
Altarnun	22	1727–1854	*c.*300
Boyton	5	1671–1707	20
Bradock	9	1778–99	30
Camborne	27	1681–1715	150+
Egloskerry	18	1755–1810	168
Illogan	12	1704–21	82
Kenwyn	2	1691–6	4+
Kilkhampton	16	1721–55	213
Landewednack	7	1678–94	17
Lanreath	20	1683–1833	93+
Lezant	54	1755–1809	1245
Linkinhorne	65	1726–1807	840+
Madron	9	1765–77	38
Morwenstow	75	1667–1752	1780
N. Petherton	1	1734	2
Padstow	5	1672–97	9
Poughill	4	1718–22	38
St Buryan	27	1717–49	216+
St Columb Min	1	1702	1
St Columb Maj	1	1704	1
St Dominic	14	1695–1718	63
St Erme	51	1733–98	424

TABLE 12—*continued*

	No. of Years	Within the Period	Total kites
St Mabyn	10	1659–81	10
St Neot	41	1648–1702	241
St Teath	19	1773–1823	73
CAMBRIDGESHIRE			
Over	14	1709–22	103
CHESHIRE			
Bunbury	8	1715–22	698
Eastham	36	1693–1738	523+
Tarporley	19	1662–81	872
KENT			
Benenden	3	1668–91	3
Charing	9	1694–1715	14
Doddington	2	1781–6	2
Tenterden	24	1655–93	447
Westerham	7	1673–1705	17
DEVON			
Abbotsham	10	1758–70	34
Bere Ferrers	5	1649–55	31
Branscombe	3	1793–1845	52
Braunton	3	1676–8	60
Clawton	10	1661–1703	33
Coombe Martin	1	1739	1
Dartington	1	1722	2
Doddiscombe L	2	1746–7	2
East Budleigh	15	1664–79	192
Exeter St T'mas	10	1726–39	92
Gittisham	6	1694–1722	18
Horwood	13	1762–1807	45
Littleham	3	1658–74	20
Marystowe	18	1764–83	166
Modbury	42	1714–71	188
Satterleigh	4	1800–5	1
Sidbury	1	1686	1
Stoodleigh	23	1691–1715	150+
Teignmouth	11	1756	12
Woodbury	1	1712	1
SOMERSET			
Crewkerne	16	1649–94	c.200
Kilton	5	1691–1725	16
Luccombe	8	1691–1718	40
Street	3	1686–1710	9
Wayford	11	1686–1727	43

	No. of Years	Within the Period	Total kites
GLOUCESTERSHIRE			
Bromsberrow	1	1694	1
Eastington	1	1724	9
Kemble	2	1700–4	11
Minch'hampton	2	1627 and 1735	11
Newnham	7	1690–1709	13

churchwardens paid for 256 heads in one year alone (1720). What is more, payments for these 256 birds were actually disbursed to 58 different parishioners! In many cases they were paid for two, three, or four heads at a time, a clear suggestion that these were broods of young taken from the nest. How many, if any, were brought in from neighbouring parishes where bounties might not have been paid we shall never know, but whatever the case it is further testimony to the abundance of Kites in that era. In 1921, Ticehurst examined the accounts for Tenterden in Kent and recorded 380 Kites killed in a 13-year period from 1676 to 1688. He used this to draw the fairly safe assumption that the Kite had formerly been an abundant species in the county. There is no doubt that he was right, although the high figures killed in Tenterden are not reflected elsewhere, even in the other Wealden parishes. In this respect Tenterden remains unique outside the counties in the west of England mentioned above.

However, all these apparently impressive figures are problematical because of the duplication of birds to which the name 'kite' was applied historically. It is made even more difficult by the fact that different names were used in different parts of the country. The issue is discussed more fully in the section on Buzzard (p. 135), but the written record, as it is contained in the original documents of the churchwardens, has to be viewed with considerable caution. The totals given above *may* be attributable to Kites, but it is more likely that they include Buzzard and possibly other species. (It might be noted that over 300 can occasionally be seen in the air together in mid Wales). In Northumberland 158 birds listed as 'gleads' were paid for in the late seventeenth century; these may well all have been Kites although in the north of England the name was loosely use for harriers. In the adjoining county of Cumberland 'glead' was exclusive to the Kite. If all the records listed as 'kite' were actually Kites, the absence of Buzzards from most parish lists is difficult to understand. In clarifying this problem there is little help to be gleaned from the per capita payments. The statutory amount set out in the Acts was 1*d.* for a Kite and 2*d.* for Buzzard (was this a measure of relative abundance, an indication of priority, or a recognition of the ease of taking Kites?). However, almost without exception, from the time

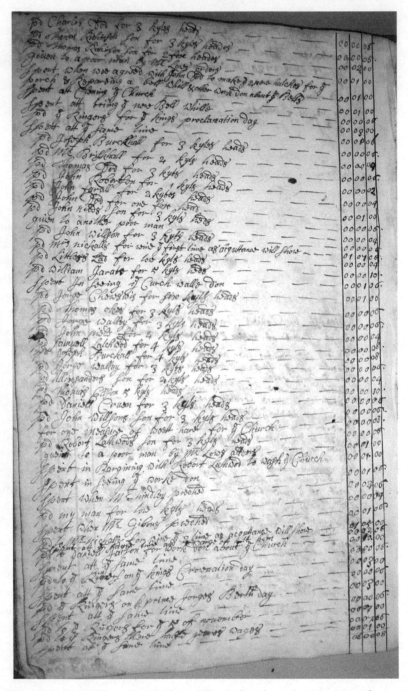

Figure 15. A page from the Bunbury (Ches) churchwardens' accounts for 1768, showing some of the large number of bounties paid for Kites.

the first payments for Kites begin to appear in the churchwardens' accounts, right up to the middle of the nineteenth century, a rate of 2*d*. was almost always paid, across the country.

By the beginning of the nineteenth century, parishes were gradually withdrawing from paying for vermin and the fashion for game shooting was flourishing. The catalogue of killing of the Red Kite (among many others) that occurred from that time is an appalling indictment of the efficiency of Hanoverian and Victorian Man's determination to obliterate species that were seen as competitors with his game-shooting interests. The example of the Burley estate in Rutland (p. 261), where 183 Kites (and 285 Buzzards) were killed between 1807 and 1816, gives an indication of the shocking level of slaughter that took place across the country in the early years of that century.

Shrubb has advanced the interesting theory that the root cause of the Red Kite's rapid demise in England lay in the dramatic changes of land use wrought by the enclosures, rather than through the efforts of gamekeepers. It is an interesting thesis which particularly focuses on the fact that enclosures revolutionized the husbandry and management of the sheep flocks, dramatically reducing the amount of sheep carrion available to birds such as Red Kite, Buzzard, and Raven. Shrubb quotes Lilford (1895) in support of this thesis, who noted that 'They (the Kites) disappeared before the advance of civilisation and the increase in the preservation of game'. Lilford recorded that the Kite 'disappeared suddenly, not gradually diminished in numbers as though shot or trapped off by 'keepers'. We know that the enclosures and the clearance of 'wastes', etc. had the effect, through habitat loss, of reducing populations of species such as Fox and Pine Marten and there is every reason to accept that the same factors affected the Red Kite (and Buzzard and Raven).

However this thesis is not necessarily convincing. Lilford was writing many decades after there was clear evidence that the Kite had been heavily persecuted in the East Midlands. Clare bemoaned its loss at the hand of Man by 1830 and the Burley figures give an indication of the huge numbers that could be killed on one estate in a brief period. The loss of sheep carrion might disadvantage Kites, but they are by no means dependent on it, as shown by the success of the recent English and Scottish reintroductions. It should also be remembered that parish enclosures, with the concomitant loss of 'wild areas', did not all happen at once, but by degrees over a long period of years. At Burley, they found abundant Kites to kill, starting in the year when enclosures took place in two adjoining parishes, Exton and Cottesmore. I believe that it was principally the early inception of shooting estates and the employment of 'keepers that successfully eradicated the Red Kite.

John Clare's lamentations for their loss referred to the adjacent county of Northamptonshire and, much later in the century, Charles Kingsley deplored their going nearby with the drainage of Whittlessey Mere. Whether they were wiped out by gamekeepers or as a result of enforced enclosures, the Kites eventually vanished. It is interesting that those counties which supported long-established 'ancient countryside', few if any parliamentary enclosures, and high populations of Kites—e.g. Cheshire, Devon—were among the earliest to lose their Kites.

No species could withstand the intensity of persecution that was suffered by the Red Kite. Even by the end of the eighteenth century its fate in England was sealed. The cul-de-sac of extinction was an inevitability. One of the tragedies, which adds insult to injury, is that the final extinction was achieved with a rapidity that has left no accurate record. In many areas the bird simply vanished without trace. Notwithstanding this, it is clear from the early county avifaunas, and other old records, that the Kite had already gone from one or two English counties (Middlesex, Cheshire, Lancashire) before the end of the eighteenth century. The last nest in London (Gray's Inn) was in 1777. The bird failed to breed in Cumberland after 1820, and a few years earlier (1815), at the opposite end of the country, a farmer near Canterbury had shot the final pair in Kent. One by one the Kite was eliminated from other English counties. The speed of extirpation can be judged by the situation in Derbyshire where the Kite was recorded as being the best known raptor in 1829, but had disappeared completely within the next few years. In Essex, the last known nest was robbed of eggs in 1854 (although there is suspicion that sporadic breeding may have taken place for another fifteen years or so). Beyond 1860, it is certainly the case that only one or two remaining areas in England could still claim an occasional pair of breeding Kites. Proven nesting had ceased in Gloucestershire by 1870 which was also the date of the last known nest in Lincolnshire, thus representing the final confirmed breeding in England although they probably survived a year or two longer in Shropshire.

In Scotland the picture was similar, but with only one significant difference. The end was achieved with such rapidity that the absence of records leaves a yawning gap in our knowledge of their path to extinction. As in England at the end of the eighteenth century, the Kite was certainly still an abundant bird over most of the country, particularly in the lowlands. It remained common in many areas until around 1840, as catalogued by Baxter and Rintoul. This is the date when the rail link to Scotland was established, which heralded an escalation in the annual migration of wealthy sports-loving Englishmen. It is from around this date that the determination of landowners and 'keepers achieved the bird's downfall at a speed that was unmatched by any other species elsewhere. A relatively modest 30 Kites were killed on Lord Melville's estate at Dunira (Perth) in 1809, but an impressive total of 275 on the Glengarry estate in 4 years, 1837–40. One hundred and five were allegedly killed on the Callander Hills in

12 months in 1875 and by 1879 the last pairs had bred in Scotland. Only ten years or so after its final demise in England, the bird was gone from Scotland too.

The basic story in Wales was no different from that in England and Scotland, with the bird being eliminated county by county through the nineteenth century. In Pembrokeshire, as in other counties, it was once a regular resident, but by 1830 it was said to be a very scarce bird. The killing of one there in 1835 was noteworthy and was then the last to be recorded from that county. On the opposite side of Wales a bird was shot in Monmouthshire in 1837 and sent to a collector in Carlisle, but this was only after he had had to wait three years or more until one could be found. The story and the timings were similar over the rest of Wales. Whereas twenty or so could be seen over the Dare valley in Glamorgan at the beginning of the century, and they still bred near Cardiff up to 1853 (when the last female was shot on the nest), they were rarely encountered thereafter. The picture in other counties was the same; before the end of the century it was only on the borders of Brecknockshire/Carmarthenshire/Cardiganshire that the last few pairs hung on.

After 400 years or so of almost unremitting effort, Man had again eliminated a species from the face of Britain. In this case, it was with the exception of a tiny handful of pairs in the refugia of the remotest and most inaccessible valleys in the heartland of central Wales: the nucleus from which this fine bird has slowly risen, Phoenix-like, into a more enlightened age.

Hen Harrier

The graceful, dove-grey male Hen Harrier and his dark, ring-tailed female have never been great friends of Man in Britain. As the name implies, the Hen Harrier was long regarded as a troublesome thief of chicks and ducklings. It was untroubled by the proximity of Man and was happy to hunt close to steadings and cottages in the areas where it bred. This reputation earned the Hen Harrier its place on the sixteenth century 'Vermin Acts' although strangely the number of bounties paid for them by the parishes in the centuries thereafter was remarkably small. The days of universal

free-ranging poultry in the countryside are now long gone, but some of the
feelings of animosity towards the bird have hardened even more. The bitterest
controversy nowadays surrounds the presence of the Hen Harrier on grouse
moors, where it can take large numbers of Red Grouse adults and chicks and is
accused of causing serious damage to the economic viability of valuable
moorland shooting estates. In the earliest years of the twenty-first century there
is no more bitter or divisive issue regarding a species that is seen by some as
unwanted vermin and by others as a symbol of conservation significance.

The Hen Harrier was a widely distributed and common bird throughout
Britain in the eighteenth and early nineteenth centuries. Around the end of
the nineteenth century there was a plethora of regional and county avifaunas
produced, and almost without exception they give us the strong impression that
this was a numerous and well-known bird up to the end of the previous century,
or even a little later. As an illustration of this, one of the fullest historical accounts
is that which Macpherson gives in his *Fauna of Lakeland*. He recounts the work
of Dr Heysham—pioneer of Hen Harrier study—on Newton Common, long
since subsumed by the urban spread of Carlisle. He was the first to realise in the
1790s, that the brown female and the dove-grey male were one and the same
species, not two separate ones as had been assumed until then (there must have
been innumerable country folk who could have put the scientific community
to right long before that!). Heysham found the Hen Harriers nesting almost
colonially and evidently polygamously, since several nests were regularly found
within a short distance of each other. Despite his regular shooting of the adults
and removal of many young, the birds continued in good numbers annually and
were obviously part of a very healthy local population. Watson, quoting Bolam
and Nethersole-Thompson, identifies Newcastle Town Moor and the heaths
now submerged within Bournemouth, as two other areas with good concentrations. The absence of detailed history from elsewhere leaves us guessing as to
how many other parts of Britain supported similar concentrations of the species.
With at least 8 million acres of 'wastes and other uncultivated land' in England
and Wales alone, before the onset of the major enclosures in the mid eighteenth
century, the Hen Harrier was undoubtedly a very familiar and plentiful species.

Three distinctly separate phases of Hen Harrier persecution can easily be
defined. The first is that which took place—albeit apparently sparingly—through
the parishes after the enactment of the Tudor Acts and the second is the period
in the nineteenth century during which the bird was exterminated by gamekeepers throughout mainland Britain. A third phase, which still continues,
relates to the killing, illegal since 1954, which began after the species enjoyed its
post-war recovery in Scotland and subsequently in northern England and Wales.

The historical churchwardens' accounts in England and Wales give only
minimal indication of bounty payments for harriers. The Orton (Cumb)

accounts show two payments in 1645 'to John Wilson for ringtails 6d' and 'to Edward Thornboro for ringtail heads 4d'. The number of birds involved is not revealed but we can assume that since the going rate in the Act was 2*d*., there may have been a total of five birds—which may well have been chicks taken from nests. At Prestwich (Lancs) there was a payment of 1/6 for 'ringtails and keits' in 1657. The only other records are from Kent where Benenden 'wardens paid one bounty in 1672 and the adjacent parish of Tenterden accounted for 20 individuals at 2*d*. each between 1680 and 1689. Several of the payments there were for four birds at a time, a clear indication that they were probably nestlings. The absence of further records throughout the country is very curious in view of the species' widespread and numerous occurrences and the strong antipathy with which the bird was regarded. It is possible that some records are hidden under bounties given for 'hawks' (see p. 132), but in any case these are few and far between and it seems more likely that, as Watson suggests, the harriers attracted little attention unless they caused a local problem with poultry.

Undoubtedly confusion arose between Hen Harrier and Montagu's Harrier, particularly as the latter was not widely recognized as a separate species until the publication of Montagu's Dictionary in 1802. However, so few records of persecution exist before that date that the possibility of confusion is little more than academic.

It was the nineteenth century that saw the rapid demise of this buoyant and agile bird of prey. MacGillivray, in his *Descriptions of Rapacious Birds in Great Britain* was lamenting the destruction of birds of prey in southern Scotland as early as 1836. Watson, quoting Richmond, exemplified the intensity with which land owners demanded the destruction of birds of prey by referring to the Marquess of Bute's instructions to his 'keepers in 1808. The Marquess required them to swear an oath of employment that ended with the words '. . . finally I shall use my best endeavour to destroy all birds of prey with their nests, so help me God'. It is small wonder that in Scotland, by the time the New Statistical Accounts were written in 1834–5, the references to Hen Harriers had decreased significantly since the time of the Old Statistical Accounts forty years earlier. Watson showed that the great decrease in Hen Harriers in southern Scotland and northern England, at the hands of the gamekeepers, occurred between the years 1820 and 1850. In Ayrshire the frequently quoted figure of 351 Hen Harriers killed on two estates between 1850 and 1854 has been questioned in the past, but we now know that such levels are perfectly feasible, assuming that they included passage birds as well as breeding pairs and young.

Whatever the accuracy of the figures, it indicates that there must have been a very healthy population. This was a population that appeared to Gray and Anderson to have virtually disappeared fifteen years later. It is a very conspicuous bird on the moors where it breeds, being bold in approaching intruders and therefore easily shot and equally easily trapped at the nest. In the Highlands, Watson believed that the major decline occurred a little later than in the south, in the latter half of the same century. Edward Ellice, in *Place-Names of Glengarry*, stated that between 1837 and 1840 the Glengarry 'keepers killed sixty-three Hen Harriers. Whereas the killing went on there for at least another 22 years (the record beyond that does not exist), the specific totals for this later period are lost within the general heading of 779 'hawks'. As the Hen Harrier became rarer it increasingly became a focus for trophy hunters and egg collectors, who often delivered the *coup de grâce* to the remaining pairs. Notwithstanding this, however, it was unquestionably the gamekeeper who was the principal cause of the bird's demise and if we have lost the bulk of the old estate vermin records in Scotland it cannot disguise the fact that similar levels of killing to those recorded at Glengarry doubtless occurred on a host of other estates in the second half of the nineteenth century. Watson quotes several other examples. On Skye, a Macdonald keeper killed thirty-two birds, young and old, in 1870; at Dunvegan twenty-five were killed on another estate in 1873; c.1887 in Caithness and Sutherland, Hen Harriers were 'killed on every possible occasion'; it had disappeared from Islay and Mull by 1890 before which it was common; on Arran, despite persecution, it may have survived until the First World War.

By 1900 this once-abundant bird was wholly eliminated from the Scottish mainland—except for a possible outpost on Kintyre—and from England and Wales. The details of its elimination in England and Wales are less well documented than in Scotland although it is evident that it had gone from the upland moors by 1900 and from its former lowland strongholds well before that. One of the principal causes of loss in England was the implementation of the Parliamentary Enclosure Acts that resulted in the loss of huge areas of 'wastes' and drainage of bogs, etc. that had previously supported many of the pairs in lowland counties. Similarly, in the uplands, the intensity of sheep grazing and the repeated moor burning that accompanied it destroyed the suitability of many areas. This was also a factor in Scotland although there it was nothing compared with the onslaught carried on by gamekeepers.

It was not until the time of the two world wars that the Hen Harrier began to gain a foothold again on mainland Britain. This recovery and subsequent spread of the Hen Harrier has, however, put it into a head-on collision with grouse moor 'keepers. Between 1990 and 1997, there were 102 reported incidents of illegal killing involving at least 131 individual birds. On one estate in the north Pennines, a former 'keeper asserted that 160 Hen Harriers had been killed on that estate alone in three years between 1995 and 1997. Not all were breeding birds or nestlings but included a number of passage birds en route north in spring. It is no surprise that on the adjacent RSPB reserve the number of breeding pairs fell from 13 in 1995 to nil by 2003. Illegal killing of this extent is an alarming echo of the days of the onslaught against harriers in Scotland in the nineteenth century, but it is probably not unique. Holmes et al. (2003), assessing the illegal killing of birds of prey in England for English Nature in 2000, found that only 44% of Hen Harrier nesting attempts on grouse moors were successful compared with 85% success on protected moors. Overall, only 27% of females holding territories on grouse moors in spring bred successfully compared with 74% elsewhere. The situation in Wales, where Hen Harriers first recolonized in 1958 and the numbers expanded to c.40 pairs in the early years of the twenty-first century, has been similar with heavy persecution throughout the latter half of the last century.

In Scotland, Etheridge et al. reviewed the effects of illegal Hen Harrier destruction between 1988 and 1995 and found that moorland managed for grouse was in effect a sink for female harriers (two-thirds of which were annual passage migrants from elsewhere), because of the high level of killing on those moors. They speculated that without illegal killing the population would increase by about 13% annually until a new equilibrium was reached. Human persecution was recorded on half of the grouse moors they investigated, with productivity of young at a low of 0.8 per nest compared with 2.4 on other moors.

The seemingly irresolvable conflict between the legitimate interests of commercial grouse shooting and the fortunes of the Hen Harrier resulted in 1992 in the setting up of a five-year study centred on the Langholm moors in south-west Scotland (discussed more fully in Chapter 11). Across the five-year programme the estate agreed that no birds of prey would be killed on the moor. Taking advantage of this respite, the number of Hen Harrier nests increased from two to more than twenty annually but it was clear that the grouse numbers suffered simultaneously. The high number of raptors there, as well as poor habitat quality, was considered to be responsible for continued low grouse density and poor bag numbers. The controversy remains unresolved. On the conservation side, the RSPB believes that the long-term solution lies in the restoration of a proper balance of heather and grass on grouse moors. Until that is achieved, the Society has argued that there should be no direct interference with harriers anywhere and that, in the interim, supplementary feeding should be provided on moors where there is a problem. Conversely, the Game Conservancy Trust believes that one solution may be to relocate surplus birds to other areas of the country, such as Exmoor and Dartmoor, from where they have been eliminated in the past. At the same time the Trust has urged the establishment of a demonstration moor to show that viable grouse moors should be able to accommodate some Hen Harriers—but not at extreme densities.

Behind it all there is a growing frustration among moor owners who believe that the only real solution to an otherwise intractable situation is a reduction of the harriers to acceptable levels, be it achieved legally or illegally. The Hen Harrier, as with all other birds of prey in Britain, is fully protected under the 1981 Wildlife and Countryside Act and remains a species of European conservation concern. Britain contains some 5% of the European population. In 2004, the police nationally launched a specific campaign seeking to tackle the issue of illegal killing of Hen Harriers head on with the aim of eliminating the problem. Only time will tell whether or not the matter can be solved this way, or if the campaign will simply widen an already serious divide in this contentious debate. It is significant that, after the first year of operation, the majority of moor owners had refused to sign up to a code of best practice.

'Hawks'

For the historical researcher attempting to catalogue the human pressure that has been exerted on birds of prey over the centuries, the word 'hawk' is frustrating and confusing. To start with, the word was not specifically included among the numerous birds of prey listed in the sixteenth century Vermin Acts. Nevertheless, and perhaps assuming a catch-all, its inclusion was clearly taken for granted, at least on the basis that payments for 'hawks' appear in various churchwardens' accounts from an early time. The most obvious assumption to make is that it is the Sparrowhawk to which such entries refer. Indeed, whenever there is precise mention in the churchwardens' accounts, it is for Sparrowhawk. However to extrapolate that for the far greater number of entries of 'hawk' would be unsafe. It is a word that was used generically throughout history and up to the present of course, to include a wide range of raptors. In the parish accounts, for example, it may well include occasional harriers, almost certainly Goshawk (it is difficult to believe that in the past Sparrowhawk was targeted while the Goshawk was ignored), and in all probability Buzzard and possibly Red Kite.

On the other hand, it could be argued that 'hawk' (interpreted as Sparrowhawk) was specifically omitted from the Tudor lists for two reasons. First it is difficult to appreciate what damage the Sparrowhawk could have been accused of in the knowledge that it preyed upon a number of the other bird species that were certainly identified as agricultural pests. Secondly, it was a bird that was valued as the 'ladies bird' for hawking. George Owen, writing in 1594 about the Pengelly Forest in Pembrokeshire, emphasized the importance of the Sparrowhawk in that implied context, 'Also there breedeth in the said woodde sparrhawks which is the lordes also'. William Linnard, writing about Welsh forests, stressed the importance therein of protecting hawks' nests for falconry. He recalled that Wales was recognized as an important source for 'goshawks, laneretts, tarcells, fawcons and other hawks', and as early as the fourteenth century Welsh Sparrowhawks were taken to Dover for export. Thus there was a degree of historical schizophrenia about the actual merits, or demerits, of the species.

Payments for hawks' heads are not numerous in the parish records in the seventeenth and eighteenth centuries, but are scattered without any consistency from county to county. Within those in which they do appear, there was equally little pattern; it is all very random. The two counties with the greatest number of records are Devon and Cornwall both with eight parishes showing payments, all for 'hawks' and without the species being named. Linkinhorne was responsible for killing high numbers although it was not possible to define the total because many are subsumed within general 'vermin payments' without giving break-down figures. In Devon, Branscombe (215 in 57 years up to 1810) and Modbury (206 between 1720 and 1771) were the most prolific (and note that both parishes killed high numbers of Kites). In three Kent parishes—Charing, Doddington, and St Lawrence—Sparrowhawks were specifically named, but the numbers were small. Generous payments of 6*d*. per head were paid in two or three parishes on the Isle of Wight, and even twice that at Brading. All payments on the island were for 'hawks' and there is considerable suspicion, at Freshwater at least, that these were Kites. In the latter part of the eighteenth century Aldworth (Berks) paid for 106 Sparrowhawks' heads, at the same time as a consistent campaign against Sparrows!

Once the mantle for predator control had effectively passed on to the new army of gamekeepers from the end of the eighteenth century onwards, the level of persecution intensified. Somewhere along the line the Goshawk disappeared, probably around the early years of the twentieth century (well after the height of the vogue for falconry). Despite the pressure from gamekeepers, the Sparrow-hawk survived surprisingly well, no doubt helped by the fact that it has a wider habitat requirement than the Goshawk and is a fairly secretive and elusive bird. Again the generic use of 'hawk' prevents an assessment of the actual numbers that were killed on most estates where records have been found. Almost inevit-ably there is no breakdown into individual species. In most cases, we can only guess at the actual proportion of Sparrowhawks. Two well-separated examples are Sandringham (Norfolk), where 1,645 hawks were accounted for between 1938 and 1950, and Langwell and Sandside (C'ness) with 1,115 killed between 1919 and 1926. On the Penrhyn estate in North Wales, Sparrowhawks were specifically listed and 735 killed on the estate between 1874 and 1902, an average of more than 26 per year. Evidence from other lowland estates suggests that such a figure was generally in line with totals elsewhere. Undoubtedly the population was reduced by such heavy annual predation, with local eliminations occurring regularly. However, there were always pairs breeding away from keepered areas and their large annual broods guaranteed continual replacement—and an annual crop for the 'keepers.

There was a recrudescence of persecution after the Second World War, but despite this the strong antipathy towards the species meant that the Sparrowhawk was the only diurnal bird of prey not fully protected by the 1954 Protection of Birds Act. However, within a few years of that Act, it was apparent that there was something dramatically wrong; there had been a catastrophic decline in numbers, which was unrelated to direct persecution. The extent of the collapse was so great that the Sparrowhawk became locally extinct, particularly in the lowland cereal areas. The Sparrowhawk was added to the protected list in 1961. It was one of the dramatic casualties of DDT and related organo-chlorine pesticides and it was not until the removal of those agricultural chemicals that the species began to recover. Pesticides had achieved, albeit thankfully only temporarily, what generations of vermin control had failed to do.

Buzzard

This is another species which presents real difficulties when trying to unravel the true picture of the geographical extent and intensity of killing to which it was subjected in England and Wales in the years following implementation of the Tudor Vermin Acts. The period is clouded in a fog of mystery and confusion. From the nineteenth century onwards, the situation becomes clearer but prior to that, and dating from the Tudor Acts which urged the killing of Buzzards amongst many other species, the payment records specifically referring to the Buzzard by name are few and far between.

The confusion centres on the duplication of vernacular names for the Buzzard that were also applied loosely to other species included on the old vermin lists. The principal confusion involves the Kite which was referred to in many parts of the country as 'gled' (glede, glead) or 'puttock', names which were also freely used for the Buzzard. To add further to the confusion, in Devon and Cornwall where they were heavily persecuted, the Buzzard was frequently referred to as 'kitt' or 'keat', although I never encountered that spelling there in searching more than 120 parish records. Nevertheless, the section on the Red Kite reveals just how many 'kites' were killed in those two counties alone in the seventeenth and eighteenth centuries. The 1566 Act itself clearly distinguishes between the two species—'Busarde' (a spelling echoing its French origin) at 2*d*. per head and 'Kyte' at 1*d*.—although this does not help us to unravel the ensuing muddle. Throughout the search of all the parish accounts I have not once found the name 'puttock', although 'kite' is very common and 'glede' fairly frequent. To complicate the matter even further, the word 'hawk' (see p. 132) is used sometimes as a generic term for all the commoner birds of prey, including Buzzard. At its simplest, and without attempting to quantify, we have to assume that the Buzzard was certainly controlled under the parish payment system but that the numbers and extent of this are hidden within the names 'kite', 'glede', and 'hawk'. However, the final observation is that the Buzzard was not always seen in the same light as the Kite. The latter was an opportunist and a thief whereas the Buzzard was recognized, with a degree of affection, primarily for its value in removing carrion and less as a snatcher of farmyard chicks and ducklings.

The main mystery surrounds the reasons for the complete absence of any payments for Buzzards (by whatever name)—or in fact other birds of prey—in the majority of counties. This is difficult to explain and has been referred to by other writers in the past, for example Steele Elliot in Bedfordshire and Tubbs, both in general terms. There is no doubt as to the Buzzard's erstwhile universal distribution. James I listed it for destruction in Scotland in 1457, William Turner (1544) said it was to be seen at all times, Willughby (1678) suggested it was widely distributed, Pennant (1774) described it as the commonest hawk in England, and Latham identified it as 'a bird known to everyone'. Despite this, there are whole swathes of the country where there is no evidence of its being targeted before the establishment of game estates and the arrival of gamekeepers. The evidence thereafter is completely different.

In only ten parish accounts in England (none in Wales) is the Buzzard mentioned by name; one each in Buckinghamshire, Dorset, Gloucestershire,

Suffolk, and Westmorland and five in Kent. Why, one wonders, was the parish of Wing (Bucks) almost unique in the Midlands of England in having a sustained campaign against the Buzzard? Here 119 were paid for from 1695 to 1722. Seventy-five are listed for Cranbourne (Dorset) in seven brief years from 1700, and they occur on the 1580 list at Cratfield (Suffolk) and sporadically at Minchinhampton (Glos) in 1575, 1596, and 1634. In Kent, the two principal parishes were Charing, where thirty-three were killed between 1692 and 1714, with a maximum of fifteen being taken in the final year, and Tenterden, with fifty-seven killed in the decade following 1683. In the north of England only one parish was found that mentioned Buzzard by name. This is Orton, high on the Westmorland fells, where we find in 1693 'ihm for 2 Busard heads iiijd' (i.e. $4d$.) and eleven years later 'Ihm ffor killing of a Busard 2d'. Other than these entries we are left to guess what might be the true interpretation of entries under synonyms. Therefore we shall probably never know precisely what effect persecution had in those centuries, on the populations locally.

On the presumption that churchwardens were not particularly keen to be duped into unnecessary payments, it is worth remembering that initially the rate for a Buzzard (which applied in all the instances given above) was $2d$. and that for a Kite $1d$. A 100% difference in these rates ought to have been sufficient for them to ensure that in the majority of cases they were paying for the right specimen. However, before long a Kite's head was fetching $2d$. or more in many areas. Of course, if the familiar name for Buzzard in Devon or Cornwall was kitt or keat, the churchwardens' problems were compounded further!

As we have seen from the comments of Pennant and Latham quoted above, and confirmed by other writers, the Buzzard was clearly widely distributed and well known in the late eighteenth century. There is no reason to doubt that this was generally the case until the end of the century. However, there is a caveat to add to that generalization, echoed by some of the ornithological writers in the early nineteenth century, which is that the bird may already have been fairly rare in parts of the east and south-east. If that was the case, there is no need to look further for a cause than the major land use changes that began with the Parliamentary Enclosure Acts from 1750 onwards. From Dorset to Yorkshire and eastwards into East Anglia, where new enclosed fields dominated the landscape, the Buzzard's preferred habitat had disappeared. Shrubb (2003) has pointed out that, as a consequence of this change, sheep were then automatically folded onto drier, better drained ground and the enormous volume of sheep carrion which characterized the pre-enclosure era was no longer available. Before the country-wide explosion of the Rabbit population, sheep carrion was almost a prerequisite for a healthy Buzzard population, certainly more so than it was for the Red Kite.

Coincident with the expanding areas of enclosure, and as a direct result of the concomitant revolution in land tenure and the evolution of large estate holdings, game preservation became a major consideration. Henceforth the Buzzard's fortunes declined rapidly. Together with other predatory birds and mammals it was then in the direct firing line of the gamekeeper's gun, trap, and poison as part of the war of extermination that was prosecuted across the land. Under the remorseless pressure from gamekeepers the speed with which the Buzzard disappeared in England, Scotland, and Wales was impressive. As with so many other predators, there was no room for them in countryside that was increasingly devoted to game preservation. With the numbers sometimes claimed to have been killed, it was little wonder that Buzzards vanished from so many areas. Macpherson described a new 'keeper on a Lake District estate killing fifty within a short time of taking up his post.

Vermin accounts from Scottish estates often lump species together as 'hawks', which doubtless embraces Buzzard, but does not allow individual species break-down. In this category, the Duniva estate claimed 21 'hawks' killed at the early date of 1809, and the Buccleuch estates in Dumfries and Galloway accounted for 1,096 'hawks' between 1819 and 1827, a total which excluded Hen Harrier, eagles, and Sparrowhawk. On Assynt, 84 'hawks' were killed between 1853 and 1868 and at Lochnaw Castle, 238 from 1853 to 1868. One Scottish estate that did name species separately was Glengarry (1837–40) where the claimed total of 285 Buzzards is impressive. The claim of 371 Rough-legged Buzzards at the same time is more difficult to validate; nonetheless, the kill was evidently very substantial.

By 1865, A. G. More, in organizing his pioneering country-wide assessment of British breeding birds, recorded that the Buzzard was 'by no means common and nearly exterminated in the eastern and midland counties of England'. In fact, it had been exterminated in Kent as early as 1810, in Norfolk by 1820, and in a whole swathe of other counties in the east of England from Northumberland to Sussex before 1850. In Scotland the picture was much the same.

Maps produced by Norman Moore in 1954, reproduced below, show that by the end of the century the Buzzard was confined to the south-west peninsula, Wales, the Lake District, and the western areas of Scotland (except for Kintyre, where it had already been exterminated by 1850). He also produced a corresponding map showing the density of game preservation throughout the country, which demonstrated the absence of Buzzards in all those areas of the most intensive game rearing. Clearly there was no room for both. Buzzards thrived only in those areas which did not suffer from gamekeeper pressure. Only after the Second World War and the passing of the Protection of Birds Act in 1954 did Buzzard distribution start to re-expand.

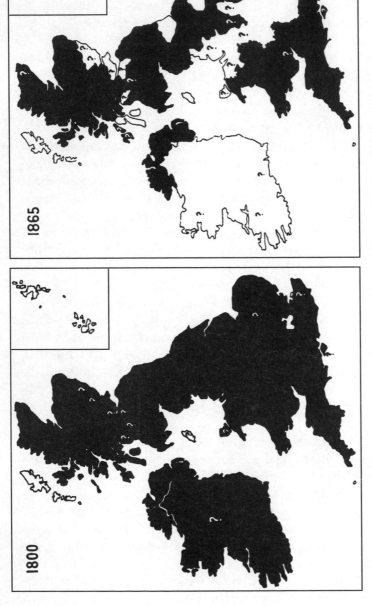

Figure 16. Changes in the distribution of Buzzard in Great Britain 1800–1954. Reproduced from Moore (1957) with the author's permission.

KEY: Black—Breeding proved, or good circumstantial evidence of breeding.
? on Black—Circumstantial evidence suggests that breeding probably took place.
? on White—Inadequate evidence of breeding.
White—No evidence of breeding.

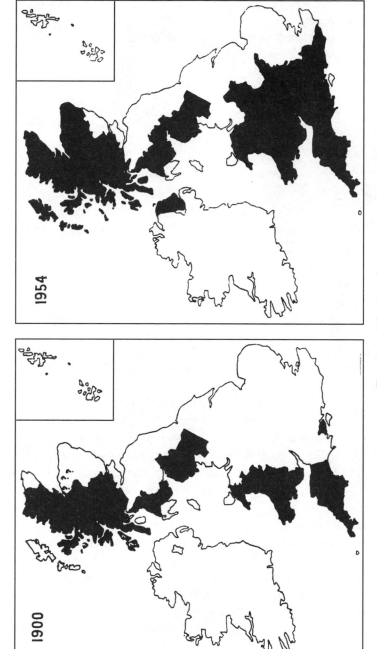

Figure 16. (*Continued*)

Ever since the introduction of the 1954 Act, which gave legal protection to the Buzzard, illegal persecution has been rife, as can be seen in Chapter 10. In addition to the figures given there, Moore himself mentioned a record of 400 being shot 'in three small areas' in Scotland in 1954. Such an instance is not unique.

Green Woodpecker—the hew hole or galley bird

Few birds have had a greater number of English vernacular names than the Green Wood-pecker: thunderbird, rain-maker, plough bird, woodwall, yaffle, galley bird et al. It has a place deeply rooted in myth and legend, as well as maintaining an ancient sacred relationship with the oak. Not-withstanding this, and in contrast to the affection with which the bird is viewed today, it was listed on the 1566 statute of vermin ('for the head of everie woodwall . . . one penny'). Although we cannot be absolutely certain in this context about the intention to identify 'woodwall' as the Green Woodpecker, it a fairly safe assumption that this is the case. This is the woodpecker that was commonest and most familiar 400 years ago, foraging part of the time on open ground, and not so exclusively an inhabitant of woodland as the Great Spotted Woodpecker.

One has to search hard to identify the justification that earned this bird a place on a sixteenth century 'Acte for the preservation of Grayne', certainly bearing in mind the almost venerable status it had always enjoyed in country lore. Needless to say it drilled holes in trees and always has done (including occasionally fruit trees) and may have attacked beehives at times (as it sometimes does in modern times). However, this hardly seems sufficient reason to castigate the bird and list it as vermin. One has to look a little deeper for a more valid cause. This can probably be found closer to home in the accounts of churchwardens over the past four centuries or so. Time and again they documented payments for supplies of roofing shingles, often on a surprisingly regular basis. Obviously the church steeples and parts of church roofs needed periodic replacement, but not normally with the frequency that many of the parish accounts show. Thin slates for roofing, Welsh ones for example, were only available from late seventeenth or early eighteenth centuries and then were prohibitively expensive for most parishes (transport being far greater than unit cost), certainly until the beginning of mass production around 1780–90. Thus, shingles were far more commonly used for roofing than they are now. As we know to this day woodpeckers are readily attracted to shingle roofs and will drill through them with ease, be they oak or cedar, not principally in pursuit of insects as often assumed, but to produce roosting or even nesting holes. Chipped and frayed edges of shingles indicate a search for insects, whereas circular chiselled holes are far more frequent and cause a lot more damage. Thus, in the days when the majority of steeples and roofs were clad with shingles the problem of woodpecker damage was much more widespread and serious than it is today. In all probability this was the reason why the Green Woodpecker was added as a supernumerary to a list of agricultural vermin.

The records of payments for Green Woodpeckers in the old parish accounts are not numerous however. Hook Norton (Oxon) clearly focused on them between 1734—the first year for which records exist—and 1739, killing twenty-three in those six years (and how many before 1734?). Once again Sherborne (Dorset) was prominent, but with only a modest scatter of seventeen birds over sixteen years or so at the end of the eighteenth century. Dursley and Easington parishes (Glos) paid 2d. per head for twenty or so individuals between them (seven in one year) around 1720 to 1740. As at Hook Norton the birds were referred to as 'Hickwalls', another common local name. Additional to these records there were a few payments at Sidbury (Devon) in 1682, Carew (Pembs) 1791–3, Crewkerne (Som) as early as 1656–69, and Tenterden (Kent) 1682–7 where the last entry used another local name 'Gallybird', for taking of which Thos Kite was paid one penny. A very early record was at Cratfield (Suffolk) in 1580, but other than these records it appears that the species was not harassed to anything like the extent it might have been once financial reward was on offer.

Writing in the middle of the twentieth century, Meinertzhagen (1959) commented on the damage being caused to a considerable number of church spires in East Anglia and blamed the Green Woodpecker. Today the bird still causes a similar nuisance. It sometimes drills holes in telegraph or transmission poles, perhaps, as some claim, attracted by the insect-like humming of the wires, and can weaken them to the point of causing them to snap. However, more serious is its continuing habit of attacking shingle-clad church steeples. Damage, which is usually concentrated in early spring, can be quite severe. Bapchild (Kent) steeple is not the only one that has been unkindly described as resembling Gruyere cheese. The cost of repair can be high in such instances. At the church of St Peter and St Andrew in Old Windsor (Berks) the cost of reshingling was £25,000 in 2003, a price similarly reflected elsewhere. The Churches Conservation Trust, responsible for the maintenance of redundant churches, had to strip completely some steeples severely damaged by woodpeckers and has reclad them in oak, interleaved with stainless steel; St Mary's at Chickney, one of the oldest churches in Essex, is one such instance. On the other hand, at All Saints, Leavesden (Herts), the churchwardens have tolerated the problem for more than a decade and since new shingles are almost immediately attacked, the solution there has been laissez-faire and the woodpeckers are apparently popular if not actually welcome. A more dynamic solution has been undertaken at Great Henny (Essex) where the steeple had to be reclad. The old shingles were used, rather optimistically, to make a, low-level, stand-alone steeple nearby, in the hope of deflecting the woodpeckers from the new shingles to their more familiar holes. So far they have ignored it.

The question as to which species of woodpecker is responsible for causing this damage is still sometimes challenged. Although it is unwise to be categorical, the overwhelming evidence points to the Green Woodpecker, in all instances where there is proof positive. In many cases, they have been seen at the scene of the crime, and in others they are regularly seen in the vicinity, whereas Great Spotteds are not. In one example a clutch of Green Woodpecker eggs was found within a hole in the steeple. However, one cannot completely rule out the possibility that Great Spotted Woodpeckers may occasionally be to blame. At Bapchild (Kent) it is suggested that it may be this species although this has not been confirmed.

The map on p. 143 shows the known distribution of current or recent damage by woodpeckers to church steeples. It shows the very heavy concentration of incidents in south-east England, especially Essex and Kent. To a degree it reflects the abundance of the Green Woodpecker but also, of course, the frequency of occurrence of shingle steeples. The map is based on information supplied by Diocesan Church Councils throughout England and Wales but it is certainly not exhaustive, since it is evident that not all dioceses have a complete picture of the problem themselves; Oxford diocese, for example, did not believe that they had a problem until some instances were pointed out to them, including the church at Ashamstead with 130 woodpecker holes! The list of affected parishes appended to the map is therefore indicative but not comprehensive.

Thus, the case of the 'Galley Bird' is an unusual one that is not widely appreciated. There is no doubt that in some places it causes mischief and incurs expense but this should in no way qualify it to be a modern pest species. One can only hope that in projecting an assumed sixteenth-century problem into a confirmed twenty-first-century one, it does not serve to propel the Green Woodpecker into disfavour. It is, of course, totally protected under the Wildlife and Countryside Act 1981.

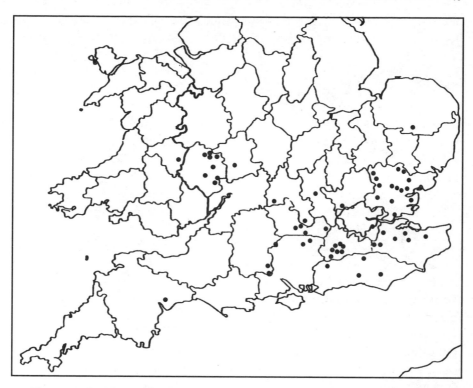

Figure 17. Parishes suffering recent woodpecker damage, represented by dots on the map above: **(Berks)**—Ashampstead, Old Windsor, Sulhamstead, Yatterdon; **(Bucks)**—Hulcott; **(Devon)**—Farringdon; **(Essex)**—Bowers Gifford, Broxted (St Mary), Broxted (St Peter), Chickney, Copford Green, Great Henny, Great Totham, Henham, Little Leighs, Margaretting, Shelley, Southminster, Terling, Ulting; **(Hants)**—Ashe, Sherfield-on-Loddon; **(Hfds)**—Eaton Bishop, Humber, Kimbolton, Puddleston, Putley, Sollars Hope, Ullingswick, Upper Sapey; **(Herts)**—Leavesden; **(Kent)**—Bapchild, Barming, Fawkham Green, Footscray, Newnham, Sundridge, West Stourmouth, Westerham; **(Norfolk)**—Quidenham; **(Oxon)**—Combe, Faringdon; **(Radnorshire)**—Knighton-on-Teme; **(Surrey)**—Albury, Dunsfold, Grafham, Hambledon, Merrow, Mickleham, Shere; **(Sussex)**—Berwick, Herstmonceux, Linchmere, Worth; **(Wilts)**—Chute Forest, Whiteparish; **(Worcs)**—Pirton.

Dipper and Kingfisher

The fact that either of these two birds should appear on vermin lists in any era— least of all in an 'Acte for the Preservation of Grayne'—is somewhat extraordinary. What is also interesting is the confusion of names and identity that occurred in the past. It was long thought that the Dipper and the Kingfisher were one and the same species; that the Dipper was nothing other than a female Kingfisher and that it was only the male Kingfisher that was resplendent in blue and orange plumage. Some hint of this confusion is easily detectable in the wording of the 1566 Act, which somewhat enigmatically determines 'for the Head of everie Byrde that is called the Kings Fyssher, one peny'. Doubtless, with the premium that was placed on fish and fisheries in medieval times, and Roman Catholic Britain, both of these species were assumed to be competitors with Man. The Kingfisher could be seen catching fish, albeit extremely small ones but sometimes from hatcheries, and the Dipper with its underwater feeding habit was presumed to take fish eggs amongst other foods. In fact, as Ormerod and Tyler have shown, Dippers feed predominantly on caddis larvae and mayfly nymphs with smaller percentages of other aquatic invertebrates. The same authors state that fish comprise only minimal percentages of Dipper food at any time of year, but may have a more prominent role in winter when young Bullheads are easily obtained and are the most frequent fish items taken. Eggs of salmonids are taken at times, but in numbers that are insignificant.

Despite the listing of these two species, the total of 1,579 English and Welsh churchwardens' records that have been examined have produced only one parish which paid out for Dippers and only three for Kingfisher. At Market Weighton in East Yorkshire, between 1681 and 1710, 307 Dippers ('water crakes' and 'water crows' were the colloquial names in that part of northern England) were killed with a maximum of 39 in one year. The earliest Kingfisher record comes from Bishop's Stortford (Herts), where five individuals comprised part of the haul of vermin for which Edward Wylley paid bounties in his capacity as one of the 'distributors' of bounty payments between 1569 and 1571. Four were taken at Cranborne (Dorset) in 1706–8 and a single bird at Great Houghton (N'hants) in 1675 for which the statutory one penny was paid.

In nineteenth-century Scotland, where the name 'water crow' was also used in some areas, little mercy was being shown to Dippers on the rivers of various large estates. By 1872, Knox was moved to lament that the Dipper—the 'Water Ouzel' as he called it—had for ages been condemned unjustifiably as a devourer of Trout and Salmon spawn. Ritchie records how the Duchess of Sutherland offered sixpence for each Dipper killed on her waters with the result that 548 were slaughtered in the years from March 1831 to 1834. It is interesting that Dippers were almost invariably referred to as 'King's Fisher', by which name the Maclaines of Lochbuie on Mull were offering 2d. per head in 1831 (Kingfishers are absent from the Highlands and most of the islands). Also in Sutherland, the Reay Country vermin lists included 368 Water Ouzels killed in the 6 years 1873–9 and in Assynt parish (Suth) 84 were shot between 1846 and 1852 together with a seemingly improbable claim for 69 Kingfishers! (Could they still have been thought of as female Kingfishers?) In the same era Ritchie recognized that the population on the Spey catchment was severely reduced by the agreement instituted by the estate which gave the right to fish the river in exchange for killing Dippers. On the Gruinard estate in Wester Ross water bailiffs shot some sixty-three Dippers in the first decade of the twentieth century. Without doubt if more estate vermin records had survived the evidence of much wider slaughter would be have been apparent.

Jay

The Jay was not actually included by name in the 1566 Act although it is there by inference within the generic inclusion of 'crows'. Plenty of early payments for its killing are to be found, for example at Minchinhampton (Glos) in 1627 when thirty-eight were killed. As we have seen, fruit, grown in both hedgerows and orchards, was at a considerable premium in the Tudor, Stewart, and later eras and there was therefore an understandable priority to protect it. This is evident from the wording in the body of the 1566 Act itself and further reflected in the accounts of other avian species covered in this book. By any standard the Jay causes fairly low-level nuisance, although its predilection for soft fruit, and occasional pecking at other fruit, together with a habit of stripping rows of peas, etc. has long antagonized gardeners. A fascinating aspect of the picture revealed through an examination of historic churchwardens' accounts is the distribution of killing as represented by bounty payments. Once again it was focused on the core of 'ancient country-side' areas with almost none having taken place outside five counties—Devon, Somerset, Dorset, Gloucestershire, and Kent. In Devon, almost 30% of parishes were killing with enthusiasm for variable periods from the middle of the seven-teenth century, for the next hundred years or so. Numbers varied from a few dozen annually to 587 in 10 years (High Week) and 2,210 in various years between 1761 and 1820 at Ashburton. In Dorset, the numbers killed were not usually of this magnitude, although several parishes undertook limited control. At Beaminster (1651–1719) bounties were paid for a total of 960 birds. Num-bers in a handful of parishes in Somerset and Gloucestershire sometimes reached as many as 50 per year but the totals were seldom more than a few hundred over a span of 30–50 years. In Kent, it was again Tenterden where the maximum numbers were taken, 1,775 individuals in a short span of years from 1682 to 1693, an annual average of 148 with a maximum of 267 in 1687. None of the other available Kentish parishes approached anything like this figure.

Nowadays it seems a little hard on the Jay to maintain it on the list of pest species. It is predominantly an acorn-feeding bird with a strong symbiotic relationship with the oak. Although it is well distributed in Britain south of the Highlands, its stronghold is in the heavily wooded counties of the south-east.

With the increasing vogue for country sports from the late eighteenth century onwards there were further pressures applied to Jays. They are egg thieves, and although this predisposition principally affects woodland passerine species, Jays will exploit the woodland edge, where any suspicion of predating Partridge or Pheasant clutches or chicks puts them into immediate conflict, especially with lowland gamekeepers. For this reason they became legitimate targets and although in this context Jays are not seen to be nearly as threatening as Carrion Crows or even Magpies, the numbers killed on some estates have been high. Table 13 gives some examples of these levels.

TABLE 13. Numbers of Jays killed on six game estates.

Burley, Rutland	1807–16	428
Highclere, Hampshire	1840–6	234
Penrhyn, Caernarvonshire	1874–1902	306
Atholl, Perthshire	1894–1904	2783
Sandringham, Norfolk	1938–50	1998
Holkham, Norfolk	1953–60	1550

Control of Jays is still undertaken on lowland Pheasant and Partridge shoots, particularly in the more wooded areas of southern England. Game Conservancy Trust figures indicate that this control is at a gradually reducing level over the past four decades.

The other reason why Jays are occasionally targeted is for the value of their blue and black primary coverts used for fly tying. These bright feathers are important constituents of some of the popular salmon flies such as Silver Invicta and Golden Olive Bumble. However, none of the levels of killing undertaken nowadays are likely to impact on the overall numbers of this successful woodland bird, the population of which is put at around 160,000 pairs.

Magpie

The Magpie is a good example of a bird whose public image has swung, pendulum like, over the years as its relationship with Man has evolved with the broadening of Man's activities and priorities. It does not have a great number of supporters nowadays, nor does it enjoy general popularity. However, before the era of game preservation the most frequent occasional charge against the Magpie was as a petty thief of eggs and fruit, especially cherries. The Breadalbane court book of 1621 identifies more general reasons for discouraging it: 'Item it is statute and ordanit that na tennent within the boundis respective forsaides suffer nather ruck, hoddit craw nor pyatis to big (breed) nor clek (hatch) in thair rowmes or possessiounes at any tyme hairefter'. William Lawton writing in 1617 warned that 'your cherries when they bee ripe will draw all the blacke-birds, Thrushes and May-pyes to your orchard'. That petty crime apart, the Magpie was always broadly welcomed as a popular and confiding neighbour of rural folk, fulfilling a degree of usefulness in helping to remove carrion, feeding on various invertebrates, and taking a number of small rodents. Its host of familiar local names such as 'chatterpie', 'piet', and 'maggie' testify to the popular image it enjoyed. It is a colourful, attractive, and jauntily self-assured bird inscribed in country folklore in jingles such as 'One for sorrow, two for joy, three for a girl, four for a boy, five for silver, six for gold, seven for a secret that's never been told'. But there is also the slightly more sinister side in which the Magpie was considered to be a manifestation of the Devil, sent to Earth to do mischief, and to this day old countrymen will still tip their cap and greet the 'gentleman' Magpie when encountered, to negate that ancient power.

Although the Magpie was specifically named in the 1566 Act, an examination of the record of bounty payments thereafter indicates that there was very little take-up in the centuries that followed. Indeed, of all the parish records checked, only forty-seven make any mention at all of bounties for Magpies and of them, twenty produced no more than one or two occasional individuals across the whole of the seventeenth and eighteenth centuries. Only two parishes had records that indicated that Magpies were killed in substantial numbers: Bunbury

(Ches), where 3,055 were taken in the 16 years between 1675 and 1691 with an impressive maximum of 452 in one year and Croston (Lancs) where the inhabitants disposed of 5,452 in 26 years (1681–1707) at a rate of 1*d*. each and ½*d*. for young, with a maximum of 617 removed in the most prolific year. Elsewhere there were short bursts of activity or very short-term campaigns in a few other counties. Abbotsham (Devon) parishioners killed 555 in 3 years around 1769 and the churchwardens paid for a large number of eggs. In the same county, at Sidbury, the record is unclear, but it appears that there were some large kills there for a short time in the 1670s. Elsewhere in Derbyshire, Somerset, and Kent the churchwardens paid for small numbers. The general picture gained from the churchwardens' records throughout the country is that the great majority of parishes simply left the birds alone. However, this probably paints a simpler picture than was actually the case. It is difficult to accept that for all its supposed popularity in the past, the Magpie's habits did not lead to a wider persecution than the parish archives reveal. In the literature there are numerous references to alternative methods of trapping and taking Magpies and allusions to killing. Macpherson, for example refers to 'this persecuted bird . . .' in Lakeland and quotes the deerkeeper in Martindale having exterminated the Magpie from the valley although the reasons for such action is obscure.

It was the advent of widespread game preservation in the latter years of the eighteenth century that changed the Magpie's fortunes. With a priority on the raising of high numbers of ground-nesting game for sporting purposes, the Magpie was quickly identified as an egg thief and as a predator of chicks, whose depredations conflicted directly with the maximizing of Partridge and Pheasant numbers. Together with the Carrion Crow and Fox, overnight the Magpie became an undesirable competitor and has remained a target for gamekeepers ever since. The universal efforts to eliminate Magpies from game estates throughout Britain in the nineteenth and twentieth centuries had a serious effect on its numbers. By the time of the First World War it was severely reduced or even extinct in parts of Scotland outside the industrial lowlands, virtually extinct in East Anglia—the most intensively gamekeepered area of the country—and much reduced elsewhere. As was the case with other persecuted species, numbers began to recover from the time of that war. They have continued to do so since, notably since the 1960s and the birds have spread to many urban and suburban areas at the same time. Here they are safer from persecution and Birkhead has shown that densities can reach up to 16 pairs per square kilometre. However, it is principally in these suburban areas that the final reason for its modern dislike arises. The Magpie is an expert nest finder and will patiently watch nesting birds, not only game species, but Blackbirds, Chaffinches, etc. as they fly back to the nest which it will then plunder of eggs or chicks. Not only is this discomforting and frustrating to the human watcher whose primary interest is usually the promoting of songbird populations in the garden, but the assumption is made that Magpies must be depleting the populations of these garden species. However, Birkhead's studies have shown that no such impact can be found and that in some cases songbird species actually did better in areas where Magpie density was higher! None of this has, up to now, gone far in reducing the ill-feeling towards the species however.

Chough

There is a problem in interpreting the past records of Chough because it was not until the end of the fifteenth century that separate words began to be used to differentiate between Chough and Jackdaw. Until the sixteenth century both were simply referred to as 'choughes'. It is fairly safe to assume that both species were included under the word 'choughes' in Elizabeth's Act of 1566; were this not so it would have meant that the Jackdaw, in particular, would have been omitted from her list of 'noyfull Fowles'. Under the intentions of the Act this would be highly unlikely, bearing in mind the Jackdaw's constant proximity to rural man and its liking for grain.

It seems remarkable to us, 400 years later, that Tudor antipathy should be directed against a bird like the Chough which is now seen as both harmless and engaging—an aerial acrobat of wild cliff coasts, with iridescent black plumage and flamboyant crimson bill and legs. The Chough feeds on a wide variety of soil invertebrates, broadening its diet to include grains and berries in winter and hard weather. However, historically, it was a bird that engendered not only antipathy as a putative agricultural pest but also a considerable degree of dread. As a ground feeder, foraging among growing crops or on stubbles (predominantly probing for soil invertebrates) it was accused of taking grain. Even worse, its habit of taking blowflies, ticks, or other insects from newly dead or sickly animals was readily misinterpreted as indicating that the bird had been the cause of their demise. Still more damning though was the unshakeable conviction of the bird's incendiary capabilities. Was it not possessed of a fiery red bill? And did it not have a Magpie-like reputation for stealing or collecting anything that glitters, including lighted sticks and similar? So its long but undeserved history as an agricultural pest (the first traceable reference can be found in the Durham Account Rolls of 1400–13) was greatly exacerbated by the accusation that it was a fire raiser. William Camden in his *Britannia* (1586) acknowledged the Chough as 'an incendiary thievish bird, often setting fire to houses and stealing and hiding small money'. These were sentiments repeated all too frequently. Even Defoe writing in the early decades of the eighteenth century reaffirmed that 'it will steal and carry away anything it finds (about the house) that is not too heavy, tho' not fit for its food (and) sometimes they say it has stolen bits of firebrand or lighted candles and lodged them in stacks of corn and the thatch of barns and houses and set them alight'. In the days before the understanding of spontaneous combustion the Chough would be a present and convenient scapegoat. The bird's scientific name *Pyrrhocorax* from the Greek means simply 'fire-crow'. Let us not forget however that we now recognize the occasional tendency of Rooks and other members of the crow family to pick up lighted cigarette ends, etc. and indulge in smoke bathing.

There are only two mentions of the word 'chough' in all the parish records that I searched. Both are on the Devon coast, certainly former Chough areas, but neither of them rings particularly true. At Branscombe, the unlikely total of ten 'choughs' were paid for in 1846. In the following six years, thirty or forty Jackdaws are listed annually but no further 'choughs' appear. The strong probability is that the 1846 birds were Jackdaws also. Two hundred years earlier at East Budleigh a payment was made 'for choughs 10/-'. There are no similar payments for many years on either side of that date and the veracity of the record remains unproven. Therefore the churchwardens' accounts do not give any help in assessing the extent to which the Chough was persecuted under the provisions of the Tudor Acts in the sixteenth, seventeenth, and eighteenth centuries.

Not until the nineteenth century do we again pick up the threads of dislike for the bird and the campaigning that was carried out against it. We can only surmise, through the gradual disappearance of the bird both inland and coastally, that persecution to unknown degrees across the country had continued in the intervening years.

So, the innocent, crimson-billed Chough was long pilloried as an agricultural anti-agent and a dangerous firebrand. Even up to the end of the twentieth century misunderstanding and prejudice has pursued the bird. A Cardiganshire farmer defending himself in court against a charge of shooting a Chough in the 1970s protested that 'I saw the blood on its bill'. Even the late and famous Welsh poet (and keen birdwatcher) R. S. Thomas said, 'It is not my favourite bird and I dare say they take the odd lamb!'

The Chough was formerly a widespread and fairly numerous bird both inland and coastally in Scotland. Ritchie attested to the extent to which it suffered from the zeal of vermin killers in the nineteenth century. He listed numerous inland areas previously frequented by Choughs and believed that the last inland pair was shot near Crawfordjohn in Lanarkshire in 1834. As Fraser Darling said, 'The Chough faced the blast of 19th-century game preservation. By the middle of the century it had gone from inland districts and was to be found only on the wilder coasts'. It survived longer on the wild western seaboard and was traditionally present on the east coast from Sutherland and Caithness in the north to Berwickshire in the south. However, on this coast it had disappeared by the 1850s. The Old Statistical Account listed it in western parishes such as Kilbrandon and Kilchattan as well as some of the off-shore islands. Ritchie records that it had gone from most of the main Inner Hebridean islands by the 1840s and that the last pair on Arran was shot in 1863. Since those times it has retained a fragile toe-hold on Islay and Colonsay but has been lost from Mull.

In the past two centuries, but particularly the 1800s, the persecution of this species was intensive, although the written record is poor. Not all of the persecution has been with the deliberate intention of killing individuals. Since at least the latter part of the sixteenth century, the Chough paradoxically was a popular pet and thus young birds were collected regularly from the nest for that purpose, certainly up to the passing of the Protection of Birds Act in 1954 and clandestinely since then. In Cornwall in the later decades of the nineteenth century, several dozen a year were being trapped on sites such as Perran Sands, according to Penhallurick. In parallel to that, the Victorian vogue for egg collecting and procuring specimens for mounting in display cases, added to the pressure on individual sites. With a highly sedentary species such as the Chough, strongly faithful to traditional nest sites, local exterminations were inevitable. Illegal egg collecting continued to be rife throughout the last century. In North Wales alone annual depredations at traditional nest sites have been regular up to recent years.

Gin traps (outlawed in 1958 but still used illegally throughout the rest of the century) and other Rabbit traps were a known cause for the deaths of many Choughs. For example, the harvest of Rabbits brought from the Pembrokeshire islands to Swansea market up to the 1920s not infrequently included a batch of Choughs, sold in the market as 'Billy Cocks' and allegedly a favourite with French fisherman.

Owen (1994) identifies the period between 1820 and 1840 as a period of intensive persecution and certainly there is plenty of evidence to support this claim. Bullock et al. suggest that the period 1846–70 was another time of peak losses but indeed throughout the whole of the nineteenth century there was widespread and constant attrition of the diminishing population. An often quoted instance was that of Sir William Jardine who shot thirty in one day on the Isle of Man in 1827—not too difficult an endeavour with a bird that is often as confiding as the Chough. By 1855, Morris lamented that 'a war of extermination has been waged against it and the consequence I need not relate'. A letter in *The Field* in 1871 reinforced the belief that it was a serious agricultural pest, claiming that farmers in Pembrokeshire believed them to be destructive to wheat crops and 'thus a war is waged on them in autumn and winter'. In 1895 or thereabouts, D'Urban and Matthews record the killing of six Choughs with one shot on Braunton Burrows in north Devon by a sportsman wishing to empty his gun before returning home.

Thus has the constant war against the Chough continued. We can only surmise its original numbers and widespread distribution or guess at the numbers that have been needlessly killed over the centuries. We are left with the legacy of that persecution and a fragile population of this engaging bird, now pushed to the western edge of its former range. It was only from the 1950s onwards that the population stabilized and slowly began to increase. In the early years of the twenty-first century, the Chough—Red-billed Chough to give it its full name— is one of the emblematic birds of nature conservation in Britain. Amongst our other native members of the crow family it is unique in its rarity, charisma, popularity, and harmlessness; it is the only one of its clan immune from accusation of impacting, in any form, on Man's interests. Since 1981, it has been especially protected through the Wildlife and Countryside Act and its successor legislation, and the bird is a primary focus for the restoration of its population throughout its residual British range.

Rook

Few birds epitomize the character of rural Britain more than the gregarious and clamorous Rook. It is a denizen of ancient rookeries throughout the land that animate and enliven the heart of innumerable villages, churchyards, woodlands, or the grounds of grand country houses. In so many respects Rooks embody the nature and spirit of the countryside itself. It has given its name to more farms, villages, and hamlets than any other bird. Not of course that they are exclusively rural in their living. In the past there were ancient rookeries established in the centre of several towns and cities— Edinburgh, London (Gray's Inn, etc.), Norwich—although this habit has mainly ended as distance to open-field feeding areas has increased. Cheltenham was one of the last large towns to enjoy a true town-centre rookery until, disgracefully, many of the trees on the Promenade were felled twenty years or so ago following public concerns about the mess of sticks and droppings produced. In fact, Rooks are almost as truly commensal with Man as are House Sparrows; they depend heavily on his systems of agriculture for their living and, increasingly nowadays, scavenge amongst his refuse.

Proximity does not necessarily guarantee neighbourly acceptance, and the Rook has long been seen as an agricultural pest meriting serious control. The substance of this contention, however, has been a matter of continual debate for many decades. On one hand it is indisputable that flocks of feeding Rooks cause economically significant damage on newly sown spring corn, excavating the grains from the ground in the days immediately after planting, up until the time that they sprout, at which point they leave them alone. A traditional country jingle summarizes the way in which the problem was viewed historically:

> Four seeds in a hole,
> One for the rook, one for the crow,
> One to rot and one to grow.

However, sowing patterns have changed markedly nowadays and most cereals are planted in autumn. Feare (pers com) believes that the change to autumn planting, when other food is abundant for the Rooks, has substantially alleviated the problem. However, Rook flocks also cause a nuisance in plundering lodged grain before it is harvested and will sometimes damage root crops—potatoes, swedes, etc. On the other side of the balance sheet, they spend the majority of the year following the plough for exposed invertebrates and probing on pasture-land for earthworms. They also take large numbers of wireworms, cockchafer grubs, and cranefly larvae (leather-jackets) all of which are considerable agricultural pests.

Whatever the pros and cons, Rooks have been the target of persecution for centuries. In Scotland, where the greatest density of Rooks in the country is now to be found, James I was clearly concerned about the numbers in those days. His 1424 legislation aimed at combating the perceived problem with Rooks, and preventing successful nesting or fledging of young. It was strengthened and broadened by the subsequent Act in 1457. As mentioned elsewhere, the uptake of these Acts in the years that followed is in some doubt, with no existing evidence that they were enforced or effective. In England and Wales, Henry VIII's Act of 1532 was aimed specifically at the control of 'choughes', crows, and Rooks through the requirement that 'every Town, Hamlet shall provide and maintain Crow-nets during Ten Years'. The efficacy of such nets to entrap members of a family as notoriously wary as the crows may to doubted, but the intent was clearly there. Other methods of eliminating Rooks were advocated as well. In 1759, Robert Brown advised the following solution to the farmer's problem:

When farmers are pestered with Rooks, as gentlemen keep rookeries for the sake of hearing a continual noise, without the least benefit, and will not destroy them, then the farmer must take of himself, for he may be sure the gentleman will not pay his rent, though the rookery may in great measure have ruined him. Use arsenic boiled with barley grains and spread behind the dung cart that the Rooks daily follow. In this fashion you may destroy a rookery in less than a week at the expense of two shillings.

It is evident from the parish records that Rooks were controlled throughout most parts of the country in the seventeenth and eighteenth centuries although not in great numbers and without any particular emphasis being apparent in the areas of principal corn growing. In many respects the Rook nuisance was at least as worrying, if not more so, in the pastoral counties where small areas of cereal crops were a crucial element of individual smallholders' subsistence economy. Even with the introduction of firearms the numbers killed (or at least those paid for by the churchwardens) were seldom high. One notable exception was Sherborne (Dorset) where some 36,432 birds were killed in 120 years from 1679 to 1799 with maxima of around 100 dozen in some years. Rooks are not particularly easy to shoot and the cost of shot and powder was considerable. However the payment rate was frequently 4*d*./doz which again indicates a reasonable priority, although it is clear that shooting was as frequently deployed for scaring the birds as it was for killing them. In numerous parishes, amounts were paid out regularly for powder and shot, e.g. Collingtree (N'hants) 1696 et seq; Middle Zoy (Som) 1672 'paid for powder for keeping rooks in field' (i.e. scaring); Oakley (Beds) 1793 'paid for the gun 2/6 . . . powder and shot for the crow keeping 12/6'; Naworth (Cumb) 1620 'for killing xv "crows" xv d and powder lx d'.

Killing was not the only way of defending crops and the employment of individuals for 'crow keeping' (*viz* crow-scaring) was universal with many payments across the counties being recorded in the churchwardens' accounts. The use of traditional scarecrows (which surely should be called 'scarerooks'), liberal displaying of dead Rooks, or their wings, and other static deterrents were always virtually useless for keeping any of the corvids off crops. The only efficient methods involved the employment of children, the handicapped, or the aged, to shout and wave, to use wooden clappers, sling shot, or shooting to scare the birds. These tasks were at the very bottom of the scale of rural employment and endured as awful daily drudgery for minimal return. George Edwards, later an MP, described his harsh upbringing in Norfolk in the mid nineteenth century:

I secured my first job in March 1856. It consisted of scaring crows. I was then 6 years of age and was paid 1/- for a seven day week. I had to be up very early in the morning, soon after sunrise and remain in the fields until after sunset. One day being completely worn out I unfortunately fell asleep. Equally unfortunately for me the crows were hungry and they came onto the field and began to pick the corn. Soon after the farmer arrived on the scene and caught me asleep and for this crime at six years of age he gave me a severe thrashing and deducted 2d from my wage.

Figure 18. *Bird Scaring* by George Clusen 1896.
Reproduced by courtesy of Richard Green Galleries.

Rook control certainly did not end with the demise of the churchwardens' payments, but continued actively in the nineteenth and twentieth centuries. Annual 'crow-shoots' were held in most rural areas, well up to the middle decades of the last century with the single aim of reducing Rook numbers. The usual form involved shooting young birds at the rookeries once they were out of the nest but not yet fully fledged ('branchers'). Whilst enhancing the feel-good factor by visibly reducing Rook numbers in the immediate vicinity, the effects on the whole population, even where large kills were achieved, was negligible. Summer is the most difficult time for Rooks. The ground is usually hard and soil-probing for invertebrates is difficult as worms go deeper and the availability of cranefly larvae and other soil invertebrates become scarcer, with the result that a large number of the young birds die of starvation. Killing young at the rookery gives the remaining birds a better chance of survival through the summer and merely eliminates most of those that are destined to die in any case over the following months.

However, there was another aspect to the shooting of young birds which was the active management of rookeries for economic reasons—Hampton Court was a good example. The old adage 'Shoot 'em hard to keep 'em healthy', was clearly in this context and not Rook control. Such management mainly involved protection against poaching which was rife at times, because the sale value of young Rooks was widely recognized. In Aberdeenshire, where large areas of oats, the favoured cereal seed of Rooks, have traditionally been grown, there are some very large rookeries. At Hatton Castle rookery, long recognized as the largest in Britain with 6,679 nests in 1957, as many as 15,000 young were shot in one-off annual harvests with the birds sent south to Leeds and York and finally exported to Italy for Rook pies. At other large rookeries in the county up to 4,000 young were shot annually in the past.

There were also big annual kills in the Edinburgh area; in the Earl of Haddington's woods 76,655 Rooks were shot between 1779 and 1793. Much later Gladstone recorded an organized one-day shoot on 17 estates in Dumfries-shire in 1911 that accounted for 7,949 birds, an average of over 460 per estate. One of the oldest rookeries on record, in Sanquhar parish in the same county, dates back to at least 1640. Despite the high figures of some of these kills, the same order of numbers was invariably breeding the next year. The only true local benefit from this shooting of branchers was the popularity of Rook pie as a rural delicacy certainly up to the years of the Second World War. However, organized Rook shoots on such scales are rare nowadays—challenging the old adage that if you did not shoot the Rooks they would desert the rookery thereby prophesizing death! The loss of millions of Elms through Dutch Elm Disease in the 1970s rearranged the geography of many rookeries in any case.

In addition to their main diet of soil invertebrates, grain, and other seeds, Rooks are also more catholic feeders and will take carrion, swarming caterpillars, small vertebrates, etc. However, they do not ignore the opportunity of taking the eggs of ground-nesting birds, in which context gamekeepers view them with some suspicion, even if not placing them in the same league as Magpies and Carrion/Hooded Crows. Many 'keepers undertake some culling to keep numbers down and Tapper (1992) has shown that the numbers killed in this way on shooting estates in south-east England in recent years total no more than 2–4 per square kilometre, rising to 5–8, and occasionally 12 per square kilometre in the mixed farming areas of the south-west and Scotland. Once again such levels of killing may have a temporary local benefit in reducing predation but have a negligible effect on the breeding population.

The Rook population increased considerably between the 1930s and 1960s, and especially after the 1940s due principally to increased land being brought into cultivation, especially cereals, during the Second World War. After this, there was a fairly rapid decline to a low point by 1975 attributed to the increased use of toxic chemicals in seed-dressings and/or, as O'Connor and Shrubb suggest, the more efficient mechanization of the cereal harvests. The overall decrease was some 36% in Scotland and 45% in England. Even in England, however, the declines were not evenly spread, with the most severe reductions in the cereal growing areas of the south and east (where intensive arable leaves relatively little grassland—the prerequisite feeding habitat) and the smallest losses, in western pastoral areas. The current population of Rooks in Britain is estimated to be in excess of 850,000 pairs.

Carrion/Hooded Crow

Carrion and Hooded Crows were formerly regarded as conspecific, but the more recent taxonomic view is that they are probably separate species. In Britain, the grey and black Hooded Crow is mainly restricted to the western half of Scotland with the Carrion Crow occupying the remainder of the country. There is a wide band of overlap of the two forms, broadly from Galloway northwards through western Scotland to Caithness, in which the birds hybridize freely. The Hooded Crow was at one time a numerous winter visitor, particularly in eastern England although its range in Europe has been squeezed further north and it is now no more than an occasional autumn visitor. Its former status was signified by such alternative names as 'Norway Crow', 'Winter Crow', 'Danishman', or 'Royston Crow'. It was widely recognized in winter, feeding on the ample supply of sheep carrion on the

Chiltern sheepwalks, etc. and the last mentioned local name dates back to at least 1611 reflecting its regularity on places such as Royston Heath (Herts). For simplicity in this historical account the birds are mainly referred to as Carrion Crows.

Despite the entreaties of Henry VIII's Act of 1532 that parishes should equip themselves with crow nets and take all possible steps to reduce all members of the crow family, there is disappointingly little evidence that it resulted in large-scale control. However, it should not be forgotten that there were virtually no records kept in the last half of that century as the bounty payments did not fall within the general church payments until fifty years or so later.

Nevertheless, the old parish records give only a very limited picture of the destruction meted out through bounty payments in the centuries that followed. The only trend that is evident is the concentration in sheep-rearing areas such as Westmorland, Wales, Lincolnshire, and Devon. Even in these areas numbers were almost invariably small and a much greater premium was put on Ravens, for example Wales, Westmorland. In these old accounts there is always the possibility of confusion between Carrion Crows and Rooks. However this is not a significant problem despite the fact that both species are often listed as 'crows' because the numbers quoted are usually (but not infallibly) indicative; Carrion Crows were listed in ones and twos, whereas Rooks were counted in dozens, etc. In addition, the use of colloquial names also helps. In Lincolnshire and other northern areas Carrion Crows were sometimes mentioned as 'flesh crows', 'dalps', or 'dopes' whereas Rooks were either called by that name or more frequently simply 'crows'.

There is little doubt that in the scale of unpopular birds in Britain, the Carrion Crow is high on the list. Although it fulfils a degree of usefulness in helping to dispose of carrion, for example by cleaning up road casualties, it runs head-on into conflict with Man in several fields and some of the charges levelled against it are serious.

First and foremost, apart from being seen as a petty felon in many areas of human contact, it is a traditional and long-standing enemy of the sheep farmer, with an indisputable record as a predator on lambing flocks, particularly in the uplands. In this respect it is seen as an equal partner in crime with the Fox and the Raven. Although the Raven, with which species there has frequently been confusion over the ages, is much larger and more dangerous, Crows are far more numerous and are constant, marauding camp-followers to the upland sheep industry. They are proven lambs killers, notably at the time of birth or very shortly after, and will attack ewes during parturition or when they are cast. For these reasons they are understandably hated, and have been for centuries, although the number of individual lambs and ewes actually killed in this way has been shown to be extremely small. Burgess found in a study in the Lake District that the percentage of ewes killed by crows was no more than 0.02% and lambs 0.04%, while in Argyllshire, Department of Agriculture and Fisheries surveys in the 1960s produced figures of 0.4% and 1%, albeit an order of magnitude greater but still very low. Notwithstanding this, the very fact that such killings take place, frequently in gruesome ways, has been more than enough for sheep farmers to justify the levels of retribution that have been inflicted over the centuries.

The upland sheep farmer is not the Carrion Crow's only adversary because it is the most important avian predator of game birds, and therefore one of the principal enemies for gamekeepers on account of its depredations on the eggs of game birds. In these respects it is again a predator capable of making serious inroads into wild stocks of Partridges, Pheasants, or Red Grouse, and therefore in modern times has been mercilessly persecuted both on moorland estates and on lowland shoots. Bannerman records 200 Red Grouse eggs found in one Carrion Crow egg dump. Similarly, Potts counted over 260 game bird eggs in one Sussex Carrion Crow nest in 2 years. An extension of this problem of egg thieving is the fact that such predation is not of course restricted to game bird clutches. With the severe depletion of many other ground-nesting bird species through habitat change in the twentieth century, crows, together with other corvid species, pose a particular problem to their residual populations and have been shown to put species such as Lapwing and Curlew at risk of elimination in some areas where numbers are already low. Their numbers and their effects on other species are therefore of concern to many nature reserve managers and control is increasingly undertaken for that purpose.

Even in the days of maximum intensity of gamekeeping, from the middle decades of the nineteenth century up to the period of the First World War, it was never possible to eliminate the Carrion Crow or the Hoodie completely. Nonetheless, intensive control undoubtedly had a severe impact on their numbers, notably in areas such as East Anglia and on the grouse moors of northern England and Scotland. Today the best-managed Red Grouse moors are kept clear of crows throughout the year. In Scotland, Hudson showed that there was an increase in the number of crows killed on Scottish moors, certainly in the southern and eastern counties, which began before the last war, but which he linked in a substantial part to the post-war increase in forestry planting in the uplands. One of the limiting factors controlling crow numbers in the uplands is the availability of tree-nesting sites, which the new forests rapidly provided. Hudson exemplified the effect of crows on grouse numbers by quoting one estate where crow control at a high level was undertaken in 1981 and grouse bags rose rapidly; when management changed and crow control was reduced in 1987 the grouse numbers fell. On a neighbouring estate in the same year crow control started and grouse numbers there increased accordingly.

In Scotland, the Act of 1457 directed that 'Crawys should be destroyed and prevented from building in orchards and kirkyards'. The implementation of this requirement is not known but once the sheep flocks colonized the country and game preservation became a vogue, Carrion and Hooded Crows were targeted intensively, as shown in the following extracts from Scottish estates.

TABLE 14. Numbers of crows killed on Scottish estates in periods of C18 and C20.

Five Deeside Parishes	1776–86	1347*
Langwell/Sandside	1819–26	4609**
Buccleuch estates	1829–31	863
Sutherland	1831–4	1739
Glengarry	1837–40	1431
Ardnamurchan	1872–87	2111
Ardfin, Jura	1877–87	600
Breadalbane	1891–1901	4459
Buccleuch estates	1894–1900	7596
Atholl	1894–1904	4009

* includes Ravens (numbers not separated). ** crows + other corvids.

Despite the levels of slaughter in these rural areas it is worth noting that Ritchie made it clear, through various references, that in urban areas the Carrion Crow was protected alongside the Raven and Red Kite for its contribution as a scavenger of the endless refuse and filth that characterized many sixteenth and seventeenth century urban centres.

In England, considerable reductions in Carrion Crow numbers were achieved in the nineteenth century. There were certainly attempts made to exterminate it completely in many game rearing areas and there was a marked suppression of numbers between c.1860 and the early decades of the twentieth century, across the heyday of the 'keepered shooting estates. In the hill sheep-rearing areas of the north and west, crow control has always been a tradition around lambing time and still continues. Intensive control may have a temporary effect but the numbers of Carrion Crows in areas such as mid Wales—where non-breeding flocks of over 100 are frequent—are so high that replacements are constantly available and the removal of breeding pairs immediately opens more areas for the flocks of non-breeders. The numbers killed nowadays in any locality are insignificant in the context of the overall population. The British Trust for Ornithology (BTO) enquiry into breeding numbers in Britain carried out by Prestt between 1953–63, showed that the only region where no increase was evident was East Anglia—the region of most sustained game preservation.

Jackdaw

The Jackdaw is recognized as a regular and proficient egg thief and also a predator on nestling birds when it has the opportunity. However, it was not for these reasons that it found itself on the Tudor vermin list together with every other British member of the corvid family. Rather it earned that dubious distinction as part of the campaign against all the crows initiated under Henry VIII's Act of 1532 in an attempt to mitigate the damage that corvids allegedly caused to grain crops. As a secondary reason they also took—and still do—ripe fruit, especially cherries which were an important crop in those days. It must be remembered that Henry's Act referred to the birds as 'choughs', which name at that time, as explained earlier, applied to both Jackdaw and Chough. Jackdaws can sometimes be a serious nuisance in other respects as instanced in 1607 when a Parliamentary Bill was actually thrown out in the Commons when the debate was abandoned after a group of noisy Jackdaws had invaded the chamber of the House!

Among the relatively few surviving sixteenth-century churchwardens' accounts, the Jackdaw (under whatever name) occurs on more occasions than many other regular species of 'vermin'. However, this was frequently for reasons totally unrelated to predation on agricultural crops, but to its other troublesome habit of nesting in buildings. Most of the early records, and many of the later ones, refer specifically to problems of Jackdaws in churches and the steps taken to remedy them, by shooting, nest pulling, and 'clearing'. This was the case at Worksop (Notts) as early as 1555 and at Bishop's Stortford (Herts) in 1569, Ludlow (Salop) the same year, Prestbury (Ches) in 1572—'for keeping choughs out of the church iiij viiij' (i.e. four shillings and nine pence)—and Cratfield (Suffolk) 1580 among others.

Similar records extend into the following two centuries with frequent references to the purchase of powder and shot specifically to remove 'daws' from the church or the belfry. At Mere (Wilts) the lordly sum of 10/- was paid in 1695 'to keep them out of the belfry where they were felting the bells' (a lovely use of the word 'felt' as the verb to describe their droppings encrusting the bells!). In the same county the numbers killed annually in Stockton parish, up to

14 dozen p.a., give the impression that these may indeed have been controlled for agricultural reasons and, if so, is a fairly infrequent example.

The only English county that stands out from the rest, in terms of the number of parishes that undertook Jackdaw control, is Norfolk, the county where another alternative name, 'cadow', originated which can be traced back as far as 1440. Considerable numbers were killed in parishes such as Garboldisham, Elsing, East Dereham, Sparham, and North Elmham. Some of these instances were certainly church problems but it seems likely that others may well have been agriculturally driven. Addlethorpe (Lincs), where between 2½ and 4 dozen were killed annually over four decades across the end of the eighteenth century, probably comes into the same category.

It is as a resourceful egg thief that modern gamekeepers see the Jackdaw. However, it is not regarded nearly as seriously as the Carrion and Hooded Crow and not all game estates take a serious toll of them. Tapper has shown that the numbers killed for that reason have declined sharply since the 1960s. Historically, fairly heavy numbers were occasionally killed on some estates, although in Scotland this applied in very few cases. At Burley (Rutland) 1,798 were killed in 10 years from 1807 to 1816 and 1,799 (includes Rooks) in 8 years on the Sutherland estates early in the same century. Two of the principal Norfolk shooting estates, Sandringham and Holkham, took considerable numbers in the last century; Sandringham 3,403 between 1938 and 1950 and Holkham 5,501 from 1953 to 1959.

Raven

From time immemorial, the Raven was a bird always considered to be endowed with supernatural powers, frequently associated with disease, disaster, or death. Thus it has long been viewed with suspicion, respect, and sometimes awe, but the association with doom was undoubtedly one of the reasons why it was persecuted in lowland Britain through the centuries, without any written record of its disappearance being left. In modern times its cultural connections are largely forgotten, since it is no longer associated with death, battlefield corpses, gallows, etc.

Formerly a close associate of Man and his habitations, it was in the Middle Ages that the Raven reached the zenith of it status, at least in urban areas, where its presence was greatly valued for the contribution it made in devouring the refuse and filth which characterized the unhygienic conditions of the time. For this purpose it was, like the Kite, protected by Royal Decree, with penalties awaiting any person found guilty of killing it. This position prevailed in London in the decades after 1500 although the precise date—some time in the seventeenth century—when protection lapsed is not recorded. At this stage, public perceptions reversed, and persecution was encouraged and Elizabeth's Act of 1566 established bounties for killing Ravens.

Formerly the Raven was widely distributed throughout Britain, in uplands and lowlands alike. In the wider countryside it justified a reputation as a killer of newborn lambs, poultry, rabbits, and other game and was always despised for those reasons. Time did little to soften the attitude towards the Raven, certainly among sheep farmers and shepherds. Forrest in 1907 stressed that the Raven was 'cordially detested by Welsh farmers' (although attitudes have become more tolerant in recent decades). Ridpath, in a report to the Ministry of Agriculture, Fisheries and Food in 1953, exemplified the reasons why sheep farmers in the hills so loathed the Raven. He spent many hours watching flocks during lambing time on the hills of Pembrokeshire and observed several instances of interaction. He described how the attacks by Ravens on newborn lambs concentrated on the lips, eyes, umbilical cord, and anus, often persisting despite the frantic attempts made by the ewe to protect her offspring.

Although the written records of the persecution of Ravens in England and Wales only begin after the commencement of bounty payments made by the parishes in the late sixteenth century, it is certain that the birds had been targeted in rural areas well before then. The 1566 Act, which offered bounties of 1*d*. per head, marked the start of a more intensive phase of killing at least in some parts of the country. It is clear from the records outlined below that this continued for centuries, up to the introduction of legal protection in 1954 (although this was later amended to allow killing in Argyll and subsequently also Skye—both amendments finally reversed in 1981). The absence of records of bounty payments from most of the lowland counties of England indicates either a lack of interest in controlling the bird, or, more likely, that by then they were scarce in any case. It is relevant to remember that the Raven is primarily a carrion eater and that the improvement of the streets and general sanitation of London was one of the factors causing its decline there. In the countryside the same useful function was undoubtedly appreciated, notwithstanding any accusations of predation on poultry, etc. Shrubb has shown how severely sheep farming in the eighteenth century was plagued by 'rot' (almost certainly liver fluke) which frequently caused huge losses and produced abundant carrion. Ravens were amongst the most important scavengers of such carcasses and the improved land drainage and animal husbandry that accompanied the enclosure of wastes and commons (the incubation grounds of 'rot') drastically reduced the previously bountiful food supply. This factor may also have contributed to the low number of Raven payments in many of the lowland counties.

The evidence of the parish records in England and Wales gives a clear picture of the intensity and geographical distribution of the killing of Ravens. To start with, no records have been traced in the majority (seventeen) of lowland English counties. Only in Sussex, Somerset, Nottinghamshire, Lincolnshire, and Cambridgeshire are even occasional records to be found and these total a mere twenty-three birds in six individual parishes. Despite this absence of records of killing through the parish system, there was other evidence that it was being undertaken. Robert Smith in his *Universal Directory for Destroying Rats and other Kinds of Fourfooted and Winged Vermin* in 1768 claimed that he was paid as much for Ravens as he was for Kites and boasted that he could catch large numbers in a day because it was easy to attract them to the calls of a distressed bird.

One anomalous record was found in the low-ground parish was Alrewas in Staffordshire where 110 Ravens were killed from 1702 to 1734. Devon and Cornwall, two counties which had very high kills for most other vermin species, strangely had only one parish each that showed any records of Raven; Abbotsham in Devon with sixteen birds in 1768–9 and Llanreath (C'wall), twenty-three birds between 1683 and 1688. It is tempting to postulate that the paucity of records in Cornwall in particular may have been related to the powerful superstition attached to the killing of a Raven. After all, according to legend, King Arthur would return in the guise of a Raven and it was taboo to kill the bird in the county. Such superstitions lingered a long time in some areas and Ratcliffe records how, as recently as the 1920s, one assiduous gamekeeper in Dumfriesshire would kill Peregrines and Hen Harriers whenever he could, but would never harm a Raven.

Kent was one other exception to the picture of low levels of killing in lowland England. Although only three parishes there killed Ravens, and two of them (Charing and High Halden) had only token numbers, the third parish, Tenterden, shows us a completely different picture. Here four were paid for in each year 1642, 1668, and 1669, but then a total of 208 was amassed from 1681 to 1693, and nothing thereafter. The largest number was taken in 1688, when fifty-three heads were submitted for payment. This shows that there must still have been significant populations of Ravens in at least one lowland county by the end of the seventeenth century. If there is this evidence of Ravens in one well-wooded parish, it is not unreasonable to assume that they were also present in wooded counties such as Sussex, Hampshire, or counties of the Marches, despite the absence of bounty payments records.

It is to the upland counties of the north and west that we must turn once again—the final retreat of so many of the species on the old vermin lists—to find high levels of persecution. In Wales, the records show that Ravens were heavily targeted in almost all counties. Defynnog (Brec) was still paying for Ravens' heads well into the nineteenth century (1826) with an annual total reaching fifty-nine in an exceptional year. Up to 4*d*. per head was paid in Caernarvonshire (464 were taken on the Penrhyn estate in 28 years up to 1902), the same amount as in Montgomeryshire where several parishes on the slopes of the Berwyn Mountains killed large numbers consistently in the eighteenth century; at Llangynog payments occasionally rose to 10*d*. per adult. In Merioneth annual control was regular in many parishes. At Llanfiangell-y-Traethau, where killing of any vermin was sporadic, the sums paid for a scatter of Ravens bordered on the ridiculous compared with payments elsewhere, with 1/- or 1/3 per head paid on several occasions. The level of killing reached impressive proportions at Llanfor parish, in the hills above Llyn Tegid (Bala Lake), where 1656 Ravens at 4*d*. per head were killed between 1720 and 1758. Killing at this rate occurred annually, apparently without any reduction in the totals. Many of these birds were shot, but there were also innumerable payments for groups of four, which doubtless represented broods of youngsters harvested regularly from traditional nest sites.

In northern England annual control was undertaken in many of the Lake District parishes. The levels of killing were clearly very high. Several of the huge, contiguous parishes at the heart of the Lake District—St Bees, Crossthwaite, Greystoke—together with other adjacent ones—Kendal, Barton, Bampton, Kirby Lonsdale—were responsible for killing over 5,000 Ravens in a succession of eighteenth-century years. In the nearby parish of Dent (then in Yorks) *c*.1,000 were also killed in the same period with as many as 62 being taken in one year. It is evident from the records existing from the previous century, that similar levels were being achieved then, and this 'heavy control certainly continued into the nineteenth century'. Although the Crossthwaite churchwardens' record is lost after 1788, as late as 1819 the vestry there still 'Agreed that any person destroying an old Raven shall receive 1/- and for a young one 6d'. Several Derbyshire parishes took a fairly heavy annual toll on Ravens but none could compete with Wirksworth where, in 18 successive years from 1707 the remarkable total of 1,775 individuals were taken, an average of almost 100 per year. Even in a parish of 8,210 acres (3,322 hectares) it is difficult to understand how the population could withstand this sort of predation and apparently maintain its numbers each year. In the final year for which records exist they were still able to kill 161 birds. Strangely, there is no evidence of Raven payments in Northumberland parishes, but there were several from Durham although numbers there were very modest, and never reached double figures in annual totals. In Lancashire the upland parish of Slaidburn in the Forest of Bowland was responsible for 130 Ravens between 1681 and 1728.

Persecution of the Raven in England and Wales did not stop with the withdrawal of parish payments in the early decades of the nineteenth century. On the contrary the pressure increased as the vogue for game preservation developed and gamekeepers on both lowland estates and grouse moors intensified their efforts to reduce or remove all those species which were deemed to compete with their primary concern—the raising of maximum numbers of game birds. Tantalizingly, we do not know what the status of the Raven was across different parts of the country when the slaughter really accelerated in the mid nineteenth century, although we know that it was widespread. Nor do we have records (unlike Scotland) for the numbers that were killed in different areas. The picture in East Anglia, the most intensive game preservation area in the country, gives some indication of what may have happened in other areas. The species was tolerably common in Norfolk and Suffolk until around 1830, according to Murton (1971), but declined markedly thereafter, coincident with the rise in intensive 'keepering. If the date Murton quoted is correct, the impact of the gamekeepers was very rapid since the avifaunas for both counties suggest that the Raven was extinct by 1840. However, the other factor that might have a bearing on that was the rapid expansion of enclosure systems. The main enclosures in the two counties occurred between 1800 and the middle of the century, and resulted in the conversion of very large areas of common to the widespread cultivation of grain crops, especially in the western areas of East Anglia. Such a change in agriculture, with the loss of sheep carrion, would have greatly disadvantaged Ravens.

There is little doubt, as expressed in many county avifaunas around the turn of the nineteenth century and shortly thereafter that the primary blame for the Raven's demise in lowland Britain was placed squarely at the doors of the game estates. Whatever the validity of the claim, the Raven was exterminated from counties west to the Marches and north to Lincolnshire and most of Yorkshire by 1870 and in many instances well before that. Ratcliffe described its retreat to the hills of the west 'under the almost universal and incessant persecution, especially by shepherds and gamekeepers'.

The position in Scotland was little different from that which prevailed in England, although the impact on the population began at a later time in Scotland. Baxter and Rintoul and the Old Statistical Account (from which much of their earlier information was gleaned) testify to the abundance and wide distribution of the Raven. At the same time, the Old Statistical Account alludes frequently to the fact that it was regarded as an enemy to the sheep farmer and to the developing game interests, quoting several parishes where bounties were given for its destruction. However, there are virtually no figures for that period to show what the level of persecution might have been. The overall picture at that time (the end of the eighteenth century) is of a bird that was deeply unpopular in rural areas but not yet under severe pressure. Only on an examination of the parish accounts in the New Statistical Account forty years later, is the effect of the sudden onslaught against Ravens revealed. Many of the parish accounts refer to the fact that numbers were reduced from their former levels. The increased attention that was then paid to the Raven as a result of the escalation of game interests is evident from the figures available from some estates in the first half of the nineteenth century. Table 15 shows the numbers of Ravens that were killed in a small sample of years in that period, together with one record from late in the previous century.

TABLE 15. Numbers of Ravens killed on some Scottish estates in brief periods in C18 and C19.

Crathie, Braemar, Glenmuich, Tulloch, and Glengarden parishes: Deeside	1776–87	1,347
Buccleuch estates	1819–27	69
Langwell and Sandside	1819–26	1,962
Sutherland estate	1831–4	936*
Glengarry	1837–40	475
Glenquoich (part of Glengarry)	1843–62	293

* 2/- per head

Harvie-Brown's survey of vermin kills from his analysis of returns from game-keepers in northern Scotland in 1902, throws light on the situation in the last decade or two of the previous century. It is interesting to compare the Raven totals on those returns (p. 77) with these in the table above. It is safe to presume that gamekeepers were still as interested in reducing Ravens as they had been earlier, although in most instances the totals at the end of the century had become noticeably smaller. The onslaught earlier in the century had clearly made deep inroads into the numbers. One extraordinary exception in Harvie-Brown's papers was from Lewis where the return for the 16 years 1887–1902 claimed 2,248 birds, with a maximum of 180 in one year.

Starling

In the fairly generous interpretation of what species constituted
vermin under the 1566 Act, it
was unlikely that the Starling
would avoid inclusion 'for every
12 stares heads 1d'. What is particularly interesting, as Feare has
pointed out, is that the Starling was
not at all a common bird in Britain
between the fifteenth and eighteenth
centuries. He illustrates this by his observation that classical authors such as Shakespeare,
Wordsworth, and Tennyson, all of whom made repeated references to familiar
wild birds, made scant reference to Starlings. Similarly Macgillivray in 1840
wrote of it as 'generally distributed but local'. So the question that must be asked
is why the bird was singled out for destruction on the list of vermin. The bird's
predilection for soft fruit, especially cherries, is the most likely reason. Fruits
of many kinds were important crops from medieval times onwards, grown either
in orchards or as hedgerow trees. A secondary reason may well have been
their nuisance value in churches and other buildings. 'Vermin' such as owls,
bats, pigeons, Jackdaws, and Starlings received regular attention in numerous
churches.

Whatever the reasons, it is clear that the problems with Starlings did not
greatly interest people in the parishes across those centuries. The payment of
bounties for Starlings is very rare in the hundreds of records that I examined
across England and Wales. In fact, only seven instances were found and almost
certainly, with one possible exception, they refer to the removal of Starlings from
the parish church. At Lyddington (Rut) in 1718–22 several payments of 6d. or
7d. were made 'for shooting Starlings in the church', powder and shot for
the same and other references to 'killing birds in the church'. Similar entries
involving the church apply at Bedale (Yorks), 'catching sternals', Buckden
(Hunts), and by implication Sherborne (Dorset) and Crewkerne and Shepton
Mallet (Som). The possible exception is Monks Kirby (Warks) where annual
payments were made between 1685 and 1688, in one year being as high as 5/-
which, at the rate of 1d. per dozen—if it still applied—would represent 60 dozen
birds, an impossible number to be found in a church.

From about 1830, Starling numbers increased considerably in Great Britain and its range extended to include the counties of the western seaboard from which they had previously been absent. These increases were almost certainly partly due to amelioration of the climate in western Europe, and partly as a result of agricultural changes. In particular, as shown by Shrubb, there was a greatly increased fertility of soils, especially on grassland in England and Wales. Starlings are first and foremost feeders on short grassland, taking large numbers of leather-jackets, earthworms, and other soil invertebrates. Baxter and Rintoul recorded that the expansion reached Scotland by the end of the nineteenth century and was complete by the middle of the twentieth. However, the birds were common in the northern isles and Hebrides in the eighteenth century, where Boswell shot and ate several, declaring them to be delicious. Smout attributes the increase in lowland Scotland, at least in part, to the improved fertility of topsoil and the rejuvenation of its invertebrate fauna through the deeper ploughing that became possible from the late nineteenth century.

As the numbers of Starlings increased in these later centuries they became recognized more and more as a pest species and were subject to increased control. Feare has shown that Starlings can cause serious damage on cherry crops and that such attacks are very difficult to combat. The acreage of cherries fell from 7,000 to 2,400 hectares during the twentieth century and bird damage was one of the contributory factors. In a wider agricultural context flocks will systematically dig up and eat the seed of germinating cereal crops, notably wheat, and descend in hordes at stock-feeding sites. The vast winter roosting flocks that still occur in some conifer plantation sites can actually kill the trees with the sheer volume and acidity of droppings accumulating over the years. Over a hundred years ago, Knapp described how the whirling dusk flocks attracted local slaughter, 'the thickness of the flights and the possibility of killing numbers encourages attention. Every village popper notices these flocks and fires into the poor Starlings'. Nowadays, away from farmland, over half the breeding population (currently put at some 8½ million birds) is to be found in urban and suburban areas. The most serious charge against these urban birds is the fouling of public areas and the corrosion of stonework caused by the accumulated droppings of flocks roosting on ledges and parapets. For these reasons Starlings have been increasingly subject to control in the past hundred years.

In an important investigation into the cause of decline in Starling numbers, the DEFRA report (Crick et al.) in 2002 concluded that the British population had declined by some 66% on farmland since 1965, a decrease partly attributed to the conversion of much pasture to arable (e.g. up to 36% in Lincolnshire according to Feare). This reduction has in itself had a beneficial effect in ameliorating the scale of problems with Starlings on farmland. However, they have been continuously subject to control for the reasons given above and the

DEFRA report gives an estimate of *c*.74,000 being killed annually by farmers and local authorities over the decade prior to the 2002 report. This represents no more than 0.8% of the breeding numbers and is of negligible significance to the national population.

As a tailpiece, it is interesting to note that Starlings were harvested in the past for human food and that the origins of the use of nesting pots for that purpose go back at least to the mid seventeenth century. Meiklejohn refers to Olina's *Uccelliera* (1682 edition) which gives a detailed description of specially made earthenware pots hung on walls to attract nesting Starlings; Breugel's picture (Dulle Griet) includes an image of Starlings using such pots (cf. House Sparrow).

House Sparrow

Still the most familiar species of wildlife for urban people—even if it lacks the cachet of other popular birds such as the Robin—the House Sparrow enjoys a special place in the British psyche. Street urchin, scrounger, and uninvited lodger it might be but there is no disputing its enormous success as it shares most aspects of its life with Man in both town and countryside. Its adjectival name betrays this association. Indeed it is difficult to visualize the species as a wholly independent wild bird, disassociated from Man. However, notwithstanding this, Man's relationship with the House Sparrow has traditionally been a schizophrenic one. On one hand it is welcomed as a constant companion around our dwellings and has even been transported by emigrants to the farthest corners of the old empire to foster memories of home. Simultaneously, it has been castigated as a pest and killed in almost unbelievable numbers over the past 400 years. In some counties it has been killed by the million.

The date of its arrival in Britain is not known, although it is believed to be a relatively recent colonist. Summers-Smith (1963) suggests that its westward spread across Europe probably meant that it was well established here by the time of the Roman occupation. Certainly there are legends involving it as far back as the Dark Ages. For example, in the eighth century those besieging the town of Cirencester allegedly used sparrows with lighted brands attached in an attempt to fire the town—thereafter for long known as Sparrowcester! In Britain it spread and increased over the past thousand years or so as agriculture developed and human settlements provided infinite opportunities for nesting. Writing in 1794, Turner stressed that the numbers had increased dramatically in the second half of the eighteenth century—a fact reflected by both Summers-Smith and Harrison. It is significant that this species—killed across the years in vastly greater numbers than all other vermin put together—is not specifically listed in the Tudor Acts, although there by implication. Its numbers in the sixteenth century were obviously not then of sufficient magnitude for it to be seen as a serious pest. It is a graminivorous species and its success evolved in parallel with the conversion of uncultivated land into intensive mixed farming systems, which process accelerated in the eighteenth and nineteenth centuries.

By the eighteenth century, the burgeoning populations of House Sparrows were recognized as serious pests on crops of ripening corn and at the same time were perceived as a domestic nuisance, particularly in their habit of burrowing into the thatched roofs of cottages to find nesting sites. Thus began an escalating war of attrition against the species that continued in different forms until recent decades. The irony is that however great the levels of annual killing, the impact on the population was inevitably negligible. As the record of bounty payments shows, however many were removed, the same numbers were there to be killed the next year: good for local income but futile in terms of reducing the population! There are innumerable examples of this: at Nonington (Kent) annual control began in 1706, but 131 years later they were still able to kill 211 dozen sparrows in the year; Braunston (N'hants) churchwardens began payments in 1672 and in 1787 were still paying for 258 dozen; the account at Easton (Hants) is missing after 1787, by which year they were still accounting for 180 dozen birds after at least 72 years of effort.

The fundamental reason for this fact is that most of the killing, notably at harvest time in late summer, involved huge numbers of young birds of the year that would, in any case, be subject to natural mortality in subsequent months. The months in which bounty payments were made is not usually recorded in the annual accounts of the churchwardens, but whenever they are, there is clear evidence of a very heavy bias towards the taking of young birds in the late summer when numbers were artificially high. The only significant impact on a population such as this would be made if the birds were controlled in springtime, when the population is at its lowest, so that the breeding pairs were the ones that were then targeted.

Although the large-scale slaughter of House Sparrows has long been recognized, this is the first time there has been an analysis of the country-wide distribution of the killing. It also gives a clear view of just how heavy and persistent the effort was in different areas. It has always been understood that the main areas of killing were in the corn growing regions of the south and east, but it still comes as a surprise to find that the area of most intensive killing was actually the Isle of Wight (see Table 16). The island was an important corn growing area and extensive programmes of control were initiated parish by parish, mainly in the latter half of the eighteenth century (broadly consistent with other parts of the country) and almost unbelievable numbers were killed each year up to the early decades of the 1800s. As an example, in the little parish of Freshwater (4,760 acres (1,926 hectares)) at the western end of the island, where systematic control on a substantial scale began in 1731, they were killing sparrows consistently at between 8,500 and 12,400 individuals annually, for 84 years. Brightstone, on the south coast of the island (only 2,700 acres (1,092 hectares)) killed far more in proportion to its size. Many other parishes on the island produced similar totals. In the last decade of the eighteenth century alone, more than 275,000 birds were killed on the island.

TABLE 16. Examples of high level killing of House Sparrow in nine English parishes in C18 and C19.

County	Parish	Span of years*	Years	Numbers killed
Isle of Wight	Godshill	1791–1821	33	c.14,890 dozen
	Brading	1769–1821	51	c.16,220 dozen
	Freshwater	1731–1820	84	c.16,340 dozen
	Arreton	1775–1830	55	c.17,050 dozen
	Brightstone	1758–1835	70	c.35,670 dozen
Bedfordshire	Eaton Socon	1819–1842	23	c.20,000 dozen
	Houghton Regis	1719–1836	117	c.16,650 dozen
Oxfordshire	Eynsham	1773–1836	59	c.21,360 dozen
Cheshire	Tarporley	1757–1811	55	c.10,850 dozen

* The span of years across which killing of House Sparrows is recorded.

In all the counties south-east of a line from the Humber to Exeter, House Sparrows were killed in enormous numbers, even if not quite on the scale of the Isle of Wight. Bedfordshire, Kent, Berkshire, and Suffolk were foremost in this respect with particularly high figures and the greatest numbers of participating parishes. The one exception to this catalogue of counties is Essex where, strangely, Sparrow control was negligible. Nationally, the vast bulk of killing took place in the eighteenth and early nineteenth centuries, although there is a record for the payments of bounties for Sparrows starting as early as 1613 at Cheddar in Somerset, with other early ones at Great Wigston and Wigston Magna (Leics) in 1620 and 1629 respectively. The going rate in these early years was 1*d*. per dozen rising irregularly throughout the country to 2*d*., and later to 4*d*. and eventually to 6*d*., by the nineteenth century. Rates often differed for old birds and juveniles and also for eggs that were collected in many parishes in multitudes. In many parishes (e.g. Clifton Reynes, Bucks) the local Sparrow catcher's name occurs annually, sometimes over a long period of years, in respect of substantial payments, but sparrow killing also provided an income, on a smaller scale for generations of village boys.

As usual it was invariably the vestry that determined the payment rate for sparrows. As late as 13 April 1857, the vestry committee at Great Easton, one of the few parishes in Essex where Sparrow control took place, recorded that 'at a meeting held this day it was agreed that every occupier shall kill 1 sparrow and 2 other birds to the acre or forfeit one ½ penny each'. This modest target was rapidly increased to two Sparrows per acre the following year. In the centuries before this, the vestry minutes all over the country regularly recorded the decisions agreed as to what species should be targeted, and at what rates.

The methods by which such numbers could be caught is open to speculation. However, a thoroughly commensal bird as this was not difficult to take at the nest (especially eggs and unfledged young), on limed twigs, in baited drop traps, baited hair nooses, riddle traps, by netting at the roosts in ivy-covered walls, etc. at night, or occasionally by using poisons (Swainswick, Somerset, 1778). Roost-netting techniques usually involved variants of 'bat-fowling' (the word 'bat' in this context referring to the use of a stick or bat to scare the birds out of their roost). Large nets suspended between two poles were held against the roost site and the birds were dislodged by the batman. They would fly into the folds of the net, often attracted by a lantern light and dropping into a cod-end (e.g. Loose parish, Kent 1811 'pd to Clim Elliot and co for sparrows caught by bat folding 11/1½d'). Willughby, in his ornithology of 1678, gives us a delightful description of the bat-fowling equipment and the technique:

A Bat-fowling net.

This net is to be used late in the evening, or early in the morning, by setting it against the Eves of thatcht Houses, Stacks, Hovels, Barns, Stables, Dove-coats etc and being so set knocking and thrusting the cross staves close against the same, making such a noise as may inforce the Birds to fly out of their holes or haunts into the net and then presently so shutting up the cross staves, enclose them and letting down your net, open it and take them out.

Another popular method involved a type of clap net which was set on a site and regularly baited with corn. Weston Zoyland (Som) is one parish where there are several entries in the 1800s for the purchase of corn for this purpose: '¼; of wheat for sparrows'. In this parish, Sam Pitman was the designated sparrow catcher through the first three decades of the nineteenth century, earning himself substantial sums annually. At South Elmham (Suffolk) there was expenditure 'for a bushel of oats . . . 1/9d'. Furthermore, an enigmatic entry in 1756 refers to the same process 'for catching of sparrows according to custom of neighbouring parishes by virtue of old acts of parliament by which netting on shraping for them for 7 dozen before they refused, paying at 3d per dozen . . . 1/9d'. Without doubt small birds of other species, Tree Sparrows, finches, etc. were sometimes taken in the nets as by-catch, but the extent to which this occurred will never be known, but it would have been unlikely to affect the estimates of the overall numbers of House Sparrows caught. There are many references through the parish records for the purchase of nets, sometimes stipulating where they are kept and the maximum period for which an individual might take them out. Such nets were not only used for Sparrows but also for other species, notably members of the crow family.

In the nineteenth and early twentieth centuries both this method and bat-fowling were regularly used to obtain birds for the popular practice of trap shooting, until the sport was banned by Parliamentary Act in 1921. Henry Warren gives a colourful account of watching the practice in his boyhood at Mereworth in Kent, in the early years of the twentieth century:

The village sparrow club was to hold a shoot at the Black Lion. Several times before the event which was to take place on Easter Monday, I had seen men going into the little lean-to tap-room carrying wicker baskets that were full of twittering, helpless birds. . . . Some of the trapped sparrows were on the floor, massed round the food that had been scattered for them, pecking and fighting; others flew in frenzied circles round the walls and under the low beamed roof; while yet others dashed themselves against the wired windows in an endeavour to get loose. I found the sight thrilling and at the same time a little frightening. . . . When Monday came . . . I hurried off to the field and found the men already gathered there in eager groups, passing round the beer and excitedly discussing the chances of the various club members. . . . Guns were cracked open. . . . Everybody stood ready for the match. The birds were loosed into the air and I watched the men take careful aim, holding my breath in anticipation of every explosion. Unable to control my excitement I jumped about in glee. This was manly sport indeed. . . . The second half of the match began. I moved as close to the guns as I dared, anxious to miss nothing and getting bolder now. Suddenly I noticed the sparrows that lay on the grass near my feet. Crumpled and grotesque and pitiable, the dead birds littered the ground, some with the down of their breasts ruffled and blown away, others with their small, thin legs pointing foolishly in the air. A wave of discomfort flooded my heart.

It has always been claimed that the idea of fixing Sparrow pots to the walls of houses had been introduced from the Low Countries in the seventeenth century. In fact as Barnard has shown they were deployed in some places at least a hundred years or so earlier than that. At Ingatestone Hall in Essex, Lord Petrie paid for '24 pottes for sparoweis to breed in' from Stoke-on-Trent potteries as early as 1549. These earthenware pots, some 18cm × 15cm, with a narrower neck, were hung with the open base against the wall and the neck facing outward as the entrance for the birds nesting within. The hollow base, affectionately alluded to as the 'robbery hole', enabled the nest contents to be removed at will. These artificial nest sites were found mainly in various parts of the south and south-east of England and were certainly still in operation in some localities, for example the Watford area, into the early years of the twentieth century. Their purposes were doubtless multifunctional. They certainly enabled villagers to take easy pickings of both eggs and young in order to claim head-money on them; after all the pairs would regularly produce two or three broods a year. But there were also other reasons that made them worthwhile. In the Fenland, and else-where, it is suggested that farmers and cottagers put up the pots to help to dissuade the birds from nesting in the thatches. They were also important in providing a readily accessible source of meat. The young birds, skinned and cooked, were a welcome addition to frugal diets and in some areas were regarded as a considerable delicacy. Until the time of the Great War Sparrow pie was a regular item in many rural areas.

In the late nineteenth century, national paranoia about the bird was undiminished. In 1885, the rising mood was demonstrated by the demand from the Consulting Entomologist to the Royal Agricultural Society—the formidable Mrs Eleanor Ormerod—for a campaign aimed at the total extermination of the House Sparrow; amongst the scientific fraternity she was not alone in that demand. Passions about the bird continued to run high.

As the payments by churchwardens tailed off, the campaign against the House Sparrow continued apace through the formation of locally organized Sparrow Clubs, or Rat and Sparrow Clubs. Guided and encouraged by an advisory leaflet produced by the Board of Agriculture in 1908, many parishes, mainly in the corn growing counties of south-east England, initiated these clubs and they became an integral part of village life. Some clubs had already been operating long before this date; Rudgwick (W Sussex) Sparrow Club members celebrated their annual dinner in 1865 rejoicing in the harvest of 5,313 sparrows' heads that year and awarded first prize to Mr Wooberry for his haul of 1,363 birds. Around the same time the Wirral Farmers Club (Ches) is said to have paid 4½d. per dozen for 10,000 birds annually and the Epping Club (Essex) claimed to have killed 6,000 Sparrows in the first 4 months after its establishment in 1891. Notwithstanding these and many similar figures, the clubs did not restrict them-selves to Sparrows. Members would pay a small annual subscription and be responsible for a defined number of birds, or pay a 'fine' on failure to reach their target. Some clubs also ran a points scheme, determining scores for different species killed. For example the Vines Cross (E Sussex 1925–6) points-list was hawk 6, Stoat 6, Weasel 4, Jay and Magpie 3, Rat, Mole, queen Wasp 2, Sparrow and mouse 1. Other parishes produced similar lists of costed vermin. Appledore in Kent stated that 'the object of the club is to decrease the number of Sparrows, Green Linnets, Bullfinches, Blackbirds, Chaffinches, Jays, Magpies, Rooks and Crows and as far as possible exterminate Rats, Stoats, Moles and Hedgehogs'. They set out a campaign that would have done credit to the most draconian of Tudor ambitions. It is not possible to estimate what the total kill of any of these species was, least of all the sparrows. What is a certainty is that the year-on-year kills in some parishes dwarfed the numbers for which the churchwardens had paid out in the previous century. Even as 'recently' as 1919, the Worcestershire Agricultural Executive announced the initiation of payments of 2*d*. per dozen for heads of unfledged or fully-fledged House Sparrows and 1*d*. per dozen for eggs. In some cases Rat and Sparrow Clubs persisted for many years; in Kent the Stone Street Club finally rested its guns, closed its books, and wound itself up at the end of 2003, surely the last of all? One participant there at the end had been a member for the whole of the Club's 72 years existence!

All through the decades up to and across the middle of the twentieth century, it was a common sight to see huge flocks of House Sparrows sitting in the hedgerows adjoining fields of corn in late summer and descending in clouds to feed on the ripening heads and later on the drying stooks. Areas on field edges adjacent to the hedges were frequently stripped bare of grain and, together with the additional spillage from the ears that the birds caused, these levels of loss were clearly sufficient to warrant determined efforts to reduce numbers. At the same time, Sparrows were serious pests in and around the grain stores, not only through the flocks feeding on the stored and spilled grain, but also through fouling with their droppings. Large-scale control through shooting, netting, and, later, narcotic baiting was commonplace through much of the twentieth century.

How a species' fortune can change! Although 300 years of killing had made no inroads into the overall population, by the 1990s it was evident that there was a serious problem. House Sparrow numbers were falling fast in both town and country. The population in the early 1970s was in the order of 12–13 million pairs but by the turn of the century when the Department of the Environment, Farming and Rural Affairs commissioned an investigation into the decline, numbers had fallen to around 6–7 million pairs. However, the same investigation found that the numbers killed by landowners/occupiers in 2001 and in the previous decade or so was probably no more than 16,000 annually—some 0.5% of the total population and an insignificant figure in the context of the decline. Until recently the House Sparrow was one of 13 species on the general licence list, under which provision it could legally be killed or taken at any time to prevent damage to crops or property. From early in 2005, it was removed from that list in view the serious decline in numbers and since then it has enjoyed total protection. If a case is made for the need to control, a special licence is now required.

The House Sparrow's recent decline in built up areas appears to be principally related to the failure of second and third broods, with nestlings dying of starvation. In the early days after hatching, the chicks are dependent on a diet of small insects brought to them by the parents. The main problem appears to be a reduction in the availability of the necessary insects, particularly those associated with open grassy areas, which are declining in many urban areas. Normal mortality of young House Sparrows is high and successful second broods are essential to the maintenance of a stable population. In the wider countryside the decline is attributed to poorer winter survival, a factor also affecting other farmland passerines.

How many sparrows were killed?

We shall never know, of course, how many House Sparrows were killed in the past but the number was clearly enormous. However it is possible to come up with a tentative estimate, based on the figures in historical churchwardens' accounts.

Some parishes began killing in the late seventeenth century but the bulk of the slaughter took place for a hundred years or so from the mid eighteenth century up to 1820–30, around which time most churchwardens ceased paying bounties on them. The vast majority of the slaughter was in England, south of a line from the Humber to Exeter and the level of the killing was very variable; negligible in some cases, intense in others, e.g. some 1,215,600 in 55 years at Selsey (W Sussex).

Sparrow control was undertaken south of the above line in some 350 parishes out of 970 or so that I examined there. I totalled the kill in all those parishes in which *substantial* culls were undertaken (i.e. ignoring those with relatively small numbers). In some cases I had to adjust the figures upwards, where it was obvious that the existing record stops—or starts—in mid flow and a longer period of cull was evidently undertaken. I then had a figure for those parishes in which substantial control had been undertaken, as a percentage of the total number of parishes that were examined in each county. This percentage could then be transposed to the total number of parishes in each county. *Assuming* that the overall proportion of parishes killing substantial numbers was the same as in my sample, I could produce a minimum figure of sparrows killed for each county.

Example
Berkshire: I examined 28 parish records. Sixteen of these (57%) had substantial kills. Total number of parishes in Berkshire is 180; 57% of 180 is 102. I counted 432,000 sparrows in the 16 parishes with substantial kills. Divide this by 16 and multiply by 102 = 2,754,000 birds killed.

By this calculation the minimum number of sparrows killed in *c.*100 years south of the Humber–Exeter line was in the order of 56,880,000.

However, this is only a part of the story. It must be noted that:

(i)   The token adjustments I made were almost certainly well short of the actual numbers accounted for in many cases.

(ii)   Most churchwardens' accounts that only start as late as *c*.1800 were not examined because of time constraints and the fact that they rarely contain species other than sparrows, but often have large numbers of these.

(iii) Other parishes, not included in the above calculations, killed sparrows but not in substantial numbers.

(iv)   These calculations take no account of the huge numbers killed by sparrow clubs and their successor campaigns from *c*.1860 onwards.

(v)   Neither do they include the uncountable numbers of eggs and chicks that were taken in some counties, going back to the eighteenth century.

A realistic figure for the minimum numbers of sparrows killed and eggs taken between *c*.1700 and *c*.1930 is probably well in advance of 100,000,000.

Bullfinch

The Bullfinch may seem an unlikely candidate for a list of 'noysome fowles' and vermin. However, Bullfinches were specifically listed in the Act of 1566 ('everie Bulfynche and other byrde that devoureth the blowth of the fruit') with a price of 1*d*. upon each head (the same value as the Act put on Kite and Raven). Particularly in the counties dominated by 'ancient country-side', the hedgerows were planted with a wide variety of tree species specifically to supply the needs for fuel and fruit. Thomas Tusser writing in 1573, around the same time as the above Act, stressed the importance of fruit trees in just such countryside and John Norden (1607) commented on the abundance of fruit being grown in the hedgerows of the same counties as those (see below) where the church records show high levels of payments for killing Bullfinches in the seventeenth and eighteenth centuries.

The Bullfinch was well recognised as a pest, as William Lawson knew when he wrote in 1618, 'The Bullfinch is a devourer of your fruit in the budde. I have had whole trees shald out with them in wintertime'. Undoubtedly he was correct. During the brief period of the Commonwealth (1649–60), Cromwell decreed a national initiative to increase the planting of fruit trees throughout the country. He appointed a small army of fruiterers and woodwards to prosecute the scheme but it was never fully enforced, although it is notable for the fact that it did encourage the planting of many orchards. Herefordshire, Gloucestershire, and Worcestershire were three of the counties in which a relative frenzy of orchard planting took place in the latter half of that century. However, the most important period for the expansion of orchards occurred from the second half of the seventeenth and on through the eighteenth century.

Control of Bullfinches was clearly an important requisite with these newly established orchards. The churchwardens' accounts and vestry minutes of that era testify to the efforts that were made in some areas to control the species. The peak of this activity coincided precisely with the period of orchard expansion and it is evident that the species occurred in an abundance that is not equalled today. The church accounts in different parts of the country are scattered with payments for 'malps, hoops and nopps'—all colloquial names for the Bullfinch derived from the old name 'alpe'. As Conyers recommended in 1705, the age-old method employed to catch the birds was the use of limed twigs. The doctored twigs and sticks were placed appropriately on the trees and bushes favoured by the birds or on sites where they were seen to perch regularly. In addition to catching Bullfinches, such an indiscriminate method must have been responsible for significant catches of other songbird species as well. It is doubtful whether the alternative types of traps or nets available at the time for other species would have been effective against a bird such as the Bullfinch that does not so readily come to the ground.

Throughout the seventeenth and eighteenth centuries (and occasionally into the nineteenth), there were some heavy kills of Bullfinches recorded through the bounty payments in the churchwardens' accounts. The strangest feature of this, however, is the very odd pattern of distribution of areas where killing did and did not take place. It is perplexing that the extant records in numerous counties such as Buckinghamshire, Bedfordshire, and Essex, to mention but three, produce not one record of bounties for Bullfinches among them. West Hertfordshire, formerly renowned for its fruit, produces only two records (sixteen birds)—perhaps a reflection of the fact that cherries were the most notable crop rather than pears or other fruit. These are areas where one would imagine that there was at least some expectation of a need for control, and yet there is no evidence at all from the large number of records examined, that any took place.

What is equally strange is the total absence of any reference to Bullfinch in the available accounts from the Vale of Evesham. The parish records for the area are fragmentary, and especially so for the seventeenth century, but even so it is inexplicable that there are no records whatever of bounties for Bullfinches being

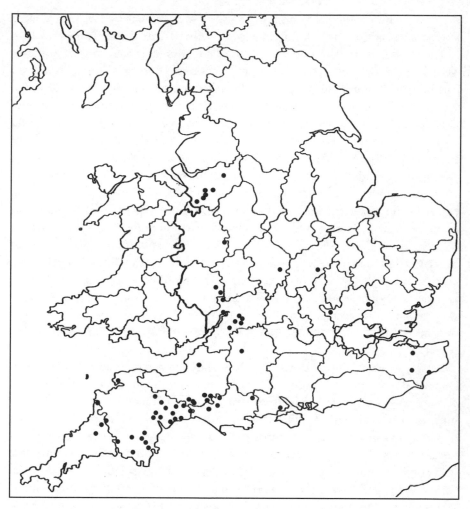

Figure 19. Map showing those parishes killing Bullfinches in C17 and C18.

paid in that important fruit growing region. One must remember that only relatively small numbers of historical parish records exist in any of the counties mentioned above and that the 'missing' ones may possibly have told a different story, although it seems unlikely, since all those that have been examined have no evidence at all. Nash, in his *History of Worcestershire* written in 1781, implies that there were considerable volumes of fruit being grown in his time; he quotes, for example, 2–3 tons of cherries being sold before 5 a.m. on Saturdays in the season. The western parts of the county were ideal for growing apples and pears, while gardens near Evesham and Pershore favoured plums, gooseberries, and currants. Cadle suggested that many Worcestershire orchards were run down in the nineteenth century but neither this, nor the statement by Nash, give clues for the surprising absence of Bullfinch persecution across the centuries.

The map on p. 181 shows the location of parishes where substantial numbers were killed and recorded in the church accounts. Principal among these are parishes in Cheshire, Devon, Dorset, Gloucestershire, and Somerset, although the number of those where bounties were paid was usually small. In some of these counties, the numbers killed over a period of years were high and bear testimony to the populations which evidently existed at the time. Three Cheshire parishes produced particularly high numbers. Bounties were paid in Rostherne (a parish of only 900 acres (364 hectares)) for 3,852 Bullfinches in 15 years including the high figure of 819 individual birds in 1687, the year before bounty payments ceased there; 6,221 in Bunbury in 35 years; and 1,198 in 20 years in Tarporley. Devon produced fairly impressive numbers from a concentration of parishes along the south coast and in the South Hams: Modbury (2,340 in 76 years), Exeter St Thomas (962 in 13 years), Dartington, Gittisham, High Week, East Budleigh, and Branscombe amongst others. In Dorset, it is once more Sherborne that is top of the list, where Bullfinches were killed at an average rate of 58 a year for 98 years; a fairly modest toll, but the longest continuous campaign against the species that my searches revealed.

Nowadays we recognize the Bullfinch as a familiar and popular bird, despite its somewhat shy and skulking habit and its unwelcome fondness for the buds of certain garden fruits. It is still a bird that arouses conflicting feelings and is not universally appreciated. Traditionally regarded as a relatively common species of woodland understorey, overgrown hedgerows, gardens, parks, etc., it has declined over the past few decades. Now, at the beginning of the twenty-first century, it is much scarcer than previously, with the population reduced from some 300,000–350,000 pairs to around 190,000 pairs by the end of the last century. It was included by conservation organizations in the UK on the Red List of Birds of Conservation Concern in 1996 with declines of 75% on farmland and 47% in woodland between 1968 and 1991. The reasons for this reduction in population over the past thirty years or so are not fully understood but are believed to be related to the loss of old hedgerows, degradation of scrubland habitats, and other countryside management and land use factors. In contrast to its recent decline, Parslow showed that the Bullfinch steadily increased in numbers and even extended its distribution northwards and westwards into new areas of Ireland and Scotland during the early years of the twentieth century. That increase was considerable in the decades of the 1950s and 1960s, coinciding neatly with the serious decline in Sparrowhawk numbers and, not surprisingly, with the increasing concern of commercial fruit growers.

At times when its numbers were much higher than they are now it was

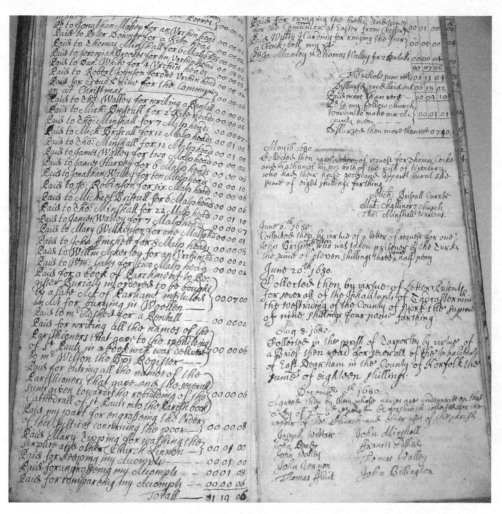

Figure 20. A page from Tarporley (Ches) churchwardens' account, 1678,
showing heavy kill of 'Malps' (Bullfinch).

regarded—with certain justification in some years—as being a considerable pest
on garden fruit trees and in commercial orchards. The Protection of Birds Act in
1954 which gave full protection to most bird species, made specific exclusion of
Bullfinch in the principal fruit growing areas of Kent and the Vale of Evesham,
where general licences were introduced for precisely that reason. Newton, writing in 1972, emphasized the seriousness of damage that could occur in extreme
cases when fruit crops on damaged trees could be reduced from the expectation
of several tons per acre to a matter of a few pounds. Damage has always been
worst in orchards situated close to extensive woodlands, where the populations

of Bullfinches are likely to be highest, and in these situations it is the peripheral rows of fruit trees nearest the woodland edge that are most severely affected. Bullfinches feed on a wide range of fruits, although the birds often demonstrate distinct preferences; the buds of pear and plum are most favoured, with goose-berries and currants also popular. As Newton shows, the birds will also display strong preferences within a crop, for example Conference and Williams pears may be severely attacked while Comice, with a slightly lower protein value, and other varieties adjacent to them, are left untouched. The birds nip out only the nutritious central part of each bud but can do so at considerable speed, such that a group of birds can cause major damage in a very short time.

We have no knowledge of the numbers that were killed by horticulturalists before the 1954 Act, when the species could be legitimately controlled any-where. Similarly, after the Act, there is no indication of numbers killed in Kent and Worcestershire as the general licence in those areas did not require returns to be made. Newton suggests that on an average fruit farm a few hundred might have been killed annually, but on one adjacent to a heavily wooded area this figure might rise to 1,000 or more. Even this level of cull would not have had a significant effect on overall numbers when the population was high and the same number could well be killed in following years. Jim Flegg (pers com) working at the Horticultural Research International at East Malling in the 1970s and 1980s, confirms that the numbers being killed in those two counties in his time were much lower than expected and that the number of incidents of serious damage reported to the Ministry was correspondingly small. As late as 1998, when Bullfinch numbers were still very low, the general licences were withdrawn but application could still be made to MAFF for individual licences in cases of serious damage.

Catching Bullfinches is relatively easy and, as Newton has demonstrated, is best carried out in the autumn, with the aim of reducing the winter numbers in a given area to levels that can be supported by the annual seed crop of docks, bramble, nettle, and ash. It is in years when these seed crops—particularly ash—are poor that damage to fruit buds is likely to be worst. Wright and Summers developed a simple type of Chardonneret trap which, when used with a decoy bird, was very selective in catching Bullfinches. This remained the most popular and efficient method of control in orchards up to the time when control in the Vale of Evesham and Kent was removed and total protection was afforded to the species in 1998. Other methods of control have also been employed. Shooting was sometimes practised and Matthews describes one farm in the 1980s which employed two men full time to shoot Bullfinches with a bounty of £1 being paid for each additional bird shot at weekends. Endrin, a pesticide with legal use only for blackcurrant treatment, was also illegally used on some farms in order to control Bullfinches.

Much as one would expect, there is no evidence of organized Bullfinch control anywhere in Wales in historical or modern times. Whereas the bird is reasonably common in the lowlands, but less so in the west, there is little likelihood of conflict with commercial interests. Similarly in Scotland, the bird is well distributed and fairly common in the lowlands, but there is little conflict with horticultural or other enterprises and no evidence of organized campaigns against it in the past. Nonetheless, at Galston (Ayr) the Old Statistical Account records that Bullfinches first appeared there around 1780 and subsequently increased 'to a considerable number wherein they do great damage to the blossoms of plums and small fruit'.

7

Mammals—individual species accounts

Hedgehog

Public attitude can be wayward and capricious. Nowadays the Hedgehog is high on the list of popular and idealized wild creatures. In the wildlife-enlightened years of the late twentieth and early twenty-first centuries, Britain abounds with Hedgehog rescue centres, Hedgehog hospitals, Hedgehog Preservation Societies, etc. Fierce campaigns have even been waged to prevent the necessary control, as opposed to translocation, of Hedgehogs unwisely introduced to Hebridean islands. In the preceding centuries, however, the animal was vilified, hunted, hounded, and killed in thousands throughout the country. The slaughter was sometimes of almost unimagined proportions. In Bunbury parish (Ches) in the late seventeenth century, for example, some 8,585 were killed in a mere 35 years.

The main charges against it were twofold. The underlying reason for the Hedgehog having being viewed in such an adverse light results from a strange misconception. For centuries it has been accused of sucking milk from the teats of recumbent cows at night. Hedgehogs are known to be fond of milk but, whereas they may lap at milk leaking from a recumbent cow, they are certainly incapable of actually milking the animal. As long ago as 1768 Robert Smith ridiculed the charge as being beyond credibility. In 1829, Knapp also condemned the killing of 'this most harmless and least obtrusive creature . . . yet (they) give rewards for the wretched urchin's head (because of) that very ancient prejudice of its drawing milk from the udders of resting cows being still entertained without any consideration of its impracticability from the smallness of the Hedgehog's mouth'. They were not alone in this; for others had long discounted the belief:

> They say they milk the cows and when they lye
> Nibble their fleshy teats and make them dry,
> But they whove seen the small head like a hog,
> Rolled up to meet the savage of a dog
> With mouth scarce big enough to hold a straw
> Will neer believe what no one ever saw.
> But still they hunt the hedges all about
> And shepherd dogs are trained to hunt then out.
> They hurl with savage force the stick and stone
> And no one cares and still the strife goes on.
>
> John Clare

In addition, the Hedgehog has been long recognized as an egg thief, stealing opportunistically from hen houses or from hens' nests concealed under hedge-rows, bushes, or barns. The hedgehog was, and still is, guilty of this charge, but it hardly seems justification for the wholesale persecution that has taken place. Nonetheless, these ancient convictions earned the Hedgehog its place on the Tudor list of vermin and it remained firmly embedded in country folklore well into the twentieth century, despite clear evidence of the animal's benefits to agriculture and forestry, and as a friend of gardeners.

The payment rate set out in the statute of 1566 was 2*d*. per head, the same as that for Otter and twice that stipulated for Polecat, Wild Cat, Stoat, or Weasel. This was a considerable sum, and seems to have put a wholly disproportionate value on the animal's misdemeanours. The Hedgehog is undoubtedly the easiest of animals to catch and innumerable parishioners made easy money, especially since in most parishes the headage payment was soon raised to 4*d*. and remained at that amount over the centuries. Despite the financial incentive the intensity of killing across Britain between the sixteenth and nineteenth centuries was curiously discontinuous. The only three counties in which no church records of Hedgehog were found were Cumberland, Durham, and Northumberland. However, other counties north of the Mersey and Humber yielded very few records, as did the whole of Wales together with counties of the north Midlands, Lincolnshire, and East Anglia. The areas of greatest killing, as shown on the map below, were in the west and south-west, Kent, and the south and east Midlands. Steele Elliott questioned how the Hedgehog had survived at all in Bedfordshire where payments were made in forty-one parishes, with relatively high levels of killing in some. His estimate of 'upwards of 10,000 victims' (seventeenth and eighteenth centuries) was certainly a considerable underestimate for the county

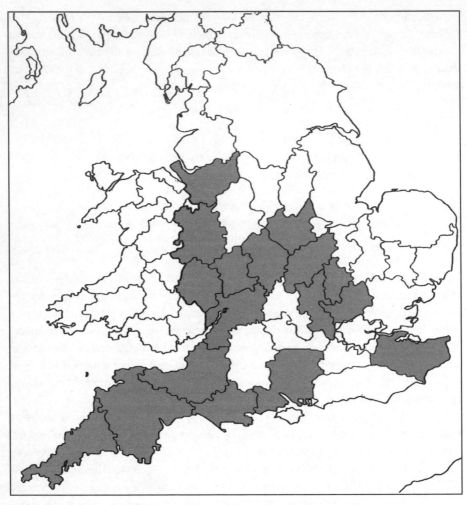

Figure 21. Map showing counties in which the heaviest killing of
Hedgehogs took place in C17–C19.

overall (many parish records did not exist) but, as ongoing annual totals showed,
there was no danger that they would be eliminated. Individual parishes such as
Eaton Socon (7,530 acres (3,047 hectares)) and Northill (4,201 acres (1,703
hectares)) were responsible for modest totals of around 1,000 animals over
periods of 160 and 120 years respectively and some parishes were still paying
bounties as late as 1833. The pattern was similar in the adjacent county of
Buckinghamshire (well over 1,000 in Hambleden and Quainton over c.70 years)
although there was a higher percentage of parishes where, apparently, no killing
took place. In Warwickshire particularly heavy kills are recorded in Tredington

and Polesworth while in Derbyshire, where several parishes killed large numbers, the churchwardens at Wirksworth paid for 571 heads between 1658 and 1677, and a further 1,011 between 1679 and 1694, at which point the killing presumably stopped abruptly, since no more bounties were recorded. The prodigious number taken in the second half of the seventeenth century at Bunbury in Cheshire (a very large parish of 17,600 acres (7,122 hectares)) at least testifies to the healthy population of Hedgehogs ('urchins', 'highoggs', 'fuzzpiggs', 'hoghogs', 'hedgepigs'—by any other name) which the countryside supported at those times. At Bunbury, where the maximum paid for in one year was 498, the numbers killed annually for 36 years were still maintained until the last available figure in 1691 (348) that year. This was not the only Cheshire parish in which large numbers were killed. Rostherne (4,064 in 24 years), Frodsham (2,816 in 24 years), Alderley (1,209 in 43 years), and Barthomley (1,953 in 15 years) all accounted for substantial numbers in the latter half of the seventeenth century. At Great Budworth, 805 were killed in only three years 1700–2. More than 50 Kentish parishes were responsible for considerable kills with Tenterden at the top of the list with more than 2,300 in the 70 years up to 1695.

South-west England was the area where the most widespread and intensive killing of many species of wildlife took place. Many parishes were active in their attempts to eradicate the Hedgehog, sometimes with open-ended campaigns which were part of the general vermin programme and at other times with short sharp drives (e.g. East Budleigh, Devon). Numbers killed were often high: 5,003 at Sherborne (Dorset), 2,557 at Painswick, and 2,696 at Great Badminton (both Glos), 9,623 at Batcombe (Som). At Branscombe (Devon) bounties for Hedgehogs were still being paid as late as 1852. In all these instances, and in many other parishes throughout the country, the main efforts were intensified from the decade 1665–75. Although it has always been relatively easy to walk around and pick up hedgehogs from pastures at night they were sometimes sought out with the help of dogs. Knapp recognized this long ago: 'some strong smell must proceed from this animal as we find it frequently with our sporting dogs even in its hibernation state; every village boy with his cur detects the haunt of the poor Hedgehog and as assuredly worries and kills him'.

We can never know the total number of Hedgehogs that were killed at the height of the implementation of the Vermin Acts in the latter half of the seventeenth and in the eighteenth centuries. However, by extrapolation from the figures in the ten counties in which the most severe regimes of Hedgehog control were pursued (including those shaded on the map) it is possible to produce a rough estimate. In these ten counties, 446 accounts were examined out of a total of some 2,760 parishes (i.e. 16%). This showed that a total of nearly 70,000 bounties were paid for Hedgehog heads. In many of these parishes the surviving documents span only parts of the period and they start or finish (or both) when

Hedgehog killing was clearly in full flow, so that the actual numbers killed were evidently considerably higher than the surviving records show. On that basis, increasing the known figure by a nominal 15,000 is not unreasonable, to produce a total of 85,000. If a further assumption is made that the level of killing was similar in the 84% of parishes for which records do not exist, then in 140 years (1660–1800) or so, more than half a million Hedgehogs could easily have been killed in those ten counties alone.

Of course, the phasing out of parish payments did not signify the end of Hedgehog persecution. Although Hedgehogs are known to be primarily invertebrate feeders, they have a more catholic diet than that. Tapper (1992) acknowledges that gamekeepers have always regarded them as significant thieves of game bird eggs and even poults and occasional incubating adults, as a result of which they have traditionally controlled them when possible. Morris (1994) suggests that up to 10,000 have been destroyed annually in this way and quotes records from an estate in East Anglia where nearly 20,000 were killed in the latter half of the twentieth century. Kills were high on two other East Anglian estates in the same century. At Sandringham, 5,904 were accounted for between 1938 and 1950 and at Holkham 5,623 were killed from 1953 to 1959. Since 1981, the Hedgehog has been partially protected under Schedule 6 of the Wildlife and Countryside Act but, notwithstanding this, Hedgehogs are still widely killed inadvertently in tunnel traps set for small mustelids and by other means. The Game Conservancy's annual returns (National Gamebag Census) from shooting estates, started in 1961, have included important data on the numbers of pests and predators killed on estates throughout the country. The Census suggests that there has been a steady reduction in Hedgehog numbers from 1961–80 (when partial protection was introduced and subsequent Hedgehog returns from estates ceased). Tapper has shown that across that period the number of Hedgehogs killed fell by 4.6% p.a. although it is not clear to what extent this reflected an overall decline in the population, or a reduced level of persecution by gamekeepers as a result of more game birds being raised in the relative security of rearing pens.

Man is also the cause of many Hedgehog deaths each year through accidental or inadvertent means. Habitat change—agricultural intensification, pesticide use (including garden chemicals), loss of hedgerows, etc.—is the principal factor causing a steady decline in numbers. Hedgehogs are frequently killed on roads too, particularly during spring and summer when they are at their most active. In the early 1990s, Morris suggested that at least 50,000 are lost each year in this way alone. Undoubtedly, the Hedgehog population in Britain is smaller now than it was even a decade or two ago. Morris believes that annual roadkill in the first few years of the present century (based on better data than previously, i.e. the Mammals on Roads survey), is probably in the region of 12,000 to 15,000. This survey has shown a significant decline (perhaps as much as 20%) in the three years 2001–4, on top of a 30% decline compared with similar data ten years earlier. The Hedgehog population appears to be in freefall.

Hedgehogs feature infrequently in the historic vermin lists in Scotland. On one or two estates where they were controlled, the numbers were quite high: 508 on Balmacaan in 8 years, 821 at Tulloch Brae in 10 years, and 2,783 on a Perthshire estate across the same period at the end of the nineteenth century. However, as a postscript to the account of the relationship between Man and Hedgehog in Scotland, it would be remiss to ignore the controversy surrounding the attempt by Scottish Natural Heritage (SNH) to exterminate the Hedgehog from the Hebridean islands of Benbecula and the Uists. They are not native to these islands but were foolishly introduced there in 1974. The resulting explosion in numbers took the population to some 5,000 by the 1990s, at which time it was shown that the Hedgehogs were heavily predating the nests of the internationally important populations of breeding wading birds. After wide consultation, SNH decided that the Hedgehogs had to be removed and that the correct strategy was extermination, rather than translocation to the mainland. Public response was swift and furious and demonstrated perfectly the quixotic evolution of public attitudes to the Hedgehog. Hedgehog support groups throughout the country were up in arms and SNH received more than 3,000 protest letters. Rescue missions were planned (and £75,000 raised to support them) with bounties of £5 in 2003—increasing the next year to £20—being offered for individual Hedgehogs captured for release on the mainland. In 2003, 156 were rescued in this way, with another 213 being taken off the islands in 2004 and a further 241 released on the mainland in 2005. At the same time, humane culling by SNH accounted for 66 animals on North Uist in 2003 and 265 in 2004 at which point the programme was extended to include Benbecula. In 2005, SNH killed 22 on North Uist and 159 on Benbecula, a total of 181. However, it is claimed that the current level of annual capture is far below that which is necessary to achieve elimination of the population. The cost of those caught and killed by SNH is about £130 per animal compared with £20 reward given for those caught and translocated. Despite official reservations about the likely success of translocating animals, a special study in 2005, of Hedgehogs taken from the islands and released on the mainland, demonstrated that relocation could be achieved entirely successfully.

With spuds and traps and horse
    hair string supplied,
He potters out to seek each fresh-
    made hill;
Pricking the greensward where
    they love to hide,
He sets his treacherous snares,
    resolved to kill;
And on the willow sticks bent to
    the grass,
That such as touched jerk up in
    bouncing springs,
Soon as the little hermit tries to pass,
His little carcass on the gibbet hings.

John Clare

Moles—'waunts' or 'mouldiwarps' to use two of their old vernacular names—
have undoubtedly been a pest on cultivated land since Man first cleared the
forests, opened up the landscape, and started to develop systems of settled
agriculture. The Mole is essentially a woodland animal and the forest floor, rich
in earthworms and other soil invertebrates, is its primary habitat, but as the
woodlands receded it readily adapted to open pastures and arable land. Since
those times this small, fodient animal has been one of the most universally
troublesome of agricultural pests. The damage it causes is clear for all to see even
though the perpetrators themselves normally remain concealed in their sub-
terranean territorial worlds. Their molehills sometimes occupy considerable
areas of pastureland, killing the grass underneath. On arable land their underground runs can directly damage crops, uproot seedlings, deprive the growing
plants of soil and moisture or leave their roots exposed, so that they wilt and die.
In our modern world the opportunities for them to cause a nuisance are widened
further. Their earth mounds, if left undisturbed in permanent pastures, often
provide ideal conditions for coarse or invasive plants to establish and the mounds
can damage farm machinery. They are also a continual problem where silage
is taken, as the soil from the mounds will invariably spoil the stored crop. Mole
activity is also a problem on lawns, golf courses, playing fields, and in gardens,
or when the animals burrow into dykes and riparian embankments, and it
has always been recognized, too, as a hazard for horse riders because both the
molehills and the subsidence of tunnels can potentially cause accidents.

Although there are plenty of detractors for the Mole, there are also those who point out that by aerating soils, helping drainage, eating some invertebrate pests, and helping to turn over the soil, it provides many benefits as well. Nevertheless, the Mole remains universally unpopular and is still heavily controlled today. When I examined payments for Moles in the old churchwardens' accounts, I was conscious of the very restricted parts of the country in which payments are recorded. The majority of the records come from the principal areas of the great open fields in the East Midlands. In these areas annual payments to mole-catchers, or for Moles brought in by individual parishioners, can be found from the early 1600s onwards. Before this, very few accounts of vermin payments have survived although the one at Bishop's Stortford (Herts) for the years 1569–71, shortly following the 1566 Act, mentions the modest number of 53 Moles amongst a range of other vermin. (This remains the only parish record of payments for Moles in the whole county of Hertfordshire in all the centuries thereafter). Dozens of parishes in Lincolnshire, Nottinghamshire, Leicester-shire, and Northamptonshire concentrated heavily on Moles, often to the exclusion of most other species of vermin. An extreme case was in Edenham (Lincs) where over a period of 68 years from 1742 to 1810 nothing except Moles were species killed and successive generations of mole-catchers were paid at the fixed rate of £3. 18s. 0d. p.a.; as was often the case, there is no record of the numbers taken. Seventeenth century Mole control at Ecton (N'hants) was achieved in an extraordinary way, by which payments of 1d. per Mole were given to an endless succession of individuals, some of whom brought a dozen or more, but many arrived with no more than a single Mole at a time. In some years between 1673 and 1703, more than 100 individual payments were made to differ-ent parishioners, but totals still only reached a maximum of fewer than 750 in a year. Other counties in the same part of England paid for Mole control, albeit at a lower intensity—Buckinghamshire, Cambridgeshire, Huntingdonshire, East Yorkshire.

In Bedfordshire, where Mole control was fairly intensive, the majority of parishes participated with payments being made across various periods from the seventeenth to nineteenth centuries. Maulden parishioners drew up a detailed agreement with John Hawkins as mole-catcher in 1710 to:

sett or cause to be sett traps and engins for the takeing and distroying all the moles that now digg or cast up moles or earth in any of the lands, meadows or pastures lying within the said parish . . . . and will spread . . . . all such earth during the said terme of six years: in consideration of such works . . . the parishioners . . . shall pay unto the said John Hawkins the summe of two pounds and seven shillings and six pence yearly.

Other Bedfordshire parishes also appointed mole-catchers or paid individually for numbers brought in; Arlesey, for example paid for 3,855 Moles between 1749 and 1769. Many other parishes made similar appointments—Barton,

Melchbourne, Streatley et al. Loughborough (Leics) is a typical example of a parish that regularly used the services of a mole-catcher. In 1653, the vestry there elected 'overseers for the moles' and renewed the post for many years thereafter. A very late parish appointment was at Selattyn (Salop) in 1882 when, after a contested election, T. Jones was appointed as mole-catcher for 21 years at ¾d. (three farthings) per acre.

Elsewhere the historical records of Mole control are very sparse. There are a few notable exceptions such as Weston Zoyland (Som) and Prestbury (Ches)—in which latter parish the vestry specifically pressed the case for controlling Moles in 1723 with enhanced payments for those individual Moles taken 'in any garden so cultivated'. The ensuing campaign was short-lived however, as 4,566 were killed in the following year but thereafter nothing happened. There was an interesting series of payments from the tiny chapelry of Middleton (Kendal parish, W'land) where disbursements for Moles did not begin until the extra-ordinarily late date of 1842 and continued with a rate of £2 or £3 annually until 1886, first to William Warrener and later to William Parker.

If the numbers killed historically in most parishes were modest by modern expectations, we should recognize that Moles were not the easiest animals to catch with devices that were available 300 years or more ago. Gervaise Markham, in his *Inrichment of the Weald of Kent* in 1636, advocated a trapping method that sounds simplicity itself but whose effectiveness requires a considerable elasticity of belief. His formula can be summarized as follows. 'During the early Spring breeding season you should take a live Mole and put it in a deep vessel from which it cannot escape, sunk below the level of a run and cover it again. The distressed calls of the captive will attract others which will fall into the vessel and the more Moles there are the more noise they make and the more will surrender themselves to the vessel.' 'I have taken 50 or 60 in a night', he affirmed. For a territorial creature such as the Mole, it is a claim that is difficult to credit.

The churchwardens' payment for Moles varied considerably. In the original Act, the stipulated rate was ½d. (i.e. 6d. per dozen) and although this rate applied in many instances across the succeeding centuries, there was frequent variation. At Eaton Bray (Beds) in the early 1800s they paid the large sum of 4d. for each Mole. Two Norfolk parishes clearly gave particular attention to Moles. At Walpole, John Harwood was employed for the generous sum of £5. 10s. 0d. each year between 1818 and 1828 while at Blickling in the early decades of the previous century the churchwardens were paying for up to 272 dozen per annum at the standard 6d. per/dozen.

The problems caused by Moles were taken seriously. As well as the innumer-able parish appointments, many of the larger estates traditionally employed their own dedicated mole-catcher and groups of farmers often co-operated to share the cost of one. The profession of mole-catcher is an ancient one, dating back to at least the time of the early parish enclosures. The fact that relatively few churchwardens' accounts show any reference to Moles reflects the knowledge that the estates employed their own Mole catchers. In this way, the parish records portray only a part of the picture. In northern areas there was intensive control. Macpherson records that many private owners and groups of farmers in the Lake District employed a mole-catcher, not only to catch the Moles but also to spread soil from the hills to facilitate harvesting and haymaking by scythe. Payment was usually on an acreage basis rather than a fixed sum for each dozen Moles. A ráte of $3d$. per acre was quoted there around 1797 compared with the $\frac{3}{4}d$. per acre at Selattyn (Salop) a hundred years earlier. The New Statistical Account in Scotland makes several references, e.g. Kirkholm in Wigtownshire, to numbers actually being reduced on many farms by the intense efforts of mole-catchers.

Historically, there was a royal mole-catcher appointed, although the post lapsed as long ago as the 1700s. The fashionable Pembroke Lodge function centre in Richmond Park now stands on the site of the original humble one-room cottage which, prior to 1754, was the home of the royal mole-catcher whose sole responsibility was to reduce the hazards to huntsmen presented by molehills in the royal park. The need for this sort of precaution was given poignancy by the fact that William III died after being thrown from his horse when it stumbled on a molehill. Although the prestigious role of royal mole-catcher lapsed shortly after this time, it was restored by Elizabeth II at Sandringham (Norfolk) in 2002 with the appointment of Victor Williamson, a long-serving operator on the estate, who was granted the royal warrant as Mole-controller to the Queen.

Although Mole control was undoubtedly undertaken in Scotland there is less historical evidence of it in the written records. Mole catchers were certainly employed on various estates where there was particular agricultural interest, for example Neill Malcolm's Poltalloch estate at Kilmartin (Argyll) where the Mole catcher was paid £7. 10s. 0d. annually in the early decades of the nineteenth century.

The number of Moles that have been killed in Britain over time is of course huge, running into many millions. It is second only to House Sparrow (p. 171) in terms of sheer numbers of mammals and birds on the old vermin lists that have been killed over the centuries. Having said this, however, it is still impossible to determine just how large the total kill of Moles has been over time. In the old parish records numbers were rarely given, but where they were these seldom amounted to more than a few hundred per parish, per year, which presumably did little more than scratch the surface of the problem. An East Midland mole-catcher mentioned by Bell claimed 40,000–50,000 in 35 years—well over 1,000 a year, but still modest in terms of the total population. He also quoted a more impressive kill of some 6,000 in one small district in East Anglia in a five-month period. In recent times one East Anglian estate of 20,000 acres (8,000 hectares) accounted for 80,000–90,000 Moles in 20 years. However, this total included only those caught in traps; poison is also extensively used underground on agricultural land and there is no figure obtainable for the number killed by that means although it was presumed to be at least as great as those killed in traps. Did this level of control have any effect on the population? The answer to the question is probably 'no', because recruitment from surrounding areas, particularly woodland and hedge banks, is continual. The number now killed annually throughout Britain cannot be calculated simply because the animals die in their underground runs and the bodies are never seen. The annual toll is doubtless in millions. Strychnine is the main chemical used, under licences issued by the Department of Environment, Food and Rural Affairs, the Welsh Assembly, and the Scottish Parliament. In 2003–4, nearly 40 kg of strychnine was issued throughout the three countries (28,524 g in England, 6,653 g in Wales, and 4,712 g in Scotland) and a similar amount in 2004–5. Strychnine was licensed on the approximate basis of 2 g for 4 hectares in England and Wales but only 1 g for 10 hectares in Scotland. However, under European legislation the substance was withdrawn in September 2006 and can no longer be used legally. Harris et al. estimated the British Mole population to be about 31 million in 1995, but since then, possibly on account of restricted access to farmland during the Foot and Mouth epidemic in 2001, numbers are now thought to be higher than that.

Another reason for killing Moles was because of the value of their skins. In the nineteenth century, huge numbers were killed specifically for the fur trade, for conversion into waistcoats (a good waistcoat required over 100 skins), gloves, or coats. The market continued, although gradually declining as fashions changed, into the early decades of the twentieth century. An Edinburgh furrier took newspaper advertisements in the south of England before the First World War, offering 25/- per 100 for good quality moleskins. In the 1920s, the mole-catcher at Malton in North Yorkshire was selling moleskins for a penny a time to Horace Friend and Son, Fur and Feather, at Wisbech. Skins from as far away as mid Wales were traded through the same firm until the 1960s. By the time of the Second World War, a Devon boy could still ask 19*d.* each for large skins in prime condition, for use in linings for gloves or flying jackets. There was always good money to be made from moleskins. A Kimbolton (Hfds) man did well selling skins at 6*d.* a time in the 1920s but then in the years of the depression that followed the value rose dramatically to 2/6 per skin. He made a lot of money, enough in fact to buy his first farm holding, acquired entirely on the back of Moles. Others recount similar gains; even the current royal mole-catcher purchased his first vehicle on moleskin money. The Wisbech firm of Horace Friend and Son continued to deal in moleskins until the early 1980s. Up to this time Norfolk mole-catchers could still command 1/6 per skin. At the same time a good winter dog Fox skin fetched as much as £16 at Friend and Son and a Stoat 2/6 to 3/-, or more if it was in ermine.

The control of Moles still continues throughout the country, and presumably always will, albeit nowadays it is largely in the hands of pest control firms. The methods remain the same as they have been for generations—spring traps placed in the tunnels and poison used in the underground runs on agricultural land. The replacement for strychnine is usually aluminium phosphide (commonly sold as Phostoxin) which is injected into the Mole runs, reacts with the damp, and gives off a short-lived toxic gas. The war against the Mole will continue, but it is in effect an annual cull, since its population is likely to remain broadly stable.

Polecat

It is a salutary measure of the totality of elimination of a species such as Polecat that it has not only been successfully exterminated from most of Britain but, over the passage of little more than 100 years, has almost been eradicated from public consciousness. Relatively few people are aware of the existence of this animal, even by name, let alone the fact that it was numerous throughout Britain until three or four generations ago. It is still one of the least studied of our native mammals. Until the second half of the nineteenth century, the Polecat was a familiar, if unpopular, creature which, evidence suggests, was widespread in most parishes. The exception to this was the south-east of England where its demise may have been earlier than elsewhere.

The depth of loathing directed towards the Polecat in the years before it was finally eliminated from England and Scotland, and reduced to a remnant in Wales, was unmatched by strength of feeling towards any other species of vermin. Its name was even used in Shakespearean times as a term of vitriolic abuse. Perusal of 1579 parish documents, numerous other written references, and 'vermin control manuals' from the sixteenth century onwards, leaves a very clear picture of the almost pathological hatred of the animal. As late as 1837, Bell deplored 'its great ravages in hen house or poultry yard where it destroys great numbers not only of chickens and ducklings but also full-grown poultry—even venturing to attack geese and turkeys'. Consequently, it is not surprising that the intensity of persecution over the centuries has been high. Langley and Yalden have demonstrated the inevitable path to extermination that occurred in most English counties around the end of the nineteenth century, with the last Polecats surviving in eastern England and in the five northern counties only five or ten years longer. Similarly in Scotland, they show that only in Perthshire, Argyll, Inverness-shire, Ross and Cromarty, and Sutherland did the Polecat hold on even into the early years of the twentieth century. By the First World War, they had disappeared even from these areas. Walton has described how the relict population in Wales was centred on the hinterland of Aberdovey, although only in south-east Wales, Flintshire, and the Isle of Anglesey did it disappear altogether. It was never extinct in some areas of the Marches, including parts of Shropshire and Herefordshire. It is interesting that the Polecat did not survive the ravages of persecution in the West Highlands of Scotland, whereas both the Wild Cat and the Pine Marten managed to maintain a fragile toe-hold there. This may be a reflection of its more southerly distribution and a preference for lowland habitats; it may never have been particularly numerous in those northern areas.

Probably no other animal on the British list has had as many colloquial names as the Polecat. In southern England it was generally referred to as 'fitchou' whereas in the north it was 'foumat' or 'foumard' (from 'foul mart' as opposed to 'sweet mart'—the Pine Marten). However there were a host of others including endless spelling variations: philbert, fulmer, fishock, filibart, poulcat, poll cat, etc. Charles Oldham identified at least 20 different versions of the name in the Hertfordshire/Bedfordshire area alone.

All species of mustelids have been in conflict with Man at some time, to some extent or other, but the Polecat was always seen as the worst offender. In the days when each smallholding and cottage had its own hen-house together with ducks or geese, the Polecat was regarded as a serious enemy, because of the difficulty of excluding it before the availability of strong wire netting. The only option was to eliminate it, whenever possible. In Kent, for example, examination of seventy-one old parish records showed that in forty-two of them bounties for Polecats were paid, sometimes for considerable numbers (e.g. West Hythe, Ospringe, Saltwood—see also Appendix 1). However, in only three instances do Kentish records of Polecat kills extend into the nineteenth century and then only for single individuals, and usually after a gap of many years. The last one to be mentioned in parish records was at Ightham in 1818. In the majority of parishes in Kent payments for Polecats disappeared one by one between 1720 and c.1760 and it is probable that the animal was already scarce by the end of that century. However, Langley and Yalden give a final extinction date for the county *c*.1870.

'The stinking Polecat, shunned by most people and persecuted by all', Charles Waterton called it in the early years of the nineteenth century. It often lived in close proximity to Man, enjoying the opportunity offered there by the resident rodent population as well as favouring the shelter of farm buildings in winter. Also, from the fourteenth century onwards, Rabbit warrens were important sustainable sources of food. The Polecat, which favoured the warrens for easy night-time hunting, was regarded there a serious pest. At a Lakeland site in the 1850s five 'Foumarts' were caught the first night that spring traps were set for Rabbits, which illustrates the point. Furthermore, as early as the end of the fifteenth century, the Pheasant was already legally protected as its sporting potential was fully appreciated. The increasing importance of Pheasant rearing was the basis of third major conflict between Man and the Polecat.

Some indication of the importance placed on the control of Polecats is suggested by the payment rates that were agreed by the vestry committees in counties throughout England and Wales, and implemented by the church-wardens. In the original statute of 1566, the stipulated rate was 1*d*. per head. Although virtually no records which catalogue the payments in the decades of the sixteenth century immediately following that Act remain, it was rare in succeeding centuries for the 1*d*. rate to be found. By the beginning of the seventeenth century, the standard rate across most parishes was 4*d*., twice that which was offered for stoats or weasels. Such a rate was not universal however and varied from 2*d*. to 3*d*. and sometimes 6*d*., as at Englefield and Winkfield (Berks) and Caddington (Beds)—the latter rate applying for over a century. At Toddington (Beds) they paid 2*d*. for youngsters and double that for females—another occasional variant from the 'standard' rate. In one or two areas the high payments made for Polecat heads make little sense. At Norton (Durham) 1/- per head was being paid regularly in the eighteenth century, an inflated sum which was also paid at Witton-le-Wear in the same county by 1811, after a century or so of paying 4*d*. The churchwardens at Llanfiangell-yr-Traethau on the Merioneth coast appear to have paid 2/6 for individual heads on the sporadic occasions on which Polecats were brought to them between 1684 and 1735—a quite extraordinary sum at today's value.

Apart from the Fox, no mammal was killed in more parishes in England and Wales between the seventeenth and nineteenth centuries than the unfortunate Polecat. Parish after parish consistently accounted for an annual succession of Polecat kills. Furthermore no other animal (except Mole) was killed in anything approaching its numbers. In only four English counties—Staffordshire, Lancashire, Derbyshire, and Suffolk—and three counties in Wales—Radnorshire, Brecknockshire, and Anglesey (surely only a reflection of the sad paucity of historical records in Wales?)—were no records of Polecat bounties found in the churchwardens' accounts. However, it must be remembered that the parish documents still in existence only represent a modest number of the total parishes in any county. Moreover, virtually none of the existing accounts covers the whole span of those centuries; they give only a partial view of a fuller picture of the extent to which Polecats were killed. Over much of England and Wales the toll taken was often consistent over a long period of years. At Eaton Socon and Northill (Beds) over 1,000 were taken in each parish over periods of around 100 years. In the adjacent county of Buckinghamshire between 1695 and 1723, the churchwardens paid for an average of 18 per year at Wing and nearby in Berkhamstead (Herts) the familiar price of 4*d*. per head was paid from 1687 to at least 1819. Many were killed in Northumberland and Durham, the maximum being at Houghton-le-Spring where a total of 563 in 24 years at the beginning of the eighteenth century averaged 23 per year. Across the Pennines in the huge parish of Kendal, 1,150 were accounted for in 1688–1705 (avg. 67 p.a.) and a further 1,149 in a second onslaught 1780–1800 (avg. 54.7 p.a.). Yorkshire too had many parishes with substantial totals killed; Cottingham, for example, averaged 25 p.a. across 33 years in the eighteenth century.

The south-west counties in common with their record of other species, once again produced high numbers. In Cornwall most parishes were killing Polecats consistently. The most notable of these were Camborne, Morwenstow (2,757 in 78 years), St Columb Minor, St Buryan, and St Neot. In Devon again the majority of parishes have Polecats on their lists; the most impressive was the huge coastal parish of Hartland (11,030 acres (4463 hectares)), where 2,329 bounties were paid over 90 years.

These are the some of the extreme examples, but the fact remains that throughout England and Wales Polecats were consistently persecuted at a greater intensity than any other species of mustelid. Did this level of persecution have an effect on overall numbers or did it purely satisfy local vengeance? In contrast to the situation with some of the other vermin species, e.g. House Sparrow, it probably did reduce populations, at least locally. The example of Kent is quoted earlier. Although few other county records indicate a similarly clear decline in numbers in the late eighteenth and early nineteenth century, the numbers controlled across that period were certainly fewer—a lot fewer in some counties—than they were in earlier years. The Polecat may be the best example of a species for which the level of killing really did make a difference to the population. The developing sporting estates then administered the *coup de grâce*.

Not only were Polecats trapped, shot, and poisoned, but they were also hunted for sport in some parts of England. Howes records such hunts from Dorset but hunts were most popular in northern counties. In Yorkshire he quotes Hatfield who claimed that Doncaster men regularly hunted Polecats in the early 1800s, 'seldom returning without securing a dozen and not infrequently a score'; such claims may have been a little far-fetched. *The Westmorland Gazette* of February 1845 gives a colourful account of 'A Grand Foumart Hunt' across the hills in the Windermere and Esthwaite area:

Long before the appointed time (ten o'clock at night) lots of hunters and hounds appeared and a large fire was lit. The hounds threw off above Colthouse and soon a merry cry proclaimed that game was stirring and over the fells the hounds flew, the hunters following as fast as they could, over ice and rocks . . . regardless of every difficulty, for the wilder the danger the sweeter the chase. They scaled the Scale where the hunters looked down upon Windermere . . . from hence they ran through the Sawrey valleys, where the hounds made a turn and ran to a place called Old Intack, where the foumart holed and the hunters did not wish to destroy the creature which had afforded this 'glorious chase'. It was left undisturbed and as the morning was now far advanced each took his way home to dream over again the pleasures of the night.

A further reason why Polecats have been killed since at least the fourteenth century was for the value of their skins, in particular the rich winter pelage, known in the trade as fitch. The Dumfries Fur market (see p. 71) was the great trading place for British furs and Polecat was one of those particularly favoured, especially when luxury imported Sables became scarcer, and the Polecat provided a cheaper and more readily available alternative. As many as 600 skins were offere[1] for sale in Dumfries in 1832. During the mid 1800s even these skins suddenly became scarcer with prices rising to reflect the market demand for a declining resource. This supports the accepted wisdom that the final demise of the Polecat was attributable to the great increase in gamekeeping on sporting estates in the middle decades of the nineteenth century. The market for fitch still remained into the next century for use in ladies' muffs, boas, etc. Howes recorded that even in 1905–6, as many as 77,578 pelts were sold on the London market although by this time the great majority originated from the continent.

The Polecat was once well distributed throughout all of Scotland, where Ritchie later documented its dramatic decline. He attributed its demise initially to slaughter because of the value of its pelt and showed graphically how the price per furriers' dozen* rose rapidly in the 1800s, plotted against equally rapidly declining populations. Before 1850, the price per furrier's dozen rarely reached 20/- whereas after 1850 it fell below 20/- only twice and one year reached as much as 45/- shillings. Across the same period, the attention it attracted from

---

* A furrier's dozen was 'twelve very best full-sized skins, or a greater number of small-sized or secondary quality, or torn skins, so that a "dozen" sometimes consisted of twenty, thirty or more inferior skins'.

gamekeepers hastened its end and Ritchie also blamed the fact that it was attracted to Rabbit warrens where it was easily caught in gin traps.

By the 1880s, Harvie-Brown believed that the Polecat was virtually extinct in all lowland areas from the Moray Firth southwards and, in parts of Argyll and Perthshire, even earlier than that. By 1920, it was scarce in the wilds of Ross, western Inverness-shire, and Sutherland where, according to Ritchie, 'it hovered on the brink of extinction'. He recorded the last Polecat in Ross-shire in 1902 and the final definite record in Scotland was in Sutherland in 1912.

The existence of feral Ferrets and hybrid Polecat-ferrets is one of the complicating factors in accurately assessing Polecat persecution. According to Blandford, Ferrets were domesticated as long ago as 2,000 years and have long been bred to favour albino varieties. The docile Ferret is still widely kept in Britain both as a pet and for rabbiting although the albino form has lost favour latterly to the Polecat-ferret. Escaped individuals will mate freely with wild Polecats to produce the hybrids which, although varying in pattern and colour, frequently resemble pure Polecats. Without doubt, some records over the centuries, including the present time, refer inadvertently to these hybrids, but this fact does not alter the overall picture significantly, since the number of hybrids at any time is relatively small. Birks (pers com) points out that the domesticated Ferret is not well adapted to life in the wild and it is therefore unlikely that it will threaten the integrity of the Polecat. It is interesting that the Polecat has never been known to occur on the Isle of Wight, although a bounty was paid for one at Freshwater in 1791. The genetic purity of that individual can never be known.

Langley and Yalden have detailed the final demise of this attractive member of the mustelid family, which disappeared from most of southern Britain by the beginning of the twentieth century. Birks suggests that the First World War came just in time to prevent its total disappearance from its last strongholds in Wales and the Marches. The departure of gamekeepers to the war marked a serious decline in game preservation. He identifies the onset of myxomatosis in the 1950s with the reduction of Rabbit trapping, and then the banning of gin traps in 1958, as the catalysts for its recovery. Since then the Polecat, with the help of various reintroductions, has made a strong recovery and continues to spread through the English counties from its refugium in the west.

Pine Marten

It is only in recent years that this attractive and elusive mustelid became known as the Pine Marten. The prefix was added to avoid confusion with its continental cousin, the Beech Marten; before this, the animal was known simply as Marten or sometimes, especially in northern England, as Sweet Mart or Clean Mart to distinguish it from the despised Foul Mart (Polecat). It appears as Martrell in some parishes in Devon and as Wood Cat in South Wales (although there may be some confusion with Wild Cat in this name). Its apogee was undoubtedly in the distant past when woodland dominated the dry-land areas of Britain, before the fragmentation of the ancient forest occurred at the hand of Man. In such times the Pine Marten prospered throughout the land, the only mustelid with a truly arboreal lifestyle and almost certainly, according to Maroo and Yalden, the second most numerous carnivore after Weasel.

Man has certainly persecuted the Marten since time immemorial, as evidenced by the remains found in archaeological excavations at classic Mesolithic sites such as Thatcham (Berks) and Star Carr (E Yorks). However, such persecution, presumably primarily for skins, was at an insignificant level, not least because of the thinly scattered population of hunter-gatherers and the vastness of the habitat available for the Martens. Several thousand years later, certainly by the Middle Ages, the Pine Marten had achieved a considerable significance. It was then killed, not so much because of any conflict with Man, but again because of its valuable pelt and the growing demand for furs, both for warmth and also, particularly in the case of the Marten furs, for fashion. As described in Chapter 1, the Marten fur was prized more highly than almost any other, apart from imported Sable. There is no doubt that this demand for its skin had an impact on the population, notably in Scotland, although it was not necessarily the principal factor that finally started to erode the numbers. Certainly, at least in southern Britain the initial factor was an indirect rather than a direct effect of Man. Knapp, writing in 1829, acknowledged the killing already being carried out by gamekeepers, but at the same time correctly put his finger on the central problem: the earlier fragmentation of the woodland cover and the loss of open heathlands and commons. He identified ongoing changes in the countryside, and lamented the loss of the commons and wastes 'wherein enclosures extirpate their haunts'. Martens are highly mobile animals with large territories and there is little doubt that they were much scarcer in the sixteenth and seventeenth centuries than in preceding times. Man's assault on it during the sixteenth and seventeenth centuries—and subsequent ones—both as vermin and for skins, simply served to accelerate its demise. To add insult, it also enjoyed popularity as a beast of the chase in some parts of the country.

By the time of the implementation of the Tudor Vermin Acts, evidence shows that the Pine Marten still occurred in every corner of Britain. In England some counties supported good populations, mainly those dominated by long-established 'ancient countryside' or which were well wooded—in particular Cornwall, Devon, Somerset, Dorset, Hampshire, Kent, East Sussex, and West-morland. The churchwardens' records in these counties show regular low-level killing in some parishes and more sporadic totals in others. In pre- and post-enclosure Britain there is little doubt that habitat loss had caused the woodland-dwelling Pine Marten to become a more thinly distributed species than the other small mustelids—Polecat, Stoat, and Weasel. Thus it is to be expected that the numbers killed were likely to be fewer too. Nowhere in the historical records are high numbers of Pine Marten bounties to be found; the picture formed is more of a sporadic, opportunistic campaign of attrition. At St Bees (Cumb), 64 bounties were paid in 13 years from 1769 (how sad that so few Cumberland records are available), while 76 were killed at Holne in Devon across a period of 60 years with maxima of 7 or 8 some years. Batcombe, Pitminster, and Locking (Som) killed moderate numbers in the early decades of the eighteenth century as did West Knoyle (Wilts) in the adjacent county. So often it was the familiar parishes which recorded major kills of a wide range of other species that also provided the highest totals of Martens; Sherborne and Melbury Osmund (Dorset) were high on the list with 64 Martens killed in 60 years from 1693 and 27 between 1696 and 1737 respectively. Once again Kendal (W'land), in one of the lingering heartlands of the species, paid for 83 heads killed in 90 years from 1689. MacPherson mentions various other records from parishes in the same county and in Cumberland, but the original documents he referred to have not been traced. In other counties there were small numbers killed, mainly in the seventeenth century. Hampshire for example produced 11 parishes out of the 57 examined in which Martens had been killed, Kent 4 out of 57, and East Sussex 4 from 28; in most cases the numbers were only in single figures. A striking revelation is the almost total absence of churchwardens' records of Pine Martens in the counties of the east of England, north from Bedfordshire as far as Yorkshire—once again, coinciding with the area dominated by the great open field systems. The Martens are known to have been there, albeit perhaps in very small numbers. Thomas Isham in his *Journal of Lamport in the county of Northampton* refers to catching four in a fortnight in December 1673 and another two months later. However, such records are few and far between. One can only speculate as to the true picture had more parishes been as assiduous in pursuing the aims of the Tudor Acts, or if we had a complete picture from the large number of parishes for which no records exist.

An analysis of all the individual records extracted from the churchwardens' accounts, given in Table 17, shows that the earliest record I found was in 1664 (Beetham, W'land) and the last one in 1824 (Kendal), with the majority occurring between 1710 and 1780. After that date the numbers decline, and although not too much should necessarily be read into this limited sample, it is consistent with Langley and Yalden's conclusions about several of the counties mentioned above, from which they suggest the species had gone completely by about 1800.

TABLE 17. Total numbers of bounties paid for Pine Martens' heads in 1579 churchwardens' accounts in England and Wales. Figures are for decades starting 1660, 1670, etc.

1660	1670	1680	1690	1700	1710	1720	1730	1740	1750	1760	1770	1780	1790	1800	1810	1820
1	5	33	57	40	22	75	79	51	67	67	50	33	31	44	13	?*

* It is apparent that the Kendal accounts contained Pine Martens beyond 1810 although the numbers are subsumed in general 'payments for vermin'.

Before guns were generally available for vermin control we can only speculate about the methods that were used to trap the Pine Marten. Certainly it was known to be vulnerable to spring traps and baited, dead-fall traps but there were other ways too of securing it. Knapp, as well as lamenting its demise, tells us of one opportunistic method: 'Yet the Marten lingers with us still and every winter's snow betrays its footsteps to those who are acquainted with its peculiar trace which it leaves. Its excursions generally terminate at some hollow tree, whence it is driven into a bag'. Presumably it was smoked out of its tree refuge. At that time (1829) Knapp, writing in Gloucestershire, quoted the local value of skins as 2/6, although he commented that they were 'only used for inferior purposes as furs from the colder regions are better and more readily obtained'. Pine Marten heads taken to the churchwardens for payment were often paid at 4*d*. so that, assuming there was a market for skins nearby, there was a far better return if it was sold as fur. This factor could be another reason for the relatively low numbers in many parish records. MacPherson's 1892 account of the fauna of Lakeland makes a similar point wherein he says that a dog Mart pelt would fetch 6/6 at Kendal in the mid nineteenth century and the smaller bitch one 5/6. In addition, one caught live could fetch as much as 10/-, to be used for baiting with dogs in the flourishing west coast towns of Workington and Whitehaven. He also extolled the sport that was occasioned in winter Marten hunts across the Lakeland hills and quotes a spine-chilling description of one lasting several hours over crags and icy screes through the early light of a bitter December day. Even occasional payments of as much as 1/- a time for heads were understandably a less attractive proposition in most parishes.

The paucity of historical records from Wales is undoubtedly a reflection, once more, of the absence of so many historical parish accounts. There are scattered records of Pine Martens from Montgomeryshire, Merioneth, Monmouthshire, and Glamorgan.

In Scotland, the picture is somewhat clearer. Ritchie, often quoting from the notes or writings of earlier naturalists, leaves us a good account of its exploitation as far back as the fourteenth century. Scottish skins were greatly valued and Martens were evidently being killed in high numbers, for there was a flourishing export trade, such that a customs levy of 4*d*. per timmer (30 skins) was imposed from around 1324, rising to 6*d*. per skin by 1424. Inverness was the principal centre for trade in Mertrick (Marten) and Beaver skins and there was also a considerable export of skins through Leith. However, the population could not sustain the continual drain on its numbers. Even in the virtually treeless Outer Hebrides the killing was rife and Ritchie quotes Donald Munro, archdeacon of the Isles, in 1549 commenting on the 'infinite slaughter of otters and mertricks' on Harris. By 1703, Martin regarded them as still 'pretty numerous' there, and little over a century later Macgillivray found them 'not very uncommon', but by 1888 Harvie-Brown in his *Vertebrate Fauna of the Outer Hebrides* regarded them as almost extinct. The pattern was paralleled on the mainland where Ritchie attributed its demise in the lowlands to the fact that it was eliminated there more as a predator of poultry and even occasionally lambs and ewes (a charge echoed in the Lake District), rather than for the value of its pelt. The nineteenth-century slaughter on some of the Highland estates was at appalling levels. In the 3 years between March 1831 and March 1834, 301 Wild Cats, Polecats, and Martens were killed on the Duchess of Sutherland's estates (individual species were not separated in the totals). Around the same time 246 Pine Martens were taken on the Glengarry estate in 4 years and another 181 on a quarter of the same estate between 1843 and 1862. On Breadalbane, 50 were killed in 1782–97, 56 on an unnamed estate in Perthshire (possibly Breadalbane?) as late as 1891–1901, and 41 on 4 contiguous shoots in Sutherland 1877–86, as mentioned in Chapter 4. Harvie-Brown's papers, containing extensive vermin records from more than seventy estates in the northern half of Scotland for the last decades of the nineteenth century, show very small numbers of Martens killed on twelve of these estates (see below), in addition to the Perthshire and Sutherland examples mentioned above. The most significant interpretation from these figures is that all these estate records are from the west and north-west of Scotland and that there were no records of kills from the other fifty-six or so estates in north Scotland from which Harvie-Brown had gleaned data for the same period. This gives further support to the claims that Pine Martens had been severely reduced or eliminated from most areas earlier in the nineteenth century except for their final footholds in the far west.

TABLE 18. Numbers of Pine Martens killed on twelve Scottish estates in late C19. Data from Harvie-Brown papers.

Kintail, Argyll	1890–1	8
Garrogie, Inverness-shire	1893–1902	1
Inverinate, Wester Ross	1874–83	6
Scourie, Sutherland	1901–2	3
North Harris	1870–80	10
Shiel, Inverness-shire	1879–88	2
Lochnell, Argyll	1878–87	2
S Morar, Inverness-shire	1885–8	1
Morar, Inverness-shire	1879–88	2
Torridon, Wester Ross	1874–1902	8
Appin, Argyll	1880–9	9
Inchnadamph, Sutherland	1880–9	7

Ritchie believed that the disappearance of the Marten was more rapid than that of the Wild Cat which suffered in a similar way, because at the time he wrote (1920) it was certainly the rarer of the two, despite the wide distribution both had shared previously. Confirmation of the earlier extinction of the species in southern Scotland can be found in the fact that on eight very heavily 'keepered Buccleuch estates in Dumfries, Galloway, Selkirk, and Berwickshire where a wide range of vermin was taken, not one Marten was killed between 1818 and 1825, the period for which those estate records exist.

The Pine Marten had been heavily plundered for centuries but its fate was effectively sealed with the upsurge of game preservation from the second half of the eighteenth century and the simultaneous employment of gamekeepers appointed to protect those interests. Figure 19 shows the heavy toll that was taken in a brief period of years on a Scottish estate, and the effect that this had on the numbers. The gamekeepers on the Burley estate in Rutland accounted for nine Pine Martens between 1807 and 1816. Langley and Yalden have shown that its final elimination, county by county, in England occurred from 1800 (Wilts) until the last ones were eliminated in the 1870s or possibly as late as 1880 (Lincs); thereafter in England the Pine Marten was restricted to the mountains

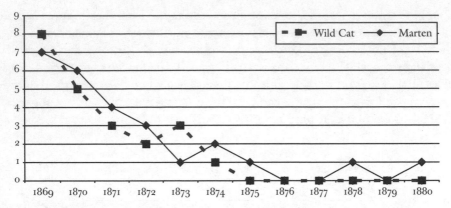

Figure 22. Decline in the numbers of Pine Marten and Wild Cat killed by
'keepers on the Assynt estate 1869–80. Adapted from Ritchie (1920).

of the Lake District, with smaller numbers persisting in the Cheviots and North
Yorkshire.

In Wales, Langley and Yalden suggest it only persisted in the fastness of
Snowdonia, but this seems increasingly unlikely since there were almost certainly
small relict populations elsewhere. Morgan, for example, has produced fairly
compelling evidence of records in Carmarthenshire and adjacent parts of mid
Wales. By 1915 in Scotland it was confined to the wild Highlands of the north-
west and arguably—in common with the Wild Cat in the same area—it may
have been saved from final extinction by the onset of the First World War, the
cessation of much of the shooting and the departure of gamekeepers to the
war front. As numbers slowly recovered in the twentieth century the Martens
were still heavily persecuted: how many were actually killed in that century, we
shall never know. McGhie analysed the records of carnivores from wide areas
of northern Scotland submitted to Macpherson, the taxidermist at Inverness,
between 1912 and 1970. He showed that 198 Pine Martens ended up there,
mostly from western areas, 40 from Assynt alone. For much of this period
Macpherson's was only one of several stuffing firms, albeit the largest.

Fox

Throughout the passage of time no animal in Britain has suffered a more schizophrenic relationship with Man than the Fox. On one hand it has been vilified since time immemorial and persecuted as one of the most despised of predators while on the other hand it has been protected with passion for Man's pleasure. Once the large predators such as Lynx, Wolf, and Bear had been eliminated from these islands it was inevitable that attention would next be directed to exterminating the Fox (with the Badger soon to follow). As long ago as 1539, Henry VIII was advised that Foxes could readily be eliminated if the landowning gentry would only agree to it. Holinshead, the royal chronicler, wrote to Elizabeth I that 'if foxes were not preserved for the pleasure of gentlemen they would be utterly destroyed manie years agone'. There were many other optimistic claims that extermination could have been achieved in those past centuries although there is no validity whatever in such claims. In any case, Man's appetite for the chase demanded that there was a continuing place for the Fox in the countryside. It was only at the time of the most intense persecution by gamekeepers and farmers with snare, poison, gun, and trap that even local extinctions were achieved.

The Fox's reputation for mischief and thievery has its origins far back in the misty reaches of antiquity and Man has waged incessant war against this troublesome neighbour from the earliest days of domesticated husbandry. Since those times, it has been widely despised for its constant depredations on poultry, lambing flocks, piglets, etc. At the same time, there has always been a sneaking respect for its legendary cunning, resourcefulness, and guile, ensuring that the Fox is woven deep into the tapestry of country lore.

In Britain hunting the Fox for sport was in vogue as early as the Middle Ages—Edward I had a pack of fox-hounds as long ago as 1280. Longrigg (1975) recounts too, that by the latter part of the Middle Ages, Henry IV and V were both enthusiastic fox-hunters. However, fox-hunting in those days was a totally different activity from the one we understand today. To quote Carr, 'Mediaeval hunting, to a modern fox-hunter, would have appeared a painfully slow affair riding through wooded country with lumbering horses, slow hounds and a bevy of hunt servants on foot'. In the fifteenth century, Carr says that the Fox was still only seventh on the list of preferred beasts of the chase, to be killed as soon as possible, not simply pursued for sport, with its greatest asset being the value of its pelt. William Harrison records that by 1586 various family hunts existed such as those run by Lord Arundel and the Duke of Buckingham. He reiterated the claim that at this early date both Fox and Badger were already being preserved in some areas for the benefit of such recreation. It is a reflective point that in such a climate, the squirearchy would have been unenthusiastic about vestry committees (on which most of them doubtless sat) paying out for the removal of Foxes through bounty payments to the villagers. There were increasing numbers of country squires such as Sir Thomas Cockaine in Derbyshire who hunted regularly with hounds in the latter days of the century and Squire Draper in Yorkshire, another name among many others prominent in the growing interest of the time. By the second half of the seventeenth century, fox-hunting was a popular pastime of the landed classes but its purpose was recreational rather than a method of control. It was not until the 1750s that the transformation to a modern form was introduced by Hugo Meynell at Corn Hall in Leicestershire and fox-hunting became the fast and furious activity that we now recognize.

It is relevant to chart this rise in fox-hunting because the seventeenth century marks the time when many parishes were active in fulfilling the requirements demanded by the Tudor legislation and were paying bounties for a wide range of vermin. In the surviving parish accounts of these vermin transactions there is no species that features more consistently than the Fox. In this respect the country-wide antipathy towards the animal can be gauged, since these individual Foxes were being killed for reasons of stock protection, not sport. Almost without exception, any parish throughout the length and breadth of England and Wales that undertook even a minimal amount of vermin control—perhaps payments for only one or two specimens in fifty years—would include Fox. If any control was being undertaken the Fox was sure to be there, sometimes in high numbers and at other times only low ones, but it would be there. A few parishes, surprisingly few, paid bounties for nothing other than Foxes over long periods of years. Lawford (Essex) in the seventy-three years between 1716 and 1809 and Phillac (C'wall) in the ninety-six years between 1741 and 1837 are two examples, although in the first case numbers rarely reached five a year, whereas at Phillac the number killed annually was in the upper teens.

It is important to note, however, that the intensity of killing through the parishes was by no means uniform across the counties of England and Wales. There are strongly marked regional differences. The records show clearly that the highest numbers were always in the areas of 'ancient countryside' in the south-west, the Marches, and Kent, and also in the upland counties of Wales and northern England. Although we do not know with accuracy the size of Fox populations in the seventeenth and eighteenth centuries in different parts of the country, it was certainly lower than at present. It is clear that even in the above mentioned areas where killing—and population levels—were highest, local control had little or no effect on the overall numbers. This can be seen from the figures in some of the parishes where there were fairly heavy annual kills but where the same numbers were killed year after year. Much Cowarne (Hfds) accounted for double figures of Foxes in most years from 1764 until 1810 but still with a maximum of twenty-nine in the final year. Hartland (Devon) was killing more than twenty annually from 1599 to 1705 and maintaining that number all the time. Corbridge (N'humb) in 1676–1723 again showed double figures most years and still killed eighteen in the last year for which records exist. Many other examples could be quoted from areas such as Cornwall, Kent, Shropshire, Durham, and the Lake District.

The age-old method that was favoured for catching the Fox in Tudor times involved the relatively simple process of netting the sides of a copse and then driving the Fox with any available dogs until it ran into the net. Here it was rapidly despatched with sticks and cudgels. Villagers readily employed this method and village Fox hunts have been likened by Carr to glorified rat-catching with participants armed with sticks or whatever other weapons came to hand. In some parishes private fox-catchers or huntsmen were employed and paid for out of the church fund. At Northill and Melchbourne (Beds), there are various references to money being paid to huntsmen for Foxes, as at Luccombe (Som) where a fox-catcher was paid 13/- p.a. from 1690 to 1692. At Great Staughton (Hunts), a handsome payment of 3/4 was made to 'ye gamekeeper for a bitch fox' in 1723. Either inflation or increasing success accompanied the fox-catcher at Bradock (C'wall) where his annual payment rose from an initial 9/- in 1673 to 10/- the next year and 15/- by 1677. Inflation evidently did not apply at Combe Martin (Devon) where the fox-catcher cost 10/- in 1719 and he (and various successors) was paid the same sum annually until 1754! At Buckland (Devon) 6d. was 'laid out to the fox-catcher' in 1631 and a few years later the record tells us that the vestry paid 4d. for 'bread and beer for the ffoxe hunters when they killed the ffoxe'; rewards in cash or beer—or both—continued in this enlightened parish for twenty or more years thereafter. Unfortunately, in none of these instances is there a record of the number of Foxes taken.

The headage payment for Fox stipulated in the 1566 Act was 1/-, far higher than the sum paid for any other species except Badger, indicating the premium that was put on controlling the animal. Throughout the following two centuries or more this remained the general rate, even up to final payments in some parishes as late as the 1830s. However, there were numerous exceptions, presumably depending on the seriousness with which individual parishes around the country regarded the damage that was inflicted by Foxes. The standard rate was then raised to 2/6 or even 5/- but differentials were initiated in many parishes where 3/4, 5/-, or 6/8 might be paid for a vixen, 2/6 for a dog Fox, and 1/- for cubs. In a rare example of co-ordination between parishes the rates of 5/-, 2/6, and 1/- for bitch, dog, and cub respectively, were agreed communally for parishes in the Vale of Clwyd in the seventeenth and eighteenth centuries. In one or two instances incomprehensible sums seem to have been paid. In a Devon parish in 1698, £1. 10s. 0d. was paid for a vixen and three cubs. The most inexplicable sum was £3 paid for a vixen and cubs at Bodfari (Flint) in 1730 for what must have been the mother and father of all Fox problems—unless the sum also provided abundant libation in celebration of success or a hidden payment for other services.

We have already seen that the countrywide effort of the parishes—uneven as it was—could have no measurable effect on the overall population of Foxes. However, the question still remains as to what the level of killing was in parishes across England and Wales. The examples below give figures for some of those English parishes where consistently high levels of control were exercised; predictably they all occur in areas of 'ancient countryside', where the majority of parishes were killing Foxes in numbers.

TABLE 19. Examples of the numbers of Foxes killed in seven English parishes C17 and C18. In considering these figures it is relevant to note that St Bees was an enormous parish of 69,260 acres (28,029 hectares) which contained 12 separate townships in the western valleys of Lakeland.

County	Parish	Span of years	Years	Numbers killed	Average p.a.
Cumberland	St Bees	1684–1775	91	1096	12
Herefordshire	Much Cowarne	1764–1810	46	298	6.4
	Aston Ingham	1771–1819	48	303	6.3
Gloucestershire	Newnham	1686–1791	105	612	5.8
Cornwall	Madron	1762–81	19	188	9.8
	St Buryan	1682–1749	57	402	7
Devon	Hartland	1627–1705	78	798	10.2

Once again records are so piecemeal in Wales that no clear picture emerges of the level of Fox control in a pastoral country where Fox predation was always of concern. Control was certainly widely practised and relatively high rates were paid in some places. In Caernarvonshire in the early years of the eighteenth century as much as 2/6 was regularly paid for an individual Fox head at Aber, in which parish landowners were subject to a Fox tax raising some £2. 10s. annually.

In contrast to the figures from the 'ancient countryside', the picture in many other areas of England was of far lower levels of control. This is particularly true of the counties of central and eastern England that were dominated by wide tracts of open fields until they were overtaken by the enclosures. The low level of Fox control is accounted for primarily by the nature of that countryside with the sparsity of woodland and scrub cover in many areas and consequent low number of Foxes, but also by virtue of farmland being predominantly arable rather than stock-rearing.

The Rabbit was another important factor determining numbers and distribution of Foxes. Up to 200 years or so ago, Rabbits were closely protected in warrens and it was only when they spread into the wider countryside that they became available as the preferred prey of Foxes, today forming 80% of their diet. (In Scotland, the spread of Rabbits only occurred 100 years or so later). Nonetheless, the exceptionally low figures of Fox payments from most counties of east and central England are still somewhat surprising. Three examples covering the same period as shown in Table 19, illustrate these differences: in Northamptonshire, Huntingdonshire, and Leicestershire only one parish in each county (Apethorpe, Great Stoughton, and Edith Weston respectively) killed Foxes with any regularity and averaged between 2.4 and 3.6 heads annually. The other 83 parish records that I examined in these three counties produced only low levels of sporadic kills or none at all; similar findings applied in other counties of the East Midlands, Norfolk, most of Yorkshire, Essex, and those south of the Thames as far as Wiltshire and Sussex.

Vermin payments from the parishes—other than for sparrows—had generally ceased by the early years of the nineteenth century. By this time the increasing numbers of gamekeepers were taking up much of the responsibility for vermin control. The Fox was one of the species that was an obvious immediate target for their attention. Lloyd has shown that, in parts of eastern Scotland and much of East Anglia, Foxes were actually eliminated during the nineteenth century. Numbers were kept low in the next century, as exemplified on the Elveden estate, where only thirteen were killed from 1903 up to the First World War. The effect of the two world wars was evident as 112 were then killed after the Second, in the 8 years from 1945. Fox control from the 1830s onward was largely in the hands of the 'keepered estates and the rising number of hunts. That century saw the formation of many more hunts in England including famous ones such as the Middleton, Belvoir, and Beaufort; the Quorn and Cottesmore hunts had been formed as early as 1688 and 1666 respectively. In Wales, the famous Wynnstay hunt was formed by 1788 and several others followed in the next decades.

Fox skins from Scotland were always highly valued and ensured that there was always a heavy kill of Foxes for that reason alone. At the beginning of the seventeenth century Ritchie recorded that they were fetching as much as forty shillings (£2 Scots) per skin when they were exported to Europe. This trade, as described in *Scottish Trade on the Eve of Union* was still running at up to 1,600 skins a year to the Baltic alone. Fox skins were also sent to Holland as well as England, together with skins of Otter, Polecat, and Wildcat. These were obviously in addition to the numbers that were traded on the home market.

The Old Statistical Account makes fairly frequent mention of the fact that some parishes in Scotland, occasionally working in combination with adjoining ones, appointed paid fox-catchers to combat the carnage that they believed was created among lambing flocks. At places such as Moffat, Lochgoilhead (Dumbarton), and Lochlee (Angus), the tackmen and tenants shared the cost and were obliged to accommodate and feed the huntsman and his dogs on a rotational basis. In lowland Scotland, several conventional hunts were set up in the later decades of the eighteenth century, for example the Edinburgh Hunt from c.1760, Mellerstain 1787, and in Fife by at least 1786 (Longrigg, 1975). However, it was the explosion of interest in the Scottish sporting estates in the 1800s, and the accompanying army of gamekeepers recruited to help manage them, that began to make serious inroads into the populations of so many predatory birds and mammals. Foxes fared better than most—at least they were not exterminated like the Polecat, or eliminated from large areas like the Wild Cat and Pine Marten. As we have seen, Foxes were wiped out from parts of eastern Scotland but elsewhere survived despite a heavy toll that was inflicted on some estates. On the Buccleuch estates between 1894 and 1900, 427 were killed, and on Glen Shieldaig Forest 247 in the last quarter of the century, with a further 201 at Gruinard 1904–12. Skye is the only Hebridean island with Foxes although there is suspicion that they may have been introduced to Harris in recent years. On Mull the island was reportedly 'full of Foxes' in 1777 but was completely cleared during the next century. As in other parts of Britain, the Forestry Commission has taken an active part in Fox control for many years and in Scotland has kept accurate records which show that the Commission kills more Foxes there than any other organization.

Through the use of gins, snares, and (from 1947) hydrogen cyanide, 'keepers throughout Britain could gain reasonable control over Foxes within their estates, albeit with constant effort. However these three methods were successively made illegal. Gins were first banned in 1958 in England and Wales (1973 in Scotland), self-locking snares in 1981, and finally cyanide gas in 1985. Since their removal 'keepers have had to rely increasingly on running snares and lamping at night with a powerful rifle and spot light. On the other side of the coin, hunts continued to prosper across the country despite setbacks in two world wars. Many of them responded promptly to local Fox problems although the effect on populations per se has been negligible (see below). Hunts, particularly mounted ones, remain, as they always have been, essentially recreational even when they shelter behind the cloak of control.

One of the paradoxical facts about hunts in the past has been that they have had to take active measures in some areas to protect Foxes, in order to ensure sufficient were available for the chase. As already mentioned the earliest examples of this go back several centuries. By the early eighteenth century, it had become commonplace to preserve cubs, import 'bagmen' (foxes brought into the area for release), or establish fox coverts. To ensure an adequate supply of Foxes for the hunt a major trade in Foxes imported from France developed between 1815 and 1914, through markets in London, notably Leadenhall. Reflecting this trade, Graham Smith (pers com) has shown through DNA analysis that Foxes in the south of England are much more closely related to French Foxes than to those in the north.

In the great hunting counties of eastern England—perfect country for the long chase over the new grassland pastures that developed after enclosures— Foxes were naturally relatively thin on the ground. To improve this situation, small areas of woodland and Fox coverts were planted and such steps were regarded as essential to maintain good hunting. Williamson suggests that in many Midland areas this may have been the first time these areas had seen woodland for a thousand years or more. The same applied in other parts of the country also; in Shropshire for example the whole county was covered by different hunts by around 1800 and the release of 'bagmen' was regular due to the lack of woodland and scrub cover and a consequently low population of Foxes. To remedy this the Shrewsbury Hunt gave 200 guineas a year from 1825 to be spent by a foxhunting committee to lease or plant coverts, of which twenty-five had already been put in place five years later. In areas such as these, the Fox was regarded as the rightful prerogative of the hunt and vulpicide was regarded, certainly by the hunts, as a morally unacceptable offence.

Lloyd describes how, during the Second World War Fox destruction societies were set up, initially with government financial support. These were mainly in the sheep-rearing areas of Wales (where there was a maximum of 139 in the 1970s), northern England (49), and Scotland (33). With echoes of past years, differential bounties were paid—£1 for an adult and 50p for cubs, although later as much as £2.50 was sometimes paid for a vixen. In Wales some 6,000 bounties were claimed in the peak years around 1970. Local Fox Destruction Societies run by farmers still operate in Wales but the number is unknown, as are the numbers of Foxes killed by them.

Baker and Harris have estimated that the current Fox population in Great Britain is in the region of 240,000 adults—195,000 in England, 23,000 in Scotland, and 22,000 in Wales—a population which they suggest is about right for a predator of that size. This population is certainly larger than that in the nineteenth and earlier centuries when 'keepers were more numerous, legal methods of controls were more varied, and upland afforestation had not begun. The same authors calculate that some 425,000 Fox cubs are born each year, in which case the same number of animals obviously needs to die annually for the population to remain stable. They suggest that each year approximately 100,000 are killed on roads, 80,000 are shot, 50,000 dug out with terriers, 30,000 snared, 10,000 killed with lurchers, and 15,000–17,000 removed by hunts (although the Burns Report puts this last figure at 21,000–25,000). This leaves well over 100,000 animals that will die by 'natural' causes each year if the population remains constant. As ever, the most efficient way of reducing a population is to cull females in the breeding season but organized hunting (184 registered hunts in England and Wales in 2005, plus six fell packs) operates between November and March (cub hunting August–October).

Most of the control by gamekeepers is undertaken across the same periods. In both instances Baker and Harris point out that a large proportion of the animals killed in these ways are youngsters dispersing from their natal areas. The situation with fell packs, up to the passing of the 2005 Act, is somewhat different and is well illustrated by the Blencathra Hunt, the most famous of all the foot packs. Across their 25 × 12 mile 'parish' the majority of their call outs during the extended lambing season are to deal with individual problem Foxes and their activity is therefore more selective and less random. This ancient hunt has killed an average of ninety to a hundred Foxes each year since around the 1960s (fewer before that), although numbers have declined slightly in recent years, because of the increase in lamping. There is the strong feeling in Lakeland that without the existence of the fell packs, the future for the Fox is bleak because of the belief that farmers will take the law into their hands and use whatever means they can to eliminate Foxes.

Notwithstanding this, the real possibility of eliminating the Fox in Britain was lost many centuries ago and the animal's place has been secured, ironically by the hunting community itself, in its determination to ensure a constant supply of animals for recreational purposes. The Fox now occupies the position of top mammalian predator in Britain while paradoxically still attracting continual persecution, favoured status, and confused public sentiments.

Rats are without question the most universally disliked of all species of vermin. They are seen as an enemy of Man almost throughout the world, both as vectors of disease and for the damage they do to his crops and stores.

In Britain, the issue nominally involves two species, the Black Rat (Ship Rat or Roof Rat) and the Brown or Norwegian Rat although, as explained at the end of this account, there is more to the story than this. Few would question why rats were listed in Elizabeth's Act of 1566, because it had been recognized ever since they first became cohabitants with Man that they were a serious pest on his grain and other supplies.

It is now widely accepted that the fleas carried by the Black Rat had been the vector for the Black Death which swept across Europe in the fourteenth century and killed in the region of 75 million people. They were also responsible for successive outbreaks of Bubonic plague. However, as Hirst points out, even at the end of the eighteenth century epidemiologists only reluctantly accepted this and therefore this could not have been a contributory reason for their inclusion on the original vermin list. The Black Rat, although not a true native, has certainly been here since before Saxon times. It was the only rat in Britain until the eighteenth century and, as an indigene of tropical and sub-tropical areas, it habitually confines itself to the warmth of dwellings. It climbs easily and is a frequent lodger in roofs, wainscots, and attics. Unlike the Brown Rat it does not burrow and is therefore more wholly a commensal with Man than the Brown Rat.

The Black Rat, which probably first arrived here with the Romans, has never been as numerous a species as the more successful Brown Rat and its distribution has been strongly governed by repeated recruitment in sea ports and onward movement from there by canal and other lines of transport. Both Bentley (1964) and Twigg have recorded its fluctuating fortunes in the second half of the twentieth century and these are summarized in Table 20.

TABLE 20. Distribution of the Black Rat in C20 from Bentley (1964) and Twigg (1992).

1951	Well established in London and 40 other locations; sporadic in a further 30 sites.
1956	Decreased to 30 localities.
1961	Further decrease. Reduction noted in port arrivals; more effective control and more modern storage buildings.
1970	Reduced to 5 sites.
1971–80	16 sites.
1981–4	8 sites.
1985–9	18 sites.

As can be deduced from Table 20, most sites are impermanent and its presence depends on regular recruitment from foreign-going ships to maintain or renew these nuclei, all of which tend to be closely related to these sea port locations. Apart from these sites, there has been a long-established and stable population on Lundy Island, off the north Devon coast; another similarly stable one on the Shiants in the Minch off western Scotland; and a small colony was identified by Gordon Corbet on the island of Inchcolm off the coast of Fife in the late 1990s. However, the Lundy animals were eliminated in the rat clearance scheme on the island in the winter of 2002–3. With Black Rats still arriving in British ports and the trend towards global warming, the environment here may become more favourable for the future of the species.

The records of historical payments of bounties for rats (they were listed at three for 1*d.* in the Tudor Acts) are virtually non-existent in the churchwardens' accounts. They were found in the records of only 16 parishes out of a total of the 1,579 examined in England and Wales. However, the reason lies in the fact that the Black Rat, despite its early arrival here, was not a widespread species throughout Britain and the Brown Rat did not arrive on our shores until the early part of the eighteenth century. Moreover, the freelance rat catcher belongs to a long-established and respected profession. In 1741, the king himself had his own appointed Rat-killer 'an honourable office', at the princely rate of £100 p.a. As is shown below, the freelance operators were frequently employed and paid directly by landowners/property owners. Also, much of the local rat destruction was carried out individually by householders without recourse to the church funds. Nonetheless, some of the very early (fifteenth century) churchwardens' accounts testify to the fact that Black Rats were a considerable problem in churches, at least in the metropolis of London, which was always the species' main stronghold in Britain. In several of the city records there is mention of payments for traps and 'beytes' (baits) and occasionally for the purchase of fine linens to repair rat damage, or for the replacement of antiphon sheets damaged by the rats.

There was a rare rat catcher
Did about the country wander,
The soundest blade of all his trade
Or him I should deeply slaunder

Upon a poale he carryd
Full fourty fulsome Vermine
Whose cursed lives without any knives
To take he did determine.

What Mise or Rattes or Wild Polcats
What Stoates or Weasels have yee?

(*c*.1615 ballad from Rollins, *A Pepysian Garland*)

The plethora of seventeenth and eighteenth century manuals of vermin control are full of inventive and innovative methods for catching or killing rats. George Conyers, in his engaging treatise *c*.1705, lists twenty-four allegedly efficacious ways of ridding properties of them, mainly with different types of trap. He also includes the two following ideas in a different vein:

Take a penny worth of treacle and mix it with unslaked lime till it is pretty thick; then lay pieces as big as a hazel nut on a piece of paper the breadth of a shilling and lay it about their holes or where they come from; they will tread on these papers and the stuff sticks to their feet which they will lick off and it burns their guts out.

In Staffordshire they place Birdlime about their holes and they, (the rats) running amongst it, it sticks to their skins and they will not leave scratching till they kill themselves.

Plagiarism was rife in these manuals and Conyers had clearly borrowed much of his material directly from 'W.W.' 1680. Robert Brown, a farmer from Somerset, added his contribution to this extensive field in 1759 (some forty years after the Brown Rat had landed on our shores) in his 'Compleat Farmer or the Whole Art of Husbandry'. As well as advocating the usual methods of control, he added words of caution directed to any employers of the old profession of rat catchers:

the rat catcher . . . makes a good living . . . for when not employed his leisure hours are taken up in catching rats and keeping them alive which he keeps by him until sent for again and the morning after he has set his traps he carries his live rats in a bag and imposes upon his employers a certain number, perhaps not one of them taken in his traps the night before. Therefore I would recommend to those who employ these people to see the head of every rat cut off, else he may be assured of paying for the same rats half a dozen times . . .

Similarly,

I have been told of a famous gypsy rat-catcher who will put live rats in the outhouses of gentlemen (whom he knew would employ him) to breed, so that he was immediately sent for, and as soon as he catched them, without reducing their number, perhaps he increased them for his going to and fro gave him the opportunity of conveying more into the building, heavy with young.

The Brown Rat first arrived in Britain around 1720, having spread across Europe from its original range in Central Asia. It spread rapidly throughout the country and was probably ubiquitous within twenty to thirty years. The new arrivals began to displace the Black Rat, a fact remarked upon as long ago as 1776 by Pennant, and were a contributory factor in the latter's demise. It was an ecological parallel to the modern replacement of our native Red Squirrel by the introduced Grey Squirrel

Since its successful colonization there has been a ceaseless war against the Brown Rat and it has been, and continues to be, killed in large numbers. Boelter, writing in 1909, was the first to suggest that there was at least one rat for every human on our islands (an erroneous belief that is still current). Boelter also pursued a protracted but unsuccessful campaign for the introduction of a Rat Act, based on an existing Danish model, which would have aimed at total extermination. In the nineteenth century, the Victorians found a recreational use for live-caught rats which were sold by rat catchers to ratting pits, where dogs were introduced to kill as many as they could in a given time. This provided both a spectator sport and a popular medium for gambling.

However, there is more to the story of this ongoing war against rats—in fact, an unexpected twist to it. It is best illustrated by the payments made in two or three parishes in Dorset. At Sherborne (4,900 acres (1,983 hectares)), the churchwardens paid out for an unbelievable number of 'rats'—135,890 in 35 years between 1762 and 1797, with an annual maximum of 9,335 in 1795. At Frome, Vauchurch, a small parish of only 1,080 acres (437 hectares), the more modest number of 861 was killed between 1792 and 1796, while in Puddletown parish (8,030 acres (3,249 hectares)) over 9,000 were slaughtered at $3d$. per dozen in 29 years from 1781 and another 10,497 in a second campaign from 1817 to 1823. These records present an interesting question because it is inconceivable that these numbers could be attributed to a combination of Brown Rats (which had only arrived in Britain c.1730) and Black Rats. In any case it is highly unlikely that there would have been a great many Black Rats in these inland parishes, even before the arrival of the Brown Rats. The answer, without question, is that the payments were being made for 'water rats'—what we now call Water Voles. Strange as this may seem, this vole was at one time a very serious pest on growing crops. The explanation for this lies in the fact that there are two forms of the Water Vole, one of which is the amphibious animal with which we are familiar— 'Ratty' of *Wind in the Willows*—and a fossorial form which is strictly terrestrial. This latter form, still common on the Continent, lives not on watersides but in open country where it can occur at very high density and burrows into pastureland and arable, causing considerable damage to growing crops. Although it had been eliminated by Man from mainland Britain by the 1920s, a few vestigial populations are known to remain on six small islets off the coast of Jura in the Inner Hebrides. It was at one time abundant, although declining, through land use change and persecution. Jefferies (pers com) has recently established that there was a very large population of this fossorial form in pre-Roman times, which dwindled gradually thereafter. Without firm evidence, there is no proof, of course, that the Dorset animals were fossorial Water Voles. However, the supposition that this is what they were, is a very strong one.

The aquatic form was regarded as a pest because it stripped bark on osier beds and both forms were intensively hunted, frequently with dogs, when winter floods drove them out into the open. Knapp, writing in 1829 and probably referring to the aquatic form, says they were 'shot daily by dozens'. The Dorset 'rats' were undoubtedly Water Voles and the beguiling question still remains: if this animal was so important a pest and killed in such numbers in a handful of Dorset parishes, why are 'rats' not represented in the churchwardens' accounts elsewhere? This remains an enigma.

This also raises another interesting point. It has always been assumed that the listing of 'rats' in the 1566 Act for 'The Preservation of Grayne' referred to rats as we now understand them. It is more likely, however, that the word was intended generically to include both Black Rat and the agricultural pest of 'water rat', with the emphasis probably on the latter. Perhaps the hunting with dogs—as with several other 'vermin' that were hunted for sport, e.g. Polecats in Lakeland—was reward in itself and did not merit payments from the church in most parishes.

By the end of the nineteenth century, when the more wide-ranging vermin payments in the parishes were being gradually reduced and eventually terminated, the network of Rat and Sparrow Clubs was being set up around the country, with the express aim of targeting those two species (although many other 'vermin' were also accounted for – see p. 176). Consequently overall numbers of Brown Rats killed each year were high, reflecting the fact that there was a proliferation of the clubs in the early decades of the twentieth century, added to which there was the encouragement of individual competition within the clubs. The few surviving club records make it clear that many of the clubs were killing rats at a rate running into several hundreds every year; money prizes for the most successful members were popular incentives. At the annual dinner of the Elham Rat and Sparrow Club in 1956 it was reported that the total bag for the year was 555 rats, 431 sparrows, 53 Grey Squirrels, 19 Carrion Crows, 10 Stoats, 96 Magpies, 171 Jays, 56 Jackdaws, 239 queen Wasps, and 788 Moles.

Rats have always been heavily targeted on lowland game estates and the numbers killed are testimony both to the levels of populations and to the animal's ability to reproduce at an immense rate. Burley estate (Rutland) accounted for 17,108 in 1807–16 (were they 'rats' or fossorial Water Voles?), Holkham (Norfolk) killed 21,714 between 1953 and 1959, and Elveden (Suffolk) 101,834 from 1903 to 1915 and 106,770 between 1927 and 1952. Many other estates killed at similar rates.

As the twentieth century progressed, local authorities were obliged to take the matter more seriously and bureaucratically usurped part of the functions of the Rat and Sparrow Clubs. Furthermore, during the Second World War successive legislation in 1940 and 1941 imposed obligations on farmers and their tenants to fence securely each corn rick before threshing took place thus enabling a maximum kill of rats (and mice) as the end of the rick was exposed. In the days before the introduction of the combine harvester, rats and mice were very serious pests on corn ricks and in 1939 the Agricultural Research Council contracted Venables and Leslie to assess the rat and mouse populations of such ricks. In their study in Oxfordshire and Berkshire they showed that individual ricks could, in some cases, hold up to 150–90 rats, plus innumerable mice, at any one time.

After the Second World War years, the development of new chemical baits (rodenticides) and anticoagulants (e.g. Warfarin) proved welcome and effective weapons against rats. However, a few years later, in the 1950s, genetic mutations began to produce Warfarin-resistant animals, first in the lowlands of Scotland (where they still exist forty years later) and subsequently around Welshpool in Montgomeryshire and thereafter in an increasing number of other centres countrywide. Thus the growing problem of resistance to both first generation and second generation rodenticides has become widespread and is of grave concern. Not the least of the concerns is that in 1998 the government withdrew funding for further monitoring of rodenticide resistance, genetic research, and the development of strategies to overcome resistance. Resistance is already a serious problem nationwide. In the worst area in the country, around Newbury on the Hampshire/Berkshire borders, it is now shown that rats there are wholly resistant to *all* rodenticides that can be used legally out of doors. Using available data, some of which are necessarily crude, Roger Quy at the Central Science Laboratory estimates the current population of the Brown Rat in England, Scotland, and Wales at somewhere in the region of 10 million. Control by rodenticides is not always without problems. In many cases rats are consuming ever-increasing loads of toxins which are not having the lethal effect intended. They become, in effect, living toxic time bombs, retaining these loads until their eventual death through age or predation, thereby opening the door to secondary poisoning of a wide range of scavengers and predatory mammals and birds higher up the food chain.

Rats or mice, ha' ye any rats, mice, polecats or weasels
Or ha' ye any old sows sick of the measels?
I can kill them, and I can kill moles, and
I can kill vermin that creepeth up and creepeth down,
And peepeth into holes.

(*c.*1615 ballad, from Brit. Mus. MS 29376 (fol 73))

Wild Cat

The Wild Cat is probably still a critically endangered animal in Britain, being confined nowadays to the Highlands of Scotland, north of the central lowlands. At the nadir of its fortunes, around the time of the First World War, it survived only as a fragile remnant in the wild country in the extreme north-west Highlands, although small pockets of Wild Cats may have survived elsewhere. However, its current restricted status belies a former distribution that saw the Wild Cat occurring commonly throughout the whole of Great Britain, at least up to the nineteenth century in parts of Wales, northern England, and Scotland. At one time, it was esteemed as an animal of the chase; Morton, for example, records that Richard I gave a charter to the Abbot and Convent of Peterborough permitting the hunting of Hare, Fox, and Wild Cat. The Wild Cat has a well-earned reputation for ferocity and untameability—even kittens show naked aggression if threatened. Always substantially larger than the domestic cat, an individual sometimes reached impressive proportions; one Lakeland male weighed 17 lbs (7.6 kg). It was sometimes referred to as the 'British Tiger' and was even reputed to be responsible for human deaths on more than one occasion. A popular local legend at Barnburgh in South Yorkshire is immortalized on a memorial tablet in the church there. It recounts the fate of Sir Percival Cresacre who, it is claimed, was attacked by a Wild Cat in the woods at High Melton as he rode home. A furious fight followed which ended at the church porch at Barnburgh where both Sir Percival and the Cat were found dead the following morning!

Whatever the veracity of such stories, the Wild Cat is a formidable animal and was regarded as a serious and dangerous predator on domestic stock and game. It was sufficiently feared and disliked—as well as presumably being plentiful—to be included in the 1566 Act where it was listed by its common name and also by an older one, 'Fayre Bade', a strange name the origins of which are obscure. Only in one case have I found reference to it by this name in respect of church-wardens' payments: Liskeard (C'wall) 1671 'four wild cats or bades and four fitches 8d'. Under the Act, a price of 1d. was put on its head, but in very few instances in churchwardens' accounts was this sum paid out; it was almost invari-ably more, and frequently as much as a shilling (1/-).

There is always suspicion that there may have been confusion in the past between genuine Wild Cats and domestic ones. Although this cannot be ruled out in every case there is no reason for supposing that there was more than occasional confusion. A Wild Cat in the hand, or its head alone, with white whiskers, could not readily be mistaken. Furthermore, the payments referred to below come from exactly those counties where one would expect to find them at those times and churchwardens were normally fairly cautious as to what they paid out for and were not too easily duped.

The churchwardens' accounts for England and Wales show records of pay-ments for Wild Cats from the sixteenth to nineteenth centuries across a number of counties. However, there are two facts that are immediately striking. The decline in numbers across those centuries is very clear (Table 21) and, perhaps unsurprisingly, there is a very strong bias of records on the wilder western and northern parts of the country.

TABLE 21. A summary of payments for Wild Cat heads from churchwardens' accounts in England and Wales, C17 to C19.

C17	1701–50	1751–1800	C19
670	322	109	4

However, in interpreting the above figures as an index of decline at the hand of Man, we need to exercise caution. On one hand, it must be remembered that surviving parish records are almost invariably piecemeal and rarely extend con-tinuously over the whole period. Thus they are, at best, only a part of the story, frequently commencing or curtailing abruptly. At the same time, the average number of parish records examined in each county is usually only c.14% of the total number. Nonetheless, the figures probably reflect fairly faithfully the actual progress of its decline in southern Britain. The British Wild Cat is essentially a forest animal and there can be little doubt that the removal of woodland in

England was the first major factor that accounted for its decline there. The onset of parliamentary enclosures, from 1750 on, and the accompanying reclamation of remaining 'wastes' for improved grazing land, undoubtedly proved a telling nail in the coffin—something bemoaned by John Clare in Northamptonshire. However, much of the damage through habitat removal had occurred far earlier than this, and the vast, treeless, open field areas of central and eastern England were totally unsuitable for the Wild Cat, so that the real decline in population had probably begun several hundred years earlier. In this respect, it is perhaps significant that parish records of Wild Cat are scarce or non-existent for most counties in the eastern half of England. Only in Suffolk (Cratfield 1585), Norfolk (N Elmham 1568), Nottinghamshire (Worksop 1586 and Cuckney 1732), Buckinghamshire (Newton Longville 1694, 1698, 1701), and Berkshire (Stratford Mortimore 1771) is there a meagre scatter of records and it is noteworthy that the first three of these are from very early sixteenth century dates. It seems slightly odd that no records at all were found in the 104 parishes examined in the heavily wooded counties of Kent and East Sussex. The Victoria County Histories mention records from these areas although Langley and Yalden, probably correctly, choose to discount them as being extremely late and almost certainly referring to feral animals.

On the western side of the country the historical picture is very different. Here in landscapes relatively untouched by eighteenth century enclosures and with long-established 'ancient countryside', characterized by small fields, coppices, woodland, and mature hedgerows, it is evident that the Wild Cat survived well until much later than in other parts of the country. In Devon, and especially Cornwall, high numbers were killed in many parishes in the seventeenth, and the first half of the eighteenth, centuries. At Morwenstow, 66 bounties were paid between 1667 and 1725 after which there were no more records. Ninety-two were killed at St Neot and heads were still being paid for there up to 1708, after which date the record no longer exists. Among the other ten parishes in Cornwall where Wild Cats were being killed regularly, Camborne was foremost with 37 individuals up to 1711. In Devon the impressive total of 311 Wild Cats were killed between 1629 and 1699, although it should be noted that the majority of these were in one parish: Hartland, on the north Devon coast, is a large parish of some 11,030 acres (4,463 hectares) with a historical record, almost second to none, for the breadth and intensity of killing. A total of 291 Wild Cats were paid for there in the seventeenth century. There is one early Devon record of 18 being killed at Dawlish in 1590–1610 and a fairly late record of one animal paid for at Branscombe in 1815—the latest of any records I found. The possibility that this animal may have been a hybrid or a feral beast cannot be discounted. Elsewhere on the western side of the country all counties, including those in the Marches (except Shropshire and Cheshire), were killing Wild Cats in small or moderate numbers until the end of the eighteenth century (to 1803 at Aston Ingham in Herefordshire).

The Wild Cat's lingering stronghold in northern England is reflected in the numbers that were killed in the four northern counties. In the 100 years from 1685, 142 were taken in the huge western parish of St Bees (Cumb) and possibly high numbers at Addingham where, frustratingly, most individual species totals are frequently buried in an annual summary of 'vermin payments'. Sadly, most of the church records from Cumberland north of the Lakeland hills are unavailable. However, Macpherson quotes various writers: Clarke, who recalled 12 being killed near Ullswater in Whitsun week 1759; Defoe, who extolled their great size and found them plentiful in the eastern fells; and Pennant who testified to their relative abundance at least up to the middle of the eighteenth century. Paradoxically, Macpherson also made the point that the price fetched in the Brampton area for a Wild Cat skin (4/-) in 1629 when Fox skin commanded only 3/-, may have indicated relative scarcity there even at that early date.

In Westmorland the Wild Cat was heavily targeted. Forty were taken at Barton in the 30 years up to 1739 with other Lakeland parishes—Kendal, Kirby Lonsdale, Beetham, Burton-in-Kendal, Heversham, Orton, Appleby—all accounting for considerable numbers and, although they were alluded to regularly in other parishes, many are again hidden under 'annual vermin payments'. The latest record mentioned was in 1759 at Burton-in-Kendal although the great majority of payments in the county were in the previous century. In Co Durham, Ryton parish was killing consistently in the late seventeenth century and in Northumberland Corbridge amassed the impressive total of 124 in the 50 years from 1676, with an annual maximum of 14 individuals in 1692.

Most Welsh counties, usually lacking in extant documents, do however provide evidence of consistent kills of Wild Cat. In Caernarvonshire, the rate in 1729 was given as 1/- per head although one paid for the following year attracted 7/6. At Llanstephan on the Carmarthenshire coast, there was a steady trickle of kills up to 1800. Most records, however, come from the border counties (where existing documents happen to be more extensive anyway), especially Montgomeryshire and Monmouthshire. In the former county, it was parishes in the east, Llansantffraid, Guilsfield, Meifod, and Kerry, that produced the most records. The majority of payments were in the eighteenth century; Meifod paid for twenty-nine heads between 1718 and 1749 and Llansantffraid twelve in forty-three similar years.

These records beg the question as to what effect the implementation of the Vermin Acts may have had on this species. It seems certain that habitat loss, not direct persecution, was the main factor responsible for the demise of the Wild Cat in most of southern Britain. Langley and Yalden suggest that the species may well have been extinct in some areas as long ago as the sixteenth century and there is no reason to doubt this. However, it appears from the records extracted from the parish accounts in western counties of England, that the efforts of parishioners could have been the cause of its final demise in some of these counties, even before the *coup de grâce* delivered with the arrival of gamekeepers.

In summarizing the history of the Wild Cat in Britain, Kitchener (1995) identifies the increase in sporting estates in the nineteenth century as being the catalyst for final extirpation. Langley and Yalden give the last dates for records of the Wild Cat in England as 1843 in Co Durham and Cumberland, and 1853 in Northumberland. No dates are suggested for the much earlier disappearance further south although, as mentioned above, there are church records of payments for individuals in 1803 from Herefordshire and 1815 in Devon. The same authors mention the somewhat enigmatic record of two that were shot in wild country around Hutton Roof near Kirby Lonsdale (W'land) in 1922 and, while accepting it as a genuine record, they resist speculating as to their origins. Were they Lakeland relicts or long-distance Scottish emigrants? Kitchener, however, has examined one of the skins in Lancaster Museum and believes it to be a feral domestic cat. The same account in the *Lancashire and Cheshire Naturalist* (Robinson 1925) refers to two identical cats being killed two years earlier than the Hutton Roof animals. Ten years earlier it is known that a landowner released a pair near Windermere but both were trapped nearby soon after.

In Wales, the record of the Wild Cat's demise is vague, with the suggestion that small populations probably survived in most counties until at least the middle of the nineteenth century. The last definite record is for 1862 at Abermule in Montgomeryshire. Scattered individuals may well have survived later in the century in some of the wooded, mountainous areas and there is one intriguing record of a cat shot near Aberystwyth in 1895 which was examined by Professor Salter, a notable naturalist at the university there, who believed it to be a genuine Wild Cat.

In 1920, Ritchie catalogued the decline of the Wild Cat in Scotland. In the heavily populated and industrialized lowlands he believed it had long been extinct. Elsewhere it was direct persecution by Man, not habitat loss, that was responsible for its disappearance. As early as 1790–7, the Taymouth estate in Perthshire was responsible for killing at least fifteen Wild Cats. In the Southern Uplands, the south-west counties, and along the English borders—areas rich with place names reminiscent of the Cat's past association—nineteenth century persecution to protect game stocks was intensive. The Wild Cat had gone from many of these areas by 1830 and held on little more than a further twenty years or so in others, the last recorded one having been killed in Berwickshire in 1849. It is worth remembering that Wild Cat skins attracted good prices in the fur trade and that the Dumfries Fur Market had long been a regular outlet. The final references to Cat skins there were 1855, 1856, and 1857, although their origins are unknown and they could easily have come from further north.

At the same time, intensive persecution by the burgeoning game estates was making serious inroads into the populations north of the Central Lowlands. In the less mountainous counties of the east Ritchie recorded it as being eliminated one by one—Fife, Kinross, Stirlingshire, Angus, Kincardineshire—mostly before 1830 and the last no later than 1850. In Aberdeenshire it was only in the mountainous inland regions where small numbers persisted as late as 1891 (Langley and Yalden).

Throughout the Highlands, the slaughter of Wild Cats by gamekeepers in the nineteenth century was unremitting. They were regarded, understandably, as prime predators on ground game and were afforded no mercy. On the Sutherland estates, for example, a reward of 2/6 was paid for all Wild Cat heads in the early decades of the century and in a mere 3 years from March 1831 to March 1834, 910 Wild Cats, Polecats, and Martens were killed (no individual species breakdown was given). The prodigious number of Wild Cats (198) claimed on the Glengarry estate between 1837 and 1840 is interesting because there is no mention of numbers of Feral Cats being killed, as there was on almost every other estate, in considerable numbers. It is abundantly clear, however, that the animals were being removed all the time throughout shooting estates across the Highlands, as shown in Table 22, which summarizes figures from estates somewhat later in the century.

TABLE 22. Numbers of Wild Cats killed on ten Scottish estates in brief periods in late C19 to early C20. From data collected by Harvie-Brown, c.1903.

Torridon (Ross & C)	1874–1902	34
Inverinate (Ross & C)	1874–83	51
	1892–1900	29
Four Sutherland shoots	1877–86	27
Inchnadamph (Inv'ness)	1880–99	16
South Morar (Argyll)	1885–8	10
Fosnakyle (Inv'ness)	1894–1902	36
Kishorn (Ross & C)	1898–1902	47
Eigg (Inv'ness)	1898–1903	9
Strathaird (Skye, Iv'ness)	1902	6
Gruinard (Ross & C)	1902–3	26

The effect of such persecution was inevitable, for no species could withstand such relentless levels of killing. Even in the Highlands the Wild Cat was eliminated area by area. Figure 22 on p. 208 shows the decline in numbers over a twelve-year period on the Assynt estate (Suth). Here the Wild Cat was almost

eliminated by 1880, albeit in a far corner of Scotland that was destined, fortuitously, to become part of the species' last refuge. An earlier record from the
same estate showed that fifty-two Wild Cats were slaughtered there between
1846 and 1852. We can only imagine the full picture on this one estate alone and
how it was obviously replicated on many others across the same era.

By the onset of the First World War the species was confined to the far north-
western corner of the Highlands. The speed with which it was eliminated in such
formidable countryside as the Highlands is testimony to the determination with
which it was hunted down.

The First World War saw the departure of many of the gamekeepers to fight at
the Front and the numbers employed after the War were never the same again.
The Wild Cat's recovery and spread stimulated by this change in intensity of
control was remarkably rapid and in twenty-five years or so it had recolonized
most of the areas north of the Central Lowlands. This remains its present distribution. The urbanized lowlands continue to represent a barrier to its more
southerly spread. Since the recovery of its population, the attitude of game
estates towards the Wild Cat has changed little; it is still regarded as a problem.
The Game Conservancy Trust recorded 274 killed on 40 Scottish estates in
central, eastern, and north-eastern Scotland in 1984–5. When Easterbee et al.
were carrying out their survey of the status and distribution of Wild Cats in
Scotland between 1983 and 1987 they found that persecution was taking place
in 62% of their survey area, mainly to protect rearing pens but sometimes also as
part of a continuing general campaign against predators. Kitchener showed that
snares set for Foxes accounted for considerable numbers of Wild Cats on one
estate in eastern Scotland. The Borobol estate in Sutherland was killing up to
eight a year until the 1960s, since when it has been rarely seen. McGhie, who
analysed Macpherson's taxidermy records at Inverness between 1912–70, found
records of 1,237 Wild Cats at the very time the species was beginning to recover
its numbers. In 1988, the Wild Cat was added to Schedule 5 of the Wildlife and
Countryside Act which gave it full protection in Britain. Since then, of course,
there are no available data although persecution, both deliberate and accidental,
still undoubtedly occurs.

In summary, the Wild Cat was lost from most of England several hundred
years ago, predominantly through land use change and consequent habitat loss.
Elsewhere in southern Britain, it was finally eliminated by deliberate persecution,
after habitat reduction had decreased its numbers. In Scotland, outside the
urbanized belt of the Central Lowlands, intensive campaigns of destruction
exterminated it from the remainder of the country, apart from a small area in the
far north-west of the Highlands. Even here it probably only survived because of
the outbreak of the First World War. As it spread out from this far corner in the
twentieth century, assisted by the reafforestation of conifer plantations, another

problem arose. In many areas, it has clearly interbred with feral domestic cats and the pure form of the truly wild animal may now be restricted to no more than a few hundred individuals.

The population at present, at the beginning of the twenty-first century, could be as low as 400 genetically pure Wild Cats, based on the proportion of pure individuals in an estimated total population of 3,500 found in surveys carried out by Harris et al. in 1990s. At this level, the animal is indeed probably critically endangered and current concern focuses on introgressive hybridization with feral domestic animals or other hybrids.

Badger

The Badger is one of the most familiar wild animals in Britain, even though people view it in different lights; there are as many who have reservations about its harmful aspects as there are those who admire it. It is also a numerous animal nowadays and its population is higher now than at any time in recorded history; the combined British and Irish populations are numerically the most important in Europe. Although it is essentially a woodland creature, the Badger has increasingly become habituated to more open environments and even to visiting suburban gardens at night, often taking advantage of food provided for it and thereby further enhancing its general popularity.

It was not always thus. For centuries the Badger was hunted mercilessly and it is small wonder sometimes that it survived at all and did not go the same way as the larger predators. It was yet another wild animal that improbably—as with Polecat and Pine Marten—was used as a beast of the chase; sometimes, as a nocturnal species, it was hunted with hounds at night.

As long ago as 1846, the sportsman/naturalist Charles St John predicted the imminent extinction of the Badger, believing it to be well down that road in England and not far behind in Scotland. He was wrong of course, but it underlined the fact that the Badger was severely persecuted by Man and, although certainly scarce, it was probably under-recorded in many areas. Later in the nineteenth century, Brown attempted to assess its status, county by county, in Scotland and concluded that although it was less widespread and numerous than formerly, it was still relatively common. Pease writing around the same time, disagreed and thought that by then it had disappeared from counties in the north-east of Scotland, but was still to be found occasionally in the west. In 1920, Ritchie was of the same view, but he thought that the effect of expanding cultivation was as much to blame as the continual direct persecution. He wrote that in the early part of the nineteenth century, before the main onslaught by 'keepers, it was sufficiently common that many villages had their own 'brock-hunter'. He listed the catalogue of reasons why the Badger was so heavily persecuted: 'It was hunted for sport, it was caught for baiting, it was destroyed for its destructiveness, it was killed for food and its skins were of marketable value'. In 1882, although Brown had thought the remaining Scottish Badgers to be most plentiful in the border counties, Robert Service asserted that they maintained only a precarious existence in Kirkcudbrightshire and were actually extinct in Dumfriesshire. He reported the presence (followed by inevitable slaughter) of one near Dumfries in 1887 as a remarkable occurrence.

In England at the end of the nineteenth century, various naturalists lamented the severity with which the Badger was being, and had been, harried and commented on its scarcity. Bell thought it nowhere abundant, rare in some places, but still occurring widely. Some suggested that it was already locally extinct but Harting and Pease were among those who maintained that it still occurred widely, particularly, according to Pease, in the south-west, Wales and the Marches, Kent, and parts of the Midlands. Gamekeeper pressure had been severe in the prime shooting counties of East Anglia, although against all the odds the Badger managed to maintain a tenuous hold there. At Hambleden (Bucks) Cocks believed, 'It is not impossible that there may still be a Badger or two lingering in the parish, in spite of the gamekeepers. One was captured here about three years ago, which I am afraid was kept for baiting for some time in Marlow and was then sent to a well-known place of entertainment in London.' In Essex, various writers regarded it as rare at best and bordering on extinction, at least locally, while prospering only in the more wooded areas. It was claimed by some to be extinct in much of the Lake District well before 1900, where persecution had certainly been severe. However this view was probably too pessimistic and Graham, among others, believed that it had always survived in a few remote woodlands. Nonetheless, in 1892 Macpherson lamented 'the extermination of these poor Badgers' and commented on 'districts from which all tradition of their former presence has long died out'. He believed that individual records in the previous two decades were the result of attempted reintroductions. Certainly in 1905, Millais mentioned their reintroduction into Lakeland and Ritchie makes reference to the same course being taken in parts of England where a few estates had always given rigorous protection to them. On the east of the Pennines they were reputedly exterminated in Co Durham, and virtually so in Northumberland, by the end of the nineteenth century.

Thus, by 1900 direct persecution by Man had taken the Badger to a position—at least in parts of Britain—where it was clearly disappearing. In Wales, western Scotland, western England, and some local pockets where it had been strongly protected, it survived to provide nuclei for recovery. In the early twentieth century, Blakeborough and Pease maintained that Badgers were hounded in at least 90% of setts so that it was unsurprising that many county mammal recorders of the time regarded them as rare or on the verge of extinction.

Of course the Badger had already been subject to persecution by Man for many centuries before this. On the list of vermin in the Tudor Acts, it was subject to a payment of 12 pence per head—a price shared only with the Fox, which was three times that stipulated for any other species of mammal or bird—indicating the priority that was placed on its removal. It is a sad reflection that Man is often all too ready to focus on the damaging aspects of a species and overlook the greater benefits it may provide. The Badger is a case in point. It is a true omnivore with a very wide range of food items, feeding principally on earthworms, a wide range of other invertebrates, and a variety of vegetable matter. Much of what it eats is clearly beneficial to our interests—slugs and snails, young rabbits dug from their nests, wasps nests, small rodents, various beetles, larvae, etc. The main charges against it are that it takes poultry, kills young lambs, and will plunder game birds' nests. There is no argument that it does all of these things, but the frequency with which such occurrences happen is strongly disputed. Assessments of the first two charges indicate that these are rare events that are too easily exaggerated, and that the Fox is often the true culprit. Badgers certainly take eggs from ground-nesting birds if they come across them, which is the main concern of gamekeepers, but the Game Conservancy Trust considers the damage done in this way to be insignificant and not enough to justify repressive measures. Badgers do not hunt for nests specifically and one helpful factor is the increased number of game birds that are now produced in rearing pens. These are not just modern concerns; their roots run deeply. The Devonshire poet W. Browne wrote in the first years of the seventeenth century,

> That Beast hath legs (which shepherds feare
> Yeleep'd a Badger, which our lambs doth teare)

This probably reflected the popular opinion of the time and helped explain why such a high price was put on its head.

Historically, the churchwardens' accounts across the country give us a clear picture of the extent to which the control of Badgers was undertaken after the implementation of the Vermin Acts from the sixteenth century onward, as well as giving indications of the local intensity with which control was carried out. In summarizing the parish records that I have examined, the first striking fact is the relatively low numbers that were killed, certainly in many areas of the country. The bounty of 1/- was generous and one would have expected higher numbers to appear overall (obviously there are individual parish exceptions) on that account alone. Was the reason that, although considered as high priority vermin, Badgers were already reduced in numbers by then? Or were the country folk just not as concerned about them, even at 1/- a head, as the legislators thought they should be? In the parish documents examined, there were three English counties with no mention at all of Badger—Hertfordshire, Lancashire, and Staffordshire. It must be remembered again, of course, that there are many more parishes in those counties (as in others) where the parish records for the centuries in question no longer exist, or for other reasons cannot been examined.

Elsewhere Badgers—'greys', 'bagerts', 'pates', and 'brocks' to use some of their many colloquial names—were killed with greatest apparent enthusiasm in Cornwall, Devon, Kent, and Westmorland. Table 23 lists some of the principal parishes in those counties together with two from north-east England which are interesting because virtually no other Badger payments were found in Durham or Northumberland.

TABLE 23. Highest kills of Badgers in English parishes in C17 and C18.

Morwenstow (C'wall)	1705–52	187
St Buryan (C'wall)	1692–1749	172
Ashburton (Devon)	1761–1820	153
Branscombe (Devon)	1793–1882	260
Combe Martin (Devon)	1714–54	151
Hartland (Devon)	1630–1705	216
Lustleigh (Devon)	1753–1820	172
Ryton (Co Dur)	1638–99	171
Saltwood (Kent)	1726–1807	139
Aylesford (Kent)	1691–1779	102
Corbridge (N'humb)	1676–1724	157
Beetham (W'land)	1618–1760	c.200
Heversham (W'land)	1628–1737	122
Kirby Lonsdale (W'land)	1669–90	127

By modern standards these totals do not seem particularly high and across all those parishes where Badgers were killed it was exceptional for one to have an average of even three per annum, however short or long a period over which their cull took place. Only four parishes, Hampstead Norreys (Berks) 5.7, Morwenstow 5.4, Kirby Lonsdale 6.0, and Branscombe 4.4 produced annual averages of more than four. Elsewhere killing was generally more sporadic, with fairly low numbers, occasional pulses of activity, but few signs of planned or co-ordinated action. Again it raises the intriguing questions about the levels of local populations in the seventeenth and eighteen centuries in different parts of the country and what the public attitude towards them really was.

Figure 23. A Badger baiting scene on the Cotswolds in the 1920s. Squire Gist sits in the centre. The Badgers are held with tongs and the Bull Terrier on the left awaits his time for the baiting. Photograph reproduced with permission of the Fred Archer Trust: www.fredarcher.co.uk.

Apart from this historic killing of Badgers as vermin—perceived or otherwise— they have for long been taken by digging from their setts both as a 'sport' for its own sake, and as means of obtaining the animals for Badger baiting. Longrigg describes how Badgers were hunted widely for sport in Dorset in the first half of the seventeenth century. This is an important point because the same clearly applied to other parts of the country as well and the churchwardens certainly did not pay out for animals dug for sport, but only for heads that were submitted to them as vermin. We can speculate that for this reason alone the actual numbers taken in the countryside were considerably higher than indicated by their appearance on the churchwardens' lists. The high numbers taken for baiting, in particular the larger males, obviously did not attract headage payments from the churchwardens. This barbaric activity, sometimes delivered with unbelievable cruelty, occasionally long drawn-out, and frequently inflicting severe injury to both Badgers and dogs, was a popular spectator sport until 1835 when it was finally made illegal under the Cruelty to Animals Act. Macpherson describes the process as it was practised in the north of England in the nineteenth century and had been for centuries beforehand:

The plan adopted for drawing the Badger was a simple one. The contest took place in a wooden structure something like an old-fashioned clock-case in appearance. It measured in length some 7 to 8 feet. The depth and height were about 3 feet. One extremity of this case was partitioned off for the Badger's den. This recess was entered by a hole, either round or square, through which the dog had to seize the Badger and drag it forth.

The appalling fact is that 170 years or so after it was outlawed, the activity is still practised today, although the scale has been reducing in recent years. The principal areas in which Badger baiting is still carried out are mainly indus-trial—particularly former mining—parts of Lancashire, Yorkshire, Glamorgan, Derbyshire, and Durham but also in Cheshire. Scottish Natural Heritage has recently expressed its concern at the amount that is still taking place in parts of Lowland Scotland and the Borders, where it is said to attract crowds of up to forty people.

During the national Badger survey in the 1980s, Cresswell et al. (1989) found high levels of persecution at setts by digging, hole blocking, and occasional illegal snaring. They believed that as many as 9,000+ setts were dug each year with the assumption that at least one Badger was killed at each dig. By the time of the 1990s survey Wilson et al. calculated that the incidence of digging had declined by about half, with only 4% or so of setts being attacked overall, although in the north and north-west the figure was as high as 25%. They believed that persecution by gamekeepers in the nineteenth and early twentieth centuries, together with ongoing digging, had a significant impact on Badger numbers. Despite these estimates of direct persecution, together with high numbers killed on roads, the Badger population in Great Britain now is at a high level.

Badgers were still persecuted illegally by fox-hunts blocking setts—at least up to the passing of the 2005 Hunting with Dogs Act—and by both Badger digging and illegal 'lamping' at night. After 170 years Badger digging and night shooting are among the most seriously abused pieces of wildlife legislation in Britain.

Three hundred and fifty years after the Tudor government introduced legis-lation to provide a bounty for killing Badgers as vermin, the animal has now been afforded almost total legal protection. Notwithstanding this, the govern-ment itself in the early years of the twenty-first century, has been paying for the

Figure 24. Sett digging, Blacklands 1920. Reproduced by kind permission
of Sue Boyes-Korkis and Malcolm Clarke.

widespread killing of Badgers in an attempt to reduce the spread of bovine TB in
which the Badger is implicated. The connection between Badgers and bovine
TB was first identified in 1971. The initial step in attempting to control the
outbreaks in cattle was the issuing of licences to farmers in affected areas permitting them to kill Badgers. The total number of animals killed by farmers at this
time is not known. Between 1975 and 1997 several different culling strategies
were implemented in areas of TB outbreaks in cattle, which resulted in a total of
49,000 Badgers being killed. Despite this, there was no reduction in the number
of outbreaks; in fact the incidence of cases rose. In 1998 therefore, the government initiated a series of large-scale trials in ten selected areas in England with
each trial area containing reactive, proactive, and survey-only sites. Until the
cessation of killing in reactive sites in November 2003 (the incidence of TB
outbreaks had actually *increased* in these areas by some 27%) 2,066 Badgers had
been killed. Killing continued beyond that date in the proactive sites, where
7,692 Badgers were killed up to January 2005. Since the middle of the 1990s there
has been a dramatic increase in the incidence of this strain of TB in cattle herds
which not only has serious implications for the livelihoods of cattle farmers but
also for human health, and the contentious issue remains unresolved. In the
meantime the numbers of Badgers killed continues to increase. Since the first
identification of the link between Badgers and bovine TB in the 1970s more than

118,000 cattle have been slaughtered despite the killing of more than 59,000 Badgers. Early in 2006, the Department of Environment, Food and Rural Affairs (DEFRA) went out to public consultation on a proposal for a total cull of Badgers in 'hot-spots' of bovine TB. Some 35,000 submissions were made by the public, 96% of which were opposed to the cull. With an unexplained drop in the incidence of bovine TB in the first half of 2006, still no decision has been made at the time of writing.

Weasel

In Britain Man's attitude to the Weasel has always been somewhat ambivalent: an uncertain love-hate relationship. This, the smallest of the mustelid family, is magnificently engineered as a quicksilver killer. Long, lithe, and lightning fast, it is a predator supreme; evolved to kill and perfectly designed for the job. Despite its diminutive size it has been widely viewed as a blood-thirsty villain and a ferocious killer, and for these reasons alone has attracted opprobrium and enmity across the years. Paradoxically, however, it has always been recognized as a potential ally, essentially because its main prey species are small rodents which were assumed to be nuisance pests. In fact this has always been a fallacy, as their main prey is voles which cause negligible damage in agricultural terms. In former times the Weasel may have been beneficial in predating the large colonies of fossorial Water Voles. In Britain, Weasels have often had bad press but much of this prejudice is unjustified. Whilst they are undoubtedly guilty of occasionally killing chicks or ducklings, this is outweighed by the numbers of rodents that are taken. This was certainly the view of Ritchie who was writing in 1920 about the situation in Scotland. King too has pointed out that Weasels are more sympathetically regarded in some other European countries than they are in Britain, and in the Middle East they were even domesticated as commensal rodent catchers.

In the process of searching the vermin payments through sixteenth to nineteenth century churchwardens' accounts for the whole of England and Wales, one is left with the strong impression that, historically, the killing of Weasels was not encouraged, despite the fact that they were specifically listed in Elizabeth's Act of 1655. In only one parish (Arksey, Yorks) out of 1,579 examined, is it clear that Weasels were specifically targeted and 685 were paid for, usually at the going rate of 2*d*. per head, between 1722 and 1767, with a maximum of 60 killed in a single year. Even at this level the effect on the population would be negligible, as shown by the continuing numbers killed each successive year. Elsewhere modest numbers were killed in several parishes in Kent (St Lawrence-in-Thanet, Tenterden, Northbourne), Bedfordshire (Clifton, Eaton Bray), Buckinghamshire (Newton Longville, Wing), and Nottinghamshire (Everton, Hayton) all in the late seventeenth and early eighteenth centuries. Numbers recorded in another ten counties were negligible and give the impression that the few accounted for were probably caught fortuitously or as the by-catch in traps set for Polecat and Stoat. In the majority of counties they did not feature at all, including, surprisingly, Devon, Cornwall (with one interesting exception mentioned below), Dorset, and Shropshire, where the overall levels of killing were particularly high and the range of other species taken was very wide.

It seems clear that across the country Weasels were regarded as beneficial around houses and farms and their presence was therefore not only tolerated but probably even encouraged. They were almost certainly abundant in most areas, taking advantage of many ideal habitats and profiting from a profusion of small rodents. They are first and foremost farmland animals where their preferred prey is Field Voles (Day, King) found in rank grassland, which they pursue both on the surface and through the little rodents' tunnel systems. Opportunistically they also take Wood Mice and other mouse species, Water Voles, Bank Voles, and to a lesser extent Moles (Weasels are occasionally caught in Mole traps) and other small prey species, including birds. When need or occasion arises they may also prey on larger animals out of proportion to their size, e.g. young rats and young Rabbits. In the past they were believed to suck blood from their prey, but this is a fallacy. However, they are skilled climbers and swimmers, hyperactive, intelligent, investigative, and resourceful. In the days when corn ricks and stackyards were ubiquitous on farms, such sites were a paradise for Weasels. The ricks were warm and dry, already provided with rodent tunnel systems in which to hunt, and teeming with an endless supply of rats and mice (see p. 222). It is hardly to be wondered that the Weasel was seen in very positive light, despite its bloodthirsty reputation, welcomed by most country people and usually absent from the churchwardens' lists of vermin payments.

Robert Smith, in his *Universal Directory* (of vermin destruction) published in 1768, described the Weasel as a 'noxious little animal—too small to do much mischief . . . (but) . . . can be a problem in hen houses and chicken gardens by sucking eggs'. In spite of this he advocated no particular methods for its control. George Conyers, in his modestly titled volume *The Complete English and French*

Vermin Killer written 60 years earlier, was less ambivalent: 'To drive away the Weasel. Cut off his stones and tail and he'll be gone and fright away all others about your house'. Alternatively he recommended the ultimate usefulness of a cat: 'The smell of a burnt cat frights them away'.

Historical research of the nature involved in this book will always produce surprises, and the occasional unexpected gem. As we have seen, Cornish parishes have revealed exceptionally large numbers of bounties for vermin covering a very wide range of species in the seventeenth and eighteenth centuries. Although I would never question the undoubted presence of 'little people' in this land of myth and legend, my credulity was stretched when I found them listed under bounty payments in the nineteenth century. On the north coast, adjacent to Tintagel, the parish accounts of St Teath for the year 1812 contain the unambiguous entry shown in Figure 25: 'To 2 Fairy's Heads 4d'. It took time to get to the root of this entry but the solution is no less interesting than the entry itself.

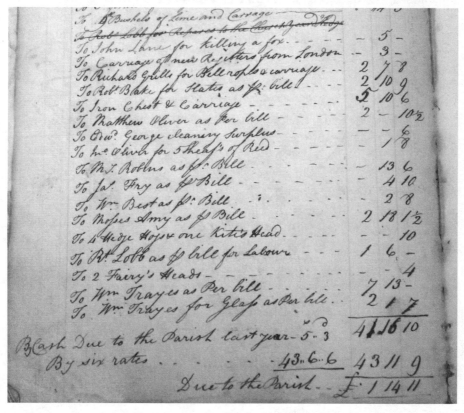

Figure 25. An entry from a page of the St Teath (C'wall) churchwardens, showing payment for fairies heads (aka Weasel). Reproduced by courtesy of the Cornwall Record Office.

'Vair', more frequently 'vairy' or other similar variants, was a dialect word, now obsolete. It was used in south-west England, Glamorgan, and Pembrokeshire as vernacular for Stoat or, more frequently, Weasel. *The Oxford English Dictionary* suggests origins linked to French (*vair* or *vaire*), which introduces another interesting reference. The story of *Cinderella* was written by a Frenchman, Charles Perrault. In it, as we know, Cinderella had a pair of delicate glass slippers. However the truth is that in the translation into English 'vair' was misinterpreted as the similar-sounding '*verre*', i.e. glass, a mistake that has been perpetuated ever since. Cinderella was not in fact shod in delicate footwear of glass but in dainty slippers of the most beautiful fur—in all probability the fur of Vairy, the Weasel.

The rise in the importance of game preservation in the nineteenth century heralded a hardening attitude towards this species, in common with that towards many other predators. Its usefulness in controlling rodents was too easily forgotten under an increasing degree of character assassination as it became a perceived enemy of game interests. The primacy of producing maximum bags of game rapidly ensured the Weasel's place on the list of undesirable vermin. The twentieth-century practice of 'keepers displaying their kills on gibbets often testified to the high numbers of the small mustelids that have been killed.

Although there seems little reason for confusing Stoats and Weasels, certainly when handled as corpses, it is odd that so many of the Scottish vermin records for the nineteenth century refer to the two species simply as 'Weasels' and do not differentiate. Even in the New Statistical Account it is claimed that 'The resemblance between these animals are so great that some consider them as of the same species'. The following examples of combined Stoat/Weasel figures show that on the Scottish estates fairly heavy control was exercised. An unnamed Perthshire estate accounted for 9,852 between 1891 and 1901, Atholl 7,198 in 1894–1904, and Buccleuch 2,526 in 1818–27. On those shoots where the differentiation was made, Stoats outnumbered Weasels by fewer than 2:1. Figures for two East Anglian estates in the following century illustrate similar levels of continuing annual control: Sandringham 1938–50, 2,641 Weasels and Holkham 1953–60, 929.

Tapper, writing in 1992, acknowledged that Weasels certainly kill Partridge and Pheasant chicks, whilst suggesting that the problem they pose is probably small in comparison with that of more serious predators such as crow or Fox. Nevertheless, a Weasel that finds itself among Pheasant or Partridge chicks will kill relentlessly. As King has put it: 'A Weasel in a pen full of chicks is psychologically unable to ignore the flutterings of the live ones in order to settle down and eat . . . It must kill . . . because killing is instinctive'. However, it is worth noting that both historically and at the present time, Weasels are probably blamed for some damage that should be more accurately attributed to Stoats.

The Game Conservancy's Partridge Survival Project undertaken by Potts between 1971 and 1976 was in response to a sudden and dramatic collapse in Partridge populations. It was a situation in which one of the main fingers of suspicion pointed to predators. Between 1971 and 1974, Tapper analysed the gut contents from 151 Weasels taken on the study site in Sussex and found remains of game bird chicks in only 2.1%. Potts eventually identified the major cause of the decline as the disappearance of the insect food supply for Partridge chicks, as a result of the use of agricultural pesticides (herbicides). At the same time, it was clear that the decline was being accelerated by predation—mainly by corvids—during the critical period of nesting and chick rearing. Weasels, as minor predators on chicks, probably had very little part to play in that.

Weasels are numerous mammals although their population levels are volatile, being quasi-cyclic and linked to the fluctuations of Field Voles. Harris et al. estimated the pre-breeding season population for Britain to be in the region of 450,000 individuals. The current levels of control have negligible effects on the overall numbers.

Stoat

The Stoat has long been an adversary of Man, specifically because it took poultry and invaded Rabbit warrens. Robert Smith, writing in 1768, saw them as 'the worst of small vermin, plundering warrens, pheasantries and chicken runs and being prone to wanton killing'. He reminded us that another old name for the Stoat was 'Cain'—echoing the murderous son of Adam and Eve and clearly reflecting the popular view of the animal. Much later, and in the era of maximum predator control on sporting estates, the Badminton Library volume on game rearing, used a more fanciful description of the Stoat. With unashamed hyperbole, they described it as a predator 'with the ferocity of a tiger, swiftness and activity of a greyhound and the nose of a bloodhound. A more lithe, active, crafty and bloodthirsty foe to all other animals has never been constructed'.

In view of the strength of the sentiments expressed, it is curious that the parishes did not persecute Stoats more than they did. Whatever the feelings expressed about the Stoat, it was the Polecat that was far more reviled and that was killed in parishes across the country in much greater numbers. Only 115 parishes out of all those I examined, revealed any payments for Stoats and 81 of these parishes were in only 5 counties: Bedfordshire 12, Dorset 26, Devon 12, Hampshire & Isle of Wight 19, and Somerset 12. In other counties it was only a scatter of parishes that undertook any serious Stoat control and across the majority of England and Wales it seemed that Stoats did not cause great concern in the seventeenth or eighteenth centuries. The levels and the patterns of killing both varied enormously. Some parishes pursued intensive short-term campaigns (e.g. Cranbourne (Dorset) 236 Stoats in 8 years 1700–7; Pyrford (Surrey) 173 in 15 years), while others maintained much longer periods of general killing. Arreton on the Isle of Wight killed 1,841 over 55 years, Sherborne (Dorset) 1,940 across 124 years, and Stockton (Wilts) the modest total of 125+ in 73 years. As with some other vermin species there were occasionally individuals who 'specialized' in Stoats; at Morwenstow (C'wall) Thos Trumble was personally responsible for 34 in 1694 out of a total of 41 that year.

It is worth making specific mention of the Isle of Wight (also quoted in Chapter 6 for its exceptional kills of House Sparrows) because on this small island there were nine parishes that focused particular attention on Stoats. Four of them caught only modest numbers, Gatcombe, Saint Helens, Northwood, and Freshwater, but the other five pursued sustained campaigns through the last quarter of the eighteenth century and the first decade or two of the next and killed several thousand, on average as many as thirty-seven per year. Newchurch, Arreton, Brading, Yaverland, and Godshill, between them, accounted for at least 5,378 Stoats in that period, considerably more than the accumulated totals for any mainland county.

The Isle of Wight figures are impressive, but even they do not compare with those that were attainable once gamekeepers were active on shooting estates and equipped with gin traps and guns. Before gin traps were made illegal many Stoats were caught incidentally in gins set for Rabbits. Harrison Matthews suggested that this reason alone accounted for the fact that they were temporarily exterminated after the Second World War in south-west Wales, at which time Rabbit catching was an important rural industry. In Scotland, the earliest estate vermin records show the steady beginnings of regular control although, irritatingly, Stoats and Weasels were almost always lumped together as 'Weasels'; John Sinclair at Taymouth killed a modest forty-five between 1782 and 1796 together with a similar number of Martens and six times as many Polecats. The records up until 1818 on the Buccleuch estates in south-west Scotland have been lost, but in the 10 years thereafter 2,526 Weasels/Stoats were killed, totals that derive from seven shooting estates, although the majority—1,786 individuals—

came from just one estate at Bowhill. Atholl (7,198 in 11 years) and the un-named Perthshire estate (9,852 in 11 years) killed at even more impressive rates.

Old estate vermin records are rare documents in England and Wales. On the Penrhyn estate (Caerns) records, 3,116 Stoats are listed for 1874–1902, with 1,289 at Burley (Rutland) 1807–16, 4,544 in thirteen years from 1938 at Sandringham, and 1953 at Holkham (both Norfolk) from 1953 to 1960.

In his Memoirs of a Gamekeeper, Turner gave a breakdown of the months in which 8,883 Stoats were killed on the Elveden estate between 1920 and 1930. This emphasizes the time of year at which the population is highest, the animals are most active, family dispersals are taking place, and 'keepers are keenest to deplete the numbers at the peak time for breeding game birds.

TABLE 24. Breakdown of seasonal killing of Stoats on Elveden estate, 1920–30.

Jan	320	Apr	446	July	1386	Oct	607
Feb	305	May	708	Aug	887	Nov	530
Mar	400	June	2258	Sept	623	Dec	353

Tapper (1992) acknowledges that gamekeepers, particularly on upland moors, regard Stoats as serious game predators that will kill incubating birds, and take eggs as well as poults, if they find the opportunity. On lowland shoots, where the majority of Pheasants are nowadays captive-bred and released, Stoats are seen as less of a problem than formerly for that very reason. The same does not apply when the main quarry is wild Grey Partridge, when Stoats are still regarded as a major threat. However, if a Stoat breaks into a Pheasant rearing pen it can inflict serious damage as a result of wanton killing. It is not surprising therefore that, where appropriate, game estates make intensive efforts to reduce Stoat numbers in Spring and Summer, echoing the pattern that was shown at Elveden.

The annual National Game Census results from 1961 to 2002 indicate an overall decline in Stoat numbers in the first twenty years, based on returns from shooting estates, after which the populations stabilized.

Trawling through the dusty pages of original documents several centuries old is fascinating in its own right, often tempered by an uneasy feeling of invading the privacy of the past. However, nothing can bring the past to life more than interpreting the personal or community tribulations, laboriously recorded by a succession of worthy villagers and townsmen. Unexpected revelations abound and even the vermin entries are liable to turn up occasional surprises.

Blickling is an inland parish in north Norfolk. In terms of vermin control in the sixteenth and seventeenth centuries (its existing churchwardens' records only cover the years 1667–1786) it produced modest totals of Foxes, Hedgehogs, Polecats, and vast numbers of Moles. But suddenly in 1729 the churchwardens documented a series of payments of 2*d*. each for lobsters. Blickling is 10 miles from the sea and lobsters are far removed from being classed as vermin in anybody's book! The explanation gradually emerged: 'lobster' is another of these strange old colloquial names. Its use is first recorded in the *Paston Letters*, dating from *c.*1490. (The Paston family came from the coastal village of the same name, south of Cromer). It is derived from another colloquial name, 'clubster', in which the first element alludes to 'head', especially its prominence, and the second element to tail (as the 'start' in Redstart). In old Norfolk dialect, lobster was simply a Stoat! As late as 1864 the word was still in local use—'Even now it is said that farmers in England complain of the "lobsters" sucking eggs and killing chickens' (C. Elton). But the parishioners of Blickling were not really serious in their pursuit of Stoats, since the only other record is for five taken in 1744.

Otter

Nowadays, the Otter is a totemic symbol of successful wildlife conservation in Britain, a very recent icon of conservation success and an animal held in great affection by the public. The fact that it is held in such esteem—a reversal of its former position—owes much to books such as *Tarka the Otter* and *Ring of Bright Water*, together with their film adaptations. With this in mind it is salutary to realize that the Otter has been hunted continuously from the time of the arrival of Mesolithic Man more than 6,000 years ago until it was given full legal protection in England and Wales in 1978. (Full protection in Scotland was not afforded until 1982). Grigson and Mellars' excavations on Oronsay in the Hebrides are one example of Otter remains being found in middens from the distant past. In those days, Otters were undoubtedly hunted, albeit at low levels by a small human population, both for their pelts and for the meat they provided for the hunter/fisherman settlers. Even in medieval times their flesh was valued since they were conveniently deemed to be 'fish' and could thus be eaten on Fridays. Across the intervening centuries Otter pelts have always been highly valued and, as a result the animal was hunted expressly for that purpose. However, in more recent times the species has also been increasingly castigated as a pest of fisheries and at the same time periodically accused of preying on lambs and farmyard fowl; the aquatic equivalent of the wily Fox and therefore to be eradicated at every opportunity.

Although the Otter feeds primarily on fish it will opportunistically take small mammals and birds. Freshwater fish formed a very significant part of human diet in medieval and post-medieval Roman Catholic Britain, both for the privileged classes who reared and guarded them and for those less elevated on the social scale who sought them as items of wild food. In rivers and lakes there was an abundance of fish that was harvested in fish traps, nets, and by other means, and the great manor houses and monastic establishments all placed great importance on their fishponds. At the same time, the Otter was a numerous and widely distributed animal throughout all river catchments and clearly competed for the same fish stocks. Artificially stocked waters are an irresistible attraction to such a resourceful piscivorous species and the effect that Otters could have on a stocked stew pond can be readily imagined. The problem still occurs today with the recovery of Otter populations; fish farms, carp ponds, and ornamental pools are all sometimes affected. Thus, for hundreds of years the shy Otter has been a direct competitor with Man, with the inevitable result that persecution increased and there were serious attempts to reduce its numbers. Inevitably, the Otter was included on the list of vermin in Elizabeth's 1566 Act.

Well before this time, Otter hunting had been organized as a sport, certainly as far back as the high Middle Ages when Henry II had his own 'Otter Master' and this form of recreational hunting—initially on horseback—was very much a sport of kings. Henry IV too had his master of Otter hounds; in 1410 William Melbourne was employed in this role and was dispatched around the country to kill Otters and Foxes for their pelts.

From the late sixteenth to the early seventeenth century, the interests of recreational Otter hunting began to merge with remunerated control, as the churchwardens began to pay for Otter heads in parishes throughout many English counties. (In Wales, the fragmentary records produced only one Carmarthenshire record and a couple in the Marches county of Monmouthshire.) Although there are a significant number of records of such payments, they are not as numerous as might have been expected. This is presumably due to the concurrent efforts of individual landowners and Otter hunts, whose activities were, of course, unrecorded in parish payments or elsewhere. The standard rate recommended in the 1566 Act was 2*d*. a head but such payment was rare and the universal rate, once vermin payments began to appear in the church accounts (around 1600), was almost always 1/-. Higher payments were occasionally given: 2/6 at Ash (Kent) in 1689 and various other parishes from time to time, 5/- for one head at Plymouth in 1706. In 1731, the vestry at Prestbury (Ches) was offering the lordly sum of 7/6 for each head. They agreed that:

... for encouraging persons to destroy otters with which this parish is now much infested it is ordered that the sum of 7/6 shall be paid by the churchwardens for every otter (come to his full growth) taken and killed within the said parish of Prestbury within the space of 6 days after the otter is taken and killed and no more than 5/- for any otter ... within the precincts of the parish that is not come to full growth provided always that he who brings the otter shall ... declare on oath before a lawful magistrate that the said otter was taken and killed within the parish precincts ...

Even this inducement produced only eight Otters over the succeeding three years from this huge parish—hardly evidence of serious attention to the 'infestation'. However, it should be noted that Otters are not always easy to trap and 'accidental' catches in eel traps may account for many of these old records.

The distribution of the persecution of Otters through the parishes was very uneven. Whether this is a genuine reflection of activity across the country or a function of the limited extent of existing records is unclear, but the discontinuous pattern of parish control that emerges in those past centuries has no ready explanation. It could of course be a reflection of the uneven distribution of Otters themselves after 1,000+ years of continuous persecution, with fish-trap and fish net casualties accounting for many of the bounties claimed. In most counties there are either occasional single payments recorded or a scatter of entries over a long period of years in the seventeenth and eighteenth centuries. Sometimes there were pulses of activity such as at Prestbury, and also at Kingswood (Glos) where thirteen were killed in five years and then nothing further recorded. At Kirby Lonsdale (W'land) the only payments were for thirteen in three brief years, 1679–81. Exceptions to this pattern were principally to be found in south-west England. Here there were parishes where more intensive and protracted killing took place. Several parishes in Cornwall—Altarnun, Egloskerry, Lezant, Linkinhorne, Morwenstow, St Buryan, St Columb Minor—were killing Otters consistently throughout the eighteenth century. However, total numbers were still low, no more than 134 in those 7 parishes across more than 70 years in the eighteenth century.

Devon parishes had a similar pattern, widespread but not intensive, although at Topsham the churchwardens paid the remarkable sum of 6/8 per head for six Otters in 1747 and five in 1750. Sherborne (Dorset) claimed seventy-seven in thirty-four different years between 1701 and 1790 with a maximum of ten in any one year. The greatest number however was at Kendal between 1723 and 1761 when ninety-five were killed (plus another twenty in a wider scatter of years between 1699 and 1796). Elsewhere, the churchwardens at Chilham in Kent paid for fifty-one Otters in seventy years and at Arksey (Yorks) for twenty-nine in forty-two years. The latest payments by churchwardens which have been found were in 1820 at Blisland (C'wall) and Eaton Socon (Cambs). We shall never know how many were killed at this time by private individuals, landowners, or evolving hunts; presumably it was many more than were accounted for by the parishes. It is clear that the efforts of parishioners across the country, presumably perceived to be useful contributions locally, had no significant impact on the overall population levels.

Bell states that hunting with properly organized packs of Otter hounds did not really get under way until around 1796. Chanin (pers com) has shown that the first 'modern' hunt was established at Culmstock (Devon) in 1790 although there is evidence that at least one south Devon pack was operating from 1740. Again, no records exist of the numbers that were killed by these early packs. Jefferies (1989) suggests that the population of Otters remained at a high level until at least the middle of the eighteenth century. After this, fuelled by the growing desire to protect fish stocks, landowners pursued more serious persecution and for the first time real pressure began to be exerted on local populations in some areas, with the aim of complete elimination (the first extinctions on individual rivers had occurred by 1800). Furthermore the rapid expansion of sporting estates meant that the nineteenth century saw a great increase in fishing and shooting interests with even further pressure from game-keepers being felt by the Otter (as with many other species). A marked decline in numbers of Otters towards the end of that century was being recognized by the Otter hunts themselves. So, by this time Man's direct persecution of the Otter was already having a serious effect. The situation was also exacerbated indirectly by the long-term drainage of marshes, fens, and other wetlands and by the first manifestations of the pollution of waterways in the principal areas affected by the industrial revolution. Notwithstanding this decline, the Otter's real nadir awaited it in the twentieth century.

In the early years of the twentieth century there were some twenty-three packs of Otter hounds in Britain. In analysing the results of these hunts, Chanin and Jeffries have shown that in total these hunts were killing an average of around 430 Otters annually. There was still a fairly healthy population across the country and the reduction in hunting and shooting activity during the First World War also helped a modest recovery in numbers. The period between the two world wars in the 1920s and 1930s has been regarded as the heyday of Otter hunting in Britain, although Chanin suggests that the level of killing by individual hunts in the second half of the preceding century was of the same order. However, it is very likely that the numbers of Otters killed by gamekeepers and river bailiffs between the wars, dwarfed those taken by the hunts. However, after the Second World War—and another lapse in the intensity of persecution—the number of active hunts had been reduced to eleven in England, Wales, and Dumfriesshire.

By the 1950s, the numbers of Otters killed by the hunts was falling and Chanin and Jeffries have shown that in the 6 years up to 1957 the 11 hunts killed a total of 1,212 Otters (Table 25) at an annual average of 202. However, during the following 6 years to 1963 the number killed had fallen to 1,065. By the early 1960s, it was increasingly clear that there was something seriously wrong with the Otter population on many river systems. Hunts were having increasing difficulty in 'finding' Otters and agreed to kill a smaller percentage of those they did succeed in finding.

TABLE 25. Otters killed by hunts in six years between 1950 and 1957 (records for the first six years in which hunting took place, in each case). Reproduced from Chanin and Jeffries (1978) with permission.

Otter hunts	Number of Otters killed 1950–5	Number of otters killed as percentage of those found
Hawkstone	256	62
Courtney Tracy	163	58
Buckinghamshire	154	58
Eastern Counties	125	50
Pembroke and Carmarthen	90	57
Border Counties	85	46
Culmstock	84	35
Dumfriesshire	79	48
Dartmoor	67	36
Kendal and District	57	40
Northern Counties	50	38

After 1969, the maximum killed by hunts in any one year was thirteen. From around 1957, the population had slipped into catastrophic decline. It reached its nadir in the west around 1966–70 and between 1978 and 1980 in eastern England. Otters disappeared from many entire river systems in south and central England and showed marked reductions in other areas, with the exception of Scotland, parts of Central Wales, and the south-west peninsula. The continuance of hunting and killing by gamekeepers and river bailiffs in the face of declining population may have exacerbated the position, but it was not in fact direct human persecution that precipitated the final crash. Chanin and Jeffries have shown that the sudden collapse of the population (as with various other wildlife species at the same time) resulted from the widespread agricultural use of cyclodiene organochlorine insecticides, especially dieldrin and aldrin. Both these highly toxic chemicals were leaching into watercourses and entering the aquatic food chain with lethal effects for a species such as the Otter at the top of that chain. Dieldrin was finally banned from use in sheep dips in 1966.

Scotland has always been one of the strongholds for the Otter in Britain where it is now more numerous in coastal areas than it is on freshwaters. Nowhere is this truer than on some of the offshore islands. On Shetland, for example, Berry and Johnston suggest that the outer islands probably have a higher density than anywhere else in Britain, at perhaps one Otter per mile of coastline. The Orkneys too have a reasonably good population, as do many of the Hebridean islands, but even here Man has long exploited Otters. Berry quotes the *Orkneyinga Saga* that describes Otter hunting more than a thousand years ago when, on Rousay '. . . nineteen men had gone to the south of the island to hunt the otters that lay under the headland'. Here Otters were also regularly caught in stone traps— 'otter houses'—almost identical in structure to the heavy stone traps, described on p. 57, used against terrestrial mustelids hundreds of years later on Dartmoor. Ritchie quotes Brand as claiming that as early as 1701 the population in the Orkneys had already greatly declined. The Orkney population is still moderately low compared with that on Shetland. McGhie's analysis of Macpherson's taxidermy records at Inverness showed that between 1912 and 1970, 1,425 Otter corpses from wide areas in the north of Scotland were sent to be stuffed.

Otter skins were an important item of trade in Scotland for many hundreds of years and Ritchie describes how, long before the commercial exploitation of pelts from Arctic countries, Scotland had a European reputation for its skins. He cites the fact that the fourteenth-century trade in Otter skins alone was sufficient to attract customs duty of one halfpenny per skin, which had increased modestly to sixpence for ten skins by the next century. In the early seventeenth century skins were exported annually, by which time they fetched the good price of some 40 shillings Scots (i.e. *c*.6/8 equivalent in English currency) per skin. In the vicinity of Kilmory on Arran, the Old Statistical Account comments on the excellent price that Otter skins from there commanded on the market at the end of the eighteenth century. As late as the 1970s, before legal protection, Jefferies recorded that they were still being snared commercially in the Hebrides for their pelts.

The Dumfries Fur Market gives some indication of the rate at which Otters were being caught in the nineteenth century in south-west Scotland and traded as skins through this market every winter. The earliest traceable record is 1816 (skins at 11/- each) although the market had been in existence long before this, and probably more intensively for mustelid skins in the eighteenth century than in the nineteenth. Subsequent numbers varied annually, peaking at an abnormally high 226 in 1831, but often attracting the comment that they were 'fewer than previous years' or 'scarce'. The effects on the population in this part of Scotland are evident from the fact that they no longer appeared in the market at all after 1867. The realization of the sporting potential of Scottish estates that occurred in the early decades of the nineteenth century, bolstered as it was by the opening of the railways in the 1840s, was a heavy blow to other inland populations of Otter—as with many other species—both in the Highlands and

TABLE 26. Otters killed on seven Scottish estates, C19.

Duke of Sutherland's estates	1831–4	263 Otters killed @ 5/- per head
Glengarry	1837–40	48 killed
Harris and Lewis	1876–1902	464 killed
Glenshieldaig Forest	1874–1902	208 killed
Ardfin, Jura	1877–86	40 killed
Glen Borrowdale	1862–81	118 killed
Morar	1880–9	98 killed

Lowlands. Impressive figures testify to the extent to which Otters were slaughtered.

So the Otter, hunted by Man at varying intensities for millennia, has had a chequered history in Britain, eventually being brought to the edge of extinction, certainly in many parts of lowland England, by the middle of the twentieth century. Only at the eleventh hour was its imminent demise realized and steps taken to halt and reverse the decline, first of all by the introduction of bans on the use of organochlorine chemicals and secondly through permanent legal protection for the Otter. Since then a series of surveys has been undertaken to ascertain the extent of any recovery. The first national survey in 1977–9 found evidence of Otters at no more than 6% of sites examined in England, 20% in Wales, and a healthier 75% in Scotland (where the Highland and Islands populations appeared to be reasonably intact). Further surveys in the 1980s and 1990s identified a gradual recovery, so that, by the time of the most recent surveys in England and Wales (both in 2002) the percentage of sites with evidence of Otter presence had risen to 34% and 71% respectively. In Scotland, the population has always been less affected by chemical pollutants than that south of the border. The 1984–5 surveys showed that the strongholds were in the Highlands and Islands and also in Dumfries and Galloway, a startling recovery since the days of the Dumfries Fur Market. By the time of the 1991–4 surveys, 88% of the monitored sites produced positive signs of Otter presence, a 15% rise since the first survey, and the area of Scotland without Otters had decreased to 1.8%.

8

Local patterns of persecution: England and Wales

ONE of the many unexpected findings of the historical searches, particularly through examination of more than 1,500 parish records, has been the enormous differences in the intensity of persecution in different areas. Naturally, agricultural practices and systems vary from one part of the country to another, depending on climate, soils, altitude, etc. and these factors help to determine the species of mammals and birds that occur there, and those that have been regarded as pests, and are persecuted as vermin. In terms of wildlife management (aka vermin control), upland sheep-rearing areas, for example, have totally different priorities from corn-growing or fruit-growing ones. Nonetheless, the difference in the intensity of control, from almost wholesale slaughter in some counties to virtually none in others, is sometimes difficult to explain. Why should widescale control throughout many parishes in Kent and Hampshire, for example, not be matched by anything approaching that in East or West Sussex, where there was almost none? This chapter gives a brief summary of these regional differences.

South-west England

Unquestionably, in terms of both range of species and sheer numbers, the four south-west counties were the heartland of vermin control between the sixteenth and nineteenth centuries. Very few of the parishes whose records I have examined in Cornwall, Dorset, and Somerset (see Appendix 1) were not killing vermin in the years for which records exist. In Devon, the figure was a little different, with twenty-five parishes out of the eighty examined not recording any vermin. Hedgehogs were continually slaughtered over a long period, for example at Luccombe (Som) where the modest number of 737 was killed in 43 years. In Cornwall, there were fewer killed than elsewhere in the region. Appendix 1 testifies to the heavy culls of Foxes and mustelids throughout the

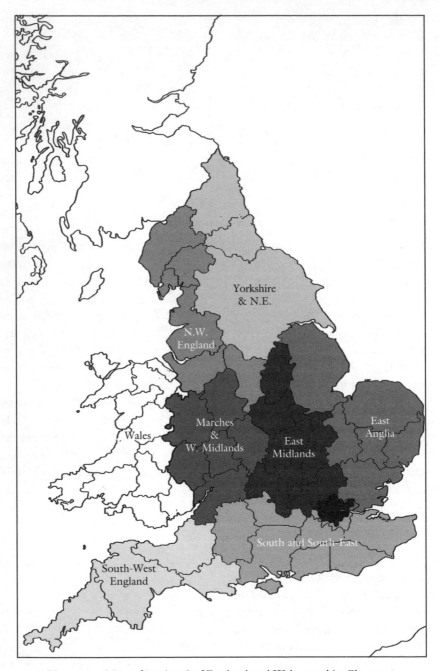

Figure 26. Map of 'regions' of England and Wales used in Chapter 8.

region. At Piddlehinton (Dorset), the vestry committee decided in 1740 that 'we do agree no more to pay for Stoats heads, Polecats or Sparrows'. However, 2 years later they were in full flow again and, uniquely for anywhere else in the country, were killing far more Stoats than Polecats—276 Stoats in 21 years against 74 Polecats in the same period. The abundance of Polecats in the seventeenth and eighteenth centuries is evident from the enormous numbers that were killed in many parishes. Hartland, on the north Devon coast, accounted for 3,061 between 1597 and 1750, and although this may be exceptional, many other parishes attained similar averages annually, albeit for shorter periods. Mullion (C'wall) churchwardens paid for 628 in the 60 years 1701–62 and in St Neot there were payments for 1,776 in 82 years in the previous century.

In this region it was predominantly mammals that were the principal targets—all the mustelids, plus Fox, and Wild Cat—although one or two bird species featured prominently on the lists. Unlike many other areas of England, House Sparrows did not attract wide attention except in the east of the region, where the majority of parishes in Dorset and a number in Somerset regularly killed high numbers, especially in the latter half of the eighteenth century and the early years of the following one. One exception in Devon was Butleigh, where a short burst of enthusiasm in 1742 yielded a total of 951 dozen House Sparrows in the following 6 years, with the high figure of 356 dozen in one year alone. Surprisingly, no members of the corvid family were particularly targeted in the south-west, but again these were one or two notable exceptions. In Devon, and in two or three parishes in Dorset, there was very heavy killing of Jays and some of the totals achieved were impressive. At Modbury, in the South Hams, twopence a head was paid and some 1,480 Jays were killed between 1726 and 1771 with a maximum of 104 in one year; Exeter St Thomas churchwardens paid for 563 in a mere 14 years, 1726–38. Both parishes also took a heavy toll of Bullfinches ('Hoops') and, unaccountably, at St Thomas', 998 'tomtits' in the same period. Other Devon parishes, but few elsewhere in the region, were responsible for targeting the Bullfinch in considerable numbers.

The Kite is the other bird that dominates the churchwardens' accounts in Devon and Cornwall—but not in Dorset or Somerset, where it rarely appeared. There is a problem here, as discussed on page 135 because of the local use of the word 'kite' for both Red Kite and Buzzard. It seems impossible that the number of 'kites' listed in the accounts of parishes such as Morwenstow, Linkinhorne, Lezant, or Modbury, could be ascribed to the Red Kite, however numerous they may have been. The numbers claimed were very high, 4,035 in the 4 parishes across a span of no more than 70 eighteenth-century years. The south-west peninsula has always been a stronghold of the Buzzard and the totals must include both species, but unfortunately it will never be possible to ascertain the respective proportions of each.

The following table summarizes the selected totals of vermin killed in four parishes in the south-west in the seventeenth and eighteenth centuries. Details of additional species killed in these parishes (woodpeckers, Jay, other corvids, House Sparrow, Rat (aka Water Vole)) are found under the species accounts (Chapters 6 and 7) and in Appendix 1.

TABLE 27. Vermin killed in four parishes in SW England C17 and C18.

		Bullfinch	Kite	Hedgehog	Fox	Badger
Morwenstow (C'wall)	1666–1752	3272	1780	2681	345	255
Hartland (Devon)	1597–1706	–	–	48	798	216
Cranborne (Dorset)	1700–25	–	5	417	53	–
Crewkerne (Som)	1625–94	–	123	403	33	48

		Otter	Polecat	Stoat	Marten	Wild Cat
Morwenstow (C'wall)	1666–1752	20	2757	1093	34	64
Hartland (Devon)	1597–1706	1	3061	7	–	291
Cranborne (Dorset)	1700–25	2	114	236	–	–
Crewkerne (Som)	1625–94	–	42	–	–	71

When considering these figures it must be remembered that these are only four parishes out of a total of some 1,406 in the 4 counties, albeit not all of them were persecuting species at such high levels.

Southern and south-east England

In the eight counties south of the Thames (East and West Sussex are considered independently, and the Isle of Wight as separate from Hampshire), there are remarkable differences in the amount of persecution and the range of species targeted from county to county. In all those parishes in which the vestry decided to undertake vermin control, the focus was almost invariably on the 'traditional' mammalian species, Hedgehog, Fox, Badger, Polecat, and occasional Otter; several parishes in Wiltshire, notably Stockton and Melksham took a particularly heavy toll on Otters. As in other parts of England, the Polecat was the most heavily persecuted mammal in these counties with the highest totals in Hampshire and Kent and one intriguing record in 1791 on the Isle of Wight (see p. 202). The only bounties for Pine Marten were from four parishes in East Sussex (which is surprising in itself since there appears to have been so little persecution of any description in the county) and Hampshire. In Hampshire, eleven parishes produced records of payments for Martens. None of these records was from the immediate vicinity of the New Forest, as one might have expected, but they were scattered randomly throughout the county. This is a good indication of the amount of woodland or open heathland that existed in the late eighteenth century. Of course Martens are not wholly confined to woodlands, but can exist in more open country, heathland for example, of which there was an abundance in Hampshire. The last payment for a Pine Marten here was in 1817. Stoats were specifically targeted in a number of parishes in Hampshire, Wiltshire, Surrey, and Kent, and were singled out in many parishes on the Isle of Wight. Relatively few records of Weasel were found and none at all of Wild Cat.

In Kent, many parishes were active in controlling a wide range of mammals and birds, and this was one of the few counties where Buzzards are mentioned by name. However, this fairly heavy pattern of control was not replicated in the other eight counties. In many ways, the most interesting feature of this region is the absence of many species which one would have expected to find on the killing lists. Apart from Kent, there were virtually no birds killed anywhere in the other eight counties with the exception of House Sparrows. Bounties were paid for a few Jays and even fewer Magpies in a couple of Hampshire parishes. 'Crows' and Rooks occur on the lists in Melksham and West Knoyle in Wiltshire and there were two payments for Ravens in East Sussex. It is strangely anomalous that, these apart, no other winged vermin—Bullfinch, corvids, birds of prey—are to be found in the 286 parish records that I have searched in the region. Even in Kent, traditionally the fruit-growing Garden of England, where one would expect to find Bullfinches persecuted, only in Ospringe and Tenterden is there evidence of them being taken. The Mole is another absentee from the payment rolls, although the existence of freelance operatives could account for this anomaly, as there are several parish references to annual payments to 'the molecatcher'.

As elsewhere in eastern England there were serious tolls taken on House Sparrows. Wherever vermin control took place House Sparrows were heavily persecuted, with the strange exception of East Sussex, where I found none at all in the twenty-nine parish accounts. Many hundreds of dozens of adults and innumerable young and eggs were taken annually. This was certainly true in Hampshire, Wiltshire, Kent, Berkshire, and West Sussex. The phenomenal numbers killed between 1742 and the end of the century in the corn-growing parishes on the Isle of Wight are referred to in Chapter 6.

The final point to make is to highlight again the enigmatic situation in both East and West Sussex, where so little vermin control appears to have taken place despite the fact that it was widely undertaken in surrounding counties. No explanation for this puzzling anomaly is offered, as discussions with local historians and county archivists have failed to suggest an answer. Occasionally, in other parts of the country, vermin payments are not found in the church-wardens' accounts, but are included within the constable's accounts or those of the overseers of the poor. In this case, even these sources failed to produce vermin records although a few annual payments in West Sussex parishes are to be found in the vestry minutes.

There is one interesting series of records in the churchwardens' accounts at St Lawrence in Thanet, in the north-east corner of Kent. Here, between 1704 and 1721, payments of 4*d*. per dozen were made for hundreds of 'larks', presumably Skylarks. It is well known that Skylarks were a popular delicacy at the time, but there appears to be no particular logic in the churchwardens paying for them. Larks, taken for food, were traditionally trapped in large numbers on the Downs, together with Wheatears, in nets or with the use of lures. It was a practice that continued up to the time of the First World War, when as many as 30,000 could be offered for sale on London markets. However, it seems an unlikely explanation for the toll that was taken at St Lawrence, far away from the Downs, a couple of centuries earlier. At a later date, the explanation could have been found in the fact that Skylarks were identified as pests on the new arable fields, where they damage sprouting grain. It was the only reference I found to Skylarks in any of the parish records.

Hampshire has long been an important county for partridge shooting and the following table illustrates the levels of vermin control that were operated in the past. All the species shown, with the exception of 'hawks', are still legitimate targets for gamekeepers.

TABLE 28. Vermin killed in seven years on a Hampshire estate in the mid C19. By courtesy of Lord Caernarvon.

	Weasel	Stoat	Cat (feral)	'Hawk'	Crow	Magpie	Jay
Highclere estate, Berkshire 1840–6	338	255	247	234	72	244	556

East Anglia with Lincolnshire

Since the early 1800s East Anglia, particularly west Norfolk, has been the pre-eminent game-shooting area of lowland Britain. This has meant that there have been concerted campaigns of predator control on most of the large estates, to maximize the available quarry, principally Grey Partridge. However, in the centuries before the development of the shooting estates, the amount of vermin control carried out in the name of agriculture, or for other justification, was considerably less than might have been expected. The region had always been important agriculturally. In fact, since the Middle Ages, Norfolk was one of the most heavily populated rural counties in England. Despite this fact, none of the control of species traditionally regarded as pests reached the levels that prevailed in many other areas. Open field systems, apparently poor in wildlife diversity, dominated the pre-enclosure landscapes and undoubtedly had a part to play in this, as they clearly did in the adjoining counties of the East Midlands. Nonetheless, there were still substantial areas of waste and common ground in the East Anglian counties, until at least the beginning of the parliamentary enclosure movement.

The selective differentiation between pests of agriculture and those regarded as undesirable predators on game is clearly evident when one looks at the historic lists of parish payments from the sixteenth to eighteenth centuries. Very few mustelids, and only modest numbers of Foxes and Badgers, were killed; once again it was the House Sparrow, scourge of corn crops, which was the principal casualty. Even if the House Sparrow was not slaughtered in the same numbers as in some other counties, there were high numbers killed in many parishes in Cambridgeshire, Huntingdonshire, Norfolk, and Suffolk. Strangely, relatively few House Sparrows appear in the churchwardens' accounts in Lincolnshire and, unaccountably, none at all in Essex. The whole question of historic vermin control in Essex is another enigma. As in Kent and eastern Suffolk, the county evolved out of its Saxon open field system long before other areas of eastern England. Enclosures in the distant past have produced a countryside characterized by a pattern of small fields, copses, and woodland clearings claimed from the original forest. In similar areas elsewhere in England, for example Gloucestershire or Cheshire, this long-established 'ancient countryside' has yielded impressive numbers of a wide range of vermin records. In Essex, the majority of parish records indicate that no killing at all took place and those where it did, show that little else was taken other than Foxes. The fact that more Foxes were killed here than in the neighbouring counties, suggests the existence of a countryside that was more conducive to supporting Foxes than other areas in the region.

Some early records from Cratfield, in east Suffolk, give a clue as to what may have happened more widely in the decades immediately after the Elizabethan Act in 1566. This period was one from which records are rarely found. In the 1580s, at Cratfield, payments were made for a range of Buzzards, 'Cadowes' (viz Jackdaws), Bullfinches, Magpies, and woodpeckers, together with six separate payments at 6d. per head for Wild Cats in 1585. The presence of woodpeckers might also have been expected in later dates and more widely in Essex, where even today, many shingle-clad steeples suffer woodpecker damage. However none was found. Jackdaws featured prominently in several Norfolk accounts, in most cases almost certainly indicating a problem in the church that was addressed in a single year. However, in East Dereham this was clearly not the case, as substantial payments—up to 4/10 at maximum—were made for killing Jackdaws every year from 1701 to 1753; whether this was churchwardens' licence for a more general cull of other corvid species, we can never know. Otherwise the crow family is virtually unrepresented on parish vermin lists throughout the region.

The long-standing importance of East Anglia for game shooting has meant that there has traditionally been a high level of vermin control since the nineteenth century. The three examples from notable shooting estates shown below, illustrate the intensity of control that has been applied over the years to ensure the maintenance of substantial game stocks.

TABLE 29. Vermin killed on three East Anglian estates over short periods in C20.

Elveden

	Weasel	Stoat	Hedgehog	Rat	'Hawk'	Crow	Magpie	Jay	'Various'
1903–19	2378	9905	5580	101834	875	2576	8	769	2940
1926–52	1345	17150	11143	106770	980	2518	603	1596	5899

Holkham

	Weasel	Stoat	Hedgehog	Rat	Hawk	Crow	Magpie	Jay	Jackdaw	Owl	'Various'
1953–60	929	1953	3226	21714	652	998	204	1550	5501	48	1064
1967–73	1223	1163	2397	15987	0	1458	68	758	1283	0	1963

Sandringham

	Weasel	Stoat	Hedgehog	Fox	Cat (feral)	Hawk	Crow	Magpie	Jay	Jackdaw	Owl
1938–50	2457	4554	5019	35	1566	1648	1657	1166	1998	3403	2954

Sandringham records by courtesy of the Royal Archives.

East Midlands and counties north of the Thames

The sweep of country from Nottinghamshire and Leicestershire, south to the Chiltern counties of Oxfordshire and Buckinghamshire was the heartland of the great open field systems. Here, even to this day, the ghosts of the ancient ridge-and-furrows are to be seen in the old pastures. In terms of vermin, the region is notable for the very narrow range and low numbers of birds and mammals that were recorded in the parish accounts in most of the counties.

Across these counties there were extensive areas of countryside where trees and woodland were scarce, which accounted for those being some of the least diverse wildlife areas in lowland Britain. Notwithstanding that fact, there were still some long-standing wooded areas such as the Dukeries, Bernwood, the Chiltern Hills, and Rockingham Forest. 'Wastes', private estates, and the parklands of major landowners also added important diversity and served as reservoirs for species of wildlife absent from the village fields. However, if one accepts the relative poverty of wildlife in the open fields, this could account for the general absence of vermin in the churchwardens' payments in the seventeenth and eighteenth centuries. Nonetheless, this alone is not a satisfactory answer, for it is difficult to accept that in all these counties so very few vermin were killed. Perhaps it was that from an early period, the squires discouraged freelance village vermin catchers (poachers by any other name?) from operating on their lands. Whatever the reason, the record is strangely wanting, with the major exceptions of Bedfordshire and parts of Buckinghamshire.

However, if there was a general absence of most vermin species in this region, it was one of the principal areas of House Sparrow persecution with many millions of adult birds, nestlings, and eggs being taken in all the counties in this region. Individual parishioners were paid at rates varying between 2d. and 4d. per dozen for adults (less for chicks and eggs) and many parishes also paid for a dedicated 'bird catcher'. The majority of these attempts at control—invariably unsuccessful at reducing overall numbers—began in the latter half of the eighteenth century and usually ran on well into the first half of the nineteenth. In one or two parishes, particularly in Northamptonshire, systematic control started in the early 1700s and at Wigston in Leicestershire considerable numbers were killed annually as early as 1620, but that was an exception.

Apart from House Sparrows (and what other passerines were incidentally swept up under the same head?), the only two other species targeted were Moles and Hedgehogs. Mole-catchers were employed on annual payments in many parishes and Moles were evidently regarded as serious pests in the arable strips and the meadows. Numbers killed each year were particularly high in Nottinghamshire, Leicestershire, Northamptonshire, and Rutland, with fewer in the parishes on the Chiltern Hills of Buckinghamshire and Oxfordshire, away from the clay lands. Very few parishes give any indication of numbers but the total killed annually throughout these areas must have been huge. It was much the same with Hedgehogs which were universally harassed wherever vermin were controlled; high numbers—a maximum of 162 in 1668—were killed annually at Loughborough, for example, in the seventeenth century.

Polecats, as almost everywhere else, were taken in large numbers in several parishes, as at Stewkley (Bucks) where the parishioners accounted for no fewer than 1,049 in 76 years. A few parishes in Nottinghamshire and Hertfordshire persecuted them regularly although not in such impressive numbers as in other parts of the country. The last Wild Cat to appear in the payment rolls was at Cuckney (Notts) in 1732 although six were killed at Newton Longville (Bucks) up to 1701. Occasional Otter and Marten records appear, notably in Nottinghamshire parishes, but apart from the House Sparrows there is an almost total absence of birds throughout the eight counties, except for the sporadic clearance of Starlings, owls, or pigeons from the churches. Throughout all of these counties it is quite remarkable that I found only one reference to a bird of prey—a 'hawk' at Hambleden (Bucks).

Bedfordshire needs particular mention, because it was a clear exception to the other counties; here, many parishes undertook long-running control of vermin. There were large kills of a wide range of mammals (but, other than Sparrows, only one bird—a crow—on two occasions). Parishes such as Meppershall, Northill, Eaton Socon, Kempston, and Moggerhanger produced particularly impressive totals. As ever Polecats, Foxes, and Hedgehogs (including eighty different variations of the name!) dominated the lists. Bedfordshire parishes were also responsible for huge numbers of House Sparrows killed, with payments in one parish (Tingrith) continuing until 1873.

Snakes were killed at various dates at Culworth (N'hants); 6/8 was paid for 20 old snakes in 1715 with a further 6/6 for 39 young ones. As late as 1802 the parish was still paying 10/6 for 143 young snakes.

It is rare to find comprehensive vermin records from English estates for the early years of the nineteenth century, at the very time when the intensity of persecution was building to a climax and species such as the Red Kite, Buzzard, and Polecat were being catapulted towards extinction. However, the records from the Burley estate in Rutland and Groby estate in Leicestershire provide an insight into the levels of killing that took place, even in brief periods of years. This gives an idea of what was undoubtedly happening on a host of other estates across England at the same time.

It is noteworthy that the number of Polecats killed at Groby declined noticeably from the 1820s, and none was recorded after 1842. The number of 'hawks' too diminished after 1832; peak kills of over 100 per year decreased to an average of about 33 from 1840 to 1855. Squires has stated (in Crocker 1981) that the Kite was still a common bird in the county in 1830, but had gone by about 1850, the same time as the last records for Raven.

The Marches and West Midlands

Most of the countryside of the Marches had been enclosed long before the implementation of the parliamentary acts; therefore it differed considerably in character from the lands to its east. Even in Warwickshire and Gloucestershire

TABLE 30. Vermin killed on two Midlands estates in the nineteenth century. Data for Burley estate reproduced by kind permission of A. Squires and M. Jeeves from their book, *Leicestershire and Rutland Woodlands Past and Present*. Data For Groby estate supplied by Anthony Squires (pers com).

	Burley estate, Rutland 1807–16	Groby estate, Leicester 1827–55 (13 miscellaneous years)
Red Kite	183	–
Buzzard	285	–
Hawk	340	c.996*
Owl	386	c.34*
Magpie	1530	c.1679*
Jay	428	c.2659*
Crow	1603	c.1765*
Jackdaw	1798	–
Heron	24	55
Woodpecker	103	–
Stoat/Weasel	1269/454	2197**
Polecat	206	212
Pine Marten	9	–
Feral Cat	554	1062
Red Squirrel	197	–
Rat	17108	–

* Annual totals were sometimes for more than one species.
** Combined figure.

it was only the eastern parts of those counties that were enclosed later than the middle of the eighteenth century. The historical pattern of vermin control therefore more closely resembled that of the south-west counties and Kent, than other parts of lowland England. The range of species targeted generally was fairly wide. Sparrows were not regarded as particularly important, except in Warwickshire where the focus on Hedgehogs and House Sparrows more closely resembled the pattern in the East Midlands; Staffordshire (away from its upland areas) showed a similar pattern. It is also interesting that Polecats featured less than one might have expected, bearing in mind that in all probability they were abundant in the diverse countryside of these western counties. Foxes, however, were killed consistently throughout the region, often in impressive numbers, for example at Sherbourne (Warks) where 314 were accounted for in 33 years from 1747.

The level of vermin control in some parishes in Gloucestershire was sometimes close to that in Devon or Cornwall. In the seventeenth and eighteenth centuries, Eastington churchwardens paid for 'crowes and devouring fowles', 'Hegogs', Foxes, Fitches, Woodpickers, Hoops (*viz* Bullfinch), Kites, Sparrows, the Sparrow catcher, Jays, 'sundry vermin', and Titmice. The annual bill for vermin reached as much as £4. 19s. 10d., a considerable amount at the time. Minchin-hampton was much the same and Dursley also had impressive totals. Newnham killed large numbers of Bullfinches for many years and is also notable for the number of Pine Martens (seven) and Wild Cats (twenty-five) killed in the early eighteenth century. In Herefordshire, the parish of Much Cowerne took a similar toll on a wide variety of species. It would be fascinating to know what toll was actually taken throughout the country in the years immediately following the Act of 1566, a period for which virtually no records exist, particularly in the light of the oft-quoted case at Worfield in Shropshire. In 1575, the parishioners reacted to being arraigned for not implementing the requirements of the Act, by launching a wholesale massacre of fourteen different species (see Appendix 1). It was short lived however and in subsequent years they soon relapsed into regular culls of nothing more than Foxes and Hedgehogs.

Figure 27. A 'keepers gibbet ('vermin pole'), Downton Hall, Shropshire,
about 1928. It contains some 225 vermin, mostly Magpies, Weasels,
Stoats, Crows, and Moles; other species are indistinguishable.
Photo courtesy of Shropshire Archives/Ludlow Museum.

There were staggering numbers of 'adders' for which payments were made at Tredington and Southam (Warks). Undoubtedly Grass Snakes, and probably Slow Worms, made up some of the totals in both parishes. From 1714 to 1758, 1,022 were killed at Tredington, but the Southam totals cannot be determined because most are submerged in 'payments for sparrows, urchins and snakes' without individual numbers being defined. Between 1772 and 1806, the number was clearly enormous and undoubtedly considerably greater than at Tredington. In 1733 alone, 76 'old snakes' and 233 'others' were paid for at 1*d*. and in the 2 years 1775–6 payment was made for 433 snakes at the same rate.

Wales

The saddest reflection about the historical picture of wildlife persecution in Wales is the paucity of extant records in the centuries when vermin were being killed in large numbers throughout much of southern Britain. In more than 1,000 ancient parishes in the country only about 70 have registers that go back beyond 1600. The total number of parish records that I have been able to find in the thirteen (former) Welsh counties is fewer that those that can be found in one large-sized English county. Of these, fewer than half yielded any records of vermin payments. This is particularly frustrating bearing in mind the enormous richness and variety of wildlife that probably existed throughout Wales, hinted at by the intriguing glimpses of high levels of persecution revealed by one or two of the parish records. At Llanegwad (Carm), as late as 1821, the vestry agreed rewards for a variety of vermin. Fox was put at 3/- a head, Wild Cat at 2/6, Weasel and Polecat at 1/-, and Raven, Crow, and Magpie at 4*d*. each. Carmarthenshire is a county with a fairly impressive record for remnant populations of rarer mammals; in the few seventeenth and eighteenth parish records that exist, Wild Cat and Polecat ('fitchets') were both quite commonly taken.

The reasons for the lack of existing records are not clear; county archivists themselves are generally uncertain as to the reasons. One archivist was adamant that the Welsh weather had been a major factor. The high rainfall in Wales resulted in a semi-permanently damp environment in many churches that was damaging to the long-term storage of church records. Certainly, floods took at least one set of records, Llechryd (Cards). This suggestion seems reasonable except that Cornwall and the Lake District both have similar weather conditions *and* comprehensive parish records. However, in partial support of the thesis, the majority of existing churchwardens' accounts are to be found in the eastern (drier) counties of the Marches although Radnorshire, where only three accounts can be traced, is an exception. The records are most sparse in Anglesey, Caernarvonshire, Radnorshire, Cardiganshire, and Carmarthenshire. Some records have been lost in fires, three in Carmarthenshire, two in Denbighshire, two in Flintshire and Radnorshire, and some also in Monmouthshire. At Cilmaenllwyd (Carm) and Cadoxton-next-Neath (Glam), they were apparently deliberately used to stoke the parsonage fires; in one Anglesey parish they were allegedly eaten by a cow.

Eagles of both species occurred in Wales, but unlike the legacy left in the Lake District and Scotland, there is no record of their removal other than the demise of the last pair of Sea Eagles in Glamorgan in the nineteenth century (p. 111). Wild Cats and Pine Martens feature several times in Denbighshire, Flintshire, Monmouthshire, and Montgomeryshire, and once (Pine Marten) in Glamorgan; Polecats were singled out in the same counties, although nowhere in any great numbers. One wonders just how many other records of these mammals, that could have told us much about former distribution and numbers, have been lost?

In a pastoral country such as Wales one would expect the Fox to be high on the list of targeted pest species. It is surprising, therefore, that the records show that nowhere were they persecuted in past centuries in anything like the numbers that might have been expected. Nonetheless, at Llanfair-ar-y-Bryn (Cards) the generous sum of 2/6 per head was agreed by the vestry in 1747 although various hunters were paid in ale in line with a 1749 edict that 'no alehouse keeper shall pay for ale for any person . . . except what shall be allowed for killing such vermin (Foxes) *within* the parish'. The real villain in sheep-rearing country was clearly the Raven and the numbers killed in many parishes were impressive. The details for Llanfor are mentioned in Chapter 6 but there were other examples of vigorous annual culls in other Merioneth parishes (e.g. Llangar 125 in 40 years; Llandderfyl 393 in 21 years) and also some in the hill areas of Montgomeryshire (Llanrhaeadr-ym-Mochnant 221 in 47 years) and Brecknockshire (Dyfynog, many each year—max. 60 in 1813—but numbers are usually lost under combined totals 'Crows and Ravens').

House Sparrows did not feature anywhere in Wales except at Hanmer (Flint) where the parishioners certainly made up for lack of control elsewhere, for between 1789 and 1835 the churchwardens' paid for in excess of 150,000 birds. In 1826 the yearly total was 752 dozen.

Wales was the last redoubt of the native Red Kite in Britain and even here it was wiped out except for a fragmentary population in central Wales. The progress of its decline is unrecorded, but there is no mention of it in any of the parish records available. The same applies to all other birds of prey.

The distribution of game estates in Wales from the early nineteenth century onwards was much more scattered than that in England, by virtue of the nature of much of the countryside and of the differences in land tenure. Nonetheless there were, and still are, a few famous moorland and lowland shoots. The head keeper at Penrhyn Castle estate in North Wales was a very fine naturalist as well as a 'keeper and following are his figures for vermin killed on the estate between 1874 and 1902.

TABLE 31. Vermin killed on a Welsh estate 1874–1902.

Penrhyn Castle estate 1874–1902

Weasel	4849	Sparrowhawk	735
Stoat	3116	Peregrine	16
Polecat	98	Kestrel	1988
Pine Marten	13	Merlin	228
Feral Cat	2310	Carrion Crow	1538
Fox	175	Magpie	334
Buzzard	135	Jay	306

North-west England

Stretching from Derbyshire and Cheshire to the Solway, this region of north-west England embraces the fertile lowlands of Cheshire, Lancashire, and the Cumbrian plain as well as the spine of the Pennines, the Peak District, and the mountains of the Lake District. Historically, right across this area there were high levels of vermin control involving a wide spectrum of bird and mammal species.

Although in Lancashire there are only scattered records of Fox and Hedgehog and not much else, the situation in Cheshire was very different. In every parish in which vermin were controlled, both Hedgehogs and Foxes were heavily predated throughout the seventeenth and eighteenth centuries; in several parishes this continued into the nineteenth century. At Bunbury and Frodsham, among others, there were very large kills of Hedgehogs. House Sparrows too were taken in moderate numbers in many places—9,811 dozen in Church Minshull in 21 years at the end of the eighteenth century—and there was a very heavy toll on Bullfinches in at least 5 parishes. Bunbury (detailed in Chapter 6), Eastham, and Tarporley achieved notoriety for the prodigious number of 'Kites' that they killed. Rostherne parish exemplified the wide range of species and quantities sometimes achieved. Six or eight Foxes were killed there annually from 1672 to 1758, large numbers of Bullfinches (189 in one year) were slaughtered in 15 years, and it was another parish where Hedgehogs were slaughtered in high numbers, over 4,000 in 25 years.

In upland areas the pattern was much the same although the species targeted were obviously different. In Derbyshire, Ravens were hit particularly hard. Hartington and Hathersage consistently killed high numbers and at Wirksworth, where the slaughter was greatest of all, the remarkable total of 214 was paid for in one year alone, 1724. Youlgreave also attacked Ravens although not in great numbers. In this parish the vestry committee decided in 1712 'not to pay for Hedgehogs or Ravens, not even any more Foxes found'. It was a strangely early date at which to make such a decision, at a time when vermin killing was in

full stride in most parishes. Perhaps the vestry decided that the efforts and payments were not worthwhile, or other priorities (e.g. church repairs) were of
greater priority.

The church annals in Cumberland and Westmorland provide a wealth of
data on the wide range of 'pest species' that formed the basis of so many lists.
Especially in Westmorland, but slightly less so in Cumberland, it was an
exceptional parish that did not indulge in fairly heavy persecution. The picture in
Cumberland is less complete than in its smaller neighbour only, I suspect,
because there are fewer available parish records. In both counties, Ravens were
evidently at the top of the lists and were killed in large numbers in almost every
parish. Foxes too feature numerously and there were more payments for Badgers
in Westmorland than in any other county. The Lake District was an area that saw
much less removal of native tree cover and rough commons than most other
parts of England. For this reason it maintained larger populations of Polecat,
Pine Marten, and Wild Cat than other areas, a fact reflected in the numbers of all
these species that appear on many of the parish lists. Although eagles were
subject to annual culls at some regular sites there are, strangely, no references
to other raptors, Red Kite, Buzzard, Hen Harrier, that one might have expected
to find.

Yorkshire and the North-east

The characteristics of the three north-eastern counties in terms of historical
vermin control are dominated by three mammal species, Fox, Polecat, and
Otter. The majority of parishes were killing the first two species in considerable
numbers, sometimes impressively high. Nowhere did I find Foxes killed in
greater numbers than at Ryton (628 in 64 years) or Romaldskirk (573 in 85 years)
(both Durham) although there were various other parishes in the north-east too
where the toll was heavy. The constant problem of ascertaining whether an
animal was killed within their parish boundary or outside it was addressed by the
vestry at Haltwhistle (N'humb) in 1755 when it was determined that a payment
of 2/6 per head would be paid if the Fox 'was raised in this parish but killed in
another'. In the three (former) Ridings in Yorkshire the pattern of control was
much the same, although none of the totals there was as high as those achieved
further north.

As elsewhere in the country, Polecats were invariably controlled, again in
numbers that testified to both their ubiquity and abundance. Otters too feature
on as many parish lists as those other parts of the country where the species was
principally targeted. It is interesting that there were also larger numbers of
Badgers killed in this region than in most others, almost reflecting the situation
across the Pennines in the Lake District.

However, other than these four mammals, the spectrum of species killed in the north-east in general was rather narrow, with one or two interesting individual exceptions. Wild Cat occurred on a few parish lists of bounty payments, as might have been expected in this part of the country; Pine Marten strangely only appears once, at Long Benton (N'humb) but that record of 71 individuals is extremely dubious and probably refers to Polecat.

The only parish in England or Wales where I found reference to Dippers was at Market Weighton (Yorks) where considerable numbers were killed for a period of years (see Chapter 6). Apart from six parishes—mainly in Yorkshire—where House Sparrows were killed, birds, even Ravens, were very poorly represented throughout the three counties. However, at Corbridge (N'humb) where prodigious numbers of mammals were killed, the payments included a large number of 'gleds'. Whether these referred to Red Kites, Buzzards, harriers, or all three we shall never know, but it is the only record in the three counties of the control of any birds of prey.

9

The return of the natives

IT is a sad indictment of the past abuse of wildlife in Britain, that one of the priorities for wildlife conservation in the twenty-first century has to be the recovery of species that were deliberately eliminated in previous centuries. One or two such species, for example Sea Eagle and Goshawk, were completely exterminated while a much longer list of others—Wild Cat, Polecat, Hen Harrier, Red Kite et al.—were eliminated from most of the country and driven to remote corners where they hovered on the very edge of extinction. The Red Kite is perhaps the extreme example because the population at its lowest was reduced to no more than a dozen or so individual birds.

This book focuses on those species that have been regarded as vermin at different times and in differing priorities across the centuries. However, it is relevant to remember a wider context nowadays and remind ourselves that an enormous number of other wildlife species have suffered the same fate, mainly through the loss or reduction of essential habitats—woodland, wetlands, heath-land, etc. It is true that a few, Great Bustard for example, were eliminated directly by Man although not of course as vermin. The situation regarding our native wildlife nowadays is seen as so serious that in the last decade of the twentieth century the UK government identified a list of critical species for which Action Plans have been devised. These Species Action Plans cover (in 2005) 382 individual plants, invertebrates, amphibians/reptiles, fish, mammals, and birds together with another nine grouped plans (e.g. marine turtles). Through these plans, determined efforts are made to ensure their survival and recovery. It is important to realize that the task is not simply the daunting one of retrieving species that have been exterminated through the hand of Man but, as important, ensuring that a host of other species, once common and now rare, are helped to spread back to the areas from which they have been lost. The challenge in the twenty-first century is to see the restoration of degraded habitats and the return of native species to environments that are large enough and productive enough to support them.

We have seen in Chapter 1 that all the large predators, together with one or two large herbivores were eliminated in the distant past. In most cases there is little chance, in our ever more crowded islands, that they will ever be reintroduced into the wild. However, there is a distinct possibility that Beaver, which has been successfully repopulated in many western European countries, could reappear, for such plans have been discussed for many years and several initiatives are under way. To date, there has been no modern attempt to bring back any other mammal that has been lost in the past. Wild Boar, eliminated well over 300 years ago and subject to numerous attempts to reintroduce it in the intervening period, is now, perforce, well established in several areas of southern Britain. These feral stocks originated from accidental escapes and releases, some due to the hurricane of 1987 that broke down fenced enclosures within which the animals were being reared commercially.

All species on the original Tudor Vermin List have been subject to severe persecution at different stages between then and the more recent past. However, with the exception of several birds of prey, none of the other species on that list has been completely exterminated even though, in several instances, they have been eliminated from the majority of the country. Birds of prey apart, none of the other birds on the Tudor list has suffered any perceptible population decline because of past persecution, except the Chough.

The reasons for the national decline of the Chough, and particularly its disappearance from Cornwall, included habitat deterioration as well as persecution, important though the latter factor undoubtedly was. Unexpectedly, the Chough made a sudden and welcome return of its own accord to its ancestral home in Cornwall. Forestalling a planned reintroduction, five birds reappeared on the Cornish coast in 2001, probably from the coast of Brittany where a small population still exists. A pair bred successfully in 2002 and has continued to breed successfully every year since, rearing twenty young up to 2006. That year they were joined by a second breeding pair which reared three young, leading to the hope that they will re-establish and expand more securely, especially given the continuing maintenance of improved feeding habitat on the cliff tops. The situation with the Chough in Wales is also encouraging where the population has increased steadily in recent years and pairs have spread along the South Wales coast, thereby reclaiming traditional sites last occupied some 150 years ago. The small population in western Scotland is relatively stable.

At its lowest ebb in the early twentieth century, the Raven too was driven back to the fastness of the rugged coasts and hill areas in the west and north. It was never absent from its great strongholds in Wales, south-west England, and western Scotland, although it was eliminated from the Central Lowlands and in many parts of counties in the east of Scotland. From the time of the First World War, as some of the pressure was taken off by both hill-sheep farmers and gamekeepers, Ravens enjoyed a slow and modest recovery. This has been most evident in eastward extensions of breeding ranges from the south-west and the Marches and breeding Ravens have already (2005) spread to counties as far east as coastal and inland Sussex, Bedfordshire, and Leicestershire. In Scotland too, there has been evidence of pairs re-establishing in the eastern counties, although this has been accompanied by an actual decline in south-west Scotland. Ratcliffe estimated the populations in 1997 at 777 pairs in England, 1,250 in Wales, and 1,140 in Scotland. However, it should be noted that a more recent census in N.W. Wales, 1988–2005, showed local increases of between 40% and 100%.

Birds of prey

With improved tolerance and the support of public opinion many bird of prey species that were ceaselessly harried in the past have started to prosper in recent decades and some have made impressive recoveries. The Buzzard, ubiquitous at one time, is a good example, and has slowly returned to many of its former areas. It was never eliminated from Wales, the Lake District, or Devon and Cornwall but at the height of persecution in Scotland it was lost from a number of Scottish counties. Although its recovery was hindered by the onset of myxomatosis in the 1950s and further weakened by the presence of high levels of organochlorine pesticides in the following decade, the Buzzard has steadily reclaimed ground. Freed from continual persecution, its numbers can increase rapidly and its recovery has picked up well in recent years. It is very numerous in its traditional strongholds in the west and once again breeds in every county in Britain with its numbers continuing to increase. Densities can sometimes be impressive. In Robin Prytherch's seventy-five square kilometre study area in north Somerset, the breeding population rose from thirteen pairs in 1982 to ninety pairs in 2006, making it to date the densest recorded breeding population and illustrating the enormous potential for its full recovery nationwide.

Several other birds of prey, previously exterminated, have also returned without planned assistance by Man. The Goshawk was undoubtedly enabled to do so by virtue of initial releases or escapes from falconers and has made remarkable progress. It is a denizen of extensive woodlands, particularly conifers, and is therefore one of the species that has been able to take advantage of the maturing of the extensive post-war forestry plantations. Although it was not named specifically in the Tudor Vermin Acts it was presumably, with Sparrowhawk, included among the payments made for 'hawks'. It was extinct in Britain by the early twentieth century, reduced initially by the reduction of woodland in some counties and finished off with the arrival of gamekeepers. Its tentative return from the 1950s has steadily built up to a population in the early twenty-first century that is thought to be well in excess of 500 pairs and still expanding.

The Golden Eagle, recently subject to a successful reintroduction scheme in Northern Ireland, made a bold attempt to re-establish itself in the Lake District after a gap of over 150 years. In March 1957, Derek Ratcliffe found a nest in

Mardale and a second one was discovered the same year in Eskdale. However, both sites were only tenanted by single birds. It continued thus in succeeding years, with the suspicion that breeding was not taking place because of the incidence of high levels of organochlorine pesticides. These were withdrawn in 1966 and a pair laid eggs in Mardale three years later and continued to do so every year thereafter, although moving to a site farther south near Haweswater. They continued breeding until 1996, rearing a single young on fifteen occasions. However in 2004, the old female (at least 28 years of age) failed to appear and was presumed to have died. The male failed to recruit a new female and the site is currently abandoned. In Eskdale the birds also bred, although after a much longer initial delay and also at an alternative site, having repaired the old Eskdale nest annually from 1957 to 1972. This pair bred from 1976 to 1983, rearing only two successful young and then disappearing. A pair resided in Northumbria for several years around the same period but subsequently disappeared. Thus the attempted recolonization of England, persisting over almost fifty years, has stalled. The most significant factor has been the fact that although the Haweswater birds produced fifteen young, this did not lead to any of the offspring settling in the area and attempting to breed, once they were mature.

It was the two world wars, the departure of 'keepers to the front, and the consequent reduction in vermin control that produced a chink of light for the Hen Harrier. One or two pairs had begun to nest on the Scottish mainland by the 1930s and, after the Second World War it was clear that the Harrier was enjoying a modest revival from their previous breeding outposts on Orkney and the Outer Hebrides—areas that had always been essentially free from 'keepers. Nests in Sutherland, Moray, and Perthshire in the 1940s signalled the beginning of a slow expansion in the Scottish uplands. The extensive planting of young conifers assisted this expansion by temporarily providing new nesting and hunting areas out of the reach of gamekeepers.

By the 1950s, the Hen Harrier had not only recolonized some of the uplands of Scotland but the first pairs had also moved into Wales. The first northern Pennine pairs were found in the 1960s. However, the story since then has been a vexed one as the bird has been relentlessly persecuted on grouse moors where it is viewed as the most detested of all predatory species. The main charges against it there are that it not only takes grouse, but its presence over the moor can ruin expensive shooting days by causing the grouse lie low in the heather, refusing to fly. Its foothold in many upland areas is still tenuous and, although wholly protected legally, the future of the Hen Harrier remains a very contentious subject.

The Hen Harrier's return as a breeding bird to the British moorlands has been monitored nationally three times, in 1988, in 1998, and in 2004. The second survey of the species (Sim 1999) found a population of c.570 territorial pairs (including Isle of Man) with the bulk of the territories, 436, in Scotland. The 2004 survey showed an increase to 749 territorial pairs (excluding Isle of Man) with 43 in Wales, 10 in England, and the remainder in Scotland. The English pairs totalled 15 in 2005, rearing 35 young and rose to 22 nesting attempts in 2006 with 12 successful nests raising 46 young, giving hope that their future may finally be brighter. At the same time, however, it is known that 60% of all breeding attempts in England in 2006 failed due to illegal human interference.

The return of the Osprey is one of the best known stories of the successful recovery of any species in Britain. It has become an emblematic totem of the success of wildlife conservation efforts in Britain. After the (apparent) last pair of Ospreys nested in Inverness-shire in 1916, only occasional passage birds en route to or from Scandinavia were recorded in Britain. However, it now appears that there was at least sporadic breeding in the Highlands after 1916, with good evidence of more regular, but unreported, nesting since 1947. By the early 1950s, there were increased sightings of Ospreys in the Scottish Highlands and although several birds were killed, some lingered and the hopes of recolonization were raised. It was in 1954 that a pair famously nested in Speyside and reared two young. Although the following years brought frequent disappointment and breeding failures, the pair persisted at the Loch Garten site. In a disastrous incident in 1958, an intruder climbed the nesting tree at night and stole the eggs, which were then found broken at the base of the tree. A special protection scheme was set up by the RSPB in 1959 and the pair successfully reared three young. Despite further frequent frustrations, this pair at Loch Garten has been present ever since. A pair nested at a second site in 1963 but failed to hatch the eggs, probably again because of pesticide residues. However, the breakthrough had been made and Ospreys were back. Since those early pioneering years the population has increased and expanded its range in Scotland despite the fact that over 100 clutches have been stolen since the 1950s. In 2006 there were c.190 known pairs. One of the major factors in the successful re-establishment of Ospreys—the same applies to Sea Eagle and Red Kite—is the complete change of attitude of modern landowners and their 'keepers towards emblematic species such as these. Underpinned by widespread public encouragement this active support from landowners is a crucial part of re-establishment of these fine species.

It was accepted that the Ospreys were likely to take a very long time to colonize new areas outside Scotland. As a result of this realization, the decision was made in 1995 to translocate seven young birds from Scottish nests to Rutland Water in the East Midlands. Individual Ospreys had lingered in the area the previous year or two and it was regarded as an ideal site for reintroduction with ample food, total security, and an enthusiastic partnership to run it. In the end a total of sixty-four young birds were introduced to the site between 1996 and

2001. In 1999, the first translocated birds returned to Rutland and successful breeding occurred in 2001. By 2003, this had risen to three pairs with two of them rearing five young. The position in 2005 was that one pair bred successfully and there were several other birds in the vicinity, with the imminent prospect of further breeding pairs in the following years.

Somewhat more unexpected was the discovery of a pair nesting in the English Lake District in 2001. They were accompanied the following year by a second pair but this has proved a tenuous foothold and although the original pair has bred every year since then, up to 2005 the second pair had failed to establish. These colonizers were almost certainly an overflow from pairs in southern Scotland but what was more surprising was the appearance of two pairs in different parts of Wales in 2004, one pair breeding successfully. In a telling testimony to the potential of bird of prey reintroduction schemes, it was found that males at both sites were individuals from the translocated birds at Rutland Water. One of the pairs has bred successfully each year since.

The two large raptors that needed initial intervention from Man to enable their return are the Red Kite and Sea Eagle. Their demise is described in the appropriate sections of Chapter 6. This account traces the steps that were taken— and are still under way—to enable both species to return eventually to as much of their former ranges as possible. In the case of the Sea Eagle, it was exterminated completely whereas the Red Kite maintained the tiniest of toeholds in central Wales at the end of the nineteenth century.

The history of the recovery of the Red Kite and the efforts of a handful of landowners, ornithologists, and local residents and, later in the story, the RSPB and Nature Conservancy Council (as was), is one of the great stories of the determined protection of a bird species. No other bird in the world has been subject to such an intensive and long-lasting campaign of protection as the Red Kite. For over a hundred years, since the 1890s, the remnant population in Wales, surviving only as an accident of history in the remotest valleys, but still hounded continually by egg collectors and taxidermists, was guarded and protected assiduously every nesting season. Throughout the early decades of the twentieth century, the constant assaults on the nests were so great that barely any progress was made and it was all that could be done to maintain the species in existence. However, the native Red Kites survived, but only just, to continue to grace the skies of Wales.

It was not until the late 1960s and 1970s that the Welsh population of Red Kites finally began to show a slow but genuine increase. Notwithstanding a plethora of problems—continuing robberies, afforestation of feeding areas, pesticides, myxomatosis, bad weather—the numbers steadily grew over the years. By 1990, there were seventy known pairs but even then only forty-seven young fledged that year; fledging rates in the wet climate of Wales have always been particularly poor. At the time of writing, late in 2006, the Welsh Kite population stands at around 500 occupied territories. In terms of overall recovery and spread to the remainder of the species' natural range in Britain, the problem has always been that the Welsh birds continue to fill in gaps in Wales and have not shown any signs of exporting pairs across the border. Therefore in 1989 the first steps of a reintroduction programme were undertaken. Ten young birds were brought in from Sweden, six to be reared in Scotland and four, together with one from Wales, taken to a release site in the Chiltern Hills. The process was repeated annually for six years and up to 1994 a total of ninety-three young birds from Sweden and Spain had been released at the two sites. Although inevitably there were some losses, on the whole there were very encouraging levels of survival in both Scotland and England. Four years after the first releases, success-ful breeding was taking place. Since then young birds taken from the initial release areas and some from eastern Germany, have been successfully trans-located to another four new sites, two each in Scotland and England. The Red Kite has proved itself very amenable to reintroductions of this nature and, with continuing and widening breeding success, there is a real prospect that, given reasonable freedom from illegal persecution, this magnificent raptor will once more become a familiar sight the length and breadth of the country. The population in England in 2006 was considered to be in excess of 400 pairs but in Scotland is still around 50, which, in part, reflects the amount of illegal persecution taking place there.

The spectacular Sea Eagle is a huge and awe-inspiring bird. Despite this, or perhaps because of it, it has been mercilessly persecuted in the European part of its wide Palearctic range. Attempts at its eradication were frequently encouraged by bounty systems in many countries and it was exterminated from most of western Europe by the twentieth century. Only in northern Norway did a viable population remain and in those wild and rugged coastal areas it is still a common and increasing bird. However, even there bounties were paid for killing the birds until they were afforded full protection in 1971. It was from here that young birds were sought for an intended reintroduction into Scotland. Because the species is not migratory it was considered extremely unlikely that it would ever recolonize Britain of its own accord.

The first attempt to bring in Sea Eagles was a private initiative in 1959 involving three birds that had been captured in Norway in order to claim bounties. The birds were tethered in Glen Etive, Argyllshire, for few weeks before being released. One of the youngsters was soon killed in a Fox trap and the other simply disappeared, fate unknown. The third bird, an adult, was found to be too dependent on Man and was eventually housed in Edinburgh Zoo.

The next serious attempt took place on Fair Isle in 1968 where George Waterston, the RSPB Director in Scotland and Roy Dennis, island warden at the time, introduced four young eaglets, two males and two females. In many respects Fair Isle seemed perfect: ample food supply, complete security from persecution, close monitoring, and good potential nest sites. However failure again dogged the initiative. Although three birds survived through the first winter, the fourth one disappeared early on. By next spring, seven months after release, another of the youngsters disappeared but there was still hope, as the two survivors were seen displaying and showing good signs of settling. It was not to be, however, for the female left the island in June and the last bird became liberally sprayed with Fulmar oil, was rescued once, but eventually succumbed.

It was always on the cards that there would be another attempt because, despite earlier failure there was every reason to believe that reintroduction could succeed and certainly the British coastline offered much ideal habitat and had supported very large numbers of Sea Eagles in the past. The final attempt was launched in 1975 when the Nature Conservancy Council (NCC), with the co-operation of the Norwegian authorities, decided to reintroduce young birds to the island of Rum in the Inner Hebrides. Again, it was seen as an ideal site, not least because by that time the whole island had been secured as a National Nature Reserve, and was under the complete control of NCC.

In that year one eight-week old male and three female youngsters were brought to Rum from the Bodo area of central Norway. The story thereafter is one of slow but steady success, requiring a substantial number of young birds being introduced to the site to ensure eventual success and a permanently viable population. Ninety-three young were introduced in the first ten years, followed by a further sixty in another five years. There have been many disappointments and setbacks but eventually two nests were discovered in 1983, although neither succeeded that year. A third nest, possibly used but undiscovered the previous year, was also found and there were several other pairs holding territory. By this time many of the Norwegian youngsters that had been released on Rum, had dispersed to other Hebridean islands and mainland cliffs.

The position at the time of writing in 2006 is rosy, with thirty-five breeding pairs rearing thirty young at sites along the west coast of Scotland and its islands. The Sea Eagle is at last back in the homeland from which it was eliminated a hundred years ago, with further plans for releases elsewhere.

Three rare mammals

The Polecat, Pine Marten, and Wild Cat, of all the mammals on the original vermin lists, have one thing in common. Each was driven to the edge of extinction in remote corners of the country and only saved, certainly in the case of the latter two, by the onset of the First World War and disappearance of so many of the gamekeepers. That fact, combined with the Second World War following after an interval of only twenty years, provided the catalyst for recovery. The intensity of gamekeeping was never to be the same again.

Both Pine Marten and Wild Cat are woodland species and suffered serious loss of habitat with deforestation throughout so much of Britain. The post-war reafforestation of many upland areas in Scotland, combined with reduced persecution and, latterly, legal protection, has unquestionably aided the recovery of both species. The Wild Cat was eliminated from its last refuges in northern England and north Wales by the middle of the nineteenth century and eventually also southern Scotland, so that by 1915 it was restricted to the extreme north-west Highlands. Its subsequent spread was surprisingly rapid and by the 1950s it had recolonized most of Scotland north of the Glasgow–Edinburgh conurbation, a situation confirmed in the 1980s by Easterbee et al. To the present time this densely populated and heavily urbanized belt continues to serve as an effective barrier to the southward spread of rare mammals such as the Wild Cat.

In 1995, Harris et al. estimated the population of Wild Cats in Scotland at around 3,500 individuals. Other recent estimates have ranged between 1,000 and 4,000. However, herein lies a great problem. The true Wild Cat, *Felis sylvestris*, has been resident in Britain since the time when there was a land bridge to Europe, some 6,000 years BC. Around 2,000 years ago the domestic cat was introduced and, ever since then, there has undoubtedly been hybridization between the two. Because of this fact, many of the current progeny are indistinguishable, either in the field or the hand, from the genuine Scottish Wild Cat. In this confused picture it is suggested by MacDonald et al. (2004) that there may be as few as 400 pure Wild Cats left, or in the extreme, *no* genetically pure ones. Whatever the true number, the animal is critically endangered and to quote the same authors, 'Conservationists may not have much time left . . . (and) we may be witnessing the very final stage of the virtual extinction of the Scottish Wild Cat'. After receiving partial legal protection in 1981, it was fully protected in Schedule 5 of the Wildlife and Countryside Act in 1988.

The picture of the Pine Marten's recovery is similar, certainly in Scotland. Here its range expanded steadily after the Second World War until it is to be found in suitable habitats throughout much of the area north of the urbanized Central Lowlands. Like the Wild Cat it was assumed that it had been eliminated in southern Scotland, although this was never certain and, with a secretive species like the Pine Marten, is difficult to prove. What is certain is that it now occurs in the forests in Galloway where the Forestry Commission introduced twelve individuals from northern Scotland in the early 1980s and they have flourished since. Although it is strictly a forest animal, perfectly adapted to an arboreal life and wonderfully agile, it nonetheless finds most of its varied food on the ground.

In Wales it has always been recognized that a relict population of Pine Martens existed in Snowdonia, although they were very rarely seen. However, it has slowly become apparent that the species retained a wider distribution than that and records have been proved from a variety of different areas of the Principality, although the limited indications are that the numbers are small. Why, in all the intervening years, the population has not increased more, given the large amount of suitable habitat throughout Wales and freedom from persecution, remains a mystery. It has also become more and more apparent that in addition to its other refuge in the Lake District, the Pine Marten has eked out a survival in other areas of northern England, principally the north Pennines and Cheviots, the North York Moors, and the Peak District. Like the Wild Cat, the Pine Marten was finally given full legal protection in 1988.

The final mammal of this trio of mustelids, the Polecat, has had a different pattern of recovery. From its final heartland in central Wales, freed from previous persecution, it has moved eastwards across the Marches and has already made good progress in recovering its former ground across much of the Midlands. Unofficial reintroductions into the Lake District, parts of Scotland, and possibly some English counties have hastened its spread. Although strictly nocturnal and therefore rarely seen otherwise in the open, it is clearly enjoying a renaissance. In areas where it occurs it is not infrequently found as a road casualty.

10

Modern control—legal and illegal

UNTIL now I have dealt mainly with the persecution and control of animals that have for many centuries been classified simply as 'vermin'. However, attitudes towards such species have changed with time and circumstance. This change has been increasingly reflected in a plethora of protective wildlife legislation enacted in the second half of the twentieth century. Much of it has been stimulated by the growing public concern about wildlife and the awareness of the disastrous impacts, both direct and indirect, that humans have had on many species.

All the native species that comprised the lists of vermin in the Tudor Acts and which form the focus of this book, nowadays fall conveniently into one of three categories: those that are universally accepted pests; a few predatory species which can be legally controlled at any time; a longer list of species, formerly regarded as legitimate vermin, that are now wholly or partially protected by law.

In the first category there is little argument that among native mammals the Brown Rat (assumed as 'native' for our purposes; see p. 218) and the Mole, together with the introduced species of Rabbit, American Mink, and Grey Squirrel, are widely regarded as pests and are therefore subject to unlimited control, whenever and wherever necessary. Rat control is widely practised both in rural and in urban areas and huge numbers are killed each year. Local Authorities have a statutory responsibility for their control in residential and commercial premises because of health risks. Many gamekeepers and other rural operatives have an interest in keeping numbers to a minimum. Whatever efforts are made to control the Rat, it will never be possible to eliminate it completely. However, in recent years Rats have been successfully eradicated for nature conservation purposes from several islands round the British coasts, e.g. Ramsey, Lundy, Ailsa Craig et al.

It is also difficult to envisage a time when Moles will not be regarded as serious agricultural pests, hazards on gallops, and genuine nuisances on maintained grasslands such as golf courses and lawns. The amount of Mole control that is undertaken nowadays is far less than in former times and the population is at a higher level than it has been in the past. Nevertheless, in terms of the overall population, the reduction in the level of control is probably balanced by the effects of changed farm practices in areas of intensive agriculture. The annual toll taken on Moles has a negligible effect on the overall population of over 30 million.

Under the Wildlife and Countryside Act 1981, twelve bird species are listed, which can be 'killed or taken by authorised persons at all times' under an open general licence. This is, in effect, a 'pest species' list, by any other name (in 2005, in England House Sparrow and Starling were removed from it). The list comprises six corvids, three gulls, and three pigeons: Carrion Crow, Hooded Crow, Rook, Jackdaw, Jay, Magpie, Great Black-backed Gull, Lesser Black-backed Gull, Herring Gull, Collared Dove, Feral Pigeon, and Woodpigeon, plus (in England), Canada Goose. In the context of game preservation and some elements of agriculture there is little to argue about and some of these birds are still regarded as genuine pests. Herring Gull, Lesser Black-backed Gull, and Feral Pigeon are listed because of concerns for public health and nuisance. In common with the Feral Pigeon, the two gull species nest in urban situations in some coastal areas and Herring Gulls, in particular, frequent refuse tips in large numbers and often resort to roosts on nearby drinking-water reservoirs.

Inevitably there are one or two birds whose continued inclusion in Schedule 2, Part II is sometimes questioned. The level of damage caused by Rooks and Jackdaws, either agriculturally or to game interests, is at a low level and for those reasons a case could be made for their removal from the list. Numbers of both species have fluctuated over the decades, for reasons related to changes in agricultural practices rather than the numbers that have been shot each year. Neither species is remotely at risk from the low levels of control exercised nowadays and the balance probably lies in favour of retaining the ability to control either species when local problems require it. It is interesting that there is still actually a small residual market for young birds for the traditional Rook pie. Perhaps the species that most deserves to have its place in this Schedule reconsidered is the Jay, a shy species with a wide woodland distribution. Although it is a minor garden nuisance and a known low-level egg thief, this latter habit principally affects songbird species and gamekeepers generally regard it as much less important than Magpie and Carrion/Hooded Crow.

The second category, predatory species of birds and mammals that can be legally killed at any time, obviously includes the last three species mentioned above, each of which is regarded as a serious enemy by gamekeepers for the depredations they inflict on nesting gamebirds. All three are skilled nest finders and are shown little mercy on shooting estates in both uplands and lowlands. Sheep farmers, especially those in the hills, also regard the two crows with deep suspicion. Certainly they are responsible for taking occasional lambs and for attacking ewes in parturition, as described earlier, and it is cold comfort to those farmers whose flocks are affected, to know that the overall statistical chance of such damage is extremely small.

The Fox, the largest terrestrial predator in Britain, is viewed in the same light as the three corvids, intensely disliked by both sheep farmers and game rearing concerns. It too is a legal quarry at all times of year. The two smaller mammalian predators that are legitimately targeted by gamekeepers are Stoat and Weasel. Of the two the Stoat is regarded as the most significant, despite the fact that the Rabbit is its preferred prey. As a predator on game stocks, it will not only take eggs and growing chicks but will also kill incubating hens on the nest and can cause havoc if it gets into rearing pens where it can kill indiscriminately. The map on p. 60 shows an example of the intensity with which gamekeepers attempt to control the numbers of Stoats, particularly in Spring, at the time when the gamebirds are nesting, and therefore at their most vulnerable.

The Weasel is a much smaller animal, some one third to half the size of the Stoat, and consequently preys predominantly on smaller animals—voles, song-bird chicks, and others. However it is known to take gamebird poults when it has the opportunity and, like the Stoat, can occasionally cause serious problems if it breaks into rearing pens. Tunnel traps are the most usual means by which both species are caught and whereas the Stoat may be the principal target, the traps are non-selective and catch the smaller Weasel almost as readily. Rats, of course freely investigate any sort of passage and occasionally Hedgehogs also are caught unintentionally, despite being partially protected under the 1981 Wildlife and Countryside Act. Gamekeepers still regard Hedgehogs with some suspicion, both as egg thieves and as opportunistic predators on poults. Another mammal that is caught accidentally in tunnel traps is the Polecat. Because its range and numbers are expanding across the country, it is inevitable that some are caught in this way. The Polecat has been partially protected under British law since 1981, although the Act mainly specifies certain methods by which it can or cannot be legally killed or taken.

There is a much longer list of those species that were included on the original Tudor Vermin Lists but that are now fully protected by law. They include all the birds of prey and all the 'miscellaneous' bird species such as Kingfisher, Dipper, woodpeckers, Raven, Bullfinch. Of the mammals, Otter, Badger, Pine Marten, and Wild Cat are fully protected. There is a disparity between the levels of protection given to mammals and birds. Which reflects the fact that, since the late nineteenth century, prominence has been given to bird protection, through the pressure of public bodies such as the Royal Society for the Protection of Birds. At that time there was no equivalent popular body to argue the case for comprehensive protection of mammals, with the result that it is only slowly being achieved piecemeal.

The fact that the law now protects a wide range of birds and mammals does not, sadly, mean that they are immune from all persecution. Indeed there are many species that are still subject to disturbing levels of unlawful control and a summary of some of these instances is outlined as the final part of this chapter.

In the modern world, the great levels of interest in wildlife, sympathy for the pressures on it, and concern about its future are unrecognizable compared with those of a hundred years ago. Public attitudes towards killing per se have hardened, reflected in limited but growing opposition to field sports. Even the control of introduced 'pests' such as American Mink and Grey Squirrel is frequently resisted. In Britain, the general public has to be persuaded of the need for the control of species such as these. The appearance of Grey Squirrel terrine on the menu at a Worcestershire restaurant in 2005 was rapidly followed by threats of fire bombing from animal rights activists. Even the universal abhorrence of Brown Rats was refuted by the owners of one Rat-infested Welsh island who for months declined to sell it to a conservation body unless there was absolute guarantee that no Brown Rat would be killed. The natural order of things has been so disrupted by Man's destruction of habitats, removal of species, unwise introductions of non-native ones, that only active wildlife management can offer the hope of restoring a better balance. This must include the reduction or long-term elimination of some alien species (plants and animals) and will therefore involve programmed controls. The capture and killing of introduced Hedgehogs on Hebridean islands, the reduction of numbers of feral goats in North Devon and North Wales, and the removal of thousands of naturalized feral pigeons from London's Trafalgar Square are early twenty-first century examples of actions that have to be undertaken but raise bitter public ire.

Similarly, it must remain legitimate to control accepted predators such as corvids and Fox to protect game interests. Game shooting is a deeply rooted tradition in Britain, as in most other countries, and held as a fundamental right. Moreover it is a very significant component of rural communities and economies in many parts of the country. The controversy over the introduction of an Act banning hunting with dogs—which was effectively a ban on traditional Fox-hunting—was based on both the erosion of traditional rights and the impact that the ban would have on rural economies. The success of game shooting in uplands and lowlands is inevitably dependent on the legal control of competing species, i.e. vermin control.

In a lowland situation this is well illustrated by the Game Conservancy Trust's (GCT) experimental work on Salisbury Plain between 1985 and 1990. In a carefully controlled scientific programme, the Trust selected two equivalent Grey Partridge beats each of approximately five square kilometres. A programme of intensive spring and early summer vermin control was initiated on one, while leaving the other free of control. The targeted species were Carrion Crow,

Magpie, Fox, Stoat, and Rat. After three years the control regime was switched from one site to the other and the results then compared at the end of the programme. The results in terms of Partridge success were dramatic. To quote from the Trust's summary report, 'When predation control began in each area the success rate almost doubled in one case and trebled in the other. When control ceased after the switch, breeding success decreased to less than 40% of the previous year'. There is no better example of the effectiveness of predator control, involving only species that can be legally controlled, in providing enhanced numbers of game species.

A further example is demonstrated by the GCT at the 823 acre Allerton farm at Loddington in Leicestershire. Here, for ten years from 1992, the set-aside allocation was distributed across the farm in twenty-metre strips sown with cereal-based plant mixtures and kale for winter cover. At the same time legal control of vermin was undertaken in spring and summer. Within ten years the results were dramatic. Autumn numbers of Pheasants increased from fewer than 150 to more than 600. With the removal of Carrion Crows and Magpies, overall breeding success of other birds improved markedly. Songbird populations more than doubled (while remaining unchanged on neighbouring farms), Brown Hares increased by a factor of 10, and the set-aside areas have become the best habitats for butterflies on the farm.

Illegal killing continues

The legal methods available for the control of vermin at the present time have been outlined in Chapter 3. At the same time it is common knowledge, backed up by ample fact and evidence, that illegal methods are still widely used to control both accepted vermin and, more seriously, many legally protected species of mammals and birds. There is nothing new about the three means that are regularly used to control vermin—shooting, trapping, and poisoning. They are systems that have been tried and tested legitimately by generations of land managers, gamekeepers, rodent operators, and others needing to target perceived pests. The difference nowadays lies in the series of twentieth-century Acts which have outlawed many of the previously popular and effective methods and defined the ways in which others can be deployed and the species against which they can or cannot be legally used. Poisoning, for example—specifically the setting of poison baits in the open—was outlawed by the Protection of Animals Act in 1911, although each year there are many examples of the law being ignored throughout Britain. The only legal uses of specific poisons directed against wildlife are now restricted to underground use against Moles, the widespread use of alphachloralose or other narcotics by professional operators under government licence, and rodenticides. The use of rodenticides is governed by strict guidelines, but even when these are followed correctly rats and mice poisoned in this way are not infrequently preyed on or taken as carrion by scavenging species such as Badger, Fox, Red Kite, or Buzzard, which may later die from the cumulative effects of secondary poisoning.

However, there are numerous instances of illegal uses on some farms (notably in sheep-rearing areas), too many game estates, occasional fruit farms, and even in some private gardens, where a wide range of proprietary chemicals, easily obtainable over the counter from agricultural suppliers and garden centres, are used as poison on baits placed in the open. One of the chemicals most frequently abused in recent years, carbofuran, has already been withdrawn because of misuse, but it is evident from the number of instances recorded that stocks are still in circulation. Aldicarb and mevinphos are two other chemicals regularly occurring in incidents of wildlife deaths, frequently on moorlands, despite the fact that they are designed only for use on arable crops. In view of the extent of misuse of these substances, the case for banning their possession in areas where there is no evident reason for their legitimate use would seem straightforward. The Central Science Laboratory (under DEFRA) and the Scottish Agricultural Science Agency (SASA) produce an annual report on the Pesticide Poisoning of Animals which documents the incidents of illegal killing investigated by the departments each year. Table 32 shows the number of incidents of wildlife deaths involving pesticide poisoning investigated by DEFRA and SASA over the period 1992 to 2004. Despite these figures, the likelihood of illegal poisoned baits, or incidents of careless misuse, actually being discovered and reported remains minimal. The majority of cases that are investigated are the result of information fortuitously passed to the police or other organizations by ramblers and other countryside users. The chances of the detection of illegal poisoned baits on private estate land, remote hill farms, or wide expanses of moorland remain low

TABLE 32. Number of incidents of pesticide poisoning investigated by the Central Science Laboratory and Scottish Agricultural Science Agency, 1992–2004, in which misuse or abuse of chemicals were shown to be responsible for deaths of wild birds and mammals.

		1992	1993	1994	1995	1996	1997	1998	1999	2000	2001	2002	2003	2004
Mammals	England	11	22	11	9	15	12	3	11	9	5	10	8	8
	Scotland	4	4	4	4	1	2	2	5	0	1	0	1	1
	Wales	1	4	2	0	1	1	1	1	0	0	1	0	1
Birds	England	25	34	35	33	28	13	11	20	18	13	25	21	17
	Scotland	19	20	18	14	17	21	23	15	30	29	24	23	27
	Wales	8	9	5	3	9	3	4	6	8	2	6	8	6

Source: CSL and SASA annual reports.

and there can only be speculation about the true number of protected mammals and birds that are killed annually in this way. The number of proven cases is often referred to as the tip of an iceberg. However, it is almost certainly a very big iceberg.

Table 32 lists the number of incidents in which pesticide poisoning was shown to be the cause of wildlife deaths, but it does not quantify the actual numbers of mammals or birds that were killed in individual incidents. In many cases an incident involved only one individual, but in as many others higher numbers were involved, two, three, or sometimes more. In some notable cases there have been serious multiple kills. In January 1991, ten Buzzards were poisoned at a site in Strathclyde and the following year ninety-one Brent Geese in Lincolnshire died as the result of the misuse of the insecticide triazophos. Fifty Rooks were killed on illegal alphachloralose baits in the Highlands in 1993 and in 1998 there was an even bigger illegal kill involving some 200 Herring Gulls and Lesser Black-backed Gulls in Strathclyde. Ravens and Buzzards, both successful carrion feeders are species that are particularly vulnerable to bait laid in the open, as is evident in Table 33. In April 1999, twenty-eight Ravens were poisoned by fenthion on farmland in west Wales and ten Buzzards succumbed to carbofuran in Devon in 2001 with a further twenty-two killed on carbofuran bait in the Scottish Borders in 2004.

Table 33 lists the minimum totals of wild bird deaths resulting from illegal poisoning incidents between 1990 and 2004. Although it is not possible to discover the true number of incidents or the total of illegal wildlife kills throughout the country in any year, there is no doubt whatever that these figures represent only a bare minimum.

Although the figures for illegal poisoning of mammals are considerably less than those for birds, they still occur. In the period 1990–2003, the Central Science Laboratory/Scottish Agricultural Science Agency also recorded the deaths of 124 Foxes, a minimum of 50 Badgers, 17 bats, 5 Hedgehogs, and 1 Otter as a result of the misuse or illegal use of poisons.

No comparable figures are available for the number of protected mammals that, in addition to those being poisoned, are either shot or trapped illegally each year, although it is widely known that a problem exists. Badgers and Otters are two species that are still killed illegally, in the case of the first one, probably in considerable numbers. The RSPB keeps a comprehensive record of incidents involving birds and the figures, which again are considered to be only a small percentage of those actually killed illegally each year, show just how serious the problem is. For example, on the RSPB's data bank for the years shown on Table 34, in addition to the confirmed deaths, no fewer than 277 other incidents have been recorded where illegal trapping or shooting of victims was believed to have occurred but could not be proved. To this can also be added a

TABLE 33. Minimum numbers of wild birds killed through the illegal use or misuse of pesticide poisons in Britain 1990–2004.

	Buzzard	Red Kite	Golden Eagle	Sea Eagle	Hen Harrier	Marsh Harrier	Goshawk
1990	16	–	2	–	2	–	–
1991	29	2	1	–	1	–	–
1992	19	5	–	–	1	–	1
1993	17	5	1	–	1	–	2
1994	19	2	1	–	–	–	–
1995	18	–	1	–	2	3	–
1996	28	4	2	1	2	–	1
1997	9	6	1	–	–	–	–
1998	27	15	3	–	1	–	–
1999	15	6	2	–	2	–	–
2000	33	16	3	–	–	–	–
2001	16	13	1	–	–	–	1
2002	23	15	2	2	–	–	–
2003	20	21	–	1	–	–	–
2004	46	3	–	–	–	1	1
Total	335	113	20	4	12	4	6

	Sparrowhawk	Peregrine	Merlin	Kestrel	Corvids	Owls	Others
1990	2	–	–	3	13	1	7
1991	–	3	–	–	13	–	9
1992	3	–	1	–	–	–	94
1993	–	–	–	–	64	–	15
1994	2	6	–	1	21	1	20
1995	1	4	–	–	36	1	120
1996	–	6	–	–	45	1	4
1997	1	6	–	–	52	–	4
1998	–	3	–	–	2	–	261
1999	–	2	–	2	35	2	4
2000	1	3	–	–	8	2	3
2001	2	1	–	2	23	3	13
2002	1	2	–	3	4	–	–
2003	2	–	–	–	37	–	2
2004	–	4	–	–	51	–	1
Total	15	40	1	11	404	11	557

Sources: CSL/SASA and RSPB data.

TABLE 34. Minimum confirmed numbers of birds of prey and owls killed by illegal trapping, shooting, or nest destruction 1990–2004. Figures in parentheses show totals of nests known to have been deliberately destroyed.

	Buzzard	Red Kite	Golden Eagle	Hen Harrier	Marsh Harrier	Goshawk
1990	3	–	(1)	2(9)	–	–
1991	9	–	(1)	(1)	1	1
1992	17(1)	1	–	8(5)	–	(1)
1993	17(1)	–	(1)	3(7)	–	3
1994	3	–	1	1(8)	–	1
1995	24	1	1	5(3)	1	1
1996	15	–	(1)	2(8)	–	1
1997	20(2)	1	–	1(5)	–	–
1998	27	1	(2)	7(3)	3	(2)
1999	9	1	–	2(1)	2	–
2000	11	–	–	2(3)	2	–
2001	11	–	–	–	–	–
2002	21	3	–	–	–	–
2003	10	1	–	1(1)	1(1)	–
2004	11(1)	1	–	(2)	1	1
Total	208(5)	10	2(6)	34(56)	11(1)	8(3)

	Sparrowhawk	Peregrine	Merlin	Kestrel	Owls
1990	1	1(2)	(2)	2	2
1991	8	5(4)	1(1)	8	12
1992	6	13(6)	–	7	4
1993	4	20(8)	–	5	3
1994	2	5(6)	(1)	–	2(1)
1995	3	8(3)	1	8	(1)
1996	5	9(5)	(2)	5(1)	4
1997	10	5(4)	–	9	6
1998	9	15(9)	1	5	18(1)
1999	5	5(3)	–	4	14
2000	8	5(2)	–	–	6
2001	7(1)	2	–	–	4
2002	3	8(4)	–	2	3(1)
2003	1	6(4)	–	1	3(1)
2004	1	3	–	5	5
Total	73(1)	110(60)	3(6)	61(1)	86(5)

Source: Data from RSPB records.
In addition to the above there were also recorded deaths of 1 Sea Eagle, 5 Ospreys, 3 Hobbies, and 1 Rough-legged Buzzard.

further 182 reports of the confirmed presence of pole traps or Larsen traps set in illegal circumstances.

Two examples have been given above of lowland shoots where legal vermin control has been undertaken, no protected species persecuted, and profitable game shooting, together with generally enhanced biodiversity, has followed. There are many other lowland examples in England and Wales where similar criteria apply. In the uplands however, especially in Scotland, the situation is very different. In fact, it is so different that it has not been possible to identify a single grouse moor north of the Border where there is certainty that no killing of protected birds or mammals takes place. Even within the industry employees will quietly acknowledge that they regard the continued killing of raptors and/or Pine Marten, Wild Cat, etc. risky as it is, as a clandestine prerequisite of the job. The number of cases of illegal poisoning investigated in Scotland in 2006 was the highest to date in the present century and included 14 Buzzards, 4 Red Kites, 2 Golden Eagles, 2 Ravens, and a Tawny Owl.

The maps on the following pages show the distribution of poisoning and other illegal killing of birds between 1995 and 2004 that emphasize the focus of the problem on grouse moorlands in England, Scotland, and Wales. In general, the public is ignorant of the scale of illegal persecution of wildlife, in the name of vermin control, that is still being carried out.

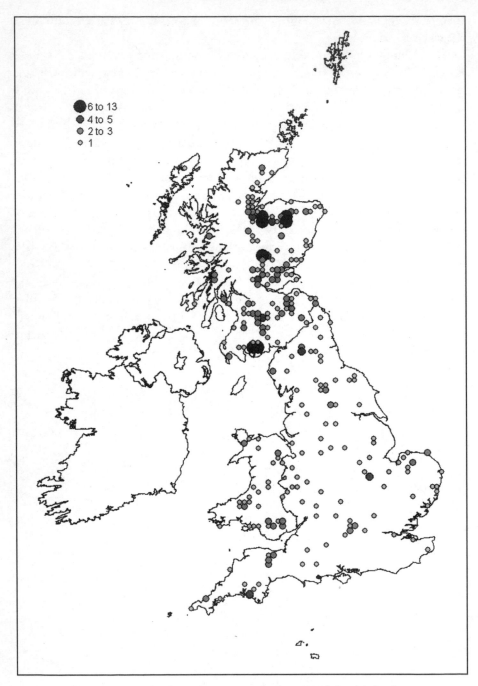

Figure 28. The number of poisoning incidents involving birds of prey
1995–2004. Each dot refers to an incident in an individual 10 km².
Map reproduced by courtesy of RSPB

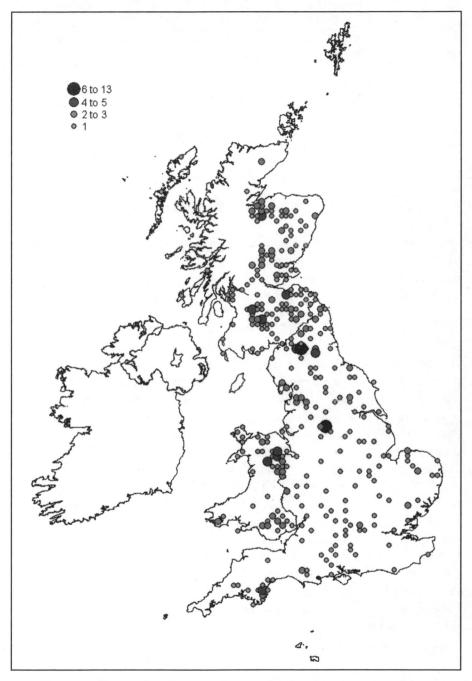

Figure 29. The number of prosecutions involving trapping, shooting, or nest destruction of birds of prey 1995–2004. Each dot represents the number of incidents in an individual 10 km². Map reproduced by courtesy of RSPB.

11

Vermin control and wildlife management: where next?

THERE was never an issue about controlling undesired wildlife in the era of the Tudors, Stuarts, and Hanoverians; vermin was what vermin was, and should be killed by whatever means were most effective. There was no question of right or wrong, even when rays of enlightenment started to lance the traditional views as the years passed. Moreover there was little thought that individual species—Hedgehog, Otter, Chough, or Kite—might actually disappear, despite the fact that some of the formerly widespread mammals, such as Pine Marten, were already rare in lowland parts of southern Britain. Several bird species certainly disappeared, but these were mainly wetland ones, lost due to the drainage of fens, open waters, and marshes. The only ones to disappear through direct persecution were the largest birds of prey—Osprey, Sea Eagle, and Golden Eagle—and some had probably already gone from wide areas of England and Wales well before the Tudors came to power. So, however energetic the varied levels of persecution in this era, it was prosecuted untrammelled by concerns for morals, public attitudes, legal constraint, or thoughts of extinction.

It was in the ensuing Victorian and Edwardian years that the campaign for the destruction of vermin, notably four-legged and winged predators, was elevated to the heights of perfection. Now, the possibility of exterminating species demonstrably became an achievable reality. The levels of all-round persecution that were carried out—killing, egg collecting, taxidermy, etc.—may revolt us nowadays, but we must accept that values then were very different and little wrong was seen, least of all by those involved. Certainly the focus swung away dramatically from the villager with his net, dog, trap, or gun and was vested in the new body of gamekeepers, full-time employees dedicated and directed to the protection of their masters' game stocks.

This sea change marked the evolution of wildlife management away from the long era of generalized village vermin killing, into a new, more clinical one of emphatic predator control. By the end of Edward VII's reign there were over 23,000 gamekeepers whose primary function was to remove predators. Their efficiency in this respect is legendary and is evidenced sufficiently in preceding chapters to render further repetition unnecessary. There were wilderness voices lamenting the evident demise of so many species. Nonetheless, the killing went on, essentially unhindered and, in many cases, for example in the remoteness of the Scottish Highlands, unseen and out of mind. It is worth noting that even the earliest bird protection legislation did not include raptors or other 'vermin'. The heyday of the 'keepered estate was the earliest years of the twentieth century, although it came to an abrupt end with the First World War and the ensuing decline in the number of effectively managed game estates. By then, however, the damage had been done to a wide range of native species. In many respects it was only the vagaries of European history that fortuitously enabled the last fragmented populations of several birds and mammals to survive in far corners of the country. In several cases they had been left clinging to the very brink of extinction: Red Kite, Hen Harrier, Wild Cat, Pine Marten, Polecat.

If it was the gamekeeper and his master who bear the responsibility for the elimination of such species, we must remember that they were not alone but were assisted in the final stages by the greed and selfishness of collectors. The Victorian and Edwardian era heralded the high vogue for egg collecting and the acquisition of mounted specimens to display in glass cases in the rooms of country houses. The rarer the species, the better and both fashions hastened the demise of numerous birds and mammals. Lasting pleasure and satisfaction, for many sportsmen, was to be found in displaying the rewards of their successful plundering in an artificially preserved form.

The post-war years from the 1940s onwards witnessed a new set of values with regard to the countryside and its wildlife. The Nature Conservancy Council was established in 1949 on the back of the growing study of ecology; the National Parks and Access to the Countryside Act introduced the first National Park in 1951; and a raft of County Wildlife Trusts was launched around the same time. Stimulated by ease of travel, access to the countryside, abundant published material, high profile campaigns by voluntary bodies such as Greenpeace, and pioneering television programmes, public awareness of wildlife issues rapidly matured into a substantial political voice, which has continued to grow. As evidence of that, one only has to consider the apparent influence of a body like the Royal Society for the Protection of Birds (RSPB), with a membership of 1 million+.

TABLE 35. Growth in RSPB membership since the Second World War. RSPB is the largest voluntary wildlife conservation body in Britain.

1945	1970	1980	2005
5,900	67,000	320,000	1,050,000

The general climate of public opinion in Britain in the early years of the twenty-first century is very interesting. The nineteenth- and early twentieth-century acceptance of unrestricted vermin killing has essentially been reversed to a new climate in which the predominating ethic is the recovery and return of lost or diminishing species. There is a proportion of the public that is unhappy about some aspects of wildlife management. At one extreme there are those—often among the most vociferous—who are strongly opposed to almost any killing. For such people even the necessary control of unarguable pests, and alien species, which are clearly detrimental to other aspects of our wildlife or to human interests—Rat, American Mink, Grey Squirrel—is apparently unacceptable.

Whatever the understandable sentiments that underlie voices supportive of reduced predator control, game shooting, and/or other field sports, the fact remains that the taking of wildlife for various purposes is perfectly legal in Britain and likely to remain so. For centuries it has been an unchallenged right to take game and wildfowl, to catch fish, and to remove those species that compete to the detriment of those interests. To what extent should we continue to protect these rights through our management of other species? Where these two philosophies collide they frequently meet at impasse and the imperative for a mature and measured national debate on a range of sensitive issues is clear. One of the serious challenges in the early years of the twenty-first century is to find genuine consensus on the complex issues relating to the management of wildlife. Nowhere will the confrontation be sharper than on issues related to various field sports—angling, hunting, and shooting. The bitter divisions that surfaced during the protracted debate on the Hunting with Dogs Bill revealed the depths of feeling on either side and the width of the gulf between them. Similar divisions exist in other fields, and we can explore some examples.

Since the collapse of Otter populations from the 1950s to 1970s and the withdrawal of the most damaging chemicals in 1966, the recovery of numbers has been gradual but widespread and sustained. Otters are steadily reclaiming their lost homelands. Barely has the corner in their fortunes been turned, before there are the first signs of renewed conflict with angling interests. In East Anglia, where many angling pools have been created as stillwater put-and-take fisheries, returning Otters have soon moved in to take advantage of them. Some of these waters are stocked with long-lived Carp; an individual fish may live to 20 years, grow to 80 cm, and be valued at as much as £2,000. Although an Otter cannot take a fish of that size, it can certainly predate them at a younger age and can mutilate and devalue the oldest ones by removing chunks. The Specialist Anglers' Alliance lobbied the Department of the Environment, Food and Rural Affairs (DEFRA) to assist with the cost of providing Otter-proof fencing for the limited number of specialized pools containing the most valuable specimen fish. These approaches for finance have not been successful at the time of writing and a solution to safeguard these valuable fisheries is still being sought. Counter to the search for government assistance is the argument that such interests have to take the responsibility for finding the legal means for protecting their own stocks from wildlife predation, as is accepted in fields as diverse as trout farms and Herons, or strawberry beds and Blackbirds. In this difficult scenario where valuable fish are involved, the question of compensation has even been breathed. However, there can be no future in this, for to do so would be to open a door which could never be closed. If it were to be agreed, why not compensate other interests: pheasant poults taken by Goshawks or racing pigeons killed by Sparrowhawks?

Similarly at fish farms—which are almost invariably near to watercourses or on the open coast—Otters quickly locate them and can cause serious depredations on fish stocks. Both situations have powerful echoes of the reasons why the animal was so disliked in medieval times and was later firmly embedded on the original Tudor vermin lists. Is the twenty-first-century Otter, helped back from the brink in southern Britain, immediately at risk of earning the sobriquet of 'vermin' once more? One sincerely hopes not and, at the time of writing, discussions are in progress to find answers to prevent ongoing conflicts of this nature.

Angling in its various forms is an enormously popular sport, practised by in excess of two million fishermen. It has more practitioners than any other countryside activity. As wild fish stocks in freshwater systems have fallen, notably migratory species such as Salmon, anglers have become increasingly concerned about the effects of piscivorous birds such as Grey Heron, Goosander, and, particularly, Cormorant. The last species is much persecuted in areas where Salmon and Trout fishing is economically important and is particularly berated for its predation at put-and-take fisheries and fish farms. To the alarm of conservation bodies, the government suddenly reversed its licensing policy in 2004 and decided to make it easier for fishery owners to obtain licences to cull Cormorants in England. Until then, limited licences were issued for killing in cases where serious damage to a fishery was proved and alternative scaring devices and other deterrents had been unsuccessful. The new policy was seemingly based solely on the assumption that, if Cormorants were present at a fishery, damage would occur and therefore a licence could be issued. Seen against a UK breeding population of just under 9,000 pairs (an increase of 15% in the past twenty years) and a wintering population of c.17,000 birds in England, the Westminster government set a ceiling for killing 3,000 Cormorants a year. Public reaction, particularly through non-governmental bodies, was predictably strident, not helped by the timing of the announcement in the middle of the fierce debate about fox-hunting. It was thus seen by many as little more than a cynical compensatory sop to field sports interests, with the clear aim of encouraging a reduction of the Cormorant population. On the other side it was argued by the Atlantic Salmon Trust, that Cormorant numbers had risen considerably in recent years and posed a genuine threat to Salmon populations already depleted by overfishing at sea and other factors. Furthermore, the Trust claimed that Cormorants predate fish in catchments notified as Special Areas of Conservation for their migratory fish species and thereby devalue them. The debate is sharpened when they accused the RSPB, in particular, of tunnel vision in respect of species other than birds.

Pigeon racing is an ancient and popular sport. Although the numbers involved are reducing (fewer young people are becoming involved) it is still predominantly a working-class activity (not forgetting that Queen Elizabeth II is a keen practitioner!) with main strongholds in some industrial areas. Despite this traditional following, it involves considerable sums of money both in maintaining the birds and their high quality facilities, and in the costs involved in racing. Prize money for the winner of some of the most prestigious races can reach £30,000, while in exceptional circumstances, at the highest level, a champion bird may change hands for as much as £120,000.

The two real enemies of the pigeon fancier are the Peregrine and Sparrow-hawk, of which the latter is generally the more detested. The populations of both species declined catastrophically in the 1950s and 1960s through the build-up of organochlorine pesticides ingested with their prey so that for several decades, until their eventual recovery, the problem of predation on pigeon lofts was virtually non-existent. Both species readily take pigeons and, since their recovery and spread into urban and suburban areas, they have presented a serious problem to some pigeon fanciers. Through the 1980s and 1990s, and to date, there have been innumerable examples of the illegal killing of Peregrines (in particular) and destruction of their nests, driven by sheer frustration. In South Wales, where Peregrines have recolonized sites in many of the valleys and thirty-six nests are monitored regularly each year, the problem with pigeons is an obvious one. The monitoring has revealed that fewer than 37% of sites were successful between 2000 and 2004. There were at least twenty-six instances of known or suspected destruction of nests/pairs in that period while a further sixty-one sites failed for unknown reasons but where human interference was regarded as probable. Another example of the problems facing pigeon racers is demonstrated by the fact that by 2001 the Scottish Homing Union lost 251 members, 67 of whom attributed their resignation to the frustration of trying to maintain their pigeons in the face of the depredations by Sparrowhawks and Peregrines. Once again the knotty question arises as to the moral legitimacy of affording unchallengeable primacy to protected species in the face of serious detriment to a perfectly legal and economically significant activity. The Scottish

Homing Union lobbied the Scottish Parliament for licences for the control of Sparrowhawks in specific circumstances, but so far has been unsuccessful. In this context it is interesting to note that in Denmark, derogation under Article 9 of the European Birds Directive has been granted on a number of occasions precisely for that purpose.

Whatever one's individual view of the merits of the 2005 Hunting with Dogs Act, there is no doubt that it represented a major landmark in the issues surrounding vermin control and associated countryside activities. It not only disabled traditional fox-hunting but also gave positive encouragement to a growing lobby of anti-field-sports activists. Fox-hunting is the outstanding example of a rural activity, nominally centred on vermin control, with important economic elements upon which some countryside communities depend, and with implications for a wider spectrum of social activities. Its significance to rural communities extends beyond the simple process of thinning out Foxes. The 2005 Act was promoted on the basis of concerns about animal welfare, not on the actual question of control of Foxes as vermin. (The Act also covered the use of dogs in hunting deer, Mink, and Hare). Its promotion was redolent with political overtones and stimulated high emotions, fierce opposition, and charges of an urban administration failing to understand the essential pulses of rural life. At its core, the Act struck at the heart of a rural tradition that has existed for hundreds of years, providing a service which is valued by farmers, a nucleus for social activities, and major recreation opportunities. In overall respects it is perhaps a moot point as to what proportion of fox-hunting is strictly vermin control and how much is principally recreational. If the point is worth pursuing, however, the easiest separation involves the foot packs (Wales) and fell packs (Lakeland) where there is especial concern among farmers that, with the passing of the Act, effective Fox control by traditional methods ceased and they will henceforward suffer increased predation among lambing flocks. A counter view that has been expressed in Lakeland is that farmers there will be forced to resort to other means of control, some of them illegal, and that Fox populations may be wiped out locally. In the hill areas which are home to these foot packs there is an important social aspect to the existence of the hunts through hound trails, social evenings, and a host of other events. They provide one of the catalysts for social gathering among communities in remote hill areas. This social aspect is similarly apparent in the rural areas in which mounted hunts predominate. Here they organize point-to point events, hunter trials, hunt balls, pony trials, dog shows, dinners, etc. although it is equally fair to note that such events also take place in areas where there are no hunts. The Countryside Alliance listed 27 examples of the different activities organized by hunts, which they claim involve upwards of 5,000 events per year attended by an estimated 1.5 million+ people.

The Burns Committee, set up by the government in 1999 to enquire into the implications of introducing a ban on hunting with dogs, analysed various aspects of the economic and social effects of hunts. The claim that hunts have impacts far beyond the specific control of Foxes is substantiated in many ways; the Committee's calculations of an overall average cost of £930 per Fox killed by hunts in England and Wales (minimum £100 with some hunts in Wales, and a maximum of up to £3,000 in seven English hunts) demonstrate that there are indeed other appreciated benefits. Certainly on a cost/benefit basis nobody would pay such astronomical sums to kill a single Fox. The Committee confirmed the substantial economic value of hunts within their rural communities, producing an all-inclusive spend of at least £70 million p.a. This figure included the direct costs incurred by hunts, total sums committed by followers, essential support service industries, etc. A specific example argued during the parliamentary debate was the amount contributed to the local economy by weekenders coming to Devon and Somerset staghounds. However, as well as making a contribution to rural economies, the social and cultural significance of hunts was recognized by Burns. Hunting was responsible for the employment of 6,000–8,000 full-time equivalent jobs, principally in rural areas where alternative employments were often few and far between. It was not suggested that all of these jobs would be lost, however. Other, occasionally exaggerated, claims are made about the importance of hunts in providing a cohesive role in helping to bind small rural communities together and in providing an antidote to the increased feeling of isolation that many farmers experience in periods of depressed agriculture. The repeated insistence, during the public debate on the Hunting with Dogs Bill, of a clear divide between urban and rural sentiments on the issue was spurious, for there are as many people in rural communities passionately opposed to fox-hunting as there are those who passionately support it. Similarly the converse applies in urban areas. Nonetheless, modern vermin control has greater ramifications than immediately meet the eye and fox-hunting is one example that has taken a severe knock, with potential social reverberations throughout rural England and Wales.

North of the Border, the Protection of Wild Animals Act, again fiercely opposed, was passed by the Scottish Parliament in 2002 with similar provisions to the subsequent Westminster legislation. It considered that 'economic factors alone are not enough to justify unnecessary suffering' (caused to hunted animals). Since the Act's introduction, the ten mounted hunts in the Border counties have remained in business although the numbers of employed staff and hounds have halved. Despite this the number of Foxes killed have almost doubled. Thereafter, Foxes have had to be flushed from cover by the hounds and then shot by marksmen. To quote one Master of Hounds, 'It's pest control now, not hunting as it used to be'. In addition to the number of jobs that have already been lost, the Scottish Countryside Alliance claimed that some £1 million annually had been lost to the Borders economy.

If the Hunting with Dogs Act signalled a major turning point in relation to fox-hunting, the results of the grouse moor experiment at Langholm in south-west Scotland similarly marked a significant milestone in the field of upland game shooting. A range of respected bodies, the Buccleuch Estate, Scottish Natural Heritage, the Game Conservancy Trust (GNT) and the GCT Scottish Research Trust, RSPB, the Joint Nature Conservation Committee, the Institute of Terrestrial Ecology, and Peter Buckley of Westerhall Estate, jointly sponsored the research programme. The principle of the five-year programme was that the eradication of Foxes and Crows was to continue annually but no protected species of birds, *viz* avian predators, would be controlled. The aim was to establish whether the two principal birds of prey that predate Red Grouse, Peregrine and Hen Harrier, affected the numbers of Grouse and therefore the surplus that was available for shooting in the autumn. When the programme started in 1992 five keepers were employed on the 11,000 acre Buccleuch estate. In 1990, with unrestricted 'keepering, the number of Red grouse shot was 4,038. Across the five-year period of research, Peregrine pairs doubled from three to six and Hen Harriers nests increased from two, to a maximum of twenty-two. The cost of managing the Langholm moors was put at £99,500 p.a,. making the average price of driven grouse in 1996 £40 per bird. The study showed that the two raptors removed 30% of territorial birds in spring, 37% of chicks, and then 30% of the survivors in autumn. The bag of driven Grouse in 1997 yielded a total of only 51 birds—2,420 fewer than required to balance the management costs. As a result, six gamekeepers had to be redeployed as the moor became non-viable as a commercial shoot. As management on the moor ceased, the Foxes and Crows returned, predating Red Grouse and other breeding birds including the Hen Harriers themselves.

These are the basic facts of the Langholm project, with an apparently unequivocal answer to the question, 'Is it possible to run a successful commercial grouse moor and allow raptors to breed freely?' There are always provisos to be added to any research results and Langholm is no different. The point has been made, for example, that the interpretation of results on Langholm does not necessarily apply on other moors. Each moor in its way is unique. Langholm had a higher than average proportion of grass than other grouse moors (it has lost 48% of its heather through overgrazing since the Second World War), and grass moorlands hold higher populations of Meadow Pipits and voles than heather and are the preferred prey of Hen Harriers. Nonetheless, the findings appeared damningly conclusive. Notwithstanding this, the controversy then began. Most of the organizations involved, and other bodies with a commercial interest in the issue, accepted that the Hen Harriers had clearly been the cause of the collapse in

Red Grouse numbers. The RSPB did not take that view and has been heavily criticized ever since by those concerned with the economics of upland management.

More recently, progress has been made with GCT and RSPB identifying important areas of agreement in this complex subject. The matter is made more complex by the recognition that there are two separate issues at stake, namely the short-term problem and then the search for a long-term solution. In the long term it is the quality of the restored moorland, with good heather habitat and a reduction in the current area of grassland, that will determine the carrying capacity for larger stocks of Red Grouse. The difficult short-term problem is one of operating within the law while ensuring that birds of prey (and ground predators) do not prevent the re-establishment of profitable levels of Grouse, while the moorland recovers over a longer period of years. Writing in 2002 Warren says, 'A variety of possibilities have been under discussion. These include the rearing and release of Red Grouse, relocation of raptors (either by live capture or through "nest management"), raptor "quotas" and diversionary feeding'. He quotes Tapper (1999), who argues that 'the legal protection given to raptors under the 1981 Wildlife and Countryside Act was a necessary first step, but that in the future we will need management as well as protection, if we are to retain a rich and diverse predator fauna as well as prolific game stocks'. Warren adds that 'such management may require a change in perception whereby raptors come to be seen as a renewable resource'. One encouraging possibility is that a follow-up project may be initiated at Langholm with the aim of moving the debate forward. It is clear that this crucial debate about avian predators and game, sharpest at present in the uplands, still has a long way to run.

Of the uplands of Britain, 30–40% is managed as grouse moor and Red Grouse are the economic driver of many upland estates. The commercial importance of grouse moors has certainly protected those areas from what would otherwise have been an even greater spread of upland conifer forest. The point is well made too, that many grouse moors are among the best for other wildlife species, notably breeding waders, due to the way in which they are managed. Recent RSPB figures, published by the Game Conservancy Trust (in *Nature's Gain*) show that moors properly managed for Red Grouse can support up to five times the number of breeding Golden Plover and Lapwing and about twice as many Curlew as unmanaged moors. The comparison with upland moors that are managed purely as nature reserves is unflattering.

These distant uplands are also, by definition, some of the most thinly popu- lated areas of the country and the economic contribution that is made through the existence and management of grouse moors is all the more important.

Thus, within these issues lies the core of a major debate that is emerging and cannot be pushed aside. What has to be done to find compromises and solutions to the conflicts that arise from problems presented by legally protected species? It is relatively easy to make the case for the legal protection of a native animal when it is clearly rare and endangered—Red Kite, Pine Marten, etc. However, it is a very different matter to try to reverse that situation, if recovery is so successful that a fully protected species starts to impact seriously on other species, or on legitimate human interests. In ensuring the permanent protection of the rare and endangered species are we at risk of tipping the balance too far? These are questions that are increasingly being raised and have to be addressed. In issues like these sentiment and prejudice too easily frustrate rationality and pragmatism.

As part of the growing concern about the effects of increasing populations of raptors, the (former) Department of the Environment established a Raptor Working Group in 1995. The Group, including representatives from twelve different organizations, was asked to focus on three particular issues:

- Conflicts involving Hen Harriers, Peregrines, and Red Grouse
- Conflicts involving Sparrowhawks, Peregrines, and racing pigeons
- Problems relating to bird of prey predation at Pheasant release pens

The Group made a series of recommendations, central to which was the presumption against the lethal control of any raptor species. Rather, a series of research projects and adaptive management proposals was initiated, many of which were taken up by the statutory bodies in England, Wales, and, particularly, Scotland. The aim of these initiatives has been to find longer-term, non-lethal solutions to these very difficult issues.

Several examples quoted earlier illustrate the breadth of the contentious subject of species regarded as vermin by particular interests—Cormorants and anglers, Otters and fish farms, Sparrowhawks, Peregrines, and homing pigeons. Without doubt, the most difficult area of the debate will be that concerning birds of prey, crystallized by the chasm of divergent views that the Langholm work emphasized. The issues emanating from the results of that work have already filled the pages of shooting and countryside journals and are being taken up in the wider ornithological press. It is the genesis of a process that is unavoidable and must result, eventually, in the formulation of acceptable public opinion and attitudes towards 'vermin'. In various popular articles the RSPB, the non-governmental body (NGO) with greatest interest and influence in this field, is frequently accused of intransigence, regarding all individual birds of prey as inviolate. Others point to the fact that Article 9 of the European Birds Directive permits derogation in certain circumstances. This process has already been used by at least seven European Union countries, in relation to derogation for the killing or taking of birds of prey protected under European law, involving Sparrowhawk, Golden Eagle, Hen Harrier, Peregrine, and hundreds of

Goshawks. Moorland game interests in England have proposed derogation for the Hen Harrier but it has had no support from the statutory agencies or conservation NGOs. The question is repeatedly asked, 'Is it logical to manage other forms of wildlife and regard birds of prey as inviolate?' We live in an environment that has been vastly adapted by Man and in which the management of wildlife—the ways in which, and the extent to which, we manage it—become of greater moment. As discussed in Chapter 10, there is a gulf in public understanding of this need that has to be bridged. The breaking debate to which I refer is only one aspect of this—but a vital one.

In the early exchanges delivered in this debate, in relation to birds of prey, there we three conflicting theses on the table: (i) that the only solution is to permit limited lethal control of the most problematic species, (ii) that the protected status of all birds of prey is inviolate, and (iii) that non-lethal solutions must be found, with derogation under Article 9 of the Birds Directive being a last resort. Should lethal control ever be approved, there would undoubtedly be some serious concerns. If, for the sake of argument, limited control of Sparrowhawks, or agreed quotas of Hen Harriers were established, how would they be adequately regulated? The Game Conservancy Trust has floated the idea of one pair of Hen Harriers per 6,000 acres of grouse moorland. How could society ever be sure that there was strict adherence to regulated numbers?

There is another concern too, involving gamekeepers. The majority of modern gamekeepers (and their masters) adhere to the letter of the law, so far as protected species are concerned. However, it is difficult to ignore the fact that, for the historical reasons outlined throughout the book, and the fact that there are still well publicized incidents of illegal killing, it is a profession with a lot of historical baggage. The responsible 'keeper's worst enemy nowadays is his fellow professional who breaks the law and is caught. It would be very difficult for the public to be persuaded to accept any enhanced control of birds of prey, or other protected animal, by gamekeepers so long as there is one rotten apple in the barrel. In that respect there is still a long way to go. The RSPB, in its analysis of illegal killing, has shown that 85% of those convicted of raptor persecution offences since 1985 had a game interest and most were gamekeepers.

So, the problem unfolds and there are difficult questions to be answered. What species are 'vermin' in the twenty-first century? Are there species (e.g. Jay) that should come off the present list? Are there any that should be back on it? In some circumstances are there protected species that should be controlled locally? Can we successfully resolve the complex issues surrounding the management of wildlife in publicly acceptable ways?

The general public mood is not, by nature, antagonistic towards field sports, even if there are some aspects and practices which cause concern and not forgetting that, at the extreme, there are certainly strident and unreasoned voices of opposition. On both sides of the issue, there is a real need for rational debate and discussion. Provocative statements only harden views, entrench positions, and thereby broaden the divide to make resolution ever more difficult. The *Shooting Times*, a popular and long-established field sports magazine, published an article in December 2005, which named thirty species described as 'voracious predators' that affected the economics of the game shooting and fishing interests. That list included saw-billed ducks (Goosander and Red-breasted Merganser), Grey Seal, Buzzard, Sparrowhawk, Hen Harrier, Peregrine, Goshawk, Badger, Polecat, Raven, Otter, Heron, Wild Cat, Pine Marten, Osprey, Red Kite, Hedgehog, and Golden Eagle, as well as Rat, Stoat, Magpie, Crow, and other legitimate vermin species. Although the editor has said subsequently that the *Shooting Times* would never advocate the illegal killing of a protected species, the publication of such a list is, at very least, highly provocative (as shown even by government reaction) and, at worst, easy to interpret as an invitation to illegal killing. How far have our real sentiments changed in 500 years? That list resonates very strongly with the one enacted in 1566.

Over the centuries our relationship with wildlife has swung to extremes. At times it has been dominating and subjugating, at others paternalistic, occasionally symbiotic, and often fraternal or patronizing, but we have always managed it for our own benefits, however damaging or ill-advised this might have been at times. What will define wildlife management/vermin control as we advance in the twenty-first century? What is certain is that it will be different from that which has been accepted in the past. Are we capable of finding acceptable balances and coming up with the right solutions to both satisfy human interests and sustain the damaged heritage of our splendid native wildlife?

 Appendix 1

Summary table of vermin payments extracted from churchwardens' accounts

Notes

1. Dates given against each parish are the first and last dates of existing/available accounts. These end dates do *not* necessarily signify a continuous record. Many are partial, discontinuous, or fragmentary; fewer than 50% are complete within the given dates.

2. The species are ranked on an indicative scale of abundance 1–5. This scoring is relevant only *within* individual species, i.e. it is only applicable vertically in the columns, not horizontally across rows. For example a '5' for House Sparrow indicates many hundreds of dozens whereas a '5' for Otter would indicate perhaps 6–8.

3. Former county and parish names are used, as this was the basis on which the payments were made.

4. Parishes with no vermin payments are listed at the end of each county. (f) or (h sp) indicates that there were no vermin except a very occasional Fox or a handful of House Sparrows.

N.B. *The original data sheets with the details for all individual parish records of vermin payments are housed as an archive in the Museum of English Rural Life at Reading, where they can be accessed.*

		Hedgehog	Fox	Badger	Otter	Polecat	Stoat	Weasel	Marten	Wild Cat	Mole	H. Sparrow	Bullfinch	'Crow'	Rook	Jackdaw	Raven	Magpie	Jay	Red Kite	Hawk'	Other
Anglesey																						
Holyhead	1737–1889		4																			
Llanfechell	1724–54		2																			

Aberffraw 1801–8, Heneglwys 1812–13, Llandegfan 1759–90, Llangoed 1778–1803, Rhodogeidio 1771–96

		Hedgehog	Fox	Badger	Otter	Polecat	Stoat	Weasel	Marten	Wild Cat	Mole	H. Sparrow	Bullfinch	'Crow'	Rook	Jackdaw	Raven	Magpie	Jay	Red Kite	Hawk'	Other
Bedfordshire																						
Ampthill	1718–1876	1	1	1		2	1															5
Apsley Guise	1708–9	1	1																			5
Arlesey	1735–93	1	1			1	1															5
Barton in Clay	1781–1837		1			2				4	2											2
Little Barford	1779–1804	1	1			1				1												5
Battlesden	1782–3		1							1												
Bedford St Paul	1762–1839	4	1			2	5	2														5
Biddenden	1836–87									2												5
Billington	1686–1720									2			1									3
Blunham	1696–1810	3	1		4	4	2			5	2											5
Bolnhurst	1676–1766	1	1		1	1				2												
Bromham	1680–1875	3	1		1	1																
Caddington	1717–1836	4				5				5												4
Campton	1798–1889									4												
Clifton	1710–1835	2			4	3		4														5
Cople	1812–77																					5
Cranfield	1777–1832																					5
Dean	1797–1861	2																				
Dunton	1775–1819																					5
Eaton Bray	1819–34	3				3	5	5		4												5

Parish	Dates									
Eaton Socon	1692–1854	5			5	1	5	5		5
Edworth	1725–99					1	1			
Eversholt	1758–1838	2					2			4
Everton	1797–1864	4	1							4
Flitton	1772–1876	5				1	1		2	
Harlington	1677–1831	3		1			4		5	5
Harrold	1791–3								2	
Houghton Regis	1714–1836	3		1		1	4			5
Husborne Crawley	1686–1715	3	1	1		1	4			
Kempston	1678–1771	5	1	1	1		5			5
Kensworth	1705–1810	1								5
Knotting	1838–56									5
Leighton Buzzard	1757						1			
Maulden	1803–34	1	1	1		1	1		4	5
Melchbourne	1685–1754	3	4	1			4	1	3	3
Meppershall	1692–1784	4		1			4			3
Millbrook	1794–1831									4
Milton Bryan	1678–1722	1	1	1		1	1		4	2
Moggerhanger	1712–1808	5	5	2		5	5	1	1	5
Northill	1563–1812	5	5	1	1	5	5	1	1	5
Oakley	1788–1802	3								3
Pertenhall	1727–1844	3	1	2	1		1		2	5
Potton	1787–1816	2			1		3	1		3
Pulloxhill	1628–1816		1				1			1
Ravensden	1704–1807	3	4	1			4		3	3
Renhold	1764–1828	5	4	4	5	1	5	1		3
Ridgmount	1727–32	2				1	1			2
Roxton	1740–79	5	2	2			1	1		1
Sandy	1804–66									5
Shillington	1574–1826									5
Silsoe	1731–84	2	2				3			1
Stanbridge	1733–1839	2					2		4	5

	Hedgehog	Fox	Badger	Otter	Polecat	Stoat	Weasel	Marten	Wild Cat	Mole	H. Sparrow	Bullfinch	'Crow'	Rook	Jackdaw	Raven	Magpie	Jay	Red Kite	'Hawk'	Other
Steppingley 1850–8										5											
Stevington 1849–72										4											
Streatley 1765–1852	1	1		2					3	4											
Sundon 1767–1834										5											
Thurleigh 1822–30										4											
Tingrith 1736–1893	1									5											
Toddington 1707–1845		1		2			1			1											
Turvey 1810		1		1			1														
Westoning 1743–1900		1		1					1	5											
Willington 1771–1871		1		1					5	5											
Wilshamstead 1722–78		1	1	2						4											
Woburn 1757–1831	1									5											

Great Barford (f) 1731–47, Hayne (f) 1734–66, Milton Ernest (h sp) 1801–4, Odell (h sp) 1839–51, Pavenham (f)1755–90, Stagsden (h sp) 1831–4, Studham (h sp) 1750–1834

Berkshire

	Hedgehog	Fox	Badger	Otter	Polecat	Stoat	Weasel	Marten	Wild Cat	Mole	H. Sparrow	Bullfinch	'Crow'	Rook	Jackdaw	Raven	Magpie	Jay	Red Kite	'Hawk'	Other
Aldworth 1707–1883		2				2	3	1		1											5
Arborfield 1742–1884										5											
Boxford 1756–1828		1							1	5											
Brightwalton 1606–1865		1	1	2				1		5											
Brimpton 1640–1787				2																	
Cumnor 1687–1938		1		1																	
Eaton Hastings 1727–1892		1		2						5											
Englefield 1713–85		2		1						3											
Hampstead Norreys 1636–1779		3	2	2						4											
Hungerford 1659–1818		3	2	2					1												
Marsham 1702–1835		2		4						4											

Stratford Mortimore	1681–1837	1	2		1	1	5
Swallowfield	1614–1886					1	3
Waltham St Lawrence	1708–1845	1		1			5
Wantage	1657–1758	3	2				5
Winkfield	1659–1867	3	2				5

Ashampstead 1610–1857, Caversham St Peter 1672–1707, Childrey 1568–1688, Enborne 1660–90, Great Coxwell 1703–71 Reading St Giles 1518–1808, Ruscombe 1669–81, Streatley 1723–1893, Sutton Courtney 1736–1839, Thatcham 1561–1628, Uffington 1655–1754 (h sp), Wallingford St Peter 1720–61

Buckinghamshire

Boarstall	1675–1703	3	3	2	5				
Clifton Reynes	1665–1720	2	2	2	3				
Drayton Beauchamp	1829–50								
Edlesborough	1686–1740	1		1		4			
Hambleden	1639–1832	5	3	5	5		1	1	
Hughenden	1681–1712	1	1	2	4				
Ivinghoe	1828–49				3				
Ludgershall	1668–1800	5	4	2	1	5			
Newton Longville	1693–1725	3	1	4	5		4		
Pitstone	1604–1829	2		2	3			2	5
Quainton	1668–1735	5	4	1	1			1	
Radclive	1672–1732	1							
Stewkley	1671–1750	5	1	5				5	5
West Wycombe	1663–1724	1	1		3				
Weston Underwood	1663–1724	4	2	1					
Wing	1527–1723	5	1	1	5	1	4		5

Buzzard (5)

Amersham 1541–1603, Aston Abbots 1562–1630, Bledlow 1640–75, Dinton 1650–73, Great Marlow 1593–1674, Marsworth 1786, Princes Risborough 1682–1707, Wingrave 1575–1694

		Hedgehog	Fox	Badger	Otter	Polecat	Stoat	Weasel	Marten	Wild Cat	Mole	H. Sparrow	Bullfinch	'Crow'	Rook	Jackdaw	Raven	Magpie	Jay	Red Kite	'Hawk'	Other
Brecknockshire																						
Defynnog	1774–1826		2	2													5				5	

Bryn Gwyn 1732–1800, Catherdine (f) 1786–1889, Crickhowell 1705–57, Llanfiangell Cwmdu 1797–1821

		Hedgehog	Fox	Badger	Otter	Polecat	Stoat	Weasel	Marten	Wild Cat	Mole	H. Sparrow	Bullfinch	'Crow'	Rook	Jackdaw	Raven	Magpie	Jay	Red Kite	'Hawk'	Other
Caernarvonshire																						
Aber	1703–1819		1														1					
Llandegai	1759–1790		2								1											
Llanfairfechan	1784–1827		1														1					

Llanbeblig 1771–86, Llanor 1756–1813, Ynyscynhaearn 1739–76

		Hedgehog	Fox	Badger	Otter	Polecat	Stoat	Weasel	Marten	Wild Cat	Mole	H. Sparrow	Bullfinch	'Crow'	Rook	Jackdaw	Raven	Magpie	Jay	Red Kite	'Hawk'	Other
Cambridgeshire																						
Babraham	1759–1946		2			1					5	5										
Burwell	1792–1864		1			1	2				5	5										
Chippenham	1761–1844										3	3										
Croxton	1634–1755		2	1		2		3			1	1		1			1					
Dry Drayton	1811–53		4			1	2				5											
Duxford	1738–51					1																
Ely St Mary	1828–34																					
Gamlingay	1608–84		2	1		2					1											
Hildersham	1761–1867		1									4										
Leverington	1809–72		1								3	5		1								
Lit. Wilbraham	1718–1858		2	1	3						5							1				
Lolworth	1752–1886										2	1										
Newton	1820–45										1	5										
Over	1733–1854										1	5							5			

Rampton 1783–1843 · 5
Soham 1663–1762 · 1 · 4
Swaffham 1823–38 · 5
Welney 1734–5 · 1 · 1
Wisbech St Peter 1620–1805 · 3 · 1 · 1

Barton 1784–1908, Burrough Green 1579–1632, Chatteris (h sp) 1811–19, Cheveley 1725–1888, Coton 1576–1817, Downham 1674–1726, Elm (f) 1759–1812, Ely Holy Trinity 1565–1738, Kirtling 1669–1856, Landbeach 1741–1805 March 1541–1679, Oakington 1717–1857, Stetchworth 1651–1751, Tydd St Giles 1644–1701, Wood Ditton 1668–1703

Cardiganshire

Llanfair-ar-y-Bryn 1766–79 · 1 · 3 1
Llanfarian 1720–30 · 1 1 · 2 1 · 1 · Kestrel(1)
Llangwyryfron 1873–1916 · 1 1 · 1 1

Cilcennin 1837–55, Llandysiliogogo 1766–79, Llanrhystyd 1737–1802

Carmarthenshire

Llanegwad 1732–1886 · 1 1 · 3
Llangadog 1785–1801 · 1 1
Laugharne 1783–1816 · 4 4 · 4 1 · 2 · 'Owl' (2)
Llansawel 1752–82 · 1 1 2 · 1 2 2 · 3
Trellech 1823–35 · 2 5 · 5 · 1

Abernant (f) 1733–78, Carmarthen St Peter 1778–1803, Llanfiangel Cilfargen 1797–1836, Llanpumpsaint 1802–29 (f), Llanstephan 1756–88, Merthyr 1756–1801, Myddfai 1653–86

Cheshire

Alderley 1682–1801 · 5 4
Barthomley 1662–1738 · 5 1
Bunbury 1655–1813 · 5 5 · 4 · 4 5 5

	Hedgehog	Fox	Badger	Otter	Polecat	Stoat	Weasel	Marten	Wild Cat	Mole	H. Sparrow	Bullfinch	'Crow', Rook	Jackdaw	Raven	Magpie	Jay	Red Kite	'Hawk', Other
Church Lawton 1681–1743	1	1																	
Church Minshull 1756–1823	5	1																	
Davenham 1685–1748		1								4	1	5				5			
Eastham 1691–1731	1	3																5	
Frodsham 1609–1756	5	4																	
Great Budworth 1699–1738	5	1											5						
Middlewich 1635–64	2	1																	
Over Peover 1674–1737	1	1																	
Prestbury 1728–1800	2	5	3	3	1					5	1			4					
Rostherne 1672–1755	5	5	1				1				1	5							
Stoke 1677–1720	3	1																	
Tarporley 1662–1811	5	1									5	5						5	
Tilston 1615–1815	3	1									2	4							
Wilmslow 1635–1741	1	1										3							
Wybunbury 1687–1781	3																		

Baddiley 1622–1738, Daresbury (f) 1742–1831, Eccleston (f) 1634–87, Macclesfield 1686–1888, Swettenham 1633–1791, Whitegate (f) 1635–1741

Cornwall

'birds' unspecified (4)

	Hedgehog	Fox	Badger	Otter	Polecat	Stoat	Weasel	Marten	Wild Cat	Mole	H. Sparrow	Bullfinch	'Crow', Rook	Jackdaw	Raven	Magpie	Jay	Red Kite	'Hawk', Other
Altarnun 1729–65		1	1	5	5					3	2							4	2
Antony 1746–1828		1	1	1															
Blisland 1724–1840		2	2	4	5														
Boyton 1749–89		1	1	1	1					4	1							1	1
Bradock 1664–1840		1	1	1	1				1									2	1
Budock 1778–98	1	2	2	1	2														

	Hedgehog	Fox	Badger	Otter	Polecat	Stoat	Weasel	Marten	Wild Cat	Mole	H. Sparrow	Bullfinch	'Crow'	Rook	Jackdaw	Raven	Magpie	Jay	Red Kite	'Hawk'	Other
St Keverne 1721–47	5			5																	
St Mabyn 1659–82		1	1	3		1		1											2		
St Neot 1602–1708	1	4	2	5				5											5		Rat (3)
St Teath 1773–1867		3	2	1	1				1										3		
Sennen 1750–1806		1		1	1				1												
Talland 1666–1700		1		1																	

Menheniot 1556–1636, Mullion (f) 1785–1855, South Petherwin 1767–1837, St Gennys (f) 1711–86, Zennor 1768–91

Cumberland

	Hedgehog	Fox	Badger	Otter	Polecat	Stoat	Weasel	Marten	Wild Cat	Mole	H. Sparrow	Bullfinch	'Crow'	Rook	Jackdaw	Raven	Magpie	Jay	Red Kite	'Hawk'	Other
Addington 1690–1748	1		1					2								4					
Brigham 1709–1882	1															4					
Crosthwaite 1713–88	5															5					Eagle (5)
Dacre 1682–1883	1			2												4					
Greystoke 1726–1841	5						1									5					
Lazonby 1719–1819	5															4					
Penrith 1655–1801	2		1													1					
St Bees 1684–1786	5		5				5	5								5					
Threlkald 1774–1819										1											

Borrowdale 1726–1824, Castle Carrock 1699–1719, Croglin 1724–1840, Dean 1746–1887, Egremont 1765–92, Garrigill 1796–1849, Gosforth 1697–1796, Hutton-in-the-Forest 1649–1777, Kirkoswald 1641–1786, Newton Reigny 1769–1836, St John's 1732–1836, Stanwix 1685–1790, Torpenhow 1672–1814, Torver 1671–1900

Denbighshire

	Hedgehog	Fox	Badger	Otter	Polecat	Stoat	Weasel	Marten	Wild Cat	Mole	H. Sparrow	Bullfinch	'Crow'	Rook	Jackdaw	Raven	Magpie	Jay	Red Kite	'Hawk'	Other
Denbigh 1697–1852	2					1															
Eglwysbach 1698–1730						1											1				
Erbistock 1772–1852	2																				

Llanarmon D C	1739–78	2								1
Llanelian	1695–1780									1
Llanfair Talhiarn	1665–89									1
Llanferres	1673–1718	2			1					1
Llanfwrog	1703–56	2								1
Llangynhafal	1663–1727	1								1
Llanrhaeadr-ym-Mochnant	1714–86	4							1	1
Llansannan	1710–79									1
Marchwiel	1663–1777	1								1
Ruabon	1746–58				1					1

Eglwysbach (f) 1698–1730, Gresford (f) 1661–7, Gyfeiliog 1787–1843, Llanarmon yn ial 1753–60, Llanbedr D C 1684–1777, Llandegla 1754–79, Llandyrnog 1663–81, Llanfair Dyffryn Clwyd 1729–31, Llangernyw 1773–6, Llangollen 1773–1825, Llanwrst 1665–1714, Llanynys 1629–63, Ruthin 1687–1735

Derbyshire

Denby Dale	1680–1806	1				1	
Hartington	1759–1847	1	3		5		3
Hathersage	1668–1782	5	4	2		5	5
Hope	1661–1861	5	1		1		
Marston on Dove	1602–1827	5					1
Wirksworth	1658–1726	5	5		5		
Youlgreave	1604–1722	5	2		3		

Barlow (f) 1648–1751, Elmton 1724–1804, Gresley 1774–1875, Heath 1712–83, Holmsfield 1725–96, Peak Forest 1674–1773, Sawley 1743–1803, Shirland 1712–19, Stanton by Bridge 1690–1766, Whitwell 1792–1821

Devon

Abbotsham	1756–1813	2	1	1	1	3	1	3	2	5	2	2	5
Ashburton	1761–1820	5	3	5		5	3	5	5
Bere Ferrers	1632–55	1	3	1	3	1	3	4

Parish	Date	Hedgehog	Fox	Badger	Otter	Polecat	Stoat	Weasel	Marten	Wild Cat	Mole	H. Sparrow	Bullfinch	'Crow'	Rook	Jackdaw	Raven	Magpie	Jay	Red Kite	'Hawk'	Other
Bishops Nympton	1739–1884									1		5										
Branscombe	1793–1837	5	5	5		5	5			1										5	5	
Braunton	1554–1790	4	1	1		1	1			1		5							3	3	3	
Broadhembury	1662–1751	2	2		1	1						5										
Buckland	1631–1836	1	3	1																		
Clawton	1592–1846		1	1						3										2		
Clovelly	1750–1809		1	1					1													
Combe Martin	1691–1912	1	4	5	2	2						1							5	1	1	Titmice (1)
Dartington	1567–1815	3	1	5	1	1						4							5	1	1	'Hawk' (2)
Dawlish	1686–1792	4	1	5	3	3	3												1	4		
Dean Prior	1567–1815		1	1								3										
Doddiscombs-leigh	1745–1843	1	1	1	2	2														2	2	
East Budleigh	1604–1784	5	5	4	2	2						1					1		5	5	5	'small birds' (5)
Exeter St Thomas	1726–39	5			2	2	1				5								5	4	5	Titmice (5)
Exminster	1788–1880	1		1							1											
Gittisham	1649–1762	5	1	2	1	1	3				1	3							5	2		
Halberton	1632–1723	5	1	2								5							1			
Harpford	1714–1861		1	1																		
Hartland	1599–1706	1	5	5	1		1							2								
High Week	1751–1842	5	1	2	3							5							5			
Holcombe Rogus	1734–1825				1			5														
Holne	1737–1856	1	3	2	1	1														2		
Horwood	1709–1812	1	1	3	2	2	2						1					1	3	2	3	
Kentisbeare	1740–9	5																	5			
Kilmington	1557–1855		1	1	1	1					5	1										
Kingswear	1825–60	4	3	3							5	5	5						5			
Landcross	1714–1803	1	2	2	1	1					5	5										
Landkey	1757–1856		1	5																		

Parish	Period	Recorded counts	Notes
Littleham	1641–1775	5, 1, 1, 2	
Lustleigh	1753–1821	2, 2, 4, 2, 2, 5, 1	
Mamhead	1786–1843		lists only 'vermin' (5)
Mary Tavy	1664–1863	1, 1, 1, 1, 1	
Marystowe	1764–83	5, 5, 5	
Modbury	1622–1842	5, 1, 2, 2, 5, 5, 5	Titmice (5)
North Tawton	1717–87	1, 4	
Pilton	1784–1884	1	
Rattery	1769–1864	1, 1	'vermin' unspecified (5)
Satterleigh	1718–1869	1, 1, 1, 2, 1, 3	
Shaldon	1780–1835	1, 1	
Sheepstor	1718–1864	2, 3, 5, 1, 3, 1, 2	
Sidbury	1622–1724	4, 3, 2, 3, 4, 2, 5, 4	Titmice (3) W'pecker (1)
South Tawton	1567–58	1	
Stoodleigh	1685–1866	2, 3, 1, 4, 1, 2	
Tawstock	1773–1843	2, 2, 3	
Teignmouth	1667–1825	3, 1, 1, 1, 1, 1, 1	
Topsham	1738–1813	3, 1, 5, 1, 1	
Torquay	1747–1827	1, 1	
Uplyme	1633–99	3, 1, 1, 4	
Upottery	1769–1829	1, 2, 1, 1, 1	
Woodbury	1648–1713	1, 1, 1	

Bishops Tawton 1709–1812, Bow (f) 1633–60, Brushford 1682–1726, Chudleigh 1580–1650, Coldridge (f) 1681–1734, Crediton 1551–99, Cruwys Morchard 1638–48, Drewsteignton (f) 1661–98, Dunchideock 1804–31, Exeter St Edmund 1701–1834, Exeter St John 1680–1842, Faringdon 1681–1734, Goodleigh 1640–1759, Huish (f) 1688–1758, Membury 1789–1860, North Tawton 1717–87, Petrockstowe 1788–1872, Sheepwash (f) 1799–1863, Shobrooke 1562–1620, South Milton 1778–1861, Staverton 1806–55, Stoke Fleming (f) 1781–1840, Stoke Gabriel 1611–22, Tavistock (f) 1566–1627, Tedburn St Mary 1646–1718

Dorset

Parish	Dates	Hedgehog	Fox	Badger	Otter	Polecat	Stoat	Weasel	Marten	Wild Cat	Mole	H. Sparrow	Bullfinch	'Crow'	Rook	Jackdaw	Raven	Magpie	Jay	Red Kite	'Hawk'?	Other
Abbotsbury	1683–1823	4	5	3	1	2	2					2										'rats' (1)
Alton Pancras	1730–1828	1	1	1	1	1	1	1				1										
Beaminster	1646–1761	5	2	1	5			2				1	2					5				
Buckland Newton	1693–1761	1	1	1	2	1	1	1				1										'rats' (2) + vermin unspecified (4)
Burton Bradstock	1699–1797	5	1	1	1	3	1					2						1				
Canford Magna	1790–1850	4				1	2					5										
Cerne Abbas	1628–1753	5	1	1	4			1				5		1								
Charlton Marshall	1666–1782	2	1	1	2	2	4					3										
Cheselbourne	1776–1900					1	2					5										
Chickerell	1729–1859	1	1	1	1	1	1					1										
Chideock	1701–1800	1	1	3	2	2	1			1		3										
Compton Valance	1669–1765	3	1	1	2	2						2										
Corfe Castle	1563–1850	2	1	2	3	3	4					3										
Cranborne	1700–25	5	4		4	4	5					5		4	1			1	5	2	5	Kingfisher (1) W'pecker (5) Buzzard (5)
Fontmell Magna	1675–1800	1	1	1	1	1	1	1				2										
Frome Vauchurch	1679–1840	3	1	1	2		1					4										'rats' (water vole?) (5)
Hammoon	1716–78	2	1	3	2	2	1	1				3										
Kingston Magna	1673–1790	1		1	1	1	1							2								
Kinson	1722–90	1				1	1					5										

Parish	Years											Species
Long Bredy	1669–1766	4	1		3	2				3		
Long Burton	1634–1769	4	1		2	2						
Lydlinch	1701–72	4	2	1	2	1	3					
Melbury Osmond	1661–1749	5	1		4	4	5	5		5		5 1
Milton Abbas	1637–88	5	2		5	5				5		1
Netherbury	1739–1803	1	1		1	1						
Piddlehinton	1686–1765	1	1		5	5				5		
Puddletown	1781–1840									5		
Seaborough	1656–1730	1	1		1		1			1	2	'rats' (5)
Sherborne	1648–1801	4	5	4	5	5	5	5	5	5	5	'rats' (5) Starling (1) Woodpecker (2) 5 1
Stour Provost	1660–1838	1	3	3	2	2			5	5		
Symondsbury	1715–1810	1	2	3	4	1		1				
Tarrant Hinton	1658–1740	1	1		2	2		4				
Wool	1741–1806						4	2				

N.B. Some or all of the 'rats' listed under Dorset parishes may well have been Water Voles. See Rat section in Chapter 7 Askerswell 1718–94, Bere Regis 1607–57, Poole 1545–1800, West Orchard 1774–1806

Co Durham

Parish	Years							
Billingham	1675–1820	1		1	1			
Bishop-wearmouth	1661–89	1	2	2				
Branspeth	1735–1837	4	1	5	5	5		
Esh	1711–1804	1		1	1			
Houghton le Spring	1592–1733	1	1	1	5	5	1	
Hurworth	1776–1835	1		1	1			
Lamesley	1634–1715	5			5			
Lanchester	1631–1802	2	1	2	1			
Merrington	1621–1700	3	1	3				

	Hedgehog	Fox	Badger	Otter	Polecat	Stoat	Weasel	Marten	Wild Cat	Mole	H. Sparrow	Bullfinch	'Crow'	Rook	Jackdaw	Raven	Magpie	Jay	Red Kite	'Hawk'	Other
Monk Hesledon 1685–1797	3		3		1											1					
Norton St Mary 1775–1833		1		1	5		5														
Romaldkirk 1771–1871	5																				
Ryton 1597–1770	5		5	1	5			3													
Staindrop 1703–91	1															1					
Stanhope 1675–1723	4		1	5	2																
Whickham 1699–1718			1	1		1															
Witton Gilbert 1739–68	2		1	3												1					
Witton le Wear 1689–1840	1		1	4												1					
Wolsingham 1713–78	1			3	3				1												
Wolviston 1672–1842	1			1	1																

Darlington (f) 1630–92, Durham St Oswald 1580–1700, Durham St Nicholas 1665–1820, Elwick 1711–1804, Pittington 1584–1699

Essex

	Hedgehog	Fox	Badger	Otter	Polecat	Stoat	Weasel	Marten	Wild Cat	Mole	H. Sparrow	Bullfinch	'Crow'	Rook	Jackdaw	Raven	Magpie	Jay	Red Kite	'Hawk'	Other
Birch 1713–86		2																			
Bradwell 1751–1867		1	1	1																	
Braintree 1686–1793	4	5								1											
Downham 1685–1827		1		1	1	1	1														
Dunmow 1684–1874		2																			
Great Bentley 1772–1854		2																			
Great Bromley 1627–1804		2																			
Hornchurch 1590–1722		3	1	1																	
Lawford 1716–1809		4	1	1																	
Little Baddow 1743–1832		2	1																		
Little Bromley 1762–1899		2																			
South Weald 1584–1716	5												3								

	Dates					
St Osyth	1817–40				2	
Stapleford Tawney	1745–46	1			1	

Abberton 1745–1825, Alresford (f) 1679–1727, Ardleigh 1767–88, Ashdon 1730–1801, Aveley 1600–1, Buttsbury 1568 'a rate for spoyling of vermin', Canewden 1568 as Buttsbury, Coggeshall 1609–93 many annual payments for 'destroyers and distributers of vermin' but no vermin records, Colchester St Botolph 1753–82, Colchester St Peter 1753–82, Dedham 1615–1829, Elsenham 1736–60, Great Easton 1577–1770, Great Wigborough 1812–49, Heydon 1567 'a rate for the destruction of noyful fowles and vermin' (no vermin records), Little Burstead 1756–1880, Messing 1747–83, Peldon 1713–1814, Thaxted 1583–1697, Theydon Garnon 1677–1717, Thorrington 1719, Wakes Colne 1681–1741, Waltham Holy Cross 1624–70, West Ham 1643–1711

Flintshire

Parish	Dates					
Bodfari	1715–67	5				1
Caerwys	1672–1748	1	1			
Cilcain	1657–1747	2	2	1		5
Hanmer	1728–1850	1				5
Hawarden	1658–1718	2	1	2		5
Holywell	1759–69	1				
Northop	1682–1717	1	1	3		1

Flint 1760–88, Mold (f) 1654–63, Rhuddlan 1726–50, Tremeirchion (f) 1742–1802, Treuddyn 1752–87, Ysgeifiog 1687–1785

Glamorgan

Parish	Dates					
Coity	1706–53	1	1		4	
Colwinston	1783–1868	1	2			
Merthyr Mawr	1768–1813	2	1		1	
Radyr	1740–95	1			1	
St Athan	1783–1803	3	1			
Ystradyfodwg	1752–1812	1	2	3	1	3

Gelligaer 1767–1809, Llanilltern 1727–8

Gloucestershire

	Dates	Hedgehog	Fox	Badger	Otter	Polecat	Stoat	Weasel	Marten	Wild Cat	Mole	H. Sparrow	Bullfinch	'Crow' Rook	Jackdaw	Raven	Magpie	Jay	Red Kite 'Hawk'?	Other
Barnsley	1609–55		3			1														
Bibury	1655–91		1									5								
Bourton on the Hill	1685–1817	2										1								
Bromsberrow	1633–1704		2										1	1					2	
Chedworth	1645–1771		2																	
Deerhurst	1664–1781		1		1															
Dursley	1566–1758	4	2	1	1							2	1	1			4			Wood-pecker (1) Titmice (2)
Eastington	1744–1800	2	1									2		2			1		3	Wood-pecker (5) Titmice (3)
Gt Badminton	1676–1839	5	2	2	5								1	1						
Kemble	1632–1704	2	2										1	1					2	
Kingswood	1681–1724	1	1	1	3															
Minchin-hampton	1555–1770	2	5	2	2							5					2	5	2	Buzzard (3) + many 'vermin payments'
Newnham	1686–1810	4	5	1	1	1		5	2			5						5	3	
Old Sodbury	1678–1741	1	1		1	1													3	
Painswick	1681–1754	5	5		5	1						1						1	1	
Prestbury	1675–1741	1	2								3									
Standish	1642–85	1	1								5									
Stroud	1623–1716	3	2	1	1							1								
Tetbury	1589–1703	1	1		1													1		

Lechlade 1558–1672, Mickleton 1639–59, Ruardean (f) 1681–9, Withington 1636–59

Jackdaw (1)

Hampshire

Alton	1625–1826	1					1	1	
Andover	1677–1721	1	1	1			1	1	
Barton Stacey	1769–1837	1		3	3		5		
Binstead	1663–1847	1	1			1	5		
Broughton	1762–1813	1	5	5	3		5		
Burghclere	1679–1788	5	1	1			1		
Buriton	1727–1870	3	3	1	1		5		
Burlesdon	1710–18	2	2						
Chawton	1622–1832	5	5				1		
Crawley	1767–1831	2					4		
Easton	1655–1820	1	3	1	5	5	5	1	
Eling	1623–91	3	1	2	1		1	1	
Ellingham	1721–1822	3	2	2	3		3		
Fawley	1661–1716	5	4	3	1				
Fordingbridge	1602–49	1	1				1		
Grateley	1738–1852	2	2				1		
Itchin Stoke	1742–1873	1	3	1	3		1		
Kingsworthy	1726–1880	2	1				5		
Long Parish	1759–1852	1	5	5	1	1	5		
Lymington	1669–1767	5	3	2	5	1	5	3	
Mary Bourne	1664–1759	5	5				1		
Milford	1713–50	5	5	1			1		
Minstead	1641–79	3	3	1					
Newnham	1724–97	1					5		
N Baddesley	1674–1733	1	1	2	1		1		
Northington	1769–1873	2	1	1	1		4		

		Hedgehog	Fox	Badger	Otter	Polecat	Stoat	Weasel	Marten	Wild Cat	Mole	H. Sparrow	Bullfinch	'Crow'	Rook	Jackdaw	Raven	Magpie	Jay	Red Kite	'Hawk', Other
Otterbourne	1775–1847	2	5	2		2		1	5			5							1		
Ovington	1677–1768	2	2	1		1						2			1						
Petersfield	1751–79	4	1	1		2	1					3									
Rockbourne	1667–1768	4	4	1		2	2					4					1	1			
Romsey	1774–98	1	1		1	1		1				2									Rat (1)
Selborne	1687–1833		5									5									
Sherfield English	1748–1802	1	3			3			2												
Sherfield on Loddon	1758–1851	1	1			1						5									
Silchester	1698–1768	1	1						1			4									
Soberton	1658–1836	2										5									
Steep	1707–1823	1	5	1	1	1						1									
Stoke Charity	1657–1727	1	3	1	1	1						3									
Thruxton	1693–1787	2	2	1		2						4									
Warnford	1732–1872	1	1								1	5				2					
Wootton St Lawrence	1559–1675		2																		

Abbots Ann 1725–1802, Bramshott 1677–1704, Durley 1616–1752, Headbourne Worthy 1642–52, Heckfield 1746–1900, Holdenhurst 1600 and 1621 only, Hurstbourne Tarrant 1686–1797 (f), Kingsley 1737–1872, North Waltham 1593–1709, Odiham 1654–95, Overton (f) 1679–1724, Ringwood 1756–1802, South Warnborough 1663–81, Stratfield Saye 1664–1720, Upham 1640–64, Yateley (f) 1698–1800

Isle of Wight

		Hedgehog	Fox	Badger	Otter	Polecat	Stoat	Weasel	Marten	Wild Cat	Mole	H. Sparrow	Bullfinch	'Crow'	Rook	Jackdaw	Raven	Magpie	Jay	Red Kite	'Hawk', Other
Arreton	1731–1843				1		5					5									
Brading	1748–1834	1					5					5									
Brightstone	1676–1842											5									
Calbourne	1782–1818											5									
Cowes	1675–1802																		1		
Freshwater	1720–1825	1			1	1	1					5									

Gatcombe	1746–92							1							5
Godshill	1741–1821							5					1		5
Mottistone	1821–76														5
Newchurch	1767–79							5							5
Northwood	1774–1803						1	1							5
Shalfleet	1760–1800														5
Shorewell	1693–1796														5
St Helens	1763–97								1				1		5
Thorley	1613–1793														5
Yarmouth	1719–1805													2	5
Yaverland	1752–1858					5									5

Herefordshire

Aston Ingham	1771–1862	4	4	1		2	2	2					1	2	
Avenbury	1733–1807	1				1									
Bodenham	1661–1769	1	1										2		
Brampton Abbots	1673–1766	1	3	1	4	4									Wood-pecker? (1)
Eaton Bishop	1714–59	2	1			1		1							
Goodrich	1781–1856	2	2				1								
Hentland	1628–1705	1			1										
Kingsland	1700–14	1	2			2									
Ledbury	1685–1783	1	2	1		1		1	3	4			1		
Leintwardine	1666–1817	1													
Leominster	1722–98	3	1												
Much Cowarne	1723–1809	2	4	3	3	3	2	3		1	3	3			
Pencombe	1676–1757	1	1			1		1							

Ballingham (f) 1799–1833, Canon Frome 1713–96, Docklow 1777–96, Edwin Ralph 1714–1830, Ganarew 1678–84, Leinthall Earls 1762 only, Madley 1564–1669, Mathern (f) 1760–1800, Middleton on the Hill 1730–96, Stoke Edith 1532–83

Hertfordshire

Place	Dates	Hedgehog	Fox	Badger	Otter	Polecat	Stoat	Weasel	Marten	Wild Cat	Mole	H. Sparrow	Bullfinch	'Crow'	Rook	Jackdaw	Raven	Magpie	Jay	Red Kite	'Hawk'	Other
Aldbury	1720–1823	2	2			3						5										
Aldenham	1728–1845	1	1			1																
Ashwell	1562–1744	2	1			3																
Bayford	1763–1889										3											
Berkhamstead	1700–46	2		1		3	2	2			2			1								
Bishops Stortford	1569–71	4				1		2			3	1		2				2				Rat (3), Mice (3), Starling (1), Jackdaw (2), Kingfisher (2)
Braughing	1730–1861	1	1																			
Bushey	1706–1821	3			1																	
Chipping Barnet	1656–1840	2			2																	
Codicote	1692–1833										3											
East Barnet	1684–1736	1	1		1																	
Elstree	1715–55	1			1																	
Gt Gaddesden	1817–35	2	1									5										
Harpenden	1739–1853	1	3		2																	
Lilley	1674–1815	2	2		3																	
Little Munden	1629–1783				3							5										Lists only 'vermin' (5)
L Gaddesden	1675–1769	1	1				2					1										

Parish	Dates								Notes
Little Hadham	1663–1872								Lists only 'vermin' (3)
Pirton	1766–1828						5		
Rickmansworth	1824–57						5		
St Albans St Peter	1572–1871	1		2	1				
St Albans St Michael	1625–1736	3	1	1	3				
St Albans St Stephen	1742					3			
Sandridge	1687–1780	3	3	3					
Totteridge	1613–1703	3	3						Lists only 'vermin' (3)
Welwyn	1790–1810	1	1	1					

Ayot St Peter 1765–80, Barkway 1558–1820, Benington 1631–1722, Kelshall 1691–1900, Ridge 1792–1809, Royston 1697–1764, Sandon 1628–1780, Sawbridgeworth 1703–1850, Stanstead Abbots 1663–1716, Thundridge 1619–76, Watton-at-Stone 1586–1749

Huntingdonshire

Parish	Dates								Notes
Alwalton	1750–79	2			1		1		
Buckden	1627–1714	4	1	1	5	3	2		Starling (1)
Bythorn	1785–1872					5	5		
Chesterton	1776–1836						2		
Diddington	1758–1900	1	1	3	3		4		
Gr Staughton	1637–1744	2	1	3	1		1		
St Neots	1748–82	2	1	2					
Tilbrook	1724–1846	1	1	1					

Fenstanton 1627–73, Grafham 1740–81, Great Gidding 1781–1818, Holywell 1547–1667, Stanground 1636–1820

Kent

Parish	Dates	Hedgehog	Fox	Badger	Otter	Polecat	Stoat	Weasel	Martin	Wild Cat	Mole	H. Sparrow	Bullfinch	'Crow'	Rook	Jackdaw	Raven	Magpie	Jay	Red Kite	'Hawk'	Other
Addington	1764–1832	3										4										
Aldington	1700–45	3	2									5										
Aylesford	1652–1838	5	5	4	1							5		1								
Badlesmere	1680–1785	2	1	1	1	2	1					1										
Bapchild	1788–1856	1										3										
Bekesbourne	1759–1882			1								5										
Benenden	1663–1742	1	1	1	1	1							1	1			1	1				Hen Harrier (1)
Bethersden	1614–39	1	1	1	1	1		1				2	1	1			1	1				
Betteshanger	1717–1852	1																				
Biddenden	1594–1779		2																			
Birling	1663–1742	2	2	1	3																	
Bobbing	1703–99	3	1	3	5	2						3						1				
Borden	1694–1720	2	1	1	1	1																
Brasted	1733–1828	5	1	1	2	2						3		1								
Bredgar	1660–95	1	1	1																		
Charing	1590–1724	5	5	4	2	5	1					1		4			1	4	2	3	2	Buzzard (5)
Chartham	1747–77	4	1	4	2	2		2				5										
Chiddingstone	1691–1869	5	1	1	1	1																
Chilham	1699–1775	5	5	4	5	4		2				5										
Chislet	1704–1805	5	5	4	5	2						5										
Doddington	1767–1808	3	1	1	1							3								5		
Edenbridge	1697–1900	2	1		1																	
Egerton	1712–1814	3	4	4	4			1														
Elham	1729–54	2	2	3	3							5										
Elmstead	1762–1835	1	1	1	1							5										

Ewell	1759–1827	2	1	1				4					
Eythorne	1667–1847	1	1	1	1			3					
Folkestone	1763–74	3	2	1	2			3					
Frittenden	1665–1732	4	1	2	1								
Guston	1730–1801	4	2	1	2			4					
Hartlip	1667–91	1	1	1									
Hawkhurst	1621–1759	5	1		1	2							
Herne	1663–1724	5	4	2	1	2		5					
High Halden	1689–1757	1	1	1	1			1	1			1	
Hythe	1658–1718	3	1	1	1	1		2	1		1	1	1
Ightham	1708–1886	3	1	1	1								
Kingsnorth	1609–79	1	1	1	1	1							
Knockholt	1671–1824	1	1	1				1		1			
Loose	1695–1850	3	2	2				3					
Lympne	1677–1734	4	5	3	2			1	1	1			
Nackington	1704–1842	1	1	1			1						
Newenden	1673–1900	1						3					
Nonington	1706–1836	1	1	1	2			5					
Northbourne	1708–60	5	3	3	1	2	2	4					Buzzard (5)
Ospringe	1694–1807	5	3	3	1	2	2	5	1			4	
Patrixbourne	1733–1841	3					2	5					
Preston next Faversham	1717–1836	3	1	1	2	1	1	2					
Saltwood	1697–1869	3	4	4	4			1					
Smarden	1701–39	2	1	1	1			2	1				
Speldhurst	1665–1717	1				1			1	1			
St Lawrence in Thanet	1688–1724	4			4	1	1	4	4	2	5		Buzzard (1)
Staplehurst	1665–1717	2	1		1					1	1	1	
Stodmarsh	1791–1847		1	1				5		2		2	
Stowting	1765–1863		1	1				5		2		2	1	Larks!

		Hedgehog	Fox	Badger	Otter	Polecat	Stoat	Weasel	Marten	Wild Cat	Mole	H. Sparrow	Bullfinch	'Crow', Rook	Jackdaw	Raven	Magpie	Jay	Red Kite	'Hawk', Other	Buzzard (5) Hen Harrier (4) Wood-pecker (3) Other
Tenterden	1614–1779	5	4	2	4	5		5	1	1	5	1	5	4	3	5	5	5	5	3	3
Tonbridge	1698–1712	2	1	1																	
Waldershare	1784–1805	1	2									2									
Walmer	1756–1805											2									
West Hythe	1718–1817	2	2		4							1	2					1			
West Peckham	1708–96	5	1									4			1						
Westerham	1662–1710	3	2	2															3		
Wye	1663–1789	5	3	2	3							5									
Yalding	1720–1892	4	3	1	1																

Bidborough 1759–1803, Brookland 1643–90, Cobham 1663–1808, Great Chart (f) 1698–1829, Pluckley 1628–68, Sandhurst 1615–94, Sevington 1706–20

Lancashire

		Hedgehog	Fox	Badger	Otter	Polecat	Stoat	Weasel	Marten	Wild Cat	Mole	H. Sparrow	Bullfinch	'Crow', Rook	Jackdaw	Raven	Magpie	Jay	Red Kite	'Hawk', Other	Buzzard (5) Hen Harrier (4) Wood-pecker (3) Other
Church Kirk	1710–64	1																			
Clitheroe	1656–1802	2	1																		
Croston	1681–1763	1	1									3				5					
Eccleston	1712–1801	1	1									1				1					
Great Croby	1700–15	2																	2	2	
Manchester	1664–1711	5	3	2	1							5		3			1	2	2		
Middleton	1647–79	4	4	2	1							1		1			1				
Newchurch in Pendle	1735–1808	1	1																		

													Heron (1)
---	---	---	---	---	---	---	---	---	---	---	---	---	Hen Harrier (2)
Prestwich	1675–1820	5	3	1	1	1	1	2	2	2	1	2	2
Slaidburn	1756–1831	1	1	1	1				3				1

Aldingham (f) 1679–1787, Ardwick 1807–24, Aughton 1737–54, Birch in Rusholme 1667–97, Blackley 1764–1802, Caton 1714–49, Deane 1723–1890, Denton 1691–94, Eccles 1679–1728, Formby 1703–33, Goodshaw 1701–41, Halsall 1755–1823, Hoole (h sp) 1812–71, Hornby 1730–1800, Melling in Lonsdale 1696–1844, Mitton (f) 1738–1818, Newton Heath 1737–55, Padiham 1706–1834, Standish (f) 1697–1739, Tarleton 1720–67, Tatham 1751–1837, Tatham Fell 1742–1822, Upholland (h sp) 1723–1822

Leicestershire

							Rats (5)
Ashby Folville	1674–1729	1				5	
Ashby Magna	1704–52	2				1	
Branston	1677–1836	1			2		
Edmundthorpe	1677–1732	2	1	1	1		
Enderby	1675–1739	4		1	1		
Groby	1805–27	4			4		
Kirby Muxloe	1705–77	2			2		
Loughborough	1584–1686	5	1	1	5		
Lubenham	1712–65	2		1	2		
Melton Mowbray	1547–1612						Rats (5)
Morcott	1686–1773	1			3	3	
Muston	1664–1725	1	1		1	1	
Stapleton	1726–97	1			4	4	
Stathern	1629–1850	1			1	1	
Thurcaston	1680–1706	1		1	1		
Wigston Magna	1615–1704	1		2	4		

Beeby 1744–1805, Belton 1602–1739, Birkstall 1727–42, Breedon on the Hill 1676–1836, Carlton 1740,'55, '58, East Norton 1770–1832, Evington 1776–1879, Gaddesby 1652–1704, Hambledon (f) 1729–59, Market Harborough 1603–13, Newton Linford 1716 only, Peckleton 1613–1704, Rotherby 1676–1743, Whitwick (h sp) 1747–78

Lincolnshire

Parish	Dates	Hedgehog	Fox	Badger	Otter	Polcat	Stoat	Weasel	Marten	Wild Cat	Mole	H. Sparrow	Bullfinch	'Crow'	Rook	Jackdaw	Raven	Magpie	Jay	Red Kite	'Hawk'	Other
Addlesthorpe	1655–1788															5						
Bicker	1753–1880		2								4											
Billingborough	1753–1880										1											
Bracebridge	1733–79		1	1	1																	
Deeping St James	1747–1890		1	1	2	2				1												
Digby	1724–1879													3								
Edenham	1717–1812		1								5											
Friesthorpe	1727–99		1		2							3		2								
Friskney	1638–1817																1					
Glentworth	1742–82		1	1							5	5	1									
Harlaxton	1668–1737	1	2	1	3	1					1	1										
Lissington	1709–49		1		1	1							1									
Long Bennington	1670–92		1		1	1					5		1									
Martin	1675–1725		1			1							1									
Riby	1742–1835										5	4	5	1				1				
South Carlton	1685–1823		1	1			1	1					1					1				
S Cockerington	1594–1742		1	2		2																
Stow	1693–1776		2	1	1	1		1				5										
Tallington	1810–54	5									5											
Threckingham	1725–62	1																				'birds' one year, 1725

Algarkirk 1599–1677, Alvingham 1573–91, Aubourn 1795–1832, Belchford 1815–78, Broughton by Brigg 1576–1724, Burgh le Marsh 1704–1858, Burton by Lincoln 1803–70, Caythorpe 1740–80, Cowbit 1671–1707, Creeton 1766–1856, Croft 1747–87, Doddington 1732–1828, Dunsby (h sp) 1786–1892, Fenton 1751–1867, Fosdyke 1722–89, Foston 1783–1883, Gosberton 1648–1713, Goxhill 1707–85, Linwood 1714–49, Londonthorpe 1736–1870, Long Sutton 1693–1798, Morton 1717–79, North Reston 1682–1741, North Somercotes 1762–1820, Scothorn 1588–1769, Sedgebrook 1714–1871, Stickney 1766–1807, Stow in Lindsey 1777–1900, Swinderby 1663–1734, Theddlethorpe 1618–1870, Wellingore 1661–1764, Whaplode 1764–1802, Whaplode Drove 1736–46, Wickenby 1739 and 1820–32, Yarborough 1756–1801

Merioneth

Betws Gwerfil Goch 1684–1763	1					1	
Gwyddelwern 1738		1				1	
Llanderfyl 1726–56	1	3				5	
Llanegryn 1735–84	1		1			1	
Llanfihangell y Traethau 1682–1763	1	1	1			2	Cormorant (1)
Llanfor 1720–58	2		2			5	
Llangar 1703–64	1 1	1	1			5	

Llanbedr 1828–30, Talyllyn 1823–61

Monmouthshire

Cwmcarfan 1773–1805	1	1								
Itton 1727–1825	1	1								
Llanfihangell Crucorney 1750–1816	1	1								
Llanover 1701–45	1	1								
Mitchel Troy 1749–88	1	1	2	2	1	1	1		3	
Panteg 1726–58	2	1		1	1	1	1		2	
Portskewett 1739–1820	1	1	2	2			2	2		
Redwick 1785–1873	1		1							
Trevethin 1767–86	4	2	1	2			2			

Caerwent 1803–34, Chepstow 1739–83, Goetre 1726–80, Llangattwg 1705–72, Llangua 1807–70, Llansoy 1769–91, Mathern 1760–1800, Whitson 1780–1874

Montgomeryshire

Berriew 1662–1720	1		1	
Darowen 1771–82		1		4
Guilsfield 1744–90	1		1	
Kerry 1742–67	1		5	

Parish	Dates	Hedgehog	Fox	Badger	Otter	Polecat	Stoat	Weasel	Martin	Wild Cat	Mole	H. Sparrow	Bullfinch	'Crow'	Rook	Jackdaw	Raven	Magpie	Jay	Red Kite, 'Hawk'	Others
Llandinam	1723–1819								1												
Llanerfyl	1739–98				1																
Llangynog	1720–1810		1		1									1			5				
Llansantffraid	1677–1750	1	1	1	1	1			2					1							Rat (1)
Meifod	1675–1720	2	2						5					3			5				
Pennant	1712–1837	5	5		1				5					3			5				

Aberhafesp 1777–1859, Bettws Cedewain 1780–1859, Castle Caereinion 1725–1849, Hirnant 1802–40, Llanfechain 1757–1858, Llanfiangell-yng-Ngwyfa 1756–1857, Llangadfan 1804–83, Llanllwchaiarn 1733–1882, Llanwnog 1678–1834, Newtown (f) 1679, Penegoes 1766–1813, Penstrowed 1759–1850, Trefeglwys 1773–1839, Tregynon 1774–1872

Norfolk

Parish	Dates	Hedgehog	Fox	Badger	Otter	Polecat	Stoat	Weasel	Martin	Wild Cat	Mole	H. Sparrow	Bullfinch	'Crow'	Rook	Jackdaw	Raven	Magpie	Jay	Red Kite, 'Hawk'	Others
Aylsham	1636–1848		2	2	2			1			1										
Baconsthorpe	1663–1713		1	1	1			1													
Bale	1632–1763		1	1	1																
Banham	1621–1726		1																		
Barton Bendish	1805–32										5					1					
Blickling	1667–1786		3	2	5		2			5	5										
Caister	1736–1830		1	1			2														
Carleton Rode	1678–1836									5	5										
Denver	1671–1789			1		1															
Diss	1721–1846										5										
Ditchingham	1561–1759		1	1	3	1	1				1			4							
E Dereham	1701–73														5						
East Ruston	1682–1844		4		1	5															
Elsing	1663–1836		1	1	3									5							
Felmingham	1679–1788		1	1	3								1	4							

	1820–87							'Linnets' (3)
Foulden		1	1					
Foulsham 1770–1862			1	3				
Garboldisham 1622–1788			1	1	1		5	
Halvergate 1747–1836				5				
Heckingham 1758–1820	1			4				
Hellington 1761–1864	1	5		5				
Horbrook 1669–1895				3				
North Elmham 1666–1793	1		1				5	
Sparham 1664–1770							5	
Topcroft 1683–1842			2	2				
Tunstead 1672–1725							4	
Walpole St Andrews 1814–74	1	5	2			1		
Walpole St Peter 1822–33		1	1	1				
Wilton 1674–1861			3					
Witton 1688–1734	2	1	1					

Besthorpe 1672–1724, Blo Norton 1764–71, Bressingham 1581–1680, Burgh Castle 1721–1839, Carbrooke 1627–1771, Cawston 1679–1681, Colby (f) 1735 only, Dersingham 1750–1846, East Harting 1663–1736, Feltwell 1735–1868, Fersfield 1666–76, Gissing 1640–88, Hardwick 1584–1732, Heydon 1654–1727, Hilgay 1619–39, Houghton-next-Harpley 1663–1727, North Creake 1613–1842, Northwold 1627–1795, Rollesby 1761–1820, Tilney St Lawrence 1653–1831

Northamptonshire

Abethorpe 1767–1834	1	1				5		
Apethorpe 1729–1885	2	3			5	5		
Bainton 1750–1806	1	1	1	1				
Barnwell 1742–1893	1				5	5		
Bradden 1735–1831	1	1	3			4		
Braunston 1656–1787	2	1	1		3	3	1	
Bugbrooke 1632–1702	3	1				5		
Burton Latimer 1584					3			

		Hedgehog	Fox	Badger	Otter	Polecat	Stoat	Weasel	Marten	Wild Cat	Mole	H. Sparrow	Bullfinch	'Crow'	Rook	Jackdaw	Raven	Magpie	Jay	Red Kite	'Hawk'	Others
Byfield	1635–7	1	1																			
Chacombe	1705–1848	3	1								2											
Collingtree	1694–1726	1	1								5		1									
Cosgrove	1706–69	1	1			4					5											
Cotterstock	1792–1897	1	5			5																Rat (1)
Culworth	1531–1684										2											Snakes (5)
Dallington	1654–1723	1																				
Ecton	1665–1703	2	1	1		1				5	1											
Eydon	1663–78	1	1								1											
Gt. Houghton	1634–98	2	1	1		1		1		1	2	1										Kingfisher (1)
Guilsborough	1739–81	1	1								4											
Hinton	1634–1770	2	1								5											
Old	1686–98	1	1							1	1		1									
Peakirk	1708–88	1	1	1	5	1																
Radstone	1676–1771	3	1								2											

Arthingworth 1734–1900, Clipston 1758–1874, Cranford St John (f) 1753–1822, Great Billing 1771–1864, Great Brington 1600–79, Holdenby 1730–1822, Little Billing 1721–1807, Loddington 1674–1873

Northumberland

		Hedgehog	Fox	Badger	Otter	Polecat	Stoat	Weasel	Marten	Wild Cat	Mole	H. Sparrow	Bullfinch	'Crow'	Rook	Jackdaw	Raven	Magpie	Jay	Red Kite	'Hawk'	Others
Alwinton	1718–1834		4																			
Bedlington	1697–1796		4	1		4																Cormorant (2)
Bywell St Andrews	1705–50	1	1	1																		
Bywell St Peter	1683–1711	2	1	1																		

Place	Dates									Rat (1) (see text re: Kite/ Gled)
Corbridge	1676–1727	5			2	5	5			5
Earsdon	1743–1833		1	1			5			
Haltwhistle	1718–92	2	2	2	2	5	5			
Heddon on the Wall	1675–1737	1	1		5	2		1		
Kirk-whelpington	1765–1867	1	1			2				
Longbenton	1713–1837	1	1			4	5			
Ponteland	1737–81			1	1	3		1		
Simonburn	1787–1864	2				1				
Stannington	1726–65	1	1			4				

Bamburgh 1724–76, Bothal 1739–1825, Eglingham 1653–1772, Elsdon 1720–45, Felton 1597–1768, Kirknewton 1758–1800, Morpeth 1720–30, Newbiggin-on-Sea 1743–1894, Ovingham 1736–84, Stamfordham 1644–1777

Nottinghamshire

Place	Dates									Owls (1)
Cuckney	1732–49	2	1	2				1		
Elkesley	1674–1804	1	1							
Everton	1732–1884	1				4			5	
Fiskerton	1750–1813			1			1		1	
Hayton	1741–95	1	2			5			4	
Holme Pierrepoint	1739–56	2	1	1	1				3	
Norwell	1685–1724		1		1					
Ossington	1737–97	1	1				3	3	3	
Tithby	1756–1806	1		1		1		5	3	
Upton	1600–44							1		
Worksop	1544–1750	3	1	1			2			Owls (1)

Bilsthorpe 1732–1879, Bingham 1769–1859, Blyth (f) 1701–70, Coddington 1631–1754, Cossall 1717–71, Costock 1720–1855, East Stoke 1794–1856, Edingley 1774–1865, Edwalton 1725–1837, Edwinstowe 1778–1807, Granby 1691–1728, Ollerton 1638–1753, Orston 1687–1787, Screveton 1669–1879

Oxfordshire

	Date	Hedgehog	Fox	Badger	Otter	Polecat	Stoat	Weasel	Marten	Wild Cat	Mole	H. Sparrow	Bullfinch	'Crow'	Rook	Jackdaw	Raven	Magpie	Jay	Red Kite	'Hawk'	Other
Ambrosden	1550–1686	1	3																			
Ardley	1757–1888		1			1						4										
Bodicote	1767–1820	2	2									5										
Charlton on Otmoor	1747–1900	1	2		1							5										
Ewelme	1681–1768	4	1		5																	
Eynsham	1640–1836	1	1				1					5										
Finmere	1729–1884	4	1									5										
Gt Haseley	1668–1773	1	3	3																		
Hampton Poyle	1727–1860	2	1								1	4										
Hook Norton	1732–97	5	1									5										Wood-pecker (5)
Islip	1701–1807	1	1		1							5										
Kencot	1754–1900				1							2										
Langford	1626–1749				1							5										
Pyrton	1548–1833											5										
South Newington	1553–1684	1																				
Stratton Audley	1720–1821	2			1							1										
Swinbrook	1745–1900		1									1										
Swyncombe	1701–80	2			1																	
Thame	1765–1840											5										
Warborough	1600–1773				1																	
Yarnton	1610–1740	3	1																			

Chinnor 1654–1847, Harpsden 1752–1849, Marston 1529–1610, Oddington 1609–66, Shiplake 1677–1714, Spelsbury 1524–75, Stonesfield 1654–1821

		Hedgehog	Fox	Badger	Otter	Polecat	Stoat	Weasel	Marten	Wild Cat	Mole	H. Sparrow	Bullfinch	'Crow'	Rook	Jackdaw	Raven	Magpie	Jay	Red Kite	'Hawk'	Other
Chirbury	1603–1720	1	2	2						2				2								
Clungunford	1673–1769	1	1																			
Edgmond	1652–1754	3	1																			
Great Ness	1723–70	3																				
High Ercall	1685–1762	1	3																			
Kinlet	1713–73	5																				
Lillishall	1672–87	1									5											
Ludlow	1540–77		1	2						2				1		1				1		Rats and Mice (2)
Pitchford	1702–82	1	1																			
Shrewsbury St Mary	1704–52	5	5																			
Stokesay	1663–1714	1	2																			
Sutton Maddock	1668–1706	2	1																			
Tugford	1695–1774	1																				
Uffington	1638–49	1	1																			
Worfield	1648–1722	5	4	1	1	1				2			5	2		1		1		1		Rat (2), Mice (1), 'finches' (2)
Wroxeter	1720–78	4	2																			

Albrighton 1608–37, Bromfield (f) 1660–86, Cardington (f) 1693–1752, Church Pulverbatch 1653–1710, Clunbury 1620–62, Cound 1683–1811, Kemberton 1719–66, Kenley 1600–80, Lydham 1763–93, More 1651–1713, Munslow (f) 1662–1701, Quatford 1693–1830, Shawbury 1633–1711, Stapleton 1736–1852, Stottesden 1776–1852, Tong 1630–80, Upton Cressett 1751–1861, Whitchurch 1619–70

Somerset

		Hedgehog	Fox	Badger	Otter	Polecat	Stoat	Weasel	Marten	Wild Cat	Mole	H. Sparrow	Bullfinch	'Crow'	Rook	Jackdaw	Raven	Magpie	Jay	Red Kite	'Hawk'	Other
Badgeworth	1681–1779	1					4	2				1										
Batcombe	1669–1766	5	1	1	3	1	5		5			2		1								

Parish	Dates	...	Mice (5)	Wood-pecker (3)	...	Starling (2)
Butleigh	1675–1766					
Cheddar	1612–74					
Churchill	1639–76					
Crewkerne	1625–94					
Curry Rivel	1673–92					
East Brent	1677–92					
Fiddington	1674–1726					
Hinton St George	1679–1794					
Kilton	1675–1737					
Locking	1632–1862					
Luccombe	1661–1747					
Lyng	1679–1747					
Middlezoy	1672–1728					
Minehead	1756–1893					
Moorlinch	1682–1732					
N Petherton	1664–83					
N Wootton	1661–96					
Norton St Phillip	1686–1752					
Pitminster	1668–1731					
Puxton	1665–1738					
Rode	1727–73					
Seavington St Michael	1659–1706					
Shepton Mallet	1617–1704					
Somerton	1640–1747					
Stockland Bristol	1673–1732					
Street	1684–1770					
Swainswick	1631–1712					
Thornfalcon	1686–1776					
Timberscombe	1680–1807					
Tintinhull	1613–78					

	Dates	Hedgehog	Fox	Badger	Otter	Polecat	Stoat	Weasel	Marten	Wild Cat	Mole	H. Sparrow	Bullfinch	'Crow'	Rook	Jackdaw	Raven	Magpie	Jay	Red Kite	'Hawk'	Other
Wayford	1684–1894	3	1	2		3			1			2		2								2
W Buckland	1672–1748	1	1	1		1							1	1								
West Pennard	1660–1776	4		1		3																
Weston Zoyland	1699–1851	5				5	2				2	5										
Wivelscombe	1681–1741	5	1	1		5																

Charlcombe 1813–47, Charlinch 1621–65, Creech St Michael 1663–1754, Durston 1633–1719, Farrington Gurney 1676–1799, Monksilver 1660–1741, Seavington St Mary 1772–1874, Stogursey 1502–46

Staffordshire

	Dates	Hedgehog	Fox	Badger	Otter	Polecat	Stoat	Weasel	Marten	Wild Cat	Mole	H. Sparrow	Bullfinch	'Crow'	Rook	Jackdaw	Raven	Magpie	Jay	Red Kite	'Hawk'	Other
Alrewas	1673–1748	2												2			5					
Blithfield	1659–1724	1	1															1				
Checkley	1628–92	1	1																			
Gayton	1615–89	1	1																			
Gnosall	1668–1724	1	1																			
Hanbury	1634–1714	2	1																			
Kingsley	1665–74	1	1																			
Madeley	1682–1751	1	2									1										Owl (1)
Mavesyn Ridware	1643–97	1	1																			
Pattingham	1583–1646	1																				
Stone	1634–84	1	2																			

Betley 1635–1706, Biddulph 1609–1703, Norbury 1643–1756

Suffolk

	Dates	Hedgehog	Fox	Badger	Otter	Polecat	Stoat	Weasel	Marten	Wild Cat	Mole	H. Sparrow	Bullfinch	'Crow'	Rook	Jackdaw	Raven	Magpie	Jay	Red Kite	'Hawk'	Other
Assington	1755–1840													1								

Place	Dates							'vermin' unspecified / species
Bardwell	1648–1732							'vermin' unspecified (3)
Barsham	1774–1884					5	5	
Beccles	1759–1884	1					5	
Blythburgh	1753–1900	2						
Brampton	1721–1829					5		
Brantham	1728–1814		1		2			
Bungay St Mary	1640–1833		2	1		5	1	
Cookley	1672–1773			1				
Cratfield	1580–6		2		1		2	Buzzard (1) Wood-pecker (1)
Dallinghoo	1661–1753					2		
Gisleham	1640–1855	1				4		
Gislingham	1595–1848					3		
Great Barton	1622–1805							
Hawstead	1720–90			1				
Honington	1666–1736					2		'vermin' unspecified (2)
Hopton	1748–1819	1						
Huntingfield	1660–1753					2		
Ilketshall	1745–75						5	
Ingham	1690–1714					5		'vermin' unspecified (3)
Melton	1657–1758		2	1				
N Elmham	1754–1846					5		
S Elmham St Michael	1790–1900					5		
Shipmeadow	1727–1851	1					5	

Parish	Dates	Hedgehog	Fox	Badger	Otter	Polecat	Stoat	Weasel	Marten	Wild Cat	Mole	H. Sparrow	Bullfinch	'Crow', Rook	Jackdaw	Raven	Magpie	Jay	Red Kite	'Hawk'	Other
Southwold	1708–98																				
Stowlangtoft	1710–88																				
Timworth	1714–1846											3									
Uggeshall	1829–1900											5									
Wangford	1765–1833											5									
Westhall	1676–1810											5									
Westleton	1643–1778		2	1								4									
Weston	1753–1870											5									
Wissett	1799–1869											5									

Other: Rat (5), 'vermin' unspecified (3)

Benhall 1600–1731, Bramford 1729–1811, Burgate 1663–1826, Bury St Edmunds 1689–1715, Chattisham 1775–1825, Chediston 1653 only, Clare 1602–1748, Cotton 1653–74, Cretingham 1657–89, Dalham 1720–1840, Drinkstone 1598–1676, East Stonham 1621–1708, Elmswell 1724–88, Erwarton 1680–1730, Framlingham 1557–1675, Great Blakenham 1764–1862, Great Finborough 1819–24, Halesworth 1580–1610, Hepworth 1641–1745, Hessett 1724–55, Heveningham 1595–1783, Ixworth 1656–88, Kettleburgh 1659–1739, Mildenhall 1554–1562, Norton 1713–16, Peasenhall 1634–1717, Rumburgh 1682–1731, South Elmham St Cross (h sp) 1834–1900, Somerton 1756–60, Sotherton 1834–87, Stoneham Aspall 1598–1686, Stradbroke 1588–1713, Sudbourne 1631–92, Theberton 1667–1751, Thwaite St George 1627–1703, Walsham le Willows 1646–1709, Walton 1747–1852, Weybread 1588–1738, Wickham Market 1652–85, Wilby 1646–85.

Surrey

Parish	Dates	Hedgehog	Fox	Badger	Otter	Polecat	Stoat	Weasel	Marten	Wild Cat	Mole	H. Sparrow	Bullfinch	'Crow', Rook	Jackdaw	Raven	Magpie	Jay	Red Kite	'Hawk'	Other
Esher	1804–5	2	3			2	3	1				5									
Ewell	1777–1846		3				2	1				3									
Gt Bookham	1717–1800	1	1																		
Kew	1757–1820		3					1				3									
Morden	1668–1788		1									1									
Oxted	1696–1723	2	1	1																	

									'vermin' unspecified (3)
Pyrford	1786–1850	4					1	5	
Seale	1559–1723	1					1		

Albury 1717–1806, Barnes 1688–1737, Betchworth (h sp) 1655–1746, Bisley 1673–88, Bletchingley 1546–52, Chaldon 1715–67, Cobham 1588–1673, Compton 1570–1782, Cranleigh 1723–37, Elstead 1648–57, Guildford Holy Trinity 1695–1850, Guildford St Mary 1665–1862, Horsell 1600–1748, Long Ditton 1663–1794, Mortlake 1662–1799, Wandsworth 1646–1742, Weybridge 1622–1701

Sussex (East)

Ashburnham	1607 only							
Beckley	1634–1749	2	2	2	1	2		1
Berwick	1656–1743	1						
Brede	1693–1864	1	2	1				
Burwash	1673–1740	1	1	1	1			
Chiddingly	1662–1675	1	1					
Ewhurst	1727–1782	1	1	1	1			
Hastings All Saints	1572–1589	1	1			1		
Hellingly	1592–1628	1						
Peasmarsh	1706–1827	3	1	1	1			
Rye	1736–1765						1	
Sedlescombe	1712–1801	1	1	1				
Udimore	1735–1873	1	1					
Winchelsea	1683–1752	1	1	1				

Barcombe 1614–1742, Battle (f) 1736–1844, Chailey St Peter 1837–1900, Denton 1752–74, Ditchling 1760–6, Hellingly 1592–1628, Herstmonceux 1732–1897, Jevington 1676–1900, Lewes St Thomas at Cliffe 1622–1704, Northiam 1721–1836, Ripe 1723–4, Rotherfield 1579–1675, Selmeston 1709–1814, Southover 1613–19, Ticehurst 1731–81

Sussex (West)

Bury	1828	3
Chichester	1806	2

Table of vermin payments recorded in churchwardens' accounts. Columns are headed (reading across): Hedgehog, Fox, Badger, Otter, Polecat, Stoat, Weasel, Marten, Wild Cat, Mole, H. Sparrow, Bullfinch, 'Crow', Rook, Jackdaw, Raven, Magpie, Jay, Red Kite, Hawk', Other.

Place	Date	Hedgehog	Fox	Badger	Otter	Polecat	Stoat	Weasel	Marten	Wild Cat	Mole	H. Sparrow	Bullfinch	'Crow'	Rook	Jackdaw	Raven	Magpie	Jay	Red Kite	Hawk'	Other
Felpham	1807–56																	2				
Harting	1620–1799	1									2			2				2	2			
Lyminster	1834										3											
N. Mundham	1828–46										5											
Selsey	1765–1841										5											
Storrington	1760–89										2											
Stoughton	1775–85										3											
Tortington	1746–87	1									3											
Walberton	1746–1842	3									4											
Westbourne	1797–1811	3		1							5											
West Dean	1730–1840	4									5											
Wisborough Green	1792–1839										4											
Yapton	1836–65										3											

Billingshurst 1530–1742, Bolney 1536–1632, Cuckfield 1633–1719, East Marden 1659–1771, Henfield 1684–1755, Hurstpierpoint 1685–1775, Lindfield 1580–1724, Lurgashall 1695–1851, Milland 1793–1844, Pyecombe 1670–1763, Sidlesham 1662–1767, Slinfold 1792–1900, Tillington 1602–78, West Chiltington 1613–1702, West Tarring 1515–92

Warwickshire

Place	Date	Hedgehog	Fox	Badger	Otter	Polecat	Stoat	Weasel	Marten	Wild Cat	Mole	H. Sparrow	Bullfinch	'Crow'	Rook	Jackdaw	Raven	Magpie	Jay	Red Kite	Hawk'	Other
Ansley	1723–1864	2	2																			
Alcester	1651–85	1	1																			
Coleshill	1657–9	1	1																			
Gt Packington	1730–63	3												1								
Kineton	1705–24	1																				
Knowle	1674–1760	5												1								
Monks Kirby	1674–1758	1												1				1				Starling (2)
Nether Whitacre	1632–1702	5																				

Place	Dates										Notes
Oldberrow	1676–1768	4	4	1							
Polesworth	1677–1777	5	1			2	1				
Rowington	1745–1841	5	3			5					
Ruyton on Dunsmore	1615–1726	4	1		1	1					
Sherbourne	1671–1783	5	1	1		5					
Solihull	1658–76	3									
Southam	1683–1814	2	1			5					'snakes' (5)
Tredington	1677–1758	5	1								Adders (5)
Warwick St Nicholas	1547–1758	5									
Wyken	1680–1727	5	1								

Barcheston 1626–1725, Berkswell 1603–18, Castle Bromwich 1641–1805, Offchurch 1619–53, Welford on Avon 1617–18

Westmorland

Place	Dates										Notes
Appleby	1696–1757	1	3	5	5	2	1	3			
Asby	1694–1794	1	5	1			4	4			
Askham	1575–1835	1	1				1	1	5		
Bampton	1774–1825	1	2				1	1	5		Eagle (1)
Barton	1700–1900	4	4		5		3	5	5		Eagle (1)
Beetham	1617–1881	5	5	5	5		1	1			
Bolton	1707–85	1	1	5	3						
Brough	1713–1808	5	5		5						'vermin' unspecified (5)
Burton	1717–1849	1	1	1		5		5			
Cartmel	1597–1674	2							3		
Cliburn	1690–1755	1	1	1	1		2				
Clifton	1677–1709	1	1								
Crosby Garrett	1722–1879	1	1	5	5		5				
Dent	1692–1802	3	2				5				
Hawkshead	1696–1771	1	1				5				

Parish	Dates	Hedgehog	Fox	Badger	Otter	Polecat	Stoat	Weasel	Marten	Wild Cat	Mole	H. Sparrow	Bullfinch	'Crow', Rook	Jackdaw	Raven	Magpie	Jay	Red Kite	'Hawk'	Other
Heversham	1601–1828		4	5	5	4				5						2					
Kendal	1658–1840		5	5	5	5			5	5						5					
Kirby Lonsdale	1669–1840	1	5	5	5	3				5											
Middleton	1661–1900		1			1					5					1					
Morland	1610–1900		2	5	5	5				5						5					
Ormside	1704–99		1	1	1	2				1						1					
Orton	1596–1672	3	1	1						1						4	5				
Shap	1788–9		1	1												3					

Crook 1766–1872, Finsthwaite 1725–1900, Firbank 1745–1870, Grasmere 1661–1735, Kirby Thore 1737–1869, Troutbeck 1639–1758, Windermere 1748–1859

Wiltshire

Parish	Dates	Hedgehog	Fox	Badger	Otter	Polecat	Stoat	Weasel	Marten	Wild Cat	Mole	H. Sparrow	Bullfinch	'Crow', Rook	Jackdaw	Raven	Magpie	Jay	Red Kite	'Hawk'	Other
Aldbourne	1683–1827	2	1								4										Adder (1)
Alderton	1725–1900		1								2										
Brinkworth	1745–1829		1			1					5										
Calne	1527–1760		1			1					2										
Calstone Wellington	1715–1853		1	3		1		1													
Christian Malford	1666–1756		1	5		1															
Collingbourne Kingston	1711–1895										5										
Durrington	1689–1766		1	1																	
Edington	1577–1625	2				2					2										
Enford	1728–1838	5	1		2	3	5	1			5										
Farley	1683–1724		1	2		1					1										
Grittleton	1672–1799	2	3								2										
Hannington	1635–1882		1								4										

Latton	1676–1782				1			2	
Laverstock	1687–1868	2					2	2	
Leigh	1719–1811		1	3	2	2			
Luckington	1697–1882	5	1						
Market Lavington	1689–1791	2	1	1			3		
Melksham	1574–1795	2	5	5	5	1	5	3	Adder (1)
Mere	1556–1853	1	1	1	1		5	2	
Seagry	1683–1707	1	1					1	
Seend	1664–1832	1	2	1	1	1			Bats (1)
Steeple Ashton	1543–1608	2	2						
Stockton	1660–1763	4	1	4	5	5	5	4	
West Knoyle	1711–60	1	3	3		1		2	
Wilcot	1694–1797	1					5		

Beechingstoke 1678–1818, Broad Blunsden 1607–76, Chilton Foliat 1577–1688, Cliffe Pypard 1682–1820, Cricklade 1670–1730, Fittleton 1688–1761, Foxley (f) 1736–57, Highworth 1620–1705, Longbridge Deverill 1552–1667, Lyd:ard Tregoze 1668–1831, North Bradley 1620–96, North Newton 1576–1646, West Lavington 1689–1791, Wilton (f) 1651–71.

Worcestershire

Abberley	1700–1831	3	1
Badsey	1620–1813	2	
Bewdley			
Bedwardine	1539–1603		
Bengeworth	1681–1844	1	
Broughton Hackett			
Chaddesley Corbett	1703–1808	1	1
Claines	1786–1828	1	
Eckington	1757–1839	2	
Himbleton	1684–1862	1	1
Holt	1664–1735	1	2

Parish	Hedgehog	Fox	Badger	Otter	Polecat	Stoat	Weasel	Marten	Wild Cat	Mole	H. Sparrow	Bullfinch	'Crow'	Rook	Jackdaw	Raven	Magpie	Jay	Red Kite	'Hawk'	Other
Norton 1723–83	3									3											
Old Swinford 1767–1853	5																				
Peopleton 1672–1863	2	1		1																	
Ripple 1705–89	1																				
Rochford 1705–1845	1	1																			
Stoke Bliss 1761–1820	1																				
Stone 1595–1781	1	2																1			

Bredwardine 1539–1603, Clifton on Teme 1756–1844, Elmley Castle 1632–40, Halesowen 1487–1582, Lower Mitton 1781–1864, North Littleton 1717–40, Salwarpe 1633–60, South Littleton 1548–1707, Stourport 1781–1841, Tardebigge 1768–1850, Upton on Severn 1754–1832, Welland 1792–1899

Yorkshire East Riding

Parish	Hedgehog	Fox	Badger	Otter	Polecat	Stoat	Weasel	Marten	Wild Cat	Mole	H. Sparrow	Bullfinch	'Crow'	Rook	Jackdaw	Raven	Magpie	Jay	Red Kite	'Hawk'	Other
Bishop Wilton 1772–1825	1	1		3																	
Bolton Percy 1679–1787	3	1		5							2										
Burton Agnes 1776–1882	2			5																	
Cottingham 1660–1890	2	1		5							5										
Heslington 1712–1810	1			5															1		
Holme on the Wolds 1748–1861	1	1	1	4																	
Kirby Underdale 1741–1828	1	1	1	5																	
Langton 1721–82			2	3																	
Market Weighton 1681–1784	1	2		5		3											5				Dipper (5)
Millington 1622–1714	1			1													4				
Nether Poppleton 1731–1804			1	4																	
Routh 1737–1851		2		5							5										
Rudston 1746–1894				2																	
Scampston 1737–1840				5																	
Settrington 1770–1900				1													5				

'vermin'
unspecified
(1)

						'vermin' unspecified (1)
Skipwith	1731–1817		I			I
Skirlaugh	1746–97					
South Cave	1700–85	I	I	I	5	
Warter	1767–80		I			
Wheldrake	1740–1881	I				I
Wold Newton	1739–1878		I			5

Birdsall 1759–1808, Boynton 1740–76, Bubwith 1714–98, Carnaby 1744–98, Catwick (f) 1722–1807, Flamborough (f) 1738–92, Garton in Holderness 1754–1830, Hilston 1742–1900, Howden (f) 1593–1666, Humbleton 1734–99, Kirby Grindalythe 1792–1870, Lund 1736–1808, Norton 1790–1825, Ottringham 1720–68, Roos 1666–1755, Rufforth (f) 1785–1900, Sutton on Hull 1710–1803, Watton 1712–90, Weaverthorpe 1756–1837, Wilberfoss 1752–1847, Wressell 1731–97

Yorkshire North Riding

Bedale	1576–1724		I	5		I
Bossall	1738–1833			5		I
Brompton by Sawden	1748–1809			2		I
Coxwold	1632–86	5				
Crambe	1756–94	I		2		
Deighton	1665–1825	I	I	3		I
Fylingdales	1762–1833	I	I	I		
Hawes	1726–1800			I		
Helmsley	1671–1785	2		I		
Hudswell	1698–1703	I	I			
Lastingham	1693–1894	I	I	I		
Lythe	1704–1840	3		2		I
Masham	1542–1677	5	2	4		
Newton upon Ouse	1777–1845					
Skipton	1728–90	2				

		Hedgehog	Fox	Badger	Otter	Polecat	Stoat	Weasel	Marten	Wild Cat	Mole	H. Sparrow	Bullfinch	'Crow'	Rook	Jackdaw	Raven	Magpie	Jay	Red Kite	'Hawk'	Other
Topcliffe	1651–1773	1	1																			5
Wensley	1726–1877	1	1					1														

Aysgarth 1722–1878, Brignall 1700–1900, Catterick 1788–1897, East Cowton 1661–1823, Husthwaite 1794–1837, Kirklington 1694–1858, Northallerton 1687–1727, Thirsk 1771–1900, Topcliffe 1651–1773

Yorkshire West Riding

		Hedgehog	Fox	Badger	Otter	Polecat	Stoat	Weasel	Marten	Wild Cat	Mole	H. Sparrow	Bullfinch	'Crow'	Rook	Jackdaw	Raven	Magpie	Jay	Red Kite	'Hawk'	Other
Addingham	1668–1824	1	4	1		3					1											
Arksey	1674–1775	1	1	5		5		5													5	
Bingley	1652–68	3	3	1		1																
Elland	1746–51		1			1		1														
Fishlake	1699–1732	2		2		2		1														
Halifax	1620–63		2	1	1																	
Ilkley	1623–1703		1	1	1					1												
Kildwick	1600–1710	1	1	1	1	1																
Kirby Malzeard	1576–1651		5	1	1						1		1					1				
Kirby Wharf	1697–1800		1	1	1	1							1					1				
Langfield	1771–1832	3	1	1																		
Methley	1681–1705		1	1		2																
Royston	1656–1720	4	4	1		4																
Thornhill	1672–1756	1	1	1		2																

Arkendale 1751–1894, Church Fenton 1775–88, Drax 1778–1874, East Ardsley 1653–90, Heptonstall (f) 1723–75, Ledsham 1738–1875, Manningham 1773–7, Thornton in Lonsdale 1771–1850

Appendix 2

Scientific names of species mentioned in the text

Mammals

Grey Seal	*Halichoerus grypus*
Hedgehog	*Erinaceus europaeus*
Mole	*Talpa europaea*
Rabbit	*Oryctolagus cuniculus*
Brown Hare	*Lepus europaeus*
Blue Hare	*Lepus timidus*
Grey Squirrel	*Sciurus carolinensis*
Red Squirrel	*Sciurus vulgaris*
Beaver	*Castor fiber*
Coypu	*Myocaster coypus*
Water Vole	*Arvicola terrestris*
Field Vole	*Microtus agrestis*
'Mice'	*Mus/Apodemus spp*
Black Rat	*Rattus rattus*
Brown Rat	*Rattus norvegicus*
Wolf	*Canis lupus*
Red Fox	*Vulpes vulpes*
Brown Bear	*Ursus arctos*
Badger	*Meles meles*
Stoat	*Mustela ermina*
Weasel	*Mustela nivalis*
Polecat	*Mustela putorius*
American Mink	*Mustela vison*
Otter	*Lutra lutra*
Pine Marten	*Martes martes*
Sable	*Martes zibellina*
Beech Marten	*Martes foina*
Wild Cat	*Felis silvestris*
Lynx	*Lynx lynx*
Wild Boar	*Sus scrofa*
Red Deer	*Cervus elaphus*
Roe deer	*Capreolus capreolus*
Elk	*Alces alces*
Aurochs	*Bos primigenius*

Birds

Red-throated Diver	*Gavia stellata*
Great Crested Grebe	*Podiceps cristatus*
Fulmar	*Fulmarus glacialis*
Shag	*Phalacrocorax aristotulis*
Cormorant	*Phalacrocorax carbo*
Bittern	*Botaurus stellaris*
Grey Heron	*Ardea cinerea*
White Stork	*Ciconia ciconia*
Canada Goose	*Branta canadensis*
Ruddy Duck	*Oxyura jamaicensis*
Red-breasted Merganser	*Mergus serrator*
Goosander	*Mergus merganser*
Osprey	*Pandion haliaetus*
White-tailed Eagle	*Haliaeetus albicilla*
Red Kite	*Milvus milvus*
Marsh Harrier	*Circus aeruginosus*
Hen Harrier	*Circus cyaneus*
Montagu's Harrier	*Circus pygarus*
Sparrowhawk	*Accipiter nisus*
Goshawk	*Accipiter gentilis*
Buzzard	*Buteo buteo*
Golden Eagle	*Aquila chrysaetos*
Peregrine Falcon	*Falco peregrinus*
Merlin	*Falco columbarius*
Kestrel	*Falco tinnunculus*
Red Grouse	*Lagopus lagopus scoticus*
Pheasant	*Phasianus colchlicus*
Grey Partridge	*Perdix perdix*
Common Crane	*Grus grus*

Great Bustard	*Otis tarda*	Magpie	*Pica pica*
Lapwing	*Vanellus vanellus*	Chough	*Pyrrhocorax*
Golden Plover	*Apricaria*		*pyrrhocorax*
	pluvialis	Rook	*Corvus frugilegus*
Curlew	*Numeniusarquata*	Carrion Crow	*Corvus corone*
Stone Curlew	*Burhinus*	Jackdaw	*Corvus monedula*
	oedicnemus	Raven	*Corvus corax*
Great Black-backed	*Larus marinus*	Starling	*Sturnus vulgaris*
Gull		House Sparrow	*Passer domesticus*
Lesser Black-backed	*Larus fuscus*	Tree Sparrow	*Passer*
Gull			*montanus*
Kittiwake	*Rissa tridactyla*	Bullfinch	*Pyrrhula pyrrhula*
Feral Pigeon	*Columba livia*	Goldfinch	*Carduelis*
	(var)		*carduelis*
Woodpigeon	*Columba*	Chaffinch	*Fringilla coelebs*
	palumbus		
Collared dove	*Streptopelia*		
	decaocto	**Fish**	
Short-eared Owl	*Asio flammeus*		
Tawny Owl	*Strix aluco*	Dab	*Limanda limanda*
Barn Owl	*Tyto alba*	Plaice	*Pleuronectes platessa*
Nightjar	*Caprimulgus*	Flounder	*Platichthys flesus*
	europaeus	Sand eel	*Ammodytes spp*
Kingfisher	*Alcedo atthis*	Sprat	*Sprattus sprattus*
Green Woodpecker	*Picus viridis*	Herring	*Clupea harengus*
Great Spotted	*Dendrocopos*	Blenny	*Blennius spp*
Woodpecker	*major*	Salmon	*Salmo salar*
Meadow Pipit	*Anthus pratensis*	Brown Trout	*Salmo trutta*
Skylark	*Alauda arvensis*	Roach	*Rutilus rutilus*
Wheatear	*Oenanthe*		
	oenanthe	**Reptiles**	
Blackbird	*Turdus merula*		
'Titmice'	*Parus spp*	Grass snake	*Natrix natrix*
Dipper	*Cinclus cinclus*	Adder	*Vipera berus*
Jay	*Garrulus*	Slow-worm	*Anguis fragilis*
	glandarius		

 # References

Introduction

Gibson, A. J. S. and Smout, T. C., 1993: *Prices, Food and Wages in Scotland* 1550–1780, Cambridge University Press.

Thirsk, J. (ed.), 1967: *The Agrarian History of England and Wales, Vols IV, V, VI*, Cambridge University Press.

Chapter 1

Main reference sources

Abbey, G., 1909: *The Balance of Nature and Modern Conditions of Cultivation*, George Routledge & Sons, London.

Bell, T., 1837: *The History of British Quadrupeds*, Van Voorst, London.

Bramwell, D., 1960: *Proc. of Merseyside Naturalists' Association*, pp. 51–8.

Clarke, G., 1848: Fowling in Prehistoric Europe, *Antiquity*, Vol. 87, pp. 116–30.

Dent, A., 1974: *Lost Beasts of Britain*, Harrap, Edinburgh.

Fleure, H. J., 1970: *A Natural History of Man in Britain*, Collins, London.

Giraldus Cambrensis, *The Itinerary of Archbishop Baldwin through Wales*, Everyman edition, 1908.

Grigson, C. and Mellars, P. A., 1987: *The Mammalian Remains from Middens*, in Mellars (ed.), *Excavations on Oronsay*, Edinburgh.

Harting, J. E., 1880a: *British Mammals Extinct within Historic Times*, Trubner & Co., London.

—— 1880b: *A Short History of the Wolf in Britain*, Pryor.

Links, J. G., 1956: *The Book of Fur*, James Barrie, London.

Maroo, S. and Yalden, D. W., 2000: The Mesolithic mammal fauna of Great Britain, *Mammal Review*, Vol. 30, pp. 243–8.

Matheson, C., 1932: *Changes in the Fauna of Wales within Historic Times*, National Museum of Wales.

Meikle, I., 1973: Dumfries Fur Fair, *Scotland's Magazine*, Vol. 69, p. 2.

Millais, J. G., 1904: *Mammals of Great Britain and Ireland*, Longman, Green & Co., London.

Pennant, T., 1774: *A Tour in Scotland*, John Monk, Chester.

Pyle, C. M., 1994: *The Archives of Natural History*, Vol. 21, pp. 275–88.

Rackham, O., 1986: *The History of the Countryside*, Dent, London.

Ritchie, J., 1920: *The Influence of Man on the Animal Life of Scotland*, Cambridge University Press.

Rogers, T., 1884: *Six Centuries of Work and Wages*, Fisher Unwin, London.

Sibbald, Sir Robert, 1684: *Scotia Illustrata*.

Stuart, A. J., 1974: Pleistocene history of the British vertebrate fauna, *Biological Review*, Vol. 49, pp. 225–66.

Veale, E. M., 1966: *The English Fur Trade*, Oxford University Press.

Yalden, D. W., 1999: *The History of British Mammals*, T. & A. D. Poyser, London.

Chapter 2

Main reference sources

Bowen, I., 1914: *The Great Enclosures of Common Land in Wales*, Chiswick Press, London.

Chambers, J. D. and Mingay, G. E., 1966: *The Agricultural Revolution* 1759–1880, Batsford, London.

Clapham, Sir John, 1949: *A Concise Economic History of Britain*, Cambridge University Press.

Crocker, J. (ed.), 1981: *Charnwood Forest: a changing landscape*, Loughborough Naturalists' Club.

Defoe, D., 1724: *Tour through the Whole Island of Great Britain*, 1991 edn., Yale.

Dix, H., 1928: *Love of animals and how it developed in Great Britain*, Edwin Mellon Press.

Emery, F. V., 1969: *The World's Landscapes:* 2, Wales, Longman, London.

Gonner, E. K. C., 1966: *Common Land and Inclosure*, Cass & Co., London.

Hopkins, Ezekiel, 1692: *An Exposition of the Ten Commandments*.

Hoskins, W. G., 1953–4: Harvest fluctuations and English economic history 1480–1619, *Agric. Hist. Review*, Vol. II, pp. 28–46.

—— 1955: *The Making of the English Landscape*, Hodder & Stoughton, London.

—— and Stamp, L. Dudley, 1963: *The Common Lands of England and Wales*, Collins, London.

Houghton, J., 1694: *A Collection of Improvement of Husbandry and Trade*, Vol. 108.

Jack, R. I., 1972: *Mediaeval Wales*, Hodder and Stoughton, London.

Jones, E. L., 1972: The Bird Pests of British Agriculture in Recent Centuries, *Agric. Hist. Review*, Vol. 20, pp. 107–25.

Knapp, J. L., 1829: *The Journal of a Naturalist*, John Murray, London.

Lawson, W., 1618: *A New Orchard and Garden*.

Linnard, W., 1982: *Welsh Woods and Forests*, National Museum of Wales.

McEvedy, C. and Jones, R., 1978: *Atlas of World Population History*, Penguin, London.

Morgan, K. O., 1999: *The Oxford History of Britain*, Oxford University Press.

Munsche, P. B., 1981: *Gentlemen and Poachers: the English game laws* 1671–1831, Cambridge University Press.

Norden, J., 1607: *The Surveyor's Dialogue*, London.

Pennant, T., 1744: *A Tour in Scotland*, John Monk, Chester.

Plot, R., 1677: *The Natural History of Oxfordshire*, Oxford.

—— 1686: *The Natural History of Staffordshire*.

Pollard, E., Hooper, M. D., and Moore, N. W., 1974: *Hedges*, Collins, London.

Rackham, O., 1986: *The History of the Countryside*, Dent, London.

Russell, K. and R. C., 1987: *Parliamentary Enclosures and the New Lincolnshire Landscape*, Lincoln.

Sheail, J., 1971: *Rabbits and their History*, David & Charles, Newton Abbot.

Shrubb, M., 2003: *Birds, Scythes and Combines*, Cambridge University Press.

Smout, T. C., 2000: *Nature Contested*, Edinburgh University Press.

Stamp, L. Dudley, 1955: *Man and the Land*, Collins, London.

Sylvester, D., 1969: *The Rural Landscape and the Welsh Borderland*, Macmillan, London.

Tapper, S. C., 1992: *Game Heritage*, Game Conservancy Trust.

Tate, W. E., 1946: *A Handbook of Buckinghamshire Enclosure Acts and Awards*, Buckinghamshire County Council.

—— 1967: *The English Village Community and the Enclosure Movements*, Gollancz, London.

Thirsk, J., 1964: The Common Fields, *Past and Present*, Vol. 29, pp. 3–25.

—— (ed.), 1967: *The Agrarian History of England and Wales, Vols IV, V, VI*, Cambridge University Press.

—— 1997: *Alternative Agriculture*, Oxford University Press.

Thomas, K., 1983: *Man and the Natural World: changing attitudes in England, 1500–1800*, Allen Lane, London.

Turner, G., 1794: *A General View of Agriculture of the County of Gloucestershire*, Board of Agriculture, London.

Turner, M., 1980: *English Parliamentary Enclosures*, Dawson Archon, Folkestone.

—— 1984: *Enclosures in Britain 1750–1830*, Macmillan, London.

Tusser, T. (ed. Mavor, W.) 1812, *Five Hundred Points of Good Husbandry*, London.

Vandervell, C. A. and Coles, C. L., 1980: *Game and the English Landscape*, Debretts, London.

Vesey-Fitzgerald, B., 1969: *The Vanishing Wildlife of Britain*, MacGibbon & Kee, London.

Williamson, T., 2002: *The Transformation of Rural England*, Exeter University Press.

Yelling, J. A., 1977: *Common Fields and Enclosures in England 1450–1850*, Macmillan, London

Chapter 3

Main reference sources

Blundell, M., 1952: *Blundell's Diary and Letter Book*, Liverpool University Press.

Brown, R., 1759: *The Compleat Farmer or the Whole Art of Husbandry*, London.

Conyers, G. (*c.* 1705) *The Complete English and French Vermin Killer—being a companion for all families.*

Cook, R. M. L., 1964: Old vermin traps on South-West Dartmoor, *Trans. Devon Association*, Vol. 96, pp. 190–7.

Kearton, R. and Kearton, C., 1898: *With Nature and a Camera*, Cassell, London.

Mascall, L., 1590: *A Book of Engines and Traps to take Polecats, Buzardes, Rattes, Mice and all other Kindes of Vermine and Beasts whatever.*

Tapper, S. C., 1992: *Game Heritage*, Game Conservancy Trust.

Willughby, F., 1678 (trans. John Ray): *Ornithology*, John Murray, London.

W. W., 1680: *The Vermin Killer, being a very necessary Family Book containing exact rules and directions for the artificial killing and destroying of all manner of vermin.*

Chapter 4

Main reference sources

Adams, I. H. (ed.), 1979: *Peter May, Land Surveyor*, Scottish History Society.

Baxter, E. V. and Rintoul, L. J., 1953: *The Birds of Scotland*, Oliver & Boyd.

Booth, E. T., 1881–7: *Rough notes on the birds observed during twenty-five years of shooting and collecting in the British Isles*, 3 vols, R. H. Porter, London.

Brown, K. M. (ed.) et al. (in press), *The Records of the Scottish Parliament* 1235–1707, St Andrews 2007, no.1424/21 (online source).

Cole, A. C. and Trobe, W. M., 2000: *The Egg Collectors of Great Britain and Ireland*, Peregrine Books, Leeds.

Colquhoun, J., 1840: *The Moor and Loch*, Blackwood.

Dumfries Courier, 1816–74.

Eden, R., 1979: *Going to the Moors*, John Murray, London.

Gaskell, P. 1968: *Morvern Transformed*, Cambridge University Press.

Harvie-Brown, J. A., papers in the National Library of Scotland.

Henderson, D. W. and Dickson, J. H., 1994: *A Naturalist in the Highlands: James Robertson, 1767–1771*, Scottish Academic Press.

Hudson, P. J., personal communication

MacDonald, Murdo (Archivist for Argyll and Bute), personal communication and in literature.

Macintyre, D., 1925: *Highland Gamekeeper*, Seeley Service, London.

Mackenzie, O. H., 1921: *A Hundred Years in the Highlands*, E. Arnold & Co., London.

Meikle, I., 1973: Dumfries Fur Fair, *Scotland's Magazine*, Vol. 69, p. 2.

Millman, R. N., 1975: *The Making of the Scottish Landscape*, Batsford, London.

Parry, M. L. and Slater, T. R., 1980: *The Making of the Scottish Countryside*, Croom Helm, London.

Pennant, T., 1774: *A Tour in Scotland*, John Monk, Chester.

Prebble, J., 1963: *The Highland Clearances*, Secker and Warburg,

Ritchie, J., 1920: *The Influence of Man on the Animal Life of Scotland*, Cambridge University Press.

Service, R., 1891: *The Old Fur Market of Dumfries*, Scottish Naturalist.

Shrubb, M., 2003: *Birds, Scythes and Combines*, Cambridge University Press.

Skilling, D., 1998: *Notes on the Old Fur Market at Dumfries*, Trans. Dumfries & Galloway Nat. Hist. & Antiq. Soc., Series 3, Vol. LXXII.

Smout, T. C., 2000: *Nature Contested*, Edinburgh University.

St John, C., 1983: *Wild Sports and Natural History of the Highlands*, John Murray, London.

Statistical Account of Scotland (Old), 1791–9.

Statistical Account of Scotland (New), 1845.

Turner, M., 1984: Enclosures in Britain 1750–1830, Macmillan.

Walker, J., 1764 and 1771 (ed. McKay, M.M., 1980): *Report on the Hebrides*, John Donald, Edinburgh.

Warren, C., 2002: *Managing Scotland's Environment*, Edinburgh University Press.

Wight, A., 1778–84: *Present State of Husbandry in Scotland*, Vol. IV, pp.174–5, Edinburgh.

Chapter 5

Main reference sources

Blair, L., 1939: *A List of Churchwardens' Accounts*, Ann Arbor.

Cocks, A. H., 1892: Vermin Paid for by Churchwardens in a Buckinghamshire parish, *Zoologist*, Series 3, Vol. 16, pp. 61–4.

Cox, J. C., 1913: *Churchwardens' Accounts from the Fourteenth Century to the Close of the Seventeenth Century*, Methuen, London.

Ellice, E. C., 1898: *Place names of Glengarry and Glenquoich*, Facsimile edition, Glengarry Information Centre.

Galt, J., 1919: *Annals of the Parish*, Edinburgh.

Gladstone, H. S., 1922: *Record Bags and Shooting Records*, Witherby, London.

Harrison, C., 1988: *The History of the Birds of Britain*, Collins/Witherby, London.

Harvey, N., 1976: *Fields, Hedges and Ditches*, Shire Books, Buckinghamshire.

Jones, A., 2000: *A Thousand Years of the English Parish*, Windrush Press, Oxford.

Jones, E. L., 1972: Bird pests in British agriculture in recent centuries, *Agric. Hist. Review*, Vol. 20, pp. 107–25.

Langley, J., 1797: *History of the Hundred of Desborough* (publisher unknown).

Murton, R. K., 1971: *Man and Birds*, Collins, London.

Oldham, C., 1929: Payments for Vermin by Berkhamstead Churchwardens, *Trans. Herts. Nat. Hist. Soc.*, Vol. 18, pp. 45–50.

—— 1930: Payments for Vermin by some Hertfordshire Churchwardens, *Trans. Herts. Nat. Hist. Soc.*, Vol. 19, pp. 79–112.

Reese, M. M., 1940: *The Tudors and Stuarts*, Arnold, London.

Thomas, K., 1983: *Man and the Natural World: changing attitudes in England, 1500–1800*, Allen Lane, London.

Williams, C. J. and Watts-Williams, J., 2000: *Parish Registers of Wales*, National Library of Wales.

Chapter 6

Generic reference sources for the chapter

Archibald, C. F., 1892: Wild Birds Useful and Injurious, *J.R.A.E.S.*, Series 3, Vol. 3, pp. 658–84.

Baxter, E. V. and Rintoul, L. J., 1953: *The Birds of Scotland*, Oliver & Boyd.

Bewick, T., 1826: *History of British Birds*, Walker, Newcastle.

Bolam, G., 1913: *Wildlife in Wales*, Frank Palmer.

Brown, L., 1976: *British Birds of Prey*, Collins, London.

Cramp, S. et al., 1977–94: *Birds of the Western Palearctic Vol. i–viii*, Oxford University Press.

Forrest, H. E., 1907: *The Fauna of North Wales*, Witherby, London.

—— 1919: *A Handbook of the Vertebrate Fauna of North Wales*, Witherby, London.

Gibbons, D. G., Reid, J. B., and Chapman, R. A., 1993: *New Atlas of Breeding Birds*, T. & A. D. Poyser, London.

Greenoak, F., 1997: *British Birds, their Folklore, Names and Literature*, Christopher Helm & A. C. Black, London.

Harrison, C., 1998: *The History of Birds*, Collins/Witherby, London.

Harvie-Brown, J. A., papers in National Library of Scotland.

—— and Buckley, T. E., 1887: *A Vertebrate Fauna of Sutherland Caithness and Wester Ross*, Douglas, Edinburgh.

—— —— 1888: *A Vertebrate Fauna of the Outer Hebrides*, Douglas, Edinburgh.

—— —— 1891: *A Vertebrate Fauna of the Orkney Islands*, Douglas, Edinburgh.

—— —— 1892: *A Vertebrate Fauna of Argyll and the Inner Hebrides*, Douglas, Edinburgh.

—— —— 1896: *A Vertebrate Fauna of the Moray Basin*, Douglas, Edinburgh.

Hudson, W. H., 1901: *Birds and Man*, Longman, London.

Jones, E. L., 1972: Bird pests in British agriculture in recent centuries, *Agric. Hist. Review*, Vol. 20, pp. 107–25.

Lack, P., 1986: *Atlas of Wintering Birds in Britain and Ireland*, T. & A. D. Poyser, London.

Lockwood, W. B., 1984: *The Oxford Book of British Bird Names*, Oxford University Press.

Lovegrove, R. R., Williams, G. A., and Williams, I. T., 1994: *Birds in Wales*, T. & A. D. Poyser, London.

MacGillivray, W., 1840: *A Manual of British Ornithology*, Webster & Geary.

Mackenzie, O. H., 1918: *Vanishing Birds and Birds that have Already Vanished on the West Coast of Ross-shire*, Arnold & Co.

Macpherson, H. A., 1892: *A Vertebrate Fauna of Lakeland*, Douglas, Edinburgh.

Murton, R. K., 1971: *Man and Birds*, Collins, London.

Nicholson, E. M., 1971: *Birds and Men*, Collins, London.

Richmond, W. K., 1959: *British Birds of Prey*, Lutterworth Press, Cambridge.

Ritchie, J., 1920: *The Influence of Man on Animal Life in Scotland*, Cambridge University Press.

Saxby, H. L., 1874: *The Birds of Shetland*, London.

Thom, V., 1986: *Birds in Scotland*, T. & A. D. Poyser, London.

Cormorant

Main references

Bolam, G., 1912: *The Birds of Northumberland and the Eastern Borders*, Blair, Alnwick.

—— 1932: Vermin killed on the Tweed and Tributaries from 1911–1931, *Trans. Northumberland Nat. Hist. Soc.*, Vol. VIII.

Devon River Board Records, in Record Office, Exeter.

Gardner-Medwin, D., 1985: Early bird records for Northumberland and Durham, *Trans. Nat. Hist. Soc. Northumbria*, Vol. 54, pp. 5–22.

Harrison, W. (ed. G. Edelen), 1968 edn: *The Description of England*, New York.

Lambert, R. A., 2003: Seabird control and fishery protection in Cornwall, *British Birds*, Vol. 96, pp. 30–4.

Mills, D. H., 1965: *The Distribution and Food of the Cormorant on Inland Waters in Scotland*, H.M.S.O., London.

Mills, D., 1969: The food of cormorants at two breeding colonies on the east coast of Scotland, *British Birds*, Vol. 5, No. 5, pp. 268–76.

Morris, Rev F. O., 1855: *A History of British Birds*, London.

Raine, J., 1852: *The History and Antiquities of North Durham as subdivided into the shires of Norham, Island and Bedlington, which, from the Saxon period until 1844, constituted parcels of the County Palatine of Durham but which are now united in the County of Northumberland*, J. S. Nicholls & Son, London.

Wallis, J., 1769: *Natural History and Antiquities of Northumberland and such of the County of Durham as lies between the Rivers Tyne and Tweed, Commonly Called North Bishoprick*, London.

Wilson, Anne, 2005: Chapter in preparation for a book on Farne Island birds.

Osprey

Main references

Baxter, E. V. and Rintoul, L. J., 1953: *The Birds of Scotland*, Oliver & Boyd.

Dennis, R. H., 1984: *Birds of Badenoch and Strathspey*, Private publication.

—— 1991: *Ospreys*, Colin Baxter, Grantown-on-Spey.

—— personal communication.

Gray, H. D. and Anderson, T., 1869: *Birds of Ayrshire and Wigtownshire*, John Murray, London.

Harvie-Brown, J. A. and Buckley, T. E., 1887: *A Vertebrate Fauna of Sutherland Caithness and Wester Ross*, Douglas, Edinburgh.

Jardine, W., 1838–43: *The Naturalists' Library. Ornithology. Birds of Great Britain and Ireland*, Lizars, Edinburgh.

Macpherson, H. A., 1892: *A Vertebrate Fauna of Lakeland*, Douglas, Edinburgh.

Mascall, L., 1590: *A Book of Engines and Traps to take Polecats, Buzardes, Rattes, Mice and all other kindes of vermine and beasts whatever*.

Morton, J., 1712: *The Natural History of Northamptonshire*.

Service, R., 1891: The Old Fur Market of Dumfries, *Scottish Naturalist*, July 1891.

Vesey-Fitzgerald, B., 1969: *The Vanishing Wildlife of Britain*, MacGibbon & Kee, London.

Sea Eagle—Erne

Main references

Clarke, J., 1787: *A Survey of the Lakes of Cumberland, Westmorland and Lancashire Together with an Account, Historical, Topographical and Descriptive of the Adjacent Country*, published by the author.

Dennis, R. H., personal communication.
Dixon, C., 1888: *Our Rarer Birds*, Bentley, London.
Gray, H. D., 1871: *The Birds of the West of Scotland*, John Murray, London.
Hale, W., personal communication.
Harvie-Brown, J. A., papers in the National Library of Scotland.
Love, J., 1983: *The Return of the Sea Eagle*, Cambridge University Press.
MacGillivray, W., 1836: *Description of the Rapacious Birds of Great Britain*, London.
Macpherson, H. A., 1892: *A Vertebrate Fauna of Lakeland*, Douglas, Edinburgh.
Mudge, G., et al., 1996: *Sea Eagles*, Scottish Natural Heritage.
Pennant, T., 1774: *A Tour in Scotland*, John Monk, Chester.
Plot, R., 1686: *The Natural History of Staffordshire*.
St John, C., 1884: *A Tour in Sutherlandshire*, Douglas, Edinburgh.
Yarrell, W., 1837–43: *A History of British Birds*, Van Voorst, London.

Golden Eagle

Main references

Baxter, E. V. and Rintoul, L. J., 1953: *The Birds of Scotland*, Oliver & Boyd.
Campbell, L. and Dennis, R. H., 1996: *Golden Eagles*, Colin Baxter, Grantown-on-Spey.
Colquhoun, J., 1888: *The Moor and Loch*, Blackwood & Sons, London.
Forrest, H. E., 1907: *The Fauna of North Wales*, Witherby, London.
Gordon, S., 1955: *The Golden Eagle*, Collins, London.
Graham, H. D., 1890: *The Birds of Iona and Mull*, Douglas, Edinburgh.
MacGillivray, W., 1836: *Description of the Rapacious Birds of Great Britain*, London.
MacNally, L., 1977: *The Ways of an Eagle*, Collins & Harvill Press, London.
Macpherson, H. A., 1892: *A Vertebrate Fauna of Lakeland*, Douglas, Edinburgh.
Ratcliffe, D. A., 2002: *Lakeland*, Collins, London.

Red Kite

Main references

Bloomfield, Robert, 1766–1823, Suffolk poet.
Carter, I., 2001: *The Red Kite*, Arlequin Press, Shrewsbury.
Lilford, Lord, 1895: *Notes on the Birds of Northamptonshire and Neighbourhood*, R. H. Porter, London.
Lovegrove, R. R., 1990: *The Red Kite's Tale*, RSPB.
Nisbett, I. C. T., 1959: The Kites of sixteenth century London, *British Birds*, Vol. 52, pp. 239–40.
Ticehurst, N. F., 1921: Of the Former Abundance of Kite, Buzzard and Raven in Kent, *British Birds*, Vol. xiv, pp. 34–7.
Shrubb, M., 2003: *Birds, Scythes and Combines*, Cambridge University Press.
Willughby, F., 1678 (translated by John Ray): *Ornithology*, John Murray, London.

Hen Harrier

Main references

Bolam, G., 1912: *The Birds of Northumberland and the Eastern Borders*, Blair, Alnwick.

Clarke, R., 1996: *Montagu's Harrier*, Arlequin Press, Shrewsbury.

Ellice, E. C., 1898: *Place Names of Glengarry and Glenquoich*, Facsimile edition, Glengarry Information Centre.

Etheridge, B., et al., 1997: The effects of illegal killing by humans on the population dynamics of the hen harrier, *J. Applied Ecology*, Vol.34, pp. 1081–1105.

Holmes, J., Carter, L., Stott, M., Hughes, J., Davies, P., and Walker, D., 2003: 'Raptor Persecution in England at the End of the Twentieth Century', in *Birds of Prey in a Changing Environment* (eds. Thompson, D., Repath, S., Fielding, A., Marquiss, M., and Galbraith, C.), pp. 481–5, SNH.

MacGillivray, W., 1836: *Description of Rapacious Birds of Great Britain*, London.

Macpherson, H. A., 1892: *A Vertebrate Fauna of Lakeland*, Douglas, Edinburgh.

Nethersole-Thompson, D., 1933: Observations on nesting hen harriers, *Oologist Record*, Vol. 13.

Richmond, W. K. 1959: *British Birds of Prey*, London

Sim, I. M. W., 1999: *Status of the Hen Harrier in the UK and the Isle of Man*, Report to the Raptor Working Group.

Watson, D., 1977: *The Hen Harrier*, T. & A. D. Poyser, London.

'Hawk'

Main references

Linnard, W., 1982: *Welsh Woods and Forests*, National Museum of Wales.

Owen, G., 1594: Extent of Cemais, *Pembrokeshire Record Series*, 1977, Vol. 3, p. 63.

Buzzard

Main references

Elliott, J. Steele, 1936: *Bedfordshire Vermin Payments*, Luton Public Museum.

Latham, J., 1781–1801: *Essays on Natural History, chiefly Ornithology*, Longman, London.

Macpherson, H. A., 1892: *A Vertebrate Fauna of Lakeland*, Douglas, Edinburgh.

Moore, N. W., 1957: The past and present status of the Buzzard in the British Isles, *British Birds*, Vol. 50, pp. 173–97.

More, A. G., 1865: On the distribution of birds in Great Britain during the nesting season, *Ibis*, New Series 1.

Pennant, T., 1774: *A Tour in Scotland*, John Monk, Chester.

Shrubb, M., 2003: *Birds, Scythes and Combines*, Cambridge University Press.

Tubbs, C. R., 1974: *The Buzzard*, David & Charles, Newton Abbot.

Turner, W., 1544: *Avium praecipuarum*.

Willughby, F., 1678 (translated by John Ray): *Ornithology*, John Murray, London.

Green Woodpecker—Hew Hole or Galley Bird

Reference

Meinertzhagen, Col. R., 1959: *Pirates and Predators*, Oliver & Boyd, London.

Dipper/Kingfisher

Main references

Ormerod, S., and Tyler, S., 1994: *The Dippers*, T. & A. D. Poyser, London.
Ritchie, J., 1920: *The Influence of Man on the Animal Life of Scotland*, Cambridge University Press.

Jay

Main references

None

Magpie

Main references

Birkhead, T. R., 1991: *The Magpies*, T. & A. D. Poyser, London.
Gooch, S., Baillie, S. R., and Birkhead, T. R., 1981: Magpie and songbird populations, *J. Applied Ecology*, Vol. 28, pp. 817–30.
Innes, C. (ed.), 1885: *The Black Book of Taymouth with other papers from the Breadalbane Charter Room*, Bannatyne Club, Edinburgh.
Lawson, W., 1617: *The Countrie Housewife's Garden . . . together with the Husbandry of Bees*, London.
Macpherson, H. A., 1892: *A Vertebrate Fauna of Lakeland*, Douglas, Edinburgh.

Chough

Main references

Bullock, I. D., Drewett, D. R., and Mickleborough, S. P., 1983: The Chough in Wales, *Nature in Wales*, Vol. 4, pp. 46–57.
—— personal communication.
Camden, W., 1695: *Britannia*, Facsimile edition 1806 (ed. Gough R.).
Darling, F. Fraser and Boyd, J. M., 1947: *The Highlands and Islands*, Collins, London.
Defoe, D., 1724: *A Tour through the Whole Island of Great Britain*, 1991 edn., Yale University Press, London.
D'Urban, W. M. S. and Mathew, M. A., 1895: *The Birds of Devon*, R. H. Porter, London.
Ellis, M. (ed.) (no date): *Operation Chough: the Story of the Cornish chough*, Beric Tempest, St Ives.

Jardine, W., 1838–43: *The Naturalist's library. Ornithology. Birds of Great Britain and Ireland*, Lizars, Edinburgh.

Morris, Rev. F. O., 1855: *A History of British Birds*, Groombridge & Sons, London.

Owen, D. A. L., 1994: *Factors affecting the distribution of the Chough in Britain with observations on its behaviour*, D.Phil. thesis (Oxon.)

Penhallurick, R., 1978: The Cornishness of the Chough, *The Countryman*, 1978, pp. 161–7.

Ritchie, J., 1920: *The Influence of Man on the Animal Life of Scotland*, Cambridge University Press.

Rolfe, R., 1966: The status of the Chough in the British Isles, *Bird Study*, Vol. 13, p. 221–30.

Rose, L., 1995: *Where to Watch Birds in Spain and Portugal*, Hamlyn, London.

Warnes, J. M., 1983: The status of the Chough in Scotland, *Scottish Birds*, Vol. 12, p. 238–46.

Rook

Main references

Brown, R., 1759: *The Compleat Farmer or the Whole Art of Husbandry*, London.

Edwards, Sir G., 1922: *From Crow Scaring to Westminster*, Labour Publishing Co., London.

Feare, C. J., 1974: Ecological studies of the rook in N.E. Scotland: damage and control, *J. Applied Ecology*, Vol. 11, pp. 897–914.

—— Dunnet, G. M., and Patterson, I. J., 1974: Ecological studies of the Rook in N.E. Scotland: food intake and feeding behaviour, *J. Applied Ecology*, Vol. 11, pp. 867–96.

—— 1978: The ecology of damage by Rooks, *Ann. Applied Biology*, Vol. 88, pp. 329–34.

Fisher, J., 1948: The Rook Investigation, *Agriculture*, Vol. 55, pp. 20–3.

Hawkins, T. S., 1940: *My Friend the Rook*, James Clarke, London.

O'Connor, R. J. and Shrubb, M., 1986: *Farming and Birds*, Cambridge University Press.

Sage B. L., and Whittington, P. A., 1985: The 1980 sample survey of rookeries, *Bird Study*, Vol. 32, pp. 77–81.

Tapper, S. C., 1992: *Game Heritage*, Game Conservancy Trust.

Watson, A., 1967: The Hatton Castle Rookery, *Bird Study*, Vol. 14, pp. 116–19.

Carrion/Hooded Crow

Main references

Bannerman, D. A., 1952: *The Birds of the British Isles Vol. 1*, Oliver & Boyd, Edinburgh.

Burgess, D., 1963: Carrion crows in Northern England, *Agriculture*, Vol. 70, pp. 126–9.

Hudson, P. J., 1992: *Grouse in Space and Time*, Game Conservancy Trust.

Potts, G. R., 1986: *The Partridge, Pesticides, Predation and Conservation*, Collins, London.

Prestt, I., 1965: An enquiry into the recent breeding success of some of the smaller birds of prey and crows in Britain, *Bird Study*, Vol. 12, pp. 196–221.

Ritchie, J, 1920: *The Influence of Man on Animal Life in Scotland*, Cambridge University Press.

Tapper, S. C., 1992: *Game Heritage*, Game Conservancy Trust.

Jackdaw

Main reference

Tapper, S. C., 1992: *Game heritage*, Game Conservancy Trust.

Raven

Main references

Armstrong, E. A., 1958: *The Folklore of Birds*, Collins, London.

Baxter, E. V. and Rintoul, L. J., 1953: *The Birds of Scotland*, Oliver & Boyd.

Harvie-Brown, J. A., papers in the National Library of Scotland.

Murton, R. K., 1971: *Man and Birds*, Collins, London.

Ratcliffe, D. A., 1997: *The Raven*, T. & A. D. Poyser, London.

Ridpath, M. G., 1953: *The Damage by Ravens in Pembrokeshire*, unpublished MAFF report No. 36.

Shrubb, M., 2003: *Birds, Scythes and Combines*, T. & A. D. Poyser, London.

Smith, R., 1768: *The Universal Directory for the taking alive and destroying Rats and all other kinds of four footed and winged vermin*, London.

Starling

Main references

Crick, H. Q. P. et al., 2002: *Investigation into the Causes of Decline of Starlings and House Sparrows in Great Britain*, Department of Environment, Food and Rural Affairs.

Feare, C. J., 1984: *The Starling*, Oxford University Press.

Knapp, J. L., 1829: *The Journal of a Naturalist*, John Murray, London.

MacGillivray, W., 1840: *A Manual of British Ornithology*, Webster & Geary.

Meikeljohn, M. F. M., 1954: The use of earthenware pots as nesting holes for starlings and house sparrows, *British Birds*, Vol. xlvii, pp. 95–6.

Smout, T. C., 2000: *Nature Contested*, Edinburgh University Press.

House Sparrow

Main references

Barnard, E. A. B., 1948: *Sparrows and Sparrow Pots, Trans. Worcestershire Arch. Soc.*, New series Vol. 25, pp. 50–6.

Cam, H., 1916: The Legend of Incendiary Birds, *English History Review*, Vol. 31, pp. 98–101.

Clark, J. F. M., 2000: The Irish Men of Birds, *History Today*, 2000, pp. 16–18.

Crick, H. Q. P. et al., 2002: *Investigation into the Causes of Decline of Starlings and House Sparrows in Great Britain*, Department of Environment, Food and Rural Affairs.

Harrison, C., 1998: *The History of Birds*, Collins/Witherby, London.

Hodgson, G., 2004: The Stone Street Rat and Sparrow Club, *Shooting and Conservation*, May/June.

Robinson, M., 1947: *A South Down Farm in the Sixties*, Bannisdale Press.

Summers-Smith, J. D., 1963: *The House Sparrow*, Collins, London.

—— personal communication.

Tegetmeier, W. B., 1899: *The House Sparrow*, Vinton & Co., London.

Turner, G., 1794: *A General View of Agriculture in the County of Gloucestershire*, Board of Agriculture, London.

Warren, C. H., 1937: *A Boy in Kent*, Hollis & Carter, London.

Bullfinch

Main references

Cadle, C., 1867: The agriculture of Worcestershire, *J. of Royal Agric. Soc. of England*, Series 2, Vol. 3, pp. 439–66.

Conyers, G., c.1705: *The Complete English and French Vermin Killer—being a companion for all families.*

Flegg, J. J. M., personal communication.

Matthews, N. J., 1983: *The Ecology of Bullfinch Damage to Fruit*, Ph.D. thesis, London.

—— personal communication.

Nash, J. K., 1935: *The Birds of Midlothian*, Witherby, London.

Newton, I., 1966: The Bullfinch problem, *Birds*, Vol. 1, pp. 74–7.

—— 1970: Some aspects of the control of birds, *Birds Study*, Vol. 17, No. 3, pp. 177–94.

—— 1972: *Finches*, Collins, London.

Norden, J., 1607: *The Surveyor's Problem*, London.

Parslow, J. L. F., 1968: Changes among the status of breeding birds in Britain and Ireland, *British Birds*, Vol. 61, pp. 51–9.

Tusser, T. (ed. Mavor, W.), 1812: *Five Hundred Points of Good Husbandry*, London.

Wright, E. N. and Summers, D. D. B., 1960: The biology and economic importance of the Bullfinch, *Ann. Applied Biology*, Vol. 45, pp. 415–18.

Chapter 7

Main generic references for chapter

Battersby, J., 2005: *UK mammals: species status and population trends*, JNCC/Tracking Mammals Partnership.

Elliott, J. Steele, 1901: *The Vertebrate Fauna of Bedfordshire*, Birmingham.

Harris, S., Morris, P., Wray, S and Yalden, D. W., 1995: *A Review of British Mammals: population estimates and conservation status*, J.N.C.C.

Harvie-Brown, J. A., papers in National Library of Scotland.

—— and Buckley, T. E., 1887: *A Vertebrate Fauna of Sutherland Caithness and Wester Ross*, Douglas, Edinburgh.

—— —— 1888: *A Vertebrate Fauna of the Outer Hebrides*, Douglas, Edinburgh.

—— —— 1891: *A Vertebrate Fauna of the Orkney Islands*, Douglas, Edinburgh.

—— —— 1892: *A Vertebrate Fauna of Argyll and the Inner Hebrides*, Douglas, Edinburgh.

—— —— 1896: *A Vertebrate Fauna of the Moray Basin*, Douglas, Edinburgh.

Langley, P. J. W. and Yalden, D. W., 1977: The decline of rarer carnivores in Great Britain during the nineteenth century, *Mammal Review*, Vol. 7, pp. 95–116.

Lockie, J. D., 1966: Territory in small carnivores, *Symposium Zoo. Soc. of London*.

Matthews, L. Harrison, 1952: *British Mammals*, Collins, London.

McGhie, H., 2002: Changes in the distribution and persecution of carnivores in Northern Scotland, 1912–1970, *Scottish Naturalist*, Vol. 114, pp. 45–83.

Millais, J. G., 1904: *Mammals of Great Britain and Ireland*, Longman, Green & Co., London.

Ritchie, J, 1920: *The Influence of Man on Animal Life in Scotland*, Cambridge University Press.

—— 1931: *Birds and Beasts as Farm Pests*, Oliver & Boyd, Edinburgh.

Statistical Accounts of Scotland (Old), 1791–99.

Statistical Accounts of Scotland (New), 1845.

Thorburn, A., 1920: *British Mammals*, Longman, Green & Co., London.

Yalden, D. W., 1999: *The History of British Mammals*, T. & A. D. Poyser, London.

Hedgehog

Main references

Elliott, J. Steele, 1936: *Bedfordshire Vermin Payments*, Luton Public Museum.

Evans, Gwen, personal communication.

Morris, P., 1994: *The Hedgehog*, Mammal Society.

Smith, R., 1768: *The Universal Directory for the taking alive and destroying Rats and all other kinds of four footed and winged vermin*, London.

Tapper, S. C., 1992: *Game Heritage*, Game Conservancy Trust.

Yalden, D. W., 1999: *The food of the hedgehog in England*, Acta Theriologica, Vol. 21, pp. 401–24.

Mole

Main references

Harris, S., Morris, P., Wray, S., and Yalden, D. W., 1995: *A Review of British Mammals: population estimates and conservation status*, J.N.C.C.

Macpherson, H. A., 1892: *The Influence of Man on Animal Life in Scotland*, Douglas, Edinburgh.

Markham, Gervais, 1621: *Hungers Prevention and the Art of Fowling.*

Mellanby, K., 1971: *The Mole*, Collins, London.

Stone, R. D., 1992: *The Mole*, Shire Books, Buckinghamshire.

Williamson, Victor, personal communication.

Polecat

Main references

Bell, T., 1837: *The History of British Quadrupeds*, Van Voorst, London.

Birks, J. D., 1993: The return of the Polecat, *British Wildlife*, Vol. 5, pp. 16–25.

—— personal communication.

—— and Kitchener, A. C., 1994: *The Distribution and Status of the Polecat in Britain in the 1990s*, Vincent Wildlife Trust.

Blandford, P. R. S., 1987: *Biology of the Polecat in Wales*, Ph.D. thesis, Exeter.

Brown, D., 2002: The Foumart: what's in a name? *Mammal Review*, Vol. 2, pp. 145–9.

Harvie-Brown, J. A. and Buckley T. E., 1896: *A Vertebrate Fauna of the Moray Basin*, Douglas, Edinburgh.

Howes, C. A., 1980: Aspects of the history and distribution of Polecats and Ferrets in South Yorkshire and adjacent areas, *Naturalist*, Vol. 105, pp. 3–16.

Langley, P. J. W. and Yalden, D. W., 1977: The decline of rarer carnivores in Great Britain during the nineteenth century, *Mammal Review*, Vol. 7, Nos. 3 and 4, pp. 95–115.

Ritchie, J., 1920: *The Influence of Man on Animal Life in Scotland*, Cambridge University Press.

Walton, K. C., 1995: in Harris, S., et al., *A Review of British Mammals*, J.N.C.C., London.

Waterton, C., 1838–57: *Essays on Natural History, chiefly Ornithology*, Longman, London.

Pine Marten

Main references

Birks, J. D., 2001: *The Pine Marten*, Mammal Society.

—— personal communication.

Harvie-Brown, J. A., papers in the National Library of Scotland.

—— and Buckley, T. E., 1888: *A Vertebrate Fauna of the Outer Hebrides*, Douglas, Edinburgh.

—— —— 1892: *A Vertebrate Fauna of Argyll and the Inner Hebrides*, Douglas, Edinburgh.

Isham, T., 1673 (translated from Latin by Isham, R.): *The Journal of Thomas Isham of Lamport in the County of Northamptonshire.*

Knapp, J. L., 1829: *The Journal of a Naturalist*, John Murray, London.

Langley, P. J. W. and Yalden, D. W., 1977: The decline of rarer carnivores in Great Britain during the nineteenth century, *Mammal Review*, Vol. 7, Nos. 3 and 4, pp. 95–115.

MacGillivray, W., 1840: *A Manual of British Ornithology*, Scott, Webster & Geary, London.

Macpherson, H. A., 1892: *A Vertebrate Fauna of Lakeland*, Douglas, Edinburgh.

Maroo, S. and Yalden, D. W., 2000: The Mesolithic mammal fauna of Great Britain, *Mammal Review*, Vol. 30, pp. 243–8.

Martin, Martin, 1703: *A Description of the Western Isles of Scotland*, Bell, London.

McGhie, H., 2002: Changes in the distribution and persecution of carnivores in Northern Scotland, 1912–1970, *Scottish Naturalist*, Vol. 114, pp. 45–83.

Morgan, I. K., 1992: Notes on the status of the Pine Marten in South-west and Mid Wales, *Llanelli Naturalists Newsletter*, Winter.

Poulson, S., Birks, J. D. S., Messenger, J. E., and Jefferies J. D. (in press 2006): *A quality scoring system for using sightings data to assess pine marten distribution at low density*.

Santos-Reis, M., Birks, J. D. S., O'Doherty, E. C., and Proulx, G. (eds.), 2005: *Martes in carnivore communities*, Alpha Wildlife Publications, Alberta, Canada.

Ritchie, J., 1920: *The Influence of Man on Animal Life in Scotland*, Cambridge University Press.

Shaw, G. and Livingstone, J., 1992: The Pine Marten: its reintroduction and subsequent history in the Galloway Forest Park, *Trans. Dumfries & Galloway Nat. Hist. Soc.*, Vol. 67.

Velander, K. A., 1983: *Pine Marten Survey of England, Scotland and Wales* 1980–1982, Vincent Weir Trust.

Fox

Main references

Baker, P. and Harris, S., 1997: *How will a Ban on Hunting affect the British Fox Population?* University of Bristol.

Beckford, P., 1781: *Thoughts on hunting, in a series of familiar letters to a friend*.

Burns, Lord, et al., 2000: *Report of the Committee of Enquiry into Hunting with Dogs in England and Wales*, HMSO, London.

Carr, R., 1976: *English Fox Hunting: a history*, Weidenfeld & Nicholson, London.

Harrison, W., 1968 edn.: *The Description of England* (ed. G. Edelen), New York.

Hewson, R., 1984: Changes in the numbers of foxes in Scotland, *J. of Zoology*, Vol. 204, pp. 561–9.

Lloyd, H. G., 1980: *The Red Fox*, Batsford, London.

Longrigg, R., 1975: *History of Fox Hunting*, Macmillan, London.

—— 1997: *The English Squire and his Sport*, Michael Joseph, London.

McDonald, D. W., Baker, R., and Harris, S., 1998: *Is the Fox a pest?* University of Bristol.

Poulson, T. H. G., 1930: *A History of Fox Hunting in Wynnstay Country* 1800–1884/5, Robinson, Brighton.

Ritchie, J., 1920: *The Influence of Man on Animal Life in Scotland*, Cambridge University Press.

Sassoon, S., 1928: *Memoirs of a Fox-hunting Man*, Faber & Faber, London.

Smith, G., personal communication.

Smout, T. C., 1959: *Scottish Trade on the Eve of the Union*, Oliver & Boyd, Edinburgh.
Statistical Account of Scotland (Old), 1791–9.
Varty, K., 2000: *Reynard the Fox*, Berghahn Books, Oxford.
Williamson, T., 2002: *The Transformation of Rural England*, Exeter University Press.

Rat

Main references

Barkley, H. C., 1911: *Studies in the Art of Rat Catching*, Read Books, Alcester.
Bentley, E. W., 1959: The distribution and status of *Rattus rattus* in UK in 1951 and 1956, *J. of Animal Ecology*, Vol. 28, pp. 288–308.
—— 1964: A further loss of ground by *Rattus rattus* in UK 1956–1961, *J. Animal Ecology*, Vol. 33, pp. 371–3.
Blencowe, R., 1912: *An Easy and Effective Method of Destroying Rats, Mice, Polecats, Weasels, Moles, Otters etc. etc.*, published privately.
Boelter, W. R., 1909: *The Rat Problem*, Bale & Danielsson, London.
Brown, R., 1759: *The Compleat Farmer or the Whole Art of Husbandry*, London.
Claremont, C. L., 1926: *A Practical Handbook for Rat Destruction*, John Hart.
Corbet, G. B., (ed.) 1998: *The Nature of Fife*, Scottish Cultural Press/ Fife & Kinross Wildlife Trust.
Conyers, G., *c.* 1705: *The Complete English and French Vermin Killer – being a companion for all families*.
Dewberry, J., 1920: *The Prevention and Destruction of Rats*, Bale & Sons & Danielsson, London.
Drummond, D., 1992: Unmasking Mascall's mouse traps, *Proc.* 15th Vertebrate Pest Conference, University of California.
—— 2005: *Mouse traps: a quick scamper through their long history*, N. American Trap Collectors Assn. Inc.
—— personal communication.
Hirst, L. F., 1953: *The Conquest of the Plague*, Clarendon Press, Oxford.
Hovell, M., 1924: *Rats and how to destroy them*, John Bale & Sons & Danielsson, London.
Jefferies, D. J. (ed.) 2003: *The Water Vole and Mink Survey of Britain 1996–1998*, with a history of long-term changes in the status of both species and their causes, Vincent Wildlife Trust.
—— personal communication.
Knapp, J. L., 1829: *The Journal of a Naturalist*, John Murray, London.
Macnicoll, A., personal communication.
M.A.F.F., 1932: *Rats and How to Exterminate Them*, M.A.F.F. bulletin No. 30.
Matheson, C., 1931: *Brown and Black Rats in Wales*, National Museum of Wales.
Quy, R., personal communication.
Rackham, D. J., 1979: The introduction of the Black Rat into Britain, *Antiquity*, Vol. 53, pp. 112–20.
Twigg, G. I., 1992: The Black Rat *Rattus rattus* in the United Kingdom in 1989, *Mammal Review*, Vol. 22, pp. 33–42.

Venables, L. S. V. and Venables, U. M., 1942: The Rat and Mouse populations of corn ricks, *J. Animal Ecology*, Vol. 11, pp. 44–68.

Wild Cat

Main references

Defoe, D., 1724: *Tour through the Whole Island of Great Britain*, 1991 edition, Yale.

Easterbee, N., Hepburn, L. V., and Jefferies, D. J., 1991: *Survey of the Status and Distribution of the Wild Cat in Scotland 1983–1987*, N.C.C.

Harris, S., Morris, P., Wray, S., and Yalden, D. W., 1995: *A Review of British Mammals: population estimates and conservation status*, J.N.C.C.

Kitchener, A., 1991: *The Natural History of Wildcats*, A & C Black, London.

—— 1995: *The Wildcat*, Mammal Society.

Langley, P. J. W. and Yalden, D. W., 1977: The decline of rarer carnivores in Great Britain during the nineteenth century, *Mammal Review*, Vol. 7, Nos. 3 and 4, pp. 95–101.

Macpherson, H. A., 1892: *A Vertebrate Fauna of Lakeland*, Douglas, Edinburgh.

McDonald, D. W., et al., 2004: *The Scottish Wild Cat: conservation and an action plan*, Wildlife Conservation Research Unit.

McGhie, H., 2002: Changes in the distribution and persecution of carnivores in Northern Scotland, 1912–1970, *Scottish Naturalist*, Vol. 114, pp. 45–83.

Morton, J., 1712: *The Natural History of Northamptonshire*.

Pennant, T., 1774: *A Tour in Scotland*, John Monk, Chester.

Ritchie, J., 1920: *The Influence of Man on the Animal Life of Scotland*, Cambridge University Press.

Robinson, H. W., 1925: Wildcats on the Lancashire–Westmorland border, *Lancashire-Cheshire Naturalist*, Vol. 17, pp. 107–8.

Victoria County Histories, Kent and East Sussex.

Badger

Main references

Anon, 1892: The rarity of badgers, *The Field*, Vol. 80, p. 683.

Bell, T., 1837: *The History of British Quadrupeds*, Van Voorst, London.

Blakeborough, J. F. and Pease, A. E., 1914: *The Life and Habits of the Badger*, The Foxhound Office, London.

Brown, J. A. H., 1882: The past and present distribution of some of the rarer animals of Scotland. IV The Badger, *Zoologist*, Series 3, pp. 1–9 and Series 6, pp 41–5.

Cocks, A. H., 1892: Vermin paid for by churchwardens in a Buckinghamshire Parish, *Zoologist*, Series 3, Vol. 16, pp. 61–4.

Cresswell, P., Harris, S., and Jefferies, D. J., 1989: The badger in Britain: present status and future population, *Biol. J. Linnean Society*, Vol. 38, pp. 91–101.

—— —— Bunce, R. G. H., and Jefferies, D. J., 1990: *The History, Distribution, Status and Habitat Requirements of the Badger in Britain*, Nature Conservancy Council.

Donnelly, C. A., et al., 2003: Impact of localised Badger culling on tuberculosis incidence in British cattle, *Nature*, Vol. 426, pp. 834–7.

Graham, R., 1946: The Badger in Cumberland, *Trans. Carlisle Nat. Hist. Soc.*, Vol. 7, pp. 88–99.

Harting, J. E., 1888: The Badger, *Zoologist*, Series 3, Vol. 12, pp. 1–13.

Howes, C. A., 1988: A review of badger persecution in Yorkshire, *Yorks. Mammal Group Newsletter*, Vol. 10, pp. 5–12.

Jefferies, D. J., 1969: Causes for badger mortality in Eastern Counties of England, *J. Zoology*, Vol. 157, pp. 429–36.

Longrigg, R., 1997: *The English Squire and his Sport*, Michael Joseph, London.

Macpherson, H. A., 1892: *A Vertebrate Fauna of Lakeland*, Douglas, Edinburgh.

Millais, J. G., 1904: *Mammals of Great Britain and Ireland*, Longman, Green & Co., London.

Neal, E., 1958: *The Badger*, Collins, London.

—— 1977: *Badgers*, Blandford, London.

Pease, Sir A., 1898: *The Badger*, Lawrence & Bullen, London.

Pennie, I., 1950: The Tongue Badgers, *Scottish Naturalist*, Vol. 62, pp. 54–5.

Pitt, Frances, 1933: *The Badger in Great Britain*, *J. Soc. for the Preservation of Fauna of the Empire*, 18: 15–19

—— 1935: Increase in badgers in Great Britain 1900–1934, *J. Animal Ecology*.

Reason, P., Harris, S., and Cresswell, P., 1933: Estimating the impact of past persecution and habitat changes on the number of badgers *Meles meles* in Britain, *Mammal Review*, Vol. 23, pp. 1–15.

Ritchie, J., 1920: *The Influence of Man on the Animal Life of Scotland*, Cambridge University Press.

Service, R., 1891: The Old Fur Market at Dumfries, *Scottish Naturalist*, July.

Skinner, P., Jefferies, D. J., and Harris, S., 1989: *Badger Persecution and the Law*, Mammal Society.

Skinner, C., Skinner, P., and Harris, S., 1991: The past history and recent decline of badgers *Meles meles* in Essex; an analysis of some of the contributory factors, *Mammal Review*, Vol. 21, pp. 67–80.

St John, C., 1893: *Wild Sports and Natural History in the Highlands*, John Murray, London.

Wilson, G., Harris, S., and McLaren, G., 1997: *Changes in the British Badger Population 1988–1997*, Peoples' Trust for Endangered Species.

Weasel

Main references

Day, M. G., 1968: Food habits of British stoats (*Mustela erminea*) and weasels (*Mustela nivalis*), *J. Zoology*, Vol. 155, pp. 485–97.

Harting, J. E., 1894: The Weasel, *Zoologist*, Vol. 52, pp. 417–23 and 445–54.

King, C., 1989: *The Natural History of Weasels and Stoats*, Helm, London.

MacDonald, D. W. and Harris, S., 1998: *Stoats and Weasels*, Mammal Society.

Potts, G. R., 1986: *The Partridge, Pesticides, Predation and Conservation*, Collins, London.

Ritchie, J., 1920: *The Influence of Man on the Animal Life of Scotland*, Cambridge University Press.

Smith, R., 1768: *The Universal Directory for the taking alive and destroying Rats and all other kinds of four footed and winged vermin*, London.

Statistical Account of Scotland (New), 1845.

Tapper, S. C., 1992: *Game Heritage*, Game Conservancy Trust.

Stoat

Main references

Matthews, L. Harrison, 1952: *British Mammals*, Collins, London.

McDonald, D. W. and Harris, S., 1998: *Stoats and Weasels*, Mammal Society.

Paston Letters, written by the Paston family *c.* 1490: in modern edition by James Gardiner, 1904.

Smith, R., 1768: *The Universal Directory for the taking alive and destroying Rats and all other kinds of four footed and winged vermin*, London.

Tapper, S. C., 1976: The diet of weasels, *Mustela nivalis* and stoats, *Mustela erminea* during early summer, in relation to predation on game birds, *J. Zoology*, Vol. 179, p. 219–24.

—— 1982: Using estate records to monitor population trends in game and predator species, particularly Stoats and Weasels, *Proceedings of the International Congress of Game Biologists*, Vol. 14, pp. 115–20.

—— Brocklees M., and Potts, G. R., 1990: The Salisbury Plain Predation Experiment: the conclusion, *Game Conservancy Review*, pp. 87–91.

—— 1992: *Game Heritage*, Game Conservancy Trust.

Otter

Main references

Andrews, E. M. N. and Crawford, A., 1986: *Otter Survey of Wales 1984–85*, Vincent Wildlife Trust.

—— Howell, P., and Johnson, K., 1993: *Otter Survey of Wales 1991*, Vincent Wildlife Trust.

Berry, R. J. and Johnston, J. L., 1980: *The Natural History of Shetland*, Collins, London.

—— 1985: *The Natural History of Orkney*, Collins, London.

Cameron, L. C. R., 1928: *Angling and Otter Hunting Sketches in Rod, Pole and Perch*, Martin Hopkinson, London.

Chanin, P. and Jefferies, D. J., 1978: The decline of the Otter *Lutra lutra* in Britain: an Analysis of hunting records and discussion of causes, *Biol. J. of Linnean Society*, Vol. 10, No. 3, pp. 305–28.

Chanin, P., personal communication.

Coventry, Earl of, and Cameron, L. C. R., 1930: *Otter Hunting*, Seeley Service, London.

Crawford, A., 2003: *Fourth Otter Survey of England*, Environment Agency.

Green, J. and Green, R., 1980: *Otter Survey of Scotland* 1977–1979, Vincent Wildlife Trust.

—— —— 1987: *Otter Survey of Scotland* 1984–1985, Vincent Wildlife Trust.

—— —— 1997: *Otter Survey of Scotland* 1991–1994, Vincent Wildlife Trust.

Grigson, C. and Mellars, P. A., 1987: *The Mammalian Remains from Middens*, in Mellars (ed.), *Excavations on Oronsay*, Edinburgh.

Harting, J. E., 1865: Otters in Middlesex, *Zoologist*, Vol. 23, pp. 94–5.

Jefferies, D. J., 1989: The changing Otter population in Britain, 1700–1989, *Biol. J. of Linnean Society*, Vol. 38, pp. 61–9.

—— Green, J., Green, R., and Cripps, S. J., 1993: *Otter mortalities due to commercial fishing* 1975–1992, in *Proc.* of Nat. Otter Conference, Cambridge 1992, Mammal Society.

—— 1996: Decline and recovery of the Otter, *British Wildlife*, Vol. 7, pp. 353–64.

—— Wayre, P., and Shuter R., 2001: A brief history of the Otter Trust's programme of repopulating lowland England with Otters bred in captivity with a special emphasis on East Anglia, *J. of the Otter Trust*, Vol. 3, No. 4, pp. 105–17.

—— personal communication.

Lenton, E. J., Chanin, P. R. F., and Jefferies, D. J., 1980: *Otter Survey of England*, N.C.C.

Maxwell, G., 1960: *Ring of Bright Water*, Longman, London.

McGhie, H., 2002: Changes in the distribution and persecution of carnivores in Northern Scotland, 1912–1970, *Scottish Naturalist*, Vol. 114, pp. 45–83.

Ritchie, J., 1920: *The Influence of Man on the Animal Life of Scotland*, Cambridge University Press.

Statistical Account of Scotland (Old), 1791–9.

Statistical Account of Scotland (New) 1845.

Stephens, M. N., 1957: *A Natural History of the Otter*, University Federation for Animal Welfare, London.

Strachan, C., Strachan, R., and Jefferies, D. J., 1990: *Otter Survey of England* 1984–1986, N.C.C.

Strachan, R. and Jefferies, D. J., 1996: *Otter Survey of England* 1991–1994, Vincent Wildlife Trust.

Williams, J., 2000: *The Otter Among Us*, Tiercel SB Publishing, Hertfordshire.

Williamson, H., 1930: *Tarka the Otter*, Bodley Head, London.

Woodroffe, C., 2001: *The Otter*, Mammal Society.

Chapter 8

Main reference sources

Crocker, J. (ed.), 1981: *Charnwood Forest: a changing landscape*, Loughborough Naturalists' Club.

Squires, A. and Jeeves, M., 1994: *Leicestershire and Rutland Woodlands: past and present*, Kairos Press, Leicester.

Turner, T. W., 1954: *Memoirs of a Gamekeeper*, Geoffrey Bliss.

Chapter 9

Main references

Dennis, R. H., personal communication.

Driver, J., 2006: *Raven Population census of Northwest Wales, 1998–2005*, Welsh Birds Vol. 4, No. 6, pp. 442–453.

Easterbee, N., Hepburn, L. V., and Jefferies, D. J., 1991: *Survey of the Status and Distribution of the Wild Cat in Scotland* 1983–1987, N.C.C.

Harris, S., Morris, P., Wray, S., and Yalden, D. W., 1995: *A Review of British Mammals: population estimates and conservation status*, J.N.C.C.

MacDonald, D. W. and Harris S., 1998: *Stoats and Weasels*, Mammal Society.

—— et al. 2004: *The Scottish Wild Cat: conservation and an action plan*, Wildlife Conservation Research Unit.

Prytherch, R., personal communication.

Ratcliffe, D., 1997: *The Raven*, T. & A. D. Poyser, London.

Sim, I. M. W., 1999: *Status of the Hen Harrier in the UK and the Isle of Man*, Report to the Raptor Working Group.

Taylor, W. L., 1946: The Wild Cat *(Felis sylvestris)* in Great Britain, *J. Animal Ecology*, Vol. 15, pp. 130–3.

Chapter 10

Main references

Central Science Laboratory Annual Reports, *Pesticide Poisoning of Animals* 1990–2004.

RSPB Bird Crime Data Bank, 1990–2004.

Tapper, S. C., Brocklees M., and Potts, G. R., 1990: The Salisbury Plain Predation Experiment: the conclusion, *Game Conservancy Review*, pp. 87–91.

—— 1992: *Game Heritage*, Game Conservancy Trust.

Chapter 11

Main references

Newlands, W., 1997: The Loss of Langholm, *The Field*, December.

Redpath, S. M. and Thirgood, S. J., 1997: *Birds of Prey and Red Grouse*, HMSO.

Tapper, S. C. (ed.), 1999: *A question of balance: game animals and their role in the British Countryside*, Game Conservancy Trust.

—— 2005: *Nature's Gain*, Game Conservancy Trust.

Warren, C., 2002: *Managing Scotland's Environment*, Edinburgh University Press.

Bibliographic references

Anon, 1833: Abstract of the Answers and Questions, Enumeration Abstract, Vol. 1, 1831 Census, London

Anon, 1862: Mildenhall Parish Records, *East Anglian*, No. 14, pp. 185–7; and No. 15, pp. 198–9.

Anon, 1863: Weybread Parish Records, *East Anglian*, No. 32, pp. 409–11.

Anon, 1873: Accounts of Churchwardens of Melton Mowbray, *Trans. Leics. Architecture & Archaeological Society*, Vol. III, Pt. 3.

Anon, 1874: Halesworth Parish Records, *Trans. Suffolk Inst. of Arch. & History*, Vol. 5, pp. 444–6.

Anon, 1895: *Transactions of Cardiganshire Antiquarian Society*, pp. 234–6.

Anon, 1910: Winterslow Churchwardens Accounts, *Wiltshire Notes and Queries*, vi and vii.

Aplin, O. V., 1889: *The Birds of Oxfordshire*, Clarendon Press.

Archer, F., 1988: *Evesham to Bredon in Old Photographs*, Alan Sutton, Stroud.

Armitt, M. L., 1912 (ed. Rawnsley, W. T.): *The Church at Grasmere: a history*, Titus Wilson, Kendal.

A. W. P., 1937: Manchester Churchwardens' Accounts, *Manchester Guardian*, 23 November 1937.

Babbington, Rev. C., 1884–6: *Catalogue of the Birds of Suffolk*, Van Voorst, London.

Barrett, W. B., 1907: The Pepys of South Dorset, *Proc. Dorset Nat. Hist. & Antiq. Field Club*, Vol. xxviii, p. 41.

Bateman, J., 1971: *Animal Traps and Trapping*, 4th impression, Stackpole Books.

Bell, A., 1904: Pleistocene and later bird fauna of Great Britain and Ireland, *The Zoologist*, 4th series, Vol. XIX, pp. 401–12.

Blezard, E., 1943: *The Birds of Lakeland*, Carlisle Natural History Society.

Blome, R., 1686: *The Gentleman's Recreation*.

Borrer, W., 1891: *The Birds of Sussex*, R. H. Porter, London.

Brushfield, T. N., 1897: On the Destruction of Vermin in Rural Parishes, *Trans. Devon Assn.*, pp. 291–343.

Burton, J. R., 1883: *The History of Bewdley*, William Reeves, London.

Carnegie, W., 1884: *Practical Game Preserving*, Upcott Gill.

—— 1973: *Practical Trapping*, Tideline Books.

Chapman, Abel, 1928: *Retrospect—Reminiscences and Impressions of a Hunter-Naturalist in three continents 1851–1928*, Gurney & Jackson, London.

Christy, R. M., 1890: *The Birds of Essex*, Simkin, Marshall, Hamilton, London.

Clarke, G., 1948: Fowling in Prehistoric Europe, *Antiquity*, Vol. 87, pp. 116–30.

Darling, F. Fraser, 1947: *Natural History in the Highlands and Islands*, Collins, London.

Dillon, P. J. and Jones, E. L., 1986: Trevor Falla's Vermin transcripts for Devon, *The Devon Historian*, Vol. 33, pp. 15–19.

Falla, T., 1978: *Private notes*, by courtesy of his widow, Mrs G. Falla.

Fitter, R. S. R., 1945: *London's Natural History*, Collins, London.

Fletcher, Rev. W. G. D., 1882: *Historical Handbook of Loughborough*.

Gladstone, H. S., 1882: *The Birds of Dumfriesshire*, Witherby, London.

Glasscock, J. L., 1882: *Records of St Michael's Church, Bishops Stortford*, p. 156.

Glegg, W., 1935: *History of the Birds of Middlesex*, Witherby, London.

Gunther, R. T., 1917: *Report on the Agricultural Damage by Vermin in the Counties of Norfolk and Oxfordshire*, Oxford University Press.

Haines, C. R., 1907: *The Birds of Rutland*, R. H. Porter.

Hancock, J., 1874: *A Catalogue of the Birds of Northumberland and Durham*, Williams & Norgate.

Hardy, H. F. H., 1932: *English Sport*, Country Life.

Hatfield, C. W., 1866: *Historical Notices of Doncaster*, Doncaster Museum.

Hill, R. and Stamper, P., 1993: *The Working Countryside* 1862–1945, Swan Hill Press, Shrewsbury.

Jefferies, R., 1930: *Wildlife in a Southern County*, Nelson, London.

Jenkins, A., 2000: *Painters and Peasants: paintings of English country life and landscapes*, Hutchinson, London.

Jones, F., 1966: Some further Slebech notes, *J. Nat. Library of Wales*, Vol. 14, p. 3.

Journal of the Incorporated Soc. for the Destruction of Vermin, 1908–9, Vol. 1, pp. 1–4.

J. M. Esq., 1707: *The Whole Art of Husbandry*, London.

Knox, A. E., 1872: *Autumns on the Spey*, Van Voorst, London.

Langley, J., 1797: *History and antiquities of the Hundred of Desborough*, pub. for R. Faulder.

McIntyre, D., 1925: *Highland Gamekeeper*, Seeley Service & Co., London.

Manchester Guardian, 1956: *Miscellany*, 10 April and 24 April.

Mansell-Pleydel, J. C., 1888: *The Birds of Dorsetshire*, R. H. Porter.

Masefield, J. B. R., 1897: *Wild Bird Protection and Nestboxes*, Taylor Bros., Leeds.

Maxwell, A., 1911: *Partridge and Partridge Manors*, A & C Black, London.

Mayer, J., 1828: *Sportsman's Directory of Parks and Gamekeepers Companion* (publisher unknown).

Mitchell, M. S., 1885: *The Birds of Lancashire*, Van Voorst, London.

Mitchell, W. R. and Robson, R. W., 1976: *Lakeland Birds—a Visitors' Handbook*, Dalesman.

Muirhead, G., 1994: *The Birds of Berwickshire*, Douglas, Edinburgh.

Munsche, P. B., 1981: *Gentlemen and Poachers: the English game laws* 1671–1831, Cambridge University Press.

Nelson, T. H., 1907: *The Birds of Yorkshire*, A. Brown & Son, London.

Oakes, C. and Battersby, E., 1939: *The Birds of East Lancashire*, Burnley Print Co.

Oldham, C., 1929: Payments for Vermin by Berkhamstead Churchwardens, *Trans. Herts. Nat. Hist. Soc.*, Vol. 18, pp. 45–50.

Parker, E., et al., 1935: *Gamebirds, Beasts and Fishes*, Lonsdale Library, Seeley Service & Co., London.

—— 1937: *Shooting by Moor, Field and Shore*, Lonsdale Library, Seeley Service & Co., London.

Patten, B., 1981: *Clare's Countryside*, Heinemann, London.

Paton, E. R. and Pike, O. G., 1929: *The Birds of Ayrshire*, Witherby, London.

Patterson, A. H., 1929: *Wildfowlers and Poachers*, Methuen, London.

Payn, W. H., 1902: *The Birds of Suffolk*, Barrie & Rockliff, London.

Pearsall, W. H., 1950: *Mountains and Moorlands*, Collins, London.

Plot, R., 1677: *The Natural History of Oxfordshire*, Oxford.

Population Census of Great Britain, 1831: *Enumeration Abstract of Answers and Returns*, House of Commons, London

Pyle, C. M., 1994: *The Archives of Natural History*, Vol. 21, pp. 275–88.

Rackham, O., 1986: *The History of the Countryside*, Dent, London.

Ralph, P. G., 1940: *The Birds of the Isle of Man*, Douglas, Isle of Man.

Redman, J., 1966: *Fruity Stories*, Boxtree/Channel 4.

Riviere, B. B., 1930: *A History of the Birds of Norfolk*, Witherby, London.

Rossiter, B. N., 1999: Northumberland's Birds in the 18th and early 19th Centuries: the contribution of John Wallis, *Trans. Nat. Hist. Soc. of Northumberland*, Vol. 59, pp. 93–136.

Rowley, G. R., 1875: *An Ornithological Miscellany*, Vol. I–III, London.

Scott, G., 1938: *Grouse Land and the Fringe of the Moor*, Witherby, London.

Shorten, M., 1954: *Squirrels*, Collins, London.

Sibbald, Sir R., 1684: *Scotia Illustrata*, Jacobi Kniblo, Edinburgh.

Smith, A. C., 1887: *The Birds of Wiltshire*, R. H. Porter, London.

Smith, A. E. and Cornwallis, R. K., 1955: *The Birds of Lincolnshire*, Lincolnshire Naturalists Union.

Stocks, J. E., 1926: *Market Harborough Parish Records*, Oxford University Press.

Temperley, G. M., 1946: A History of the Birds of Durham, *Trans. Nat. Hist. Soc. Northumberland, Durham and Newcastle on Tyne*, Vol. 9, pp. 1–296.

Thompson, A. R., 1931: *Nature by Night*, Nicholson & Watson, London.

Ticehurst, C. B., 1932: *A History of the Birds of Suffolk*, Gurney & Jackson, London.

Turberville, G., 1575: *The Noble Art of Venerie or Hunting*, Bodleian edition.

Turnbull, W. P., 1867: *Birds of East Lothian*, privately published.

Venables, L. S. V. and Venables, U. M., 1955: *The Birds and Mammals of Shetland*, Oliver & Boyd.

Waddington, R., 1958: *Grouse Shooting and Moor Management*, Faber & Faber, London.

Walker, F. A., 1892: Churchwardens' Accounts at Dry Drayton, *Zoologist*, Vol. 16, p. 189.

Walsingham, Lord and Payne-Galwey, Sir Ralph, 1866: *Shooting*, Badminton Library, Longmans.

Watson, A. E. T. (ed.), 1912: *The Grouse*, Fur, Fin and Feather series, Longman, London.

Weaver, F. W. and Clark, G. N., 1925: *Churchwardens' Accounts of Marston, Spelsbury, and Pyrton*, Oxfordshire Record Society.

White, Rev. G., 1798: *The Natural History and Antiquities of Selborne*, White & Son.

White, W., 1859: *Northumberland and the Borders*, Chapman & Hall, London.

Whitehead, G. K., 1953: *The Ancient White Cattle of Britain and their Descendants*, Faber, London.

—— 1964: *The Deer of Great Britain and Ireland*, Routledge & Kegan Paul, London.

Wood, C., 1993: *Paradise Lost; paintings of English country life and landscape*, Grange Books.

Worlidge, J., 1697: *Systema Agriculturae: the mystery of husbandry discovered*, printed for Tho Dring, London.

Wright, J., 1650: *A Thousand Notable Things of Sundry Sorts*, London.

Wright, Sir J., 1796: *Observations upon Important Objects for Preserving Wheat and Grain from Vermin*.

Index